BARGAINING WITH THE S

BARGAINING WITH THE STATE FROM AFAR

AMERICAN CITIZENSHIP IN TREATY PORT CHINA, 1844–1942

Eileen P. Scully

Columbia University Press   New York

Columbia University Press

Publishers Since 1893

New York   Chichester, West Sussex

Copyright © 2001 Columbia University Press

All rights reserved

Library of Congress Cataloging-in-Publication Data

Scully, Eileen P.

Bargaining with the state from afar :

American citizenship in treaty port China,

1844–1942 / Eileen P. Scully.

p. cm.

Includes bibliographical references and index.

ISBN 0–231–12108–3 (cloth : alk paper)

ISBN 0–231–12109–1 (pbk. : alk paper)

1. Citizenship—United States—History.

2. Citizenship—China—History.

3. Americans—Legal status, laws, etc.—China—History.

4. Americans—Legal status, laws, etc.—Foreign countries—History.

5. Extraterritoriality. I. Title.

KF4700 .S38 2000

342.73'083—dc21   00–064464

Casebound editions of Columbia University Press
books are printed on permanent and durable acid-free paper.

Printed in the United States of America

Designed by Audrey Smith

c 10 9 8 7 6 5 4 3 2 1

p 10 9 8 7 6 5 4 3 2 1

To Clara Elspeth and Matthew Haas

CONTENTS

ACKNOWLEDGMENTS

Only with the completion of such a project does it become clear how many others contributed to it, whether in intellectual, financial or emotional ways. My greatest debt is to my graduate adviser and continuing mentor, Dr. Nancy Bernkopf Tucker, whose own good example will always be a powerful and enduring inspiration to me. Her patient listening, impatient reading, and warm kindness have contributed significantly not only to this book, but to my own personal and professional growth.

For their continuing encouragement and past sacrifices, I thank my parents. For their constancy and good humor, I thank my siblings, particularly my sisters. By the end, they were among the few who could ask without insult: "Haven't you finished that thing yet?" In the same vein, Warren I. Cohen's periodic encouragement to "just write the thing" proved very valuable, particularly at moments when I was certain that, unlike all book topics taken on by others before me, the unique subtleties of my chosen area defied words and distinct chapters.

To my teachers and fellow graduate students at Georgetown University, I owe many intellectual debts, as each in their own style taught me to seek history from the bottom up, and to temper intellectual rigor with scholarly humility. For their intellectual insights on all variety of matter, jokes both good and bad, and generous doses of timely encouragement, I thank the members of the History Department of Princeton University, particularly to Susan Naquin, Sean Wilentz, Christine Stansell, and Daniel Rodgers. Particular thanks to Dirk Hartog, for reading through versions of this manuscript and offering suggestions, not all of which I took advantage of. I also wish to express appreciation to the Social Science Research Council–MacArthur Foundation Program in International Peace and Security, which funded a year of study at Harvard Law School, as well as the East Asian Legal Studies Program at Harvard, which accepted me as a visiting fellow. I am also grateful to the Society of Historians of American Foreign Relations (SHAFR), from whom I received the 1991 Stuart L. Bernath Dissertation Grant. An added thanks to Paul Cohen, who read multiple versions of this manuscript, and to the editors and anonymous reviewers at Columbia University Press.

BARGAINING WITH THE STATE FROM AFAR

INTRODUCTION AND OVERVIEW

Most broadly conceived this is a study of the relationship between the federal government and U.S. nationals sojourning abroad, particularly those living in Western colonial enclaves during the nineteenth and early twentieth centuries. Drawing inspiration from the growing literature on American citizenship struggles, including Rogers Smith's *Civic Ideals* (1997), Gerald Neuman's *Strangers to the Constitution* (1996), and Richard Epstein's *Bargaining with the State* (1993), it explores the bargaining process between federal officials and these sojourners over the rights and responsibilities of U.S. nationality beyond the territorial confines of the American nation.[1] The focus of the work is the federal-sojourner struggle over "extraterritoriality" in certain colonial areas where the U.S. government reached into foreign lands to exercise direct legal jurisdiction over resident Americans thereby exempting them from native authority. The exercise of legal authority, done primarily through State Department consuls and ministers, emerged as the central exception to the American insistence that government authority over citizens has strict territorial and constitutional limits.

Just as resident aliens within the U.S. have so often been the object of hostility by full citizens fearing "free riders" of suspect loyalty, so too have sojourning Americans been vulnerable to allegations that they seek only the benefits of membership, evade its responsibilities and slough off its burdens.[2] The image of "expatriates" (a popular misnomer for unexpatriated sojourners) conjured up by one nineteenth-century American observer thus remains evocative today; that of a "class of persons who have never become identified in spirit and feeling with the ideas our government represents, who have contributed little or nothing to its welfare, who lend nothing to its support, and who, beyond all reach of its influence and authority, use it in a foreign land as a personal protection to themselves and their interests."[3]

A different vantage point on sojourners is offered by post-Cold War scholarship on the history of citizenship and the nation state. Here, citizenship emerges as "a set of mutual, contested claims between agents of states and members of socially-constructed categories: genders, races, nationalities, and others." In all of its variations, ranging from what historians term "thick" and "thin," this claim-based transaction is "relational, cultural, historical and contingent." Claims and assertions of identity are "strategic interaction[s] liable to failure or misfiring rather than . . . straightforward expression[s] of an actor's attributes."[4]

For sojourners in colonial areas, this claim-making translated primarily into requests for extreme diplomatic protection and indemnity demands for damage to property abroad; on the flip side were responses to the home government's demands for tax payments, military duty, and circumspect behavior. In providing these benefits and asserting these demands, the federal government acted in the name of a "greater good." As in the domestic sphere, when the federal government extended or withheld property, rights and securities, this raised difficult questions about what "conditions . . . the state [might] impose on citizens in the course of their mutual dealings."[5] Thus extra-territorial jurisdiction, an instrument of great power in a period of imperial expansion, functioned as an "anomalous zone," where the mix of rights and responsibilities for sojourning nationals was uncertain, and strenuously negotiated.[6]

Extraterritoriality (abbreviated by contemporaries as "extrality") considered not only as an instrument of imperialism but *also* as a citizenship regime affords a window into the process by which—to quote a seminal article on the subject—the state emerged in international politics and legal discourse, "as a realm to which one belongs or from which one is banned, whose interests one serves or one injures, and whose sovereignty should be respected but is persistently at risk."[7] Extrality combined an extreme form of diplomatic protection with an anomalous, almost unworkable, geographical extension of sovereign authority. As such, its operations proceeded along a three-way bargaining process between: the state and its citizens abroad; resident aliens and host authorities; and two national governments.[8]

The West-versus-the-rest paradigm of colonial studies predictably focuses on the latter two aspects, i.e. the immunity of foreigners from native law-enforcement and the inequality of coerced state-to-state treaties. This vantage point does little to illuminate the first axis, that is, the struggle between home authorities and far-off citizens over the rights and responsibilities of national membership. For metropolitan governments, imperial benefits from extrality were ultimately overshadowed by its costs: citizens under it required high maintenance and mounting protection, yet these privileged sojourners possessed the greatest resources and incentives to evade the reciprocal obligation to the state of allegiance and tractability.

Extrality's courtrooms stood at the broad juncture of two historical trajectories running through the eighteenth, nineteenth and early twentieth centuries: the first, the expansion of a Western-centric, capitalist world order to incorporate heretofore autonomous regions; the second, the solidification of the sovereign territorial nation state as the preeminent gatekeeper of power and identity in human affairs.

Beyond something the great powers "did" to countries such as China extraterritoriality was first and foremost a complicated, often contentious, relationship between metropolitan governments and their sojourning citizen-subjects. So, although the colonial courtroom is an important vantage point on imperialism, it is at the same time an integral site in the history of the modern international state system. Particularly in the late nineteenth century, extraterritorial jurisdiction became deeply implicated in the push by increasingly centralized states to harness their citizens abroad in the service of something called "the national interest."[9]

The primary beneficiaries of extrality were white colonial elites, now recalled as living in luxury in exotic climes on the perquisites and proceeds of imperialism, demanding immunity from native authority while flouting the disciplinary efforts of their own home governments. Even well-intentioned colonizers, those who labored to "uplift" indigenous

3

populations and who came to detest the imperial edifice around them, are bid good riddance as the wrong-headed architects of an age of inequality, exploitation, racism, and pervasive contempt for the non-Western world. First encouraged to flourish, Western colonial sojourners were, over time, incorporated as distant resources of home governments. Ultimately, they were jettisoned by home authorities in the service of improved state-to-state relations, and to sanctify territorial sovereignty as the organizing principle of international relations.

In portraying colonial elites as the "spoilt children of empire," scholars communicate an implicit expectation that sojourners should have been better behaved and more restrained in their demands than stay-at-homes, as the reasonable price of the state's transgressive protective reach into alien settings.[10] The unstated assumption seems to be that foreigners should have been grateful for their governments' protection, held themselves to a higher standard of behavior, and submitted to the summary justice of their own officials—if not out of a sense of decency, than at least in the interest of good state-to-state relations and long-term profits. Methodologically speaking, this seems akin to labor historians unwittingly acting as management's publicists, disparaging unruly, ungrateful, disruptive workers who did not know how darn lucky they were to have jobs.

Yet, the dictum that when "outside the family" sojourners ought to conduct themselves with their nationality in mind was contrived and coerced. The notion that extra-territorial protection obligates beneficiaries to render extra-ordinary obedience, or settle for less than the rights of stay-at-homes, was for contemporaries in the age of modern empires the bargaining position metropolitan governments occupied in their continuing struggle to control "their" citizens abroad. The presumption that travelers owe heightened obedience as the price of transported protection was historically a much-contested, much-resisted disciplinary tool in the armory of expansive governments.

AMERICAN EXTRALITY IN CASE OF CHINA

Slowly at first, then more enthusiastically, Americans obtained the same imperial legal privileges enjoyed by their European counterparts.[11] The U.S. concluded treaties embodying degrees of extraterritorial jurisdic-

4

tion with Morocco (1787), Algiers (1795), Tunis (1797) Tripoli (1805), Turkey (1830), Muscat (1833), China (1844), Borneo (1850), Persia (1856), Japan (1857), Madagascar (1867), Samoa (1878), and Tonga (1886). After 1900, the momentum was reversed. By World War I, Americans had either suspended or significantly abbreviated privileges in most of these locales, either in recognition of full equality (as in the case of Japan), or in deference to the occupation or annexation of an area by another great power (as in Algiers [France] and Korea [Japan]).[12] Only in the late 1950s, did the State Department close the last of its consular courts, those in Morocco and Tangier.[13]

American extraterritorial jurisdiction over sojourning U.S. nationals was most extensive in China. Here, the U.S. was part of a consortium of great powers collectively exercising informal domination first over the Chinese empire, then over the Republic of China under the Kuomintang. Extraterritoriality had come to China in the Treaty of Nanking* (1842), signed after the defeat of the Ch'ing dynasty in the first Anglo-Chinese Opium War. By the 1860s, and well into the twentieth century, most foreigners resident in China enjoyed virtual immunity from native law, and were instead under the extraterritorial authority of their own home governments.[14]

Unlike the more familiar "diplomatic immunity" shielding diplomatic personnel stationed abroad from local law enforcement, extrality was portable, transferable, almost irrevocable, and buttressed—not by reciprocity and custom—but by gunboats and coercive treaties. These combined qualities gave foreigners in China something of a "Midas touch," allowing them to extend their privileges and immunities to employees, protégés, institutions, businesses and land. This dynamic transformed nineteenth-century makeshift self-governance among a hundred or so foreigners in a few coastal enclaves into twentieth-century semi-colonial domination, comprising control of customs revenues, military garrisons and sizable territorial concessions whose burgeoning cosmopolitan Sino-foreign populations were shielded from indigenous fiscal and political control.[15]

---

* Consistent with the bulk of primary sources, this work uses the traditional Wade-Giles transliteration system rather than Pinyin (e.g., Ch'ing, rather than Qing). In the case of familiar Chinese names, such as Shanghai and Canton, the Anglicized versions are used.

Americans exercised extraterritorial criminal, civil and administrative jurisdiction in China for about one hundred years, beginning with the 1844 Treaty of Wanghia, and ending in 1942 during World War Two. Until 1906, State Department consuls and ministers decided cases where Americans were the defendants, settled the estates of U.S. nationals dying in China, and assisted indigenous authorities in the resolution of Sino-foreign "mixed" cases involving Chinese defendants. In 1906, in the wake of scandalous revelations that consular officials in Shanghai, Canton and Amoy had thoroughly abused the judicial powers invested in them, the 59th Congress created the U.S. District Court for China, the only institution of its kind in American diplomatic history.[16]

This Court attempted to exercise jurisdiction over all U.S. nationals in China.[17] For thirty-six years, it was the designated venue for the resolution of most civil litigation and criminal complaints brought against Americans in China by Chinese, by other Americans, and by other foreign nationals in the treaty ports. Whether the problem was personal bankruptcy or a murder spree, a dispute over the size of Grade-A hen's eggs or illegal arms sales to insurgents, if the defendant was a U.S. national it fell to the United States Court in Shanghai to determine the winners and the losers in the day-to-day adjudication of American extrality in China.

The U.S. Court in Shanghai was only one among many foreign judicial tribunals in China. There were British Supreme Courts in Hong Kong and Shanghai, a myriad of treaty port consular courts (including American, British, French, German, and Japanese), and the various permanent "mixed courts" set up in Shanghai, Amoy and Hankow to handle Sino-foreign cases. Between 1844 and 1900, over eighteen countries acquired extraterritorial privileges in China; in addition, Britain, France, and the U.S., extended these legal immunities to protégés or subjects from their respective colonies and protectorates. Each treaty power determined its own method of handling this anomalous legal authority, none effectively accountable to Chinese officials.

Extrality meant that Americans residing in China before 1942 were subject, not to Chinese law, but to an array of laws borrowed from the District of Columbia and other territorial codes, as well as to local ordinances enacted by and for foreign residents themselves. A Shanghai American charged with—for instance—murdering a Chinese, dealing in contraband, or living as a vagrant, was typically described as having "violated the peace and security of the United States," and was tried by local American officials according to American laws. If sentenced to prison, treaty port Americans served their time in the local American consular jail; longer terms were served in the U.S. prison in the Philippines or in a federal penitentiary within the continental United States.

PROGRESSIVES, EMPIRE, AND EXTRALITY

The architects of the U.S. Court for China—Theodore Roosevelt, Elihu Root, William Howard Taft and Congressman Edwin Denby (R-MI), were convinced that wayward treaty port Americans were undermining U.S.-China relations. Progressives argued that a tighter jurisdictional rein over treaty port Americans was essential to the preservation of internal authority in China, to the survival of nascent, Western-oriented elites, and to the furtherance of U.S. ambitions to play a significant, nonentangling, role in the "great game" of East Asian power politics.

From Washington's perspective, the role of the U.S. Court in Shanghai was to inculcate Chinese with an appreciation for American jurisprudence, but even more important, to punish among U.S. nationals the sort of predatory, rapacious behavior known to hinder the emergence and rise to official power of indigenous Westernizers. The first Judge of this new Court, Taft protègè Lebbeus R. Wilfley, was thus sent to Shanghai with orders to reclaim his country's "good name" there from the ranks of vagabonds, brothel inmates, casino owners, confidence men, overzealous missionaries, buccaneering legal sharks and pretenders to U.S. citizenship—most all of whom had ridden into the treaty ports on the great wave of American expansionism from Hawaii to Peking at the turn of the century. It was in this sense that Frank Hinckley, first Clerk of the Court, declared to Shanghai Americans that the United States Court for China was a court *for* China, a vehicle through which the American government could assist its Chinese counterpart in performing the essential tasks of law and order.

Ultimately, those whom Washington sought to subordinate had many resources at their disposal to resist their government's smothering embrace, not the least of which were the very legal procedures and moral principles the Court itself brought to China. The rule of law is, as a number of social and legal historians have argued, a "potent fiction" which provides the framework for societal conflict, as groups and individuals invoke its hallowed presumptions and prescriptions for divergent and sometimes subversive purposes. This is no less so when the rule of law is extraterritoriality. Thus, the imperialist agenda unfolds subject not only to the contradictions and tensions of imperialism, but also to the constraints and imperatives inherent in law as an instrument of power.

EXTRALITY'S DYNAMICS

Adjudicating colonial privilege was a complicated affair that went well beyond the stark juxtaposition of a civilized, racially and culturally superior "us" versus a barbaric, backward, indolent, darker "them."[18] Law in the imperial context was no less the balancing act that it is in domestic settings. The dynamics of foreign expansion into China, and the myriad constituencies it generated over time, imposed multiple, often contradictory, demands on the extraterritorial justice system. The claims and issues at stake in both mixed and intra-foreign cases generally confronted a foreign judge with complex challenges, not the least of which was his own pursuit of professionalism and judicial autonomy. Intertwined forces of race, class and nationality made consular courts in China a "place of contest" not only between sojourners and Natives, but among foreigners themselves.[19]

In extraterritorial tribunal such as the U.S. Court for China, the vast majority of cases were between foreigners themselves. For both the U.S. and Great Britain—the two countries with the most extensive court systems in China and Japan—upwards of 75% of the cases in consular courts did not involve Chinese litigants at all. For both countries, criminal and police cases significantly outweighed civil causes. These realities indicate that the principal day-to-day function of such courts was disciplinary and punitive. Reinforcing this conclusion is the fact, explained more fully in the work, that when the U.S. and Great Britain augmented and reformed their court systems in China, they did so by way of bringing sojourning nationals under more effective and rigorous metropolitan authority. Indirectly, of course, the goal was to save imperialism from itself.

The imperatives, contradictions, and multiple constituencies within the Western enterprise in China ensured that ultimately "justice" was more compromise than dictate. Far from being a blunt instrument imposed on a passive, victimized indigenous society by single-minded imperialists, extrality was more in fact a complex balancing act in which metropolitan governments, colonial sojourners, indigenous elites, and opportunists of all nationalities battled for advantage.

Extraterritoriality performed several vital functions in the imperialist enterprise. The first and most readily apparent role of extrality was to carve out a sanctuary where colonial sojourners could live out quite ordinary lives, sheltered from the consequences of their own and their countries' activities in China. Extrality and the treaty port concession areas it buttressed, allowed the forward agents of an implosive process to survive and even prosper in chaos. The very mundaneness of most of the tens of thousands of civil and criminal cases heard by foreign courts in China is itself a testament to extrality's role as a haven from the furious and self-destructive turmoil of a society which contemporaries described as being "midwifed" into the twentieth century.

Once the dynamic of informal imperialism was unleashed, extraterritoriality assumed more sophisticated and subtle tasks as well. It is one of the abiding contradictions of informal imperialism that even while seeking to break down the resistance of indigenous elites to external penetration, outside powers must also bolster these same elites against the civil disorder and political extremism their growing weakness occasions. Visible predatory behavior among foreign nationals against native inhabitants whether assault, rape, theft, or business fraud—although no more or less inherently brutal and exploitative than westernization itself—makes it increasingly perilous for indigenous elites to suppress anti-foreign violence without losing ground in their own society. Doing so opens them to attack from radical nationalists at either end of the political spectrum with agenda distinctly hostile to the interests of imperialism.

Outside powers, collectively unable or unwilling to rule China directly, had to reach a modus vivendi with indigenous authorities. Indirect or informal imperialism could not work by simply decimating or vanquishing indigenous elites, as the latter's "voluntary or enforced cooperation" was essential to the success of the enterprise. Absent this cooperation, raw materials could not "be transferred, strategic interests protected or xenophobic reaction and traditional resistance to change contained." These factors together required the treaty powers to concern themselves with the needs and perceptions of Chinese elites, as without their acquiescence imperialism's coastal enclaves could well have been overrun. The imperative imperialists had to preserve indigenous authority gave collaborators significant leverage in their dealings with outsiders, such that they could enlist and call upon foreign powers to combat activity inimical to their survival and efficacy. Ultimately, treaty port China, it was a Faustian bargain inasmuch as, to paraphrase Sinologist Joseph Levenson, the West historically sought to drain power from Chinese ruling circles in order to be able to give it back to them, but only for the quid pro quo of ever more far-reaching concessions.[20]

Whereas gunboat legalism bound the unequal treaty powers and their sojourning nationals together in the common cause of opening China, the project of conciliating and bolstering up indigenous elites so as to facilitate "imperialism on the cheap" generated what one scholar has described as a "harmony of interests" between metropolitan elites and their indigenous counterparts in the target society.[21] This symmetry of needs linking outside governments and internal authorities created a dynamic that crosscut nationality, the cementing force of extraterritoriality. By virtue of their essential role in suppressing antiforeignism and allowing if not actively abetting the process of penetration, indigenous elites became, paradoxically, a constituency capable of commanding the solicitous, albeit self-serving, attention of imperialists seeking to harness them.

THE EXTRALITY NEXUS

That tension between an imperialist-collaborator alliance, on the one hand, and affinities of race and culture, on the other, was reflected in, and resolved through, extraterritorial jurisprudence. This, then, was extrality's second major function in the imperialist enterprise. Whereas the essential unity of interests between governments and treaty port nationals was evident in the demand for and continued insistence upon the privilege of extrality, what some have called "the tensions of empire" were manifest in periodic efforts to reform extrality through a refinement and redefinition of the criteria used to bestow colonial privilege.

As historian Jack Greene has observed, empires are "extended polities," in which the problems of governance and membership are continuously negotiated by unequal, contending parties.[22] Historians of British imperialism have found that in the colonies, there was "[a] continuous struggle" among governing agents and their sojourning wards to "define the boundaries of law and authority, the limits of freedom, the relevance and applicability of English law, and the proper balance between" settlers' rights and colonial exigencies.[23] Expansion generates tension between frontier outposts and the "mother country." When outposts become stable political entities with their own distinctive character and concerns, they grow increasingly less amenable to control by the center, less desirous of sending home expansionism's dividend. While continuously requiring assistance to battle indigenous opposition and international rivals on the scene, colonial settlers resist and subvert curtailment by their home authorities, whose domestic constituencies seek lower costs or greater payoffs from expansion. For Americans as well, the "bargain" between sojourners and stay-at-homes, a deal mediated by the state, was in constant flux, each ever alert to shifts in costs and benefits; every new exaction and all signs of resistance confirmed the mutual feeling each had of somehow being taken advantage of by the other.

Foreign colonial elites welcomed and solicited the projection of metropolitan authority, but only to the degree this fortified power helped them to navigate their own local crises, faced as they were by mounting waves of interlopers who debased foreign nationality as the currency of privilege and brought into question the whole arbitrary rationale of colonial domination. However, to the extent this projection of power from the center challenged local elite hegemony within expatriate colonial communities, it was resisted, neutralized and appropriated.

Although overseas white communities did not wholly duplicate the metropolitan class spectrum, they contained significant fault lines of their own. In the imperial context, nationality, race, class and gender competed for loyalties, as individuals and groups experienced a "multiplicity of consciousnesses" far "more complex than the dichotomy of colonizer and colonized."[24] As between a foreign vagrant arrested multiple times in Shanghai and a wealthy Chinese merchant living in a luxurious foreign-style house in the International Settlement—who was more "privileged"? As Mary Wilkie has argued, one primary source of instability in the colonial setting was exactly this juxtaposition of white pauper and wealthy Native: both grew enraged over a frustrated sense of entitlement.[25]

The battles among Americans themselves over extrality also makes clear a point earlier obscured, that understanding the inner workings of extraterritorial jurisdiction requires attention not simply to the court-room contest between indigene and foreigner, but also to the larger forces that brought certain foreign individuals and not others into the defendant's box. The visibility of trials, and the ostensible impartiality law requires as the price of its utility, made courtrooms the least manip-ulable, and thus the riskiest, site in the exercise of legal privilege. Assess-ing the overall functioning and impact of the system means under-standing the continuing struggle between Chinese and outsiders, as well as among foreigners themselves, not so much over this or that case, but rather over what portion of Sino-foreign interaction, and of foreign activities in China, extraterritorial courts should be permitted to scruti-nize and adjudicate. Given that courts would hardly have been credible had they consistently taken the side of their own nationals, the real goal of powerful wrongdoers was to stay out of court.

Colonial sojourners were not all the "ideal prefabricated collabora-tors" some historians imagined.[26] White prostitutes, vagrants and pau-pers put a constant strain on the imperial matrix, and thus on consular jurisprudence. Though necessary as surplus labor and/or sexual subsidy, imperial loiterers "lowered the tone" of empires, and inspired among their social betters an effort "to make them invisible, to shut them up in . . . workhouses, or, a last resort, deport them," by way of sustaining "the illusion of a homogeneous white race, affluent, powerful, impeccable, aloof."[27] In fact, lower-class Westerners in this setting frequently found themselves reminding their more prosperous and "respectable" country-men that, in the words of a British sailor in 1893: "We're children of the dominant race, same as you, and more'n that we've got to show the swabs of natives all over the world we are *still* dominant."[28]

COLONIZATION OF CONSCIOUSNESS

The third crucial function extrality performed in the imperialist enter-prise involved what has come to be called by students of Western impe-rialism the "colonization of consciousness" within target societies. The critique of modernization theory in general, and Euro-centric Oriental-ism more particularly, has brought forth a nascent but diverse literature showing how transplanted Western legal systems historically forwarded the colonial enterprise by discrediting traditional customs and elites as "backward," and sanctioning integration into the world market as "progress" and "development." In general, imported capitalist laws and judicial ideologies transformed peasants into wage laborers, commodi-fied communal holdings into individual property, supplanted customary reciprocity with institutionally enforced codes of responsibilities and rights, and propped open underdeveloped markets for the benefit of international capital.[29]

However, there were inherent limitations in the system of extrality as a vehicle for capitalist penetration and transformation. British munici-pal authorities in Shanghai, for example, consistently blocked the pallia-tive changes that historians associate with "proletarianization," such as the implementation of child labor laws, factory safety codes, minimum wage requirements, and so on.[30] Further, in contrast to, for instance, the Philippines and India, where colonial powers had a virtual monopoly over transplanted legal institutions, in treaty port China the multiplicity of foreign and indigenous courts denied any one body of law or group of legal authorities the hegemony required for the "colonization of con-sciousness."[31]

IN SEARCH OF "JUSTICE"

For countries formerly burdened with this anomalous foreign justice within their territory, Western consular jurisprudence is recalled mostly as an era of humiliation and exploitation. The success with which trou-bled regimes "wave the bloody shirt" of extraterritoriality and imperial-ist oppression indicates a still deeply felt bitterness and cynicism about legal norms that once seamlessly legitimated unequal treaties and terri-torial infringements.[32] Immunity among sojourners from indigenous laws, and the general laxity of transplanted colonial self-policing regimes, provide an ever-present subtext in international politics and bilateral incidents.[33]

Chinese historical accounts in particular generally equate extraterri-toriality (*chih-wai fa-ch'üan*), and its synonym "consular jurisdiction"

13

(*ling-shih ts'ai-p'an ch'üan*), with legal laxity, arguing that foreigners' immunity from indigenous law spawned urban vice and violence, and allowed egregious crimes against Chinese to go unpunished and undeterred.[34] This perception arises not only from an enduring emphasis in Chinese jurisprudence upon crime control and society's welfare over the due process rights of individuals, but also from the very real shortcomings of under-funded and ill-supervised extraterritorial courts.[35] On the basis of both cultural perception and historical reality, Chinese have concluded that extrality permitted foreigners and their indigenous collaborators to lay claim to China's resources, while avoiding civil and criminal liabilities in matters large and small, thereby crippling that country's long-term economic, social and political development.

These views are also well represented in Western scholarship, particularly among authors trained in the era of the "New Left" and the Vietnam War. That generation firmly rejected the longstanding positive assessment of the Western enterprise in treaty port China as beneficial, if sometimes painfully so, to China's "modernization." More recent Western-language work on China's treaty ports—Shanghai in particular—ascribes much of the proliferating vice and violence of the 1920s to extrality and its byzantine system of independent national courts and overlapping jurisdictions; foreign nationals extended their legal privileges to their indigenous protèges, spawning a cosmopolitan jurisdictional netherworld in which politics, commerce and crime were inextricably linked. The collective portrait of Shanghai presented in books by Frederic Wakeman, Gail Hershatter and Brian Martin, is one of Sino-foreign gangsterism and vice-based enterprises deeply entwined in the politics and commerce of the treaty port.[36]

There have been scholarly efforts to counter the image of extraterritorial courts as accessories to imperialism. In his 1992 study of the Shanghai British-run International Mixed Court, which handled Sino-foreign cases, Thomas Stephens concludes that despite its colonial auspices, and notwithstanding a certain sensitivity to foreign interests, "[i]n its day-to-day workings th[at] court presented a very close facsimile of the Western notion of a judicial tribunal."[37] According to Stephens, the "prompt, summary, and decisive" hearings of the Mixed Court enabled Shanghai Municipal authorities, largely British, "to maintain, in a population that was 90 percent Chinese, a much higher standard of security, orderliness, cleanliness, and health than was to be

14

found outside settlement limits."[38] Along similar lines, Richard Chang's 1984 study of British and American consular courts in nineteenth-century Japan, concludes from a detailed quantitative and qualitative analysis that "less than 1 percent" of an approximate total of 3,500 mixed cases "may have been adjudicated unfairly." Contrary to "prevalent Japanese interpretations that, as a rule, no Japanese could expect justice" in these courts, in the vast majority of instances, according to the author, indigenous complainants received "fair and impartial" judgments.[39]

AMERICAN EXTRATERRITORIAL "JUSTICE"

The records of the United States Court for China—headquartered in Shanghai, and extant from 1906 to 1942—are suggestive and ambiguous. Although there are numerous decisions any historian would second-guess, those having a daily familiarity with America's domestic justice system should not be surprised: defendants were freed on legal technicalities, felons obtained early release because of crowded jail facilities, repeat offenders were simply recycled through the system. By and large, though, the Court was more friend to plaintiffs than defendants, whatever the nationality of the former. (Defendants were perforce U.S. citizens, or the venue would have been elsewhere). In fact, in spearheading the establishment of the U.S. Court, President Theodore Roosevelt set out to give Chinese a "square deal." Progressives believed that in the long run this would bring America its share of the "China Market," and provide outward-looking Chinese with a tutorial in Anglo-American jurisprudence.

The openness of the proceedings, the increasing volatility of Chinese urban nationalism, knowledge that verdicts could be overturned by the 9th Circuit Court in California—all of these factors militated against gunboat justice in the U.S. Court. This courtroom itself appeared a level playing field; one might even argue that American defendants had an uphill battle against federally appointed judges, sitting without juries, and feeling a greater responsibility to U.S. "national interests" than to any one fellow countryman.

By way of example, let us consider *U.S. v. Jones*, a 1909 case before the U.S. Court for China. This case established the landmark precedent that

"Chinese testimony must be weighed by the same rules as any other." This holding put the Court at odds with the American defendant's argument that "the Chinese mind and point of view is such that in the case of every Chinese witness a Court is bound to start with a presumption that the witness will not tell the truth."[40] The defendant, Thomas Jones, was accused of fatally shooting a Chinese sampan pilot who refused to pick him up at a dock in Chefoo. In dispute was whether Jones accidentally fired a pistol while unloading it, or—as Chinese witnesses insisted—deliberately aimed, fired and killed the pilot. Jones was found guilty of involuntary manslaughter, and sentenced to three years in the Shanghai jail.

Privately, Judge Rufus Thayer (1909–13) conceded that he had imposed what seemed to him a harsh penalty primarily in deference to Chinese public opinion. Second, even as the gavel came down on the defendant Jones, his attorney—with the full endorsement of Judge Thayer—set about lobbying Washington for a Presidential pardon for the convicted murderer on the grounds that he was an otherwise solid, reputable treaty port resident with a family to support.[41] If not for the untimely death of Jones in prison during all of this activity on his behalf, it is likely that he would have served only six months of his prescribed three-year sentence, subject to the stipulation that he not return to China until those three years had passed, so as to avoid needlessly antagonizing Chinese sensibilities.

Was this "justice"? Sympathies probably tend toward the Chinese victim. What we know about the treaty port milieu lends credibility to the version of events given by the other water-taxi pilots. So too, one might argue, the occasion and opportunity for foreign criminal behavior in China grew out of the unequal treaties, which not only sanctioned the continuing influx of privileged foreigners, but also contributed to the inability of successive indigenous governments to achieve the degree of stability and development required to throw off semi-colonial domination. On the other hand, was Jones not entitled to be "innocent until proven guilty," beyond a "reasonable doubt"? Should he have been treated more harshly than a defendant in a similar case back home, simply because he happened to be in China, and his actions had implications for Sino-American relations?

No one verdict would have been "just" to all parties. The real injustice toward Chinese in this instance was less in the court proceedings than in the fact that had Jones been the victim of the pilot, and the pilot been found guilty of the lesser charge of involuntary manslaughter, the U.S. Government and local Americans would have: a) condemned the outcome as further proof that foreigners needed protection from indigenous courts; b) pressured Chinese political officials to strong-arm their judicial counterparts into a reversal; c) demanded an indemnity from the Chinese government, arguing that in "semi-civilized or backward countries," the local government "is held a guarantor of the security of foreigners"; and, d) backed up the U.S. position with the full political, economic and military force at the collective disposal of the unequal treaty powers.

There were countless apparent miscarriages of justice involving Chinese victims, but the abiding, indisputable inequity of extrality was systemic, rather than a matter of this or that particular case. Inequity lay not in public view, but in pre-trial preemption and post-verdict maneuvering behind the scenes through channels much less visible or accessible to Chinese.[42] Financial, legal and cultural hurdles discouraged Chinese from bringing suit in consular courts against foreign nationals. Civil suits occasioned court and lawyers fees; witnesses not of the nationality of the court could not be forced to appear; each different foreign court followed its own laws and procedures; favorable judgments were difficult to collect; defendants often bought time by countersuing Chinese in foreign-dominated "mixed" courts.

INTERROGATING THE PAST

The operations of anomalies such as the U.S. Court for China inspire a multitude of questions from a variety of disciplinary perspectives. Many readers will be concerned about the fate of native litigants coming before American colonial judges. Did they find something approximating "justice" in these venues, or encounter the judicial variant of gunboat diplomacy, where the law of power ran roughshod over the power of law? While not ignoring questions of "justice," the central focus of this work is book as a whole is extrality as a citizenship regime in the changing international system of the nineteenth- and early twentieth-century. From the vantage point of indigenous groups, such as the sampan taximen in *U.S. v. Jones*, the extraterritorial courtroom functioned as one of a wide array of instrumentalities in the hands of powerful outsiders. For metropolitan governments, in this case Judge Rufus Thayer and his Washington overlords, it was a vital site in the effort by nation states to command allegiance and acquiescence from their distant wards.

To explore the intra-foreign struggles over empire and its dividends is not to minimize or ignore imperialism's destructive impact on now independent states still grappling with the aftermath. Neither does it redeem the Shanghai American who, for example, killed a Chinese, trafficked in opium, lived on the earnings of prostitutes, physically abused rickshaw pullers, embezzled money from a business, and the like. Rather, the point is that historians must now explore the naturalization of a distinction between the citizen who committed such crimes while abroad, versus those who stayed home to do the same. That contemporary governments employed a double-standard is to be expected; that most historians followed in tow is more troubling. It seems intellectually schizophrenic to invoke rampant foreign vagrants, prostitutes and street-level predators in colonial ports as proof of just how outrageous imperialism and extrality were, while granting their stay-at-home counterparts deconstruction, contextualization, and a voice of their own. There are perhaps sound reasons for scholars to insist that ultimately such distinctions be drawn, but the implicit acceptance of a state-centered world is not one.

For historians, the post-Cold War de-centering of the nation state and de-nationalization of citizenship have opened up new vantage points from which to look upon the past. As after an earthquake, it becomes clear to survivors just what their world was made of, and what it might take to go on. It now becomes less "formidable" for historians of American foreign relations to take up the challenge issued some years back by Michael Hunt and Charles Lilley, to: "find a place for nonstate actors in our hardy, state-dominated conception of foreign relations."[43] As the planks and pillars of a world built on territorial nation states become exposed to scrutiny, and the sinews of modern citizenship regimes revealed, it becomes possible to think anew about historical phenomena long considered known and understood.

Diplomatic protection and extraterritorial jurisdiction are two such phenomena inviting re-examination. Extrality was an extreme form of diplomatic protection, managing the "China district" entangled the State Department, and later the Justice Department, in constitutional dilemmas. As one law specialist summed up the dilemma in the 1920s: "[W]hile the worthy citizen abroad should be protected, the ever present problem of the government is to accomplish this while relieving itself of responsibility for the underserving one."Inasmuch as it is the stay-at-homes who ultimately bear the costs when governments assume responsibilities for sojourning nationals, "there exists a right to demand of the person proceeding abroad every reasonable guarantee against improper use of his national status. If such citizen has the proper concept of the value of his citizenship and of the government's protection of him, as well as of the obligation to his fellow citizens at home, he will be anxious to submit to reasonable regulation."[44]

There have been any number of studies of the "special relationship," the term generally used to describe Sino-American ties. Some correctly make the point that it was not "special," that it resembled U.S. relationships with most third world, revolutionary countries.[45] Others emphasize that the U.S. enjoyed all of the perquisites of imperialism obtained by powers in a less "special" relationship with China. Most far reaching has been work demonstrating how officials and interest groups on both sides of the Sino-American relationship used the mythology of the "special relationship" for their own purposes, that they were, to quote a Chinese adage, "sleeping in the same bed, dreaming different dreams."[46]

What *Bargaining with the State* offers is an understanding of the "special relationship" as a citizenship regime, one requiring the sojourning American "to submit to reasonable regulation," thereby demonstrating "the proper concept of the value of his citizenship and of the government's protection of him, as well as of the obligation to his fellow citizens at home." One does not need to order up the heavy artillery of Foucault and Derrida to appreciate that, in State Department hands, "reasonableness" is a construct open to contestation and negotiation.

CHAPTER ONE

EXTRATERRITORIALITY IN THE CHANGING
WORLD OF THE NINETEENTH CENTURY

This chapter provides the historical and international context necessary to understand the American experience with colonial legal privileges in treaty port China. The "extraterritorial enclave" was an extraordinarily complex space within the American policy, but cannot be appraised solely in those terms. The U.S. grew to great power status in an international system dominated by Western Europe. American laws and practices on nationality, citizenship and extraterritoriality were formulated within the framework of international law, as it was then being codified. Nineteenth-century extraterritoriality in China was largely shaped by the British; so too, the extrality Great Britain brought to China was the product of centuries of diplomacy and trade between Europe and the non-Western world.

In the developing international system of the nineteenth-century, extraterritoriality was an anomaly, an atavistic remnant of personal fealty in an age of territorial nation-states and modern citizenship regimes.[1] The projection by Western governments of legal authority over sojourners into the "barbarous lands" of Asia and the Middle East was the most notable exception to their abandonment of an earlier era's "vain phantom of unlimited sovereignty."[2] At the same time, the fact that national governments could promise—and threaten—sojourners with a continued connection to the home polity beyond the pale of "civilization," fused imperialism and state-building; a notion of portable, imperial citizenship made Europeans the "shareholders in hegemony" that *civitas* had made ancient Romans.

There was nothing inherently oppressive or exploitative about extrality. In the ancient world, consular jurisdiction—the predominant form of extrality—arose as a mutual concession among incompatible religious and cultural groups to facilitate trade. However, modern extraterritorial jurisdiction over sojourning nationals in the colonial setting turned upon state-to-state unequal treaties, often forced upon indigenous governments in the wake of lost wars, as was the case in the 1842 Treaty of Nanking opening China, as well as the agreements opening Japan a decade later.[3] The crucial differences in the nineteenth-century variant included: the gross disparity of power in the relationship; a shift in Western perceptions of the non-Western world; the greater numbers and diversity of sojourning communities; and the emergence of modern citizenship norms. Together, these factors made extrality an instrument of imperialism, though one that required constant attention and legitimation.

The process set in motion by the 1648 Peace of Westphalia culminated during the 1800s in the modern nation state. This territorially contained, centralized entity became (to quote philosopher John Dewey) a "Person who has a touchy and testy Honor to be defended and avenged at the cost of death and destruction."[4] Sojourners were ever more the embodiment of this "national honor," leading—in an age of expansive global commerce and travel—to more frequent conflict between governments over the activities and status of resident or itinerant foreigners.[5] Centralizing nineteenth-century governments attempted direct control over these sojourners in "barbarous lands," displacing charter companies (such as the English East India Company) which had long exercised quasi-sovereign authority. The appropriation of this far-off jurisdiction by increasingly democratic, centralized governments brought into irreconcilable conflict the perceived rights of sojourning nationals, the demands of domestic constituencies, and the metropolitan support required by ever weaker indigenous regimes on the periphery.

In China, most particularly, the "Midas touch" dynamic of modern extrality transformed it into an unstable protection racket requiring ever more metropolitan supervision, maintenance, and self-justification. Through their association with foreigners, treaty port Chinese themselves were able to evade native authority and exactions. Their relatively large numbers, and their adept manipulation of racist nationalism, gave Western sojourners in treaty port China the wherewithal to resist changes in the ethic of citizenship imposed from the center; they challenged metropolitan demands for a mounting percentage of the take and conformance to changing international norms.

As a fuller exploration of these developments, this chapter covers four major topics: the "modernization" of extrality in the eighteenth and nineteenth centuries; changes in the political and legal relationship between central governments and sojourning nationals during the era; the origins of foreign extraterritorial jurisdiction in China; and the complications of policing the protection racket extrality became in nineteenth-century treaty port China.

EXTRALITY: ANCIENT VERSUS MODERN

As its modern beneficiaries never tired of pointing out, extrality was not invented by mid-nineteenth-century Western imperialists. Historically, self-policing among migratory merchants facilitated trade among religiously or culturally incompatible groups. Ancient and premodern societies almost universally had some form of special law and status for visiting nonmembers.[6] Arabs trading in the southern ports of Tang China (618–907) were permitted special quarters and self-policing.[7] Early Egypt hosted various colonies of foreigners, including Jews, Bedouins, Phoenicians, and Greeks.[8]

In pointing to ancient precedents, nineteenth-century advocates of Western colonial privileges were disingenuous. These early forms of consular jurisdiction were neither inherently exploitative nor inevitably demeaning to host societies. Typically, the right to communal self-governance turned on unilateral concessions to geographically compact, numerically circumscribed minorities by powerful central rulers, upon whose sufferance resident aliens could be secure in person, property, and belief. The primacy of religious affiliation in the determination of legal status made it self evident to contemporaries that sojourners and migratory merchants could not enjoy the full benefits of local law and membership; at the same time, trade and comity motivated host governments to extend basic protections to visitors, and to provide legal venues for the resolution of civil and criminal cases arising between natives and resident strangers.

The more apposite ancient precedent for understanding nineteenth-century extrality is the privileged status of sojourning Romans in their age of empire. In Rome, where non-citizens far outnumbered citizens, *civitas* determined rights, duties and amenability to particular laws.[9] As "shareholders in hegemony," Roman citizens could appeal from local courts throughout the empire in capital cases.[10] In practice, this tended to preempt litigation and discourage summary justice far from Rome.[11] Recall the oft-cited instance of Paul invoking the protection of *civitas* when arrested by officials at Jerusalem. In contrast to homogeneous, religiously defined mercantile groups, Romans abroad included traders, businessmen, farmers, money lenders, bankers, semiofficials, military units, as well as troublesome individuals pushed from the center.[12] The high-handed attitude of Roman sojourners, such as roving senators wielding *legatio libera* (diplomatic immunity), and predatory generals of imperial armies, inspired Cicero to complain about "the hatred with which we are regarded by foreign peoples."[13]

The transformation of accommodationist, equitable consular jurisdiction in Asia and the Mediterranean world into a modern Euro-American variation of Roman imperial citizenship occurred over several centuries.[14] The "capitulations" Westerners enjoyed in Ottoman lands until World War I dated back to the twelfth century. When the Ottoman Turks conquered Constantinopole in 1453, they expanded and regularized a system already in use in the Mediterranean, that of issuing letters of protection to non-Muslim migratory merchants. (The term "capitulations" derives from the *capitula*, or chapters, in these documents.) Ottoman rulers used the threat of abridgment to compel good behavior and true reciprocity for their own sojourning subjects (including Armenians, Greeks, Slavs, and Jews). One detailed study of the Levantine trade has argued conclusively that Westerners "did not occupy a protected and special position in international law within the Ottoman empire" before 1700. "[T]heir rights and obligations were determined partly by the capitulations, partly by their customary place among other groups and by their ability in any given situation to adapt themselves and make the most of the existing power balance."[15]

The dynamics of the practice had been indelibly altered, however, with the decline of Italian city states and entry into the Mediterranean trade of France, the Netherlands, and England, followed by Russia and Austria. With the French capitulation of 1740, particular agreements became valid beyond the lifetime of the granting sultan, depriving Ottoman rulers of negotiating leverage. Russian and Austrian competition in the 1780s prompted each to assume control over large subject groups within the Ottoman empire through blanket grants of protection; for example, by 1800 there were 200,000 Austrian protégés in Moldavia and 60,000 in Wallachia.[16]

Beginning in the late eighteenth century, European governments successively imported into the capitulations concepts and doctrines taking hold in the Western world, such as diplomatic protection, due process, and non-Western inferiority. Prior to this, jurists argued that what put a sovereign beyond the pale of civilized intercourse was a refusal to help strangers in need, such as shipwrecked and stranded sailors. Openness to foreign trade, or full hospitality to resident aliens, did not constitute a litmus test, as a sovereign was thought to have full discretion over such matters. Thus, it was generally held that a government ought to intervene to help its own subject abroad *only* if the latter had been deprived of the remedies available to locals. Though sojourners did not owe their temporary sovereign the same allegiance and obedience that locals did, they were bound to obey the general laws of a place that had been enacted to preserve social order.[17]

In the modern era, however, there was a much wider array of concrete and abstract injuries potentially inflicted upon sojourners. One legacy of the American and French Revolutions was the principle that (white) individuals had basic rights transcending territoriality and government.[18] Thus, to mere physical safety of person and property was added enjoyment of what nineteenth-century Westerners came to think of as the "rights of man." The chief criterion for determining whether a country was modern, civilized, and thus juridically equal became the safety and liberty of a European who might find himself there.[19]

These changing notions marked a more general shift in European views of the non-Western world, from acknowledging differences to asserting cultural superiority. Before, Western Christian states had coexisted with other regional systems, such as Arab-Islamic hegemony; now the European standard of "civilization" emerged as the yardstick of international relations.[20] This marked a qualitative expansion of eighteenth-century precepts, and a jettisoning of naturalist beliefs "that a universal international law deriving from human reason applied to all peoples, European or non-European." Positivist approaches arose that demarcated civilized from noncivilized states. "[I]nternational law applied only to the sovereign states that composed the civilized 'Family of Nations.' "[21] Assimilation into this "society of nations" could come only through westernization, which in turn was to be achieved by acquiescence to treaties, colonization, and tutelage.[22]

DIPLOMATIC PROTECTION, NATIONALITY, AND JURISDICTION

These changes had dramatic consequences for the relationship between sojourners and metropoles (i.e. home governments). A regular, accepted practice of extending extraterritorial diplomatic protection to citizens abroad grew up as a legacy of the French Revolution, with its emphasis on the rights of the individual whether at home or abroad.[23] The legitimacy and survival of the modern nation-state became contingent upon its ability to protect members and provide individuals the opportunity to enjoy their "natural rights" wherever they might roam.

Nineteenth-century jurists found a doctrinal basis for modern diplomatic protection in Emmeric de Vattel's 1758 *Law of Nations*. One of its most frequently quoted precepts is this: "Whoever uses a citizen ill, indirectly offends the state, which is bound to protect this citizen; and the sovereign of the latter should avenge his wrongs, punish the aggressor, and, if possible, obligate him to make full reparation; since otherwise the citizen would not obtain the great end of the civil association, which is, safety."[24] This view combined earlier notions that migratory subjects belonged to the sovereign, and more modern theories of social contract, stipulating that state-dispensed protection was the very reason subjects agreed to be governed and circumscribed.

There was a broad effort among states to bring all individuals into evolving citizenship regimes, supplementing birthright membership with ongoing residency requirements, loyalty oaths, and declarations of allegiance at the age of majority.[25] Where before, subjects at home and abroad "belonged" to the sovereign through "many supplementary and competing systems," increasingly entitlement to protection came only by virtue of nationality.[26] With the enactment of the Napoleonic Code (1804), nationality became a primary category of individual status and identity. Modern citizenship legislation emerged almost simultaneously in European states in a short period around 1800; the citizen replaced the subject, and his relationship with government became less personal and more abstract.[27]

Concepts of sovereignty, though of classical origin, now took on a ideological and uniform character. At the start of the nineteenth century, according to David Kennedy, "there were many sovereigns and many types of sovereignty, which overlapped unproblematically." This was a carry-over from the development of the nation state around diffused authority and franchised sovereignty, with variegated pockets of autonomy within society.[28] At century's end, though, sovereignty had become "consolidat[ed] as an artificial and abstract idea located in the state." To be outside of the nation state community was to be a "pirate...native or...nomad."[29] (Hence the case of Louisa Lassone, a Swiss-born woman who had married a naturalized American in Russia in 1874, never been to the U.S. herself, and become widowed in 1897. Elderly and infirm, she was a burden neither the Swiss nor Americans wanted, leaving her to ask the American Secretary of State in 1901: "So, now, sir, I would like to know what I am.")[30]

The solidification of what Eric Hobsbawm aptly describes as "the administrative, citizen-mobilizing, and citizen-influencing modern national states" put the question of loyalty center stage.[31] Democratization and efforts by governments to involve every individual in political life focused attention on a citizen-subject's feelings toward the state.[32] Greater geographical mobility made clear demonstrations of one's allegiance to the nation more important than proof of local domicile.[33] Enlightenment views of citizenship as a volitional contract lost ground to an international law regime obligating every individual to declare clear and exclusive allegiance to one particular territorial sovereign. Displacing the precept that every man has a right to live somewhere on this earth was a hard-edged belief that every individual has the obligation to call one place "home," thereby assuming an exclusive allegiance to one nation.[34] Even international jurists still loyal to Lockean views of citizenship as a tacit or explicit contract agreed it was an obligatory, unavoidable contract that could be imposed "on whomever it will, and independently of the will of the person."[35]

In this new world order, dual nationals became, if not pitiful victims of political chaos, then conniving free riders, whom no government would tolerate. Stateless people, dual nationals, and transient sojourners were inimical to the new order—no individual could be without a country or have more than one fatherland. In the words of one U.S. official in 1849, states should "as soon tolerate a man with two wives as a man with two countries; as soon bear with polygamy as . . . double allegiance."[36] Governments within the largely Western "family of nations" shared an interest in insuring that all sojourners everywhere belonged to a territorial sovereign somewhere; national rivalries notwithstanding, state-builders viewed with palpable fear the proliferation of a "floating population" of sojourners, dual nationals and stateless persons, who would "escape every responsibility for foul deeds committed abroad should they be thought separated from their original allegiance to the laws of their mother country."[37]

State-building elites sought to "develop the capacity to 'embrace' their own citizens in order to extract from them the resources they need to reproduce themselves over time."[38] Historically, a centralized "monopoly of the legitimate means of movement," and the standardization of documents "effectively distinguishing between citizens/subjects and possible interlopers," constituted an essential pillar in the construction of modern states.[39] The 1800s thus brought the spread and institutionalization throughout most of Western Europe of passport practices first developed by sixteenth- and seventeenth-century French and German towns to regulate regional travel, keep out vagrants, and retain skilled workers.[40] Beginning with the French Revolution, and through the 1890s, successive passport laws targeted political dissidents, military deserters, and itinerant vagrants.

Extra-territorial Policing

Nineteenth-century jurists agreed that a state's duty to protect its citizen-subjects abroad "implies, as a compensation thereof, the right of a calling for account the protected ones if they turn offenders."[41] The other side of diplomatic protection for sojourning citizen-subjects was thus extraterritorial jurisdiction. Vattel himself cautioned that a state "ought not to suffer the citizens to do an injury to the subjects of another state," or "offend that state itself." Sovereigns were warned: "If you let loose the reins to your subjects against foreign nations, these will behave in the same manner to you; and, instead of that friendly intercourse which nature has established between all men, we shall see nothing but one vast and dreadful scene of plunder between nation and nation."[42]

The evolving international law regime sanctioned the extension of sovereign jurisdiction beyond territorial limits over flagships on the high seas, as well as in cases of slavery, piracy, and other international crimes. A state could legitimately claim jurisdiction over persons committing offenses within its territory, or perpetrating crimes against the state from anywhere, crimes such as counterfeiting or subversive conspiracy. In the abstract, sovereigns had the right to make all citizens fully liable to their own country's domestic laws. For example, Austria made subjects indictable upon their return for crimes committed abroad, without regard to the laws of the locale of the crime. Similar rules obtained in the German States, though the Prussian Code dictated punishment for acts abroad only if they were crimes in the place of occurrence. The 1836 Belgian Code called for punishment of crimes abroad by Belgians against countrymen, and allowed foreign victims to draw up complaints for review by Belgian authorities. Britain's 1854 Merchant Shipping Act made seamen liable to English law and British courts; Great Britain asserted universal criminal jurisdiction over its subjects, but exercised this only once, in 1807, in a case ultimately dismissed by domestic high courts.[43]

Abstract principles notwithstanding, the general practice among Western nations in this era was to assert the right of extraterritorial jurisdiction, but settle individual cases by compromise or arbitration.[44] Both "expediency and justice" constrained all but a few countries from attempting to tie "the entire criminal law of a country round the neck of a subject, and. . . making him liable to its operation, in whatever part of the world he may be."[45] Whatever theory held, in reality "every sovereign state is able to obtain obedience only to those of its commands which it has the physical might to enforce." Legitimacy and practicality mandated acquiescence to the reality that although a state might be "legally able to command," it was "powerless to control."[46] For modern Western states projecting power beyond a given "range produced defeats or fragmentation of control, with the result that most rulers settled for" much less than an integrated system of centralized control.[47] This was the object lesson for national governments to be found in the experience of treaty port China.

ORIGINS OF EXTRALITY IN CHINA

Until the 1840s, the Ch'ing dynasty was able to hold the West at bay, and remained indifferent to the evolving practices and ideas of the "Family of Nations." British victory in the Opium War yielded the first series of many "unequal treaties," signed by Ch'ing officials under great duress. Taken together, agreements concluded between 1842 and 1844 with Great Britain, the United States, and France opened five ports to foreign residence (Canton, Shanghai, Amoy, Ningpo, Foochow), conceded the privilege of extraterritoriality to treaty power nationals, and handed Hong Kong over to the British.

The infringements on Chinese sovereignty extraterritoriality ultimately wrought, though, have obscured its inauguration in the 1840s as an instrument of imperial management jointly agreed upon both by Ch'ing officials and foreign representatives, each seeking to police with greater efficacy the intersection of their peoples.[48] Although anxiously sought by Britain and the United States, they did not have to coerce acquiescence from the Chinese on this point. Not foreseeing the "Midas touch" quality of extrality, Ch'ing negotiators initially understood it only as a minor concession, well in keeping with traditional "barbarian management" techniques, and affording mutual benefit for both sides. Their greatest fear (realized in the 1860s) was not extrality, but that foreigners might obtain rights to reside in Peking. For the central government, foreigners' self-governance harkened back to earlier mutual extradition treaties with Russia, and promised to end "the extortions of rapacious underlings," "controversies between [native] persons and barbarians," and smuggling by native and foreigner alike.[49]

Concomitantly, although a few Westerners may early on have sensed the imperial possibilities involved, extrality was first and foremost an effort by commercial groups to control the more "turbulent elements" in the foreign enterprise, so as to insure continued and expanded access to the China trade. Self-discipline among foreigners centered on the class-

30

based effort of established merchant houses to keep their own quite large floating population of sailors, deserters, and mercenaries under control. Preemption, prevention, and punishment were made necessary by the simple fact that in this volatile setting minor incidents between a few individuals—foreign and local—quickly became riots involving hundreds, even thousands. Thus, a small affray in 1765, not "being adjusted to the satisfaction of the Natives," rapidly escalated with the arrival of a local "Army of 20,000 men, and 8 elephants."[50]

The implications for trade were clear. Succinctly stating the problem in 1787, an English lieutenant colonel deputed by London to obtain trade and territorial concessions reported back that such gains were unlikely "unless the Assurance of better Control over our own People is promised," as the Ch'ing could not "confide in Us at present, when they annually see, fifty or sixty Sail of our Ships in their Ports, whose Sailors are subject to no Law or authorized Coercion and Subordination."[51] The East India Company worked to limit seamen's shore leave and access to liquor, by way of preempting "all quarrells between our sailors and the Chinese," not wanting to be held accountable for incidents they lacked the power and authority to resolve.[52]

THE SPACE THAT BECAME EXTRALITY

Until the late eighteenth century, most foreigners trading at, or passing through, Canton (the only open port after 1757) were under the control of the English East India Company (EIC), which had first stationed agents in south China in 1676.[53] In general, the Ch'ing followed the traditional policy of China's rulers, allowing foreign communities autonomy in resolving disputes among themselves and punishing minor offenders.[54] The Company exercised full authority over British subjects and kept other nationals in check through licensing mechanisms and ship discipline. This was in keeping with the general practice among Western European heads of state and central governments of renting out quasi-sovereign powers over sojourners to charter companies, such as the Dutch East India Company and the Levant Company. The relationship between such charter companies and their licensing state governments was complicated and contentious: central authorities enjoyed the efficiency and predictability of returns from trading monopolies; however, there was constant domestic opposition to these commercial privileges. On their part, charter companies paid for the privilege in the form of forced loans to governments.[55]

For charter companies, this rented extraterritorial authority over sojourners and seamen was not about the Western "civilizing mission" so important later, but was rather an instrument wielded to assure shareholders and company personnel security of profit, property, person, and contract.[56] Until the mid-eighteenth century, these companies did not interfere in indigenous legal institutions, except as they directly impinged on the status and security of European traders, missionaries, settlers, or officials.[57] An early Levant Company representative, for example, was instructed that his primary duty was to protect the members of the Company, while interlopers (his own countrymen who were not members of the Company) were to be arrested.[58] In India, the EIC reserved the right to license white migration, restrict the mobility and residence of British subjects, and deport any of the latter for "good" cause.[59] The EIC enjoyed full legislative, executive, and judicial powers; the English Crown "contented [itself] with a position of overlord," stipulating only that Company rule "be reasonable and not contrary or repugnant to the laws, statutes, or customs of the realm of England."[60] The high costs and great risks involved in Asian trade provided incentives to keep sojourners under tight control.[61] The lower-class origins and social marginality of most settlers and sojourners in this early period made this heavy-handed paternal approach that much easier.[62]

Continuing difficulties on both sides of the Sino-foreign divide led in the 1750s to the establishment of the "Canton System," by which all trade was limited to port of Canton, to the busy season only, and to "factory" areas leased from Chinese merchants. Foreigners were not allowed in the city of Canton for any reason, were barred from bringing foreign (European) women with them to these factories, and were required to communicate with authorities only through Chinese merchants who, in turn, had to guarantee all debts and fees and could not borrow from foreigners. The native security merchant, linguist, and comprador assumed responsibility for foreign compliance with all Chinese laws and regulations. Those not under EIC auspices, including the Americans first arriving in the 1780s, came under the ambiguous authority of their own merchant-consuls or "taipans," whom Ch'ing agents treated unofficially as the primary liaison with a given group of foreigners. Taipans and supercargoes (men appointed by investors to oversee a ship's cargo) were made responsible for the discipline of sailors, and for turning over any sailor involved in the death of a Chinese.[63]

Most incidents involving destruction of locals' property or physical injury to Chinese were successfully resolved in this early, pretreaty period by financial compensation to the aggrieved, and payoffs to local officials. So too, contract and debt issues in this initial phase were typically worked out informally, both among foreigners and between foreigners and Chinese. Sino-foreign homicides, though, were always problematic for all parties concerned. The basic Ch'ing approach, as clearly expressed in the Sino-Russian Treaty of Nerchinsk (1689), was that "When people of one empire violate the frontier and kill the people of the other empire, they should be put to death."[64]

Though there were settlements involving lesser penalties, such as financial indemnities or deportation, such compromise was a source of continuing controversy between central and local Ch'ing officials. In a 1748 case, for example, authorities in Peking rejected a compromise reached between Portuguese and Chinese representatives in Macao to deport foreigners accused of killing two Chinese. Central officials argued that: "if after they [foreigners] have violated the basic law of our Empire, [and] we spare them simply because we fear some difficulty, the barbarians will never learn good manners. Hereafter they will become more proud and lawless and will commit more crime. Consequently, instead of diminishing trouble, we only breed it."[65]

Thus, in cases involving the death of a Chinese, Ch'ing central authorities—responding to political pressures and dilemmas of their own—almost uniformly demanded "a life for a life." Reciprocity came in the form of swift and harsh Ch'ing justice against Chinese accused of major crimes against foreigners.[66] By the principle of "collective responsibility," central to Ch'ing law codes and applied to foreigners, if a culprit was not turned over to local officials for trial and punishment (strangling, typically), punitive actions were taken against his immediate superiors; failing that, trade stoppages were then imposed. As the existing literature explains, until the late 1830s, Europeans and Americans on the scene grudgingly submitted to or worked around this policy, recognizing the realities of power and numbers, and aware of their home governments' reluctance to support overt resistance. The dilemma was explained by the exasperated British superintendent of trade in 1835: homicide cases were the "most fraught with difficulty and anxiety," as "we must give up a man or men, or certain individuals in the first instance, and, finally, the officers of the commission are threatened, annoyed, insulted, and ultimately compelled to retreat."[67]

INTRA-FOREIGN TENSIONS

The emphasis in the existing literature on the cultural differences clear in such instances of brinkmanship have obscured the equally important fissures among foreigners themselves occasioned by such exigencies. The pressure to throw over one of their own forced foreigners to experience their identity and affinities in shifting and conflicting ways—with competing pulls of loyalty to ship, shareholders, countrymen, class, and—as a last resort—to Western civilization itself.

As in a lifeboat situation, the high stakes of survival made for a certain triage, the criteria of which became ever more self-justifying and exacting. The question of who in a lifeboat is "them" and who is "us" is a fluid one, as individuals work through their full repertoire of prejudices and preferences, growing ever more convinced that some in the boat are more expendable than others, particularly when the greater "public good" is at stake. In the words of the Portuguese vicar-general of Macao, who in 1773 handed over Englishman Francis Scott for local trial and strangulation for the death of a Chinese: "Moralists decide that when a tyrant demands even an innocent person, with menaces of ruin to the community if refused, the whole number may call on any individual to deliver himself up for the public good, which is of more worth than the life of an individual. Should he refuse to obey, he is not innocent, he is criminal."[68]

This lifeboat dynamic is well illustrated by the oft-cited case of the *Lady Hughes*, erupting in 1784 when the ship's gunner killed two minor Chinese officials while firing a salute. The first response by Company authorities was protective of their man—with claims that he had fled and could not be found; these statements were augmented by protestations that the ship was, strictly speaking, not a Company vessel and thus not under their control; when local officials came to the foreign factories to demand the man, a consensus among foreigners emerged that given a guarantee that the trial would be strictly for face-saving purposes and result in acquittal or a wrist slap, they would give a man over to stand in the missing gunner's place.

No agreement reached, Chinese officials had the *Lady Hughes* super-cargo kidnapped, sealed off the foreign "factories," mobilized troops, and stopped all trade. Once apparent that protecting a common sailor would come at such a price and with such inconvenience and danger to his superiors, a second meeting of foreign (British) authorities ordered the gunner be found or a ship-by-ship search begun. A man was surrendered, tried, and strangled. One early account of the incident claims that English complaints about the supercargo being punished for a gunner's mistake and flight were met by Chinese suggestions to substitute a "servant or some person of less consequence in his place." An 1834 British source alleged that just such a substitution had occurred: that the supercargo had been "redeemed, by the surrender of another individual, equally innocent, though of an humbler station."[69]

A variation on this sacrificial lamb syndrome, wherein culprits were sacrificed to defend a larger principle and only indirectly to feed the Trade, is suggested in a case circa 1780 when a Dutch sailor found guilty of murdering a fellow crewman was not turned over to "the Mandareens but . . . [instead] executed on board one of their ships . . . in sight of the Chinese" as vivid disproof of Ch'ing complaints that "the Europeans have not the Power of punishing a criminal." This brand of demonstrative justice, and the elements of race and class involved, are even clearer in the 1805 case of a Siamese sailor (Andreas) on a Portuguese ship accused of killing a Chinese interpreter at Macao; in the course of events, the governor of the deceased's district demanded the culprit, notwithstanding precedents tacitly ceding jurisdiction in Macao to local Portuguese officials. By way of proving their point, standing their ground, the Portuguese authorities in Macao "conducted the trial of the prisoner and afterwards executed him . . . with considerable forms and parade, the Garrison under arms and the principal officers of the Macao Government being present." The execution of a Timor black slave by his Portuguese "countrymen" in Macao, reported in 1827, seems also to have been used symbolically by way of demonstrating "the right of exercising their own laws on their own subjects."[70]

Over time and under sustained pressure, the hunt for culprits, or likely substitutes, tended to flush out individuals whose hold on group loyalties was more tenuous than that of others. Given modern insights into the psychology of groups in crisis, one wonders, for example, what really went on in an 1820 incident when the search for a culprit in the shooting of a Chinese at Whampoa was settled, to the great relief of all, after a butcher on the Company ship *Duke of York* allegedly killed himself and was then identified as the wanted man.[71]

THE TERRANOVA SOLUTION

The clearest and most dramatic expression of the gestalt of Sino-foreign clashes over "justice" is the well-known but still little understood 1821 Terranova case, a high-stakes episode pitting Americans at Canton against local, provincial, and central Ch'ing authorities, ending when Americans submitted, albeit under protest. Correctly cited in the modern literature as a crystallization of incompatible Chinese and Western ideas of justice and equity, the case also highlights fissures within the ranks on both sides of the divide over the uneven costs and benefits of submission and trade.[72]

The affair involved the death of a Cantonese boatwoman killed by an earthenware jar allegedly thrown by a sailor on board the *Emily*, a Baltimore ship, anchored at Whampoa in the fall of 1821. Before 1840 the few Americans in South China considered themselves bound to obey local laws, in keeping with general U.S. policy regarding sojourning citizens. In Canton, American merchant-consul B. C. Wilcox initially deputed the ship's Chinese security merchant (Pacqua) to pay off the victim's family and prevent the viceroy from learning of events, underscoring the symmetry of interest among traders on both sides of the divide. This effort was apparently thwarted by provincial and central government Ch'ing officials, who were concerned primarily with the complicity of local authorities and merchants in covering up the fact that the *Emily* was carrying opium. Reporting to the capital on the case, Viceroy Yuan saw this as a watershed case in Ch'ing efforts to combat the proliferating opium trade.[73]

When reparation efforts failed, and pressure to turn over a culprit began, Wilcox called a meeting of resident (American) merchants, itinerant supercargoes and ship captains, for opinions "which were given in turn, according to . . . standing and age." It was at this time, and against the opposition of the *Emily*'s captain and supercargo, that Francesco

("Frank") Terranova was identified as the culprit, based on his ownership of the jar thrown from the ship. Wilcox then formed a committee of
15, evenly comprising resident merchants, supercargoes, and ship captains, to insure that whatever the eventual outcome it would be a matter
of rough consensus.

This committee met with the Hong merchants, and a trial was agreed
upon, with the Americans imposing conditions protective of Terranova.
After a "farce" of a trial by the district magistrate held on the *Emily* found
Terranova guilty, Americans resisted turning him over. Appeals that the
sailor had grown ill with anxiety were met with Chinese allegations that
this was no doubt a ruse designed to substitute for Terranova the body of
an individual fortuitously dying from one thing or another.

Local American resolve weakened when the ship's Chinese security
merchant (Co-hong guarantor) was imprisoned, and American trade
halted. American reactions were influenced by various factors: pressures
exerted by the imprisoned security merchant on his foreign creditors
(using the leverage of debts upwards of $1,000,000); the fact that at the
time, the United States had looked to China to prevent British search and
seizure of American vessels, seeking deserters; and, by fears that the
Emily's cargo of opium would ignite controversy.[74] Terranova was turned
over. A Sicilian who, after all, was a "U.S. national" only by virtue of his
employment aboard an American-owned vessel, he was ultimately
strangled after confessing before a provincial judge, although insisting to
the end that it had been an accident. That the strangling was carried out
on the precise site of the execution of five Chinese accused of pirating the
Wabash four years earlier suggests something of the political circumstances dictating the responses of local and provincial Ch'ing officials,
and helps explain their solicitude for a simple boatwoman.[75]

Long since forgotten by scholars are British claims at the time that
Terranova was not the real culprit, simply the owner of the jar, and that
the "employers of the miserable Italian . . . to secure their own individual
profits, did persuade the ignorant man to totally trust himself to a Chinese tribunal." The "eye-witness" testimonials taken as evidence all initially cleared Terranova, and those foreigners summoned by the committee as having said otherwise in various settings recanted. Further
pressure produced a second batch of testimonials implicating Terranova
in accidental homicide. Faced with the loss of the China market, such as
it was at the time, the preferred strategy among Americans on the scene

was to sacrifice one of their more vulnerable members—a sailor with borrowed citizenship and few if any local ties—in order to propitiate indigenous elites and "anti-foreign" mobs.[76]

BEFORE "JUSTICE" BECAME A COLONIAL PRIVILEGE

Although it is unknowable whether surrendered parties were always actual culprits, the allegations made in contemporary sources to the contrary reveal deep-seated mutual suspicions and animosities among foreigners themselves about the distribution of burdens and profits of submission and accommodation. Indeed, what ultimately put supercargoes, superintendents, and merchants between the devil and the deep blue sea, was less their devotion to abstract notions of due process and justice, than resistance by the "floating population" to the sacrifice of some among their numbers to appease Chinese constituencies so as to keep trade open. Sailors effectively raised the cost to their superiors of using what may be described as the "Terranova solution" to resolve Sino-foreign crises that threatened escalation and trade stoppages. British authorities may have deliberated such an option during crises, but after continued mutinies did not do so and bitterly attacked rivals who did. The impulse to jettison a fellow foreigner to appease indigenous outrage and to feed the Trade was countered by the ability and willingness among the rank and file to make their resistance felt.

In the turbulence and mutiny of crewmen there was agency and resistance, not simply the mindless self-aggrandizement suggested in standard accounts about "Happy Jack" and his "riotous conduct...[when] plunged into the attractions of a seaport in a foreign land."[77] For example, investigating a mutiny at Whampoa on board a Company ship (the *Belvedere*) just a few years after the 1784 surrender of the gunner (or his proxy) from the *Lady Hughes*, Company agents blamed the uprising on a prevailing view among the crew "that . . . they would not meet with due Punishment," that is, fair and proportionate justice, following an altercation with Chinese on shore. Nonetheless, Company commanders then imposed severe and public corporal punishment for the ringleaders, fearing the spread of this spirit of outrage and resistance to a fleet comprising over 3,000 sailors who might join in "Depredations against the Inhabitants and put a Stop to the Company's Trade."[78]

Although class solidarity may have been lacking, seamen in this area of the world often acted in concert "as a powerful pressure group" regarding decisions affecting the ship as a whole.[79] Crew members engaged in, to borrow a description from English legal historians John Styles and John Brewer, "actions deliberately undertaken as part of a *negotiative process*."[80] A sailor's sense of justice, of proportionate punishment, though not without blind spots, might well be outraged by the uncustomarily harsh, and possibly illegal, penalties imposed just to keep the peace, that is, to prevent "embarrassments in the Trade." In the continued "riotous conduct" of sailors, we may see an element of enduring resistance to the unusually coercive measures used by their own authorities to keep them in line, and deprive them of what they no doubt saw as the gleanings of empire due them, simply so that their social betters might prosper.[81]

FROM COMPANY TO CROWN

By the 1830s, the proliferation of small, independent traders and vendors on both sides—foreign and Chinese—operating on the fringes of the great monopolies had undermined existing control mechanisms.[82] To the extent "free trade" issues were at stake, as British contemporary accounts underscored, they pertained as much to Sino-foreign dealings as to the efforts by each side—merchant houses and co-hong agents—to drive out unlicensed local "shop men" and private traders from abroad. EIC representatives repeatedly beseeched London for help against "The Inconveniences to which we are constantly subject from the imprudence, or wilful misconduct of Private Traders and the accidents which may happen on board their ships."[83] At the same time, the "private sector" operations of EIC agents acting on their own accord further widened the scope and scale of non-monopoly commerce.[84]

Diversification and centralization within the Sino-foreign trade nexus contributed to the push on both sides for more formal conflict resolution mechanisms. The Crown abolished the EIC's monopoly in 1833, a landmark in the passing of the charter company era. Analogously, on the Chinese front, the debt-ridden co-hong system collapsed, no longer efficiently able to manage the increasingly complex barbarian problem in ways simultaneously beneficial for both local and central officials. (Historically, the power dynamics in force here were not unlike those that in the early Roman republic led to the creation of a special court for noncitizens. Scholars have found that it was not simply the sheer volume or complexity of cases involving non-Romans that prompted the creation of the *praetor peregrinus* in 247 B.C.E.; it was primarily an effort by governing officials to reduce the power obtained by local aristocrats through their extensive patronage and protection of individual foreigners.)[85]

For the British, and in their immediate wake the Americans, extraterritoriality emerged as a way of asserting hierarchical control among foreigners to prevent the sort of incidents leading to trade stoppages. It was the culmination of the gradual acquisition of "authorized Coercion and Subordination" by EIC official and merchant-consuls from the late seventeenth to the early nineteenth centuries in a site where distance from the center, class conflict, and cultural hybridity frayed the hold of deference and power.

With the end of the EIC's charter in the 1830s, the English Crown invested the Company's powers in a superintendent of trade, whom London urged to pursue a "quiescent policy," involving arbitration, persuasion, preemption. British subjects were expected to conform to Chinese laws and usages, provided these applied equally to foreigner and native alike.[86] Parliament established in 1833 a Court of Criminal and Admiralty Jurisdiction in Canton, to be presided over by the superintendent of trade.[87] However, this court lacked the requisite legitimacy not only from the Ch'ing perspective, but also in the view of critics in Parliament and the home judiciary.[88] It was thus wholly ineffective in resolving the volatile homicide cases that so threatened trade, and it heard no case until 1839.[89]

The 1830s and 1840s saw the transition from formal company rule to metropolitan control of consular jurisdiction. There were continued and urgent demands from the frontier for more authority over fellow nationals in the overlapping spheres of Sino-foreign interaction, and intra-foreign conflict. As the Superintendent of Trade explained to Foreign Minister Palmerston in 1837, there was a critical "necessity for the early establishment of some formal and efficacious means of maintaining a state of good order amongst His Majesty's subjects in this country, and for the adjustment of disputes involving claim of money which may arise upon the spot. . . . [N]o circumstance seemed to be better calculated to relax the anti-social jealously and alarm of the Chinese than the existence of adequate regulations for the repression of disorder." He identified the principal source of disorder as the two thousand or so British subjects who, for several months a year, populated Canton, Whampoa, Macao, and nearby anchorages.

The catalyst in the collapse of the makeshift justice system of this early era was the anti-opium campaign of "Commissioner Lin" beginning in 1839. The epidemic spread of opium addiction, and the outflow of silver to pay for imports notwithstanding an 1800 Imperial Edict outlawing the trade, eventually prompted the Tao-kuang emperor to appoint scholar-official Lin Tse-hsü to stamp out the trade. An integral part of the effort was the elevation of opium smuggling to a capital crime punishable by death; to insure foreign liability to the new laws, Lin demanded that the British superintendent of trade and the other foreign "taipans" sign bonds promising to pressure their merchants "to respect the laws of the empire" regarding opium, and in the event of transgression submit accused parties for trial and execution.[90]

Chinese convicted of opium trafficking were executed in front of the Canton foreign factories, to underscore the point. This led to riots in 1839, as "a large and desperate mob was raised by the imprudence and folly of a small number of English and American young men; the number of Chinese increased in about one hour to seven or eight thousand."[91] The specter of being handed over—like common sailors—to the Chinese as culprits awakened the mercantile community to the intolerability and "barbarism" of Ch'ing law. When a group of foreign seamen in Hong Kong, "drunken and riotous," killed a villager (Lin Wei-hi), British Superintendent of Trade Charles Elliot refused Chinese demands for the culprits; he convened the Court of Criminal and Admiralty Jurisdiction, mentioned above, and a jury trial of five seamen resulted in small fines and prison terms of from two to six months.[92] The clash over the Lin Wei-hi case, and the larger jurisdictional contest around the opium trade, became the opening salvos of the first Opium War and the harbingers of treaty port justice.

EXTRALITY'S GRAVITATIONAL PULL

Once obtained by foreigners as a more certain means of self-government, and acceded to by Ch'ing officials as a historically proven method of barbarian management, extrality became something else entirely.[93] It emerged as one of "the three pillars" of British-dominated informal empire in China, the other two being the free trade regime facilitated by control of customs and tariffs, and the omnipresence of gunboats.[94] When applied to territory held by foreigners, extrality gave de facto autonomy to enclaves such as Shanghai, despite the absence of specific treaty regulations suspending Ch'ing authority.[95]

Instances where Chinese were defendants served treaty nations as test cases to pry open China and broaden the scope of foreign privilege. Foreign powers put fiscal, military, and political pressure on indigenous officials to punish such defendants quickly and harshly, thereby perpetuating the very features of Ch'ing law that made it so barbaric and arbitrary as to necessitate extrality in the first place.[96] The most-favored-nation clause in the treaties each foreign power signed with China insured that the victories by one accrued to them all. Chinese resistance to this gunboat legalism was ascribed to a supposed inability to understand sophisticated concepts of Western law, or to a duplicitous, Confucianist, perverse unwillingness to honor contractual commitments.

Migratory merchant communities in ancient China had been numerically and geographically circumscribed. Nineteenth-century Europeans in coastal China were neither. Extrality gained territorial dimensions in the shape of treaty ports (*chiang-k'ou*), which included areas forcibly opened by unequal treaties, ports opened more or less voluntarily by the Chinese themselves, and ports of call for foreign military and trading vessels. Of all these types, there were 5 in the 1840s, 28 in the early 1890s, and 92 by 1917.[97] By 1900, China had ceded extrality to Great Britain, the United States, France, Sweden-Norway, Denmark, Russia, Germany, the Netherlands, Spain, Belgium, Italy, Austria-Hungary, Japan, Peru, Brazil, Portugal, the Congo Free State, and Mexico. Individuals claiming French or British protégé status included those from Persia, Greece, Syria, Togo, Cameroon, Memel, Monaco, Poland, Romania, Siam, Czecho-Slovakia, Yugo-Slavia; Palestine, Iraq, and British East Africa.

These extraterritorial enclaves, or what one scholar has termed "urban micro-colonies," became sanctuaries for tens of thousands of Chinese fleeing chaotic conditions and extractive demands of their own officials.[98] The presence of foreigners in China, particularly those willing to lend or rent out their privileges, made extrality ever more a quasi-legal protection racket, access to which enabled Chinese purchasers to move differently—usually more profitably and exploitatively—within their own society. Chinese in Canton were able to "rent" British nationality from willing foreigners, using the protection to evade internal taxes. So extensive was the practice that British and Ch'ing officials agreed that those Chinese who could legitimately claim British protection—by virtue of a Hong Kong domicile or British paternity, for example—were required to wear Western dress to prevent them from working both sides of the fence.[99]

Extrality's long-term, implosive danger to internal authority and national identity formation in China arose not only from foreign immunity to indigenous law, but also from the operations of "extraterritorial Chinese" able to move unimpeded in the interstices of the unequal treaty system.[100] The extension to Chinese of certain legal immunities by virtue of their presence in foreign enclaves, and the emergence of tremendously wealthy treaty port Chinese, generated constant tension centered primarily in two groups: well-off Chinese faced with racial discrimination at the hands of less well-off foreigners; and, foreign colonials less prosperous than their race and nationality led them to expect.[101]

"JUSTICE" AS A PRIVILEGE

With regard to internal discipline among foreigners, extrality also developed along lines unanticipated by the architects of the first unequal treaties but clearly presaged by pretreaty class struggles over "justice." Ironically, having exalted the superiority of Western legal mores, local foreign officials sought to subordinate their free-wheeling countrymen on the scene by meting out a much abbreviated form of the law and due process enjoyed back home in metropolitan societies.

As an intra-foreign disciplinary regime, extrality's abiding logic was to use a phrase popular in late nineteenth-century America, "when two men ride a horse, one must ride behind." If China was to be exploited without collapsing, some self-ordering and self-control among foreigners was required. The necessity of holding treaty port colonials in check, to the extent that they endangered indigenous authority and local sufferance, gave rise to a conciliatory approach to Sino-foreign legal conflicts. Complementing the aggressive use of test cases to expand and protect the foreign enterprise in China was an accommodationist tactic of sacrificing a "Terranova" close at hand. Indeed, at least one Ch'ing official recognized this dynamic early on. An 1843 secret memorial to Peking from the viceroy at Nanking (who had also negotiated the Sino-American Treaty of Wanghia) observed that greed made the English solicitous toward locals, translating into tough justice for "colored barbarians," i.e., Indiamen, Manilamen, and the outcasts of way stations between Europe and Asia.[102]

In a carryover from the pretreaty era, the primary though elusive target of extraterritorial justice comprised, "[r]unaway sailors and other lawless individuals" in the habit of "going about masked, and under the cover of night plundering the houses and persons of the Chinese," and in some instances using the British and American flags to demand "convoy money" to "protect" small Chinese vessels.[103] Piracy and growing instability created a market for protection, filled by "British and other European Subjects, generally reckless characters and under no control or feeling of responsibility." British officials and established merchants complained that such activities "tend[ed] to alienate from us the good will of the Chinese, and to degrade . . . the British National character in their eyes."[104]

As in the pretreaty era, the self-policing effort within foreign ranks was centered on controlling internal "turbulent" elements, the "band of dissolute and reckless individuals" most likely to perpetrate "assaults upon the Natives that would create a decided ill feeling against . . . [foreigners] amongst the Chinese, and perhaps lead to deplorable and serious results hereafter."[105] Chinese officials and long-term colonial settlers both felt most threatened by the union of "unscrupulous natives and lawless foreigners out of employment." The combination of local knowledge and foreign power raised the specter of "great disorders and strifes," as seen in the late 1860s when something akin to a "gold rush" erupted in what is today Shandong. American diplomats advised the imperial government to open up such areas to regulated exploitation, by way of forestalling the "multitudes of needy, reckless people from all countries [who] will swarm towards these regions, in their desire for gain."[106]

Foreign Office dispatches cautioned that "foreign vagabonds infest the open ports and constantly commit evil, greatly to the injury alike of all natives and foreigners quietly living there." So urgent was the problem, that native businesses and vendors had submitted a petition to regional officials, asking for cooperation with foreign consuls to drive out foreigners without visible means of support. In Shanghai, foreign consuls met frequently to work up preventative measures against "foreign vagabonds who are at present prowling about the settlement." The prosperity and well-being of "well-disposed persons," whether Chinese or foreign, were threatened most when unemployed outsiders "band[ed] together" with natives "to plunder and stir up the utmost disorder."[107]

RESISTANCE AND BARGAINING

There is no doubt that the era of charter company "justice" among sojourners was a more efficient form of extra-territorial self-governance than were these later efforts of metropolitan states to bring "the rule of law" to their own nationals in colonial areas. In their prime, entities such as the EIC functioned not unlike the tightly run Hanseatic League, the fourteenth-century German collective security mercantile organization. German *komtors* were established in key trade nodes, such as London, Novgorod, and Bruges; each had a constitution based on those of German parent municipalities, and were self-governing through consular jurisdiction. Collective bargaining power was sustained by periodic campaigns against "free riders" seeking the privileges but shirking the dues. Among other tactics was the use of expulsion (*verhansung*) to punish a town in the event one of its merchants refused to conform and comply with League regulations.[108] In contrast, metropolitan-controlled extrality generated what historians have identified as "a shift in the ideology justifying Empire from the vulgar language of profit to that of order, proper governance, and humanitarianism."[109] In China, this spawned sojourners less like Hanse merchants and more like "haughty" ancient Romans traveling beyond their imperial capital, their privileges in hand.

As successive Roman emperors found, so too did nineteenth-century metropolitan governments: Policing the ranks was no simple task when imperial *civitas* made every man a Midas. Those expected to "ride behind," to be latter-day Terranovas, resisted this disciplinary regime, and did so by invoking the very ideas and language of cultural and racial superiority employed against the Chinese to justify extrality and the unequal treaties in the first place. Race provided access to privilege, even when nationality claims were dubious. Although foreign offenders from nontreaty powers were supposed to be turned over to Chinese courts, treaty port types agreed that it was "unworthy of western nations to let the Chinese see that his native country thinks so little of a white man, that it will subject him to the tender mercies of a Chinese Police Court."[110]

Western contempt for Chinese sustained the imperialist enterprise there by supplying the cultural and philosophical justification for transgressing Chinese sovereignty even while pledging to uphold that country's "administrative and territorial integrity."[111] Most important, it established foreign nationality as the criterion of colonial privilege, such that diverse and rivalrous treaty port foreigners were drawn together through a *weltanschauung* of racial superiority, which endured until Japan's rise as an unequal treaty power in China in the late 1890s.[112] However, policing internal ranks required assertion of class-based summary justice, directed primarily at fellow foreigners whose unlicensed predations threatened person and property within the foreign-run settlements, and/or were deemed so egregious as to risk either native retaliation or the further collapse of internal authority. Both the British and the Americans found that harsh authoritarian rule over sojourners might help state-to-state relations, but would at the same time threaten internal control in foreign communities. The capacity of a legal system to preserve "the wider social order and system of class rule" depends not merely upon its control of the means of violence, but also upon its "ability to present itself as the guardian of the interests and sentiment of those being ruled."[113]

In China, nineteenth-century great powers faced this intractable contradiction: In order to establish, preserve, and enlarge a foothold in the target area, outsiders had to weaken the resistance of indigenous elites to Western penetration, such that they acceded to unequal treaties and foreign intrusion. On the other hand, imperialists had to bolster these same indigenous elites against the civil disorder and political extremism their growing weakness occasioned. Forcing an indigenous government into the imperialist harness required a combination of coercion and solicitude. Acquiescence to foreign intrusion undermined a regime's legitimacy, eroding its ability to collect revenues (needed to pay off foreign loans and indemnities), enforce laws, and punish anti-foreignism, i.e., the hostile and often violent reaction in a society to the presence and activities of unwanted, privileged, and well-armed foreigners. This corrosive process, in turn, left indigenous governments vulnerable to attack from radical nationalists at either end of the political spectrum with agenda distinctly hostile to the interests of imperialism.[114]

FULCRUM SHIFT OF THE 1860S

These contending imperatives came to the fore particularly in the 1860s, when a second major round of treaty revisions expanded the system beyond all previous imaginings.[115] In 1858, following the sacking of Peking by European forces, China signed the Treaties of Tientsin with Great Britain, France, the United States, and Russia. These opened up eleven new ports, affirmed the legality of the opium trade, brought China's tariff collections under the British-run Imperial Maritime Customs Service, opened up the Yangtze River to foreign navigation, allowed foreign travel and commerce in the interior under a passport system, expanded the rights and protection of Christian missionaries, and allowed foreign diplomats to reside in the capital.[116]

The expansion of the system exacerbated intra-foreign tensions, increased pressure on the Ch'ing to control the indigenous population, and awakened Chinese opposition. Complaints by the Tsungli Yamen (China's new foreign affairs ministry) cited continued missionary efforts to extend protection to native converts, unregulated travel by foreigners into the interior, and the unsupervised transfer of land to foreigners.[117] The return home of Chinese graduates from Western law schools, and the greater availability of translations of Western-language international law classics, illuminated Sino-foreign treaties as unequal and humiliating. In his 1868 "Proposals on Foreign Affairs," for example, the public intellectual Hsueh Fu-ch'eng called for an end to both extraterritorial legal privileges and the most-favored-nation provisions of these treaties.[118]

On their part, a cadre of Western diplomats identified extrality and its abuses as one of the sources of resentment leading to incidents such as the 1870 Tientsin massacre of missionaries and converts. While conceding the enormous problems that would undoubtedly arise with the abolition of consular jurisdiction, these observers foresaw with great prescience that: extrality would "sooner or later, end in the overthrow of the Government within whose jurisdiction it is exercised."[119] One incentive Chinese officials held out to foreigners was the possibility that giving up extrality would extend their access beyond the extant 14 ports into the interior.[120] These counter currents inspired the "cooperative policy" of the post-Tientsin treaties era. As Mary Wright explains, the approach meant "co-operation on the part of Great Britain, the United States, France, Russia, *and* China to secure the peaceful settlement of disputes and the gradual modernization of China."[121]

So too, did the shifting currents widen the split between British merchants and diplomats on the optimum strategy for opening up China. The Foreign Office did not want the commitments and problems of expanding extrality beyond ports, whereas business groups seemed to want to make China "into one vast Treaty Port." London waged "a constant struggle between the mercantile demand for an all-out attack on Chinese backwardness at whatever costs," and government reluctance to face the consequences of the total collapse of Ch'ing authority.[122]

Outside of China, the 1860s also brought a fulcrum shift in the development of the extraterritorial enclave. Although Western governments expanded their extraterritorial realm to include Japan, they were increasingly on the defensive on the entire issue of colonial legal privileges. Tokugawa officials, learning from China's fate, effectively restricted extraterritorialized foreigners to open ports. At this same time, Ottoman rulers endeavored to narrow and rationalize foreign privileges. Although it would be almost five decades before the final abrogation of the capitulations, between 1867 and 1900 foreigners lost a significant percentage of their immunities. The Treaty of Paris of 1856 admitted Turkey into the "concert of nations," and its rulers were able to parlay that gain into more indigenous control over mixed cases, real estate, and protégé questions.

These changes in the international system, the evolving agenda of metropolitan governments, and growing instability in China, led to widening conflict between sojourners and their home authorities—conflict inevitably spilling over into the day-to-day administration of extraterritorial justice. Before taking up this confrontation between sojourners and state-builders, let us first examine the nature of Americans' participation, and their role in the treaty port system.

CHAPTER TWO

EXTRATERRITORIAL AMERICANS,
BEFORE THE RUSH TO EMPIRE

U.S. approaches to colonial legal privileges and extraterritorial governance were shaped not only in the colonial context described in the preceding chapter, but also by late eighteenth- and early nineteenth-century
internal American struggles over federalism, race, expansionism, and the
meaning of consensual citizenship. Their war of independence from
England's claims of "perpetual allegiance" had convinced early Americans of the need to put strict constitutional and territorial limits on government authority over citizens. U.S. nationals operating abroad thus
generally held to an Enlightenment-era international law tenet that
sojourners must take local law as they found it.

Yet, by 1900, the United States was philosophically and systemically
committed to an international system of racialized, juridical hierarchies;
the American polity itself had expanded to encompass a broad array of
"anomalous zones," where the United States demanded allegiance from
"subject peoples," but exercised its jurisdiction not subject to constitutional restraints.[1] Among the more strategic of the many stepping-stones
to 1900 were palpable shifts in the relationship between the federal government and American nationals sojourning abroad. It was, in fact, the

1844 Treaty of Wanghia with China that created a great divide in the status of sojourning Americans between those in countries belonging to the "family of nations," with whom the United States sought "comity," and those in non-Christian, "barbaric" states where extrality was demanded and exercised.

Though subscribing to the prejudice against non-Western mores, American lawmakers remained unapologetically ambivalent about extrality and its imperial pretensions. This attitude was evident in the [dis]organization and deficiencies of U.S. consular courts in China. Paradoxically, domestic anti-imperialism—expressed in an unwillingness to subsidize a full-dress colonial service—gave free rein to the imperialistic activities of individual Americans. Federal control over sojourners increased during the Civil War era, however, as seen in the imposition of an income tax on absent U.S. nationals. Reconstruction era laws and court precedents made diplomatic protection for citizens a constitutional right. This, in turn, generated intense struggle between sojourners and the State Department over the terms of the exchange, particularly in extraterritorial zones.

This chapter engages four major topics: the evolution of American thinking about the status of sojourning U.S. nationals; the federal government's efforts to construct a constitutionally acceptable approach to diplomatic protection; the range of distinctions in U.S. practice as regards American nationals in the "civilized" world of the West, the imperial borderlands of Central America, and the distant markets of the Asia Pacific; and the operation of American consular jurisdiction in nineteenth-century China.

ORIGINAL INTENT AND SECOND THOUGHTS

Gauging the rights and responsibilities of U.S. nationals sojourning beyond the territorial United States was a uniquely complicated proposition. Continental expansion, as well as the constitutional division of power between federal and state government, gave "unqualified assent" to '[o]nly the minimal definition of national citizenship, meaning the individual's allegiance and the nation's reciprocal guarantee of protection."[2] Well into the century, " 'federal' relations with European powers could not be extricated from the federal bonds among Americans," one leading historian observes.[3] Until the "Civil War, states had the larger part in defining citizens. National citizenship was inchoate."[4] One of the meanings given the term "foreign" in contemporary law dictionaries, for example, was membership in a different state of the Union. As late as the 1840s, the governor of Vermont felt within his rights to settle extradition cases with Canada, a prerogative unthinkable in twentieth-century America. Only in 1856 did the Secretary of State extract from Congress a legal monopoly to issue passports. Not until the 1890s did individual states yield to central authorities exclusive and effective control over both immigration and emigration.[5]

The original Constitution was silent not only on the precise meaning of American citizenship itself, but also on the rights and responsibilities of U.S. nationals sojourning abroad. Philosophically, the prevailing influence on contemporary American thinking on the question of protecting sojourning citizens was the view propounded in Vattel's *Law of Nations*. Vattel, as noted earlier, posited the state's obligation to protect and avenge its sojourning citizens, while at the same time conceding that resident foreigners should obey local laws and call upon their own sovereign *only* when deprived of the legal remedies available to native inhabitants. These principles found concrete expression in U.S. federal law and policy. Until the 1840s, most U.S. nationals abroad were, in theory, subject to local authority. Indeed, federal officials warned sojourners in 1829 that to violate indigenous laws was also to violate "their duty to their own Government and country," and would be met with "censure and punishment."[6]

Throughout the century, Supreme Court decisions reaffirmed the territorial limits of U.S. domestic laws and jurisdiction.[7] Although the Crimes Act of 1790 extended federal authority over U.S. nationals abroad in cases of treason, piracy, slave trading, and counterfeiting, the judicial branch interpreted this power narrowly.[8] State Department jurisdiction over public or private U.S. vessels came as a continuation of territorial sovereignty; it was the flag of the vessel, not the nationality of the sailor, that occasioned the government's long reach.[9] Early exceptions to the territoriality principle came by virtue of treaties signed with Morocco (1787), Algiers (1795), Tunis (1797), and Tripoli (1805).[10] At least in this early period, though, these treaties were distinctly different from later "unequal treaties" concluded between the 1830s and the 1880s. Until mid-century there was no identifiable American community residing in

North Africa, and in practice these privileges translated simply into consular jurisdiction over seamen on U.S. public and private vessels.[11]

Broadly speaking, eighteenth- and nineteenth-century American views on the rights and responsibilities of sojourners were entangled with domestic struggles over citizenship, federalism, and expansion. In the decades after the American Revolution, domination of Congress and the courts by supporters of strong central government—the Federalists—translated into laws and precedents emphasizing individual obligation to the whole. Successive laws in the 1790s made citizenship more difficult to obtain, more demanding to possess, and more complicated to throw off. Jeffersonian republicans, generally advocates of the primacy of individual states over the federal government, supported more liberal immigration and naturalization policies. They saw as their natural constituents newer arrivals, whose numbers might counter Federalist strongholds among the monied elite. However, even after Thomas Jefferson's assumption of the presidency in 1800, continuing Federalist control of the courts insured decisions favoring strong national government over states rights, and conscriptive citizenship over individual consent.[12]

Views on Expatriation

The principal overlap between domestic partisan debates and the determination of sojourners' status came on the subject of expatriation. Created out of a revolution against the "perpetual allegiance" claims of the British Crown, early Americans embraced as a natural right the ability to leave off one nationality and take up another. Federalists and Jeffersonians disagreed as to the hurdles an individual should be faced with in exercising this right, with the latter offering a more liberal approach.[13] However, both supported Federalist court decisions denying the right of sojourning Americans to expatriate themselves in instances where to do so thwarted a coherent and consistent foreign policy. Indeed, as Secretary of State, Jefferson himself had been the driving force in the passage of the Logan Act "to Prevent Usurpation of Executive Functions," by individuals with the "temerity and impudence" to "interfere" in the federal government's dealings with other sovereigns.[14]

This near bipartisan agreement was first evident in a series of cases in the 1790s against individuals charged with privateering, thereby violating official American neutrality between France and Britain. These defendants claimed to have expatriated themselves from the United States, and so contested American jurisdiction. The questions before the courts were these: assuming, as most Americans did, that voluntary expatriation was a natural right, what constituted adequate evidence of the act, what limitations obtained, and could either side unilaterally sever the tie?[15] In *Henfield's Case*, heard by the Pennsylvania circuit court, Chief Justice John Jay asserted that individuals must heed "the will of the people" as manifest in law; a member may not unilaterally abandon the burdens of citizenship.[16] Treaties entered into by the United States bind citizens themselves, and "every virtuous citizen . . . will concur in observing and executing them with honor and good faith."[17] Similarly, in *Talbot v. Janson* (1795), the Supreme Court found that the natural right of free expatriation did not include the right to injure the country of one's native allegiance: "Can that emigration be legal and justifiable," asked the Justices, "which commits or endangers the neutrality, peace, or safety of the nation of which the emigrant is a member?"[18]

As became clear in the *Talbot* case, both Federalists and Jeffersonians found a common threat in the defendant's effort to equate citizenship with consent, but allegiance to tyranny. For Talbot, "Citizenship is a political tie; allegiance is a territorial tenure. Citizenship is the character of equality; allegiance is a badge of inferiority. Citizenship is constitutional; allegiance is personal. Citizenship is freedom; allegiance is servitude. Citizenship is communicable; allegiance is repulsive. Citizenship may be relinquished; allegiance is perpetual."[19] Despite their philosophical and partisan differences in the domestic sphere, Jeffersonians and Federalists thus agreed that no man can be without a country; to throw off one nationality required taking on another. The modern world of nation-states was no place for "a human balloon, detached and buoyant in the political atmosphere"; sovereigns could not long suffer migratory, unencumbered "citizens of the world" forever "roving on the ocean in quest of plunder."[20]

More complex still were instances when U.S. assertions of jurisdiction or extension of diplomatic protection ran up against another country's prerogatives. Such cases typically juxtaposed the federal government's obligations to a citizen against not only the demands of good state-to-state relations, but also the desire to validate international law.[21] In the Anglo-American impressment controversy leading up to the War of 1812, for example, federal officials ultimately had to choose between their obligation to protect crewmen aboard American ships from British efforts to recapture English-born subjects, and peaceful resolution of differences between the two countries. A coincidence of commercial goals and philosophical inclinations gave greater weight to the government's obligation to protect its nationals. Despite knowing that substantial numbers of sailors falsely claimed U.S. citizenship when confronted by British vessels, the great Federalist John Adams nonetheless invoked the allegiance-for-protection contract between citizen and government. In a letter to the *Boston Patriot* in early 1809, Adams wrote: these seamen "are our fellow-citizens by our laws. They have sworn allegiance to the United States. We have admitted them to all the rights and privileges of American citizens, and by this admission have contracted with them to support and defend them in the enjoyment of such rights."[22]

Evolving Federal Policy on Extraterritorial Citizenship

U.S. officials opted for a case-by-case approach to the duties and rights of sojourning Americans, sacrificing consistency for flexibility. To illustrate, until the late 1860s, there was no consensus that naturalized U.S. citizens who returned to their country of birth were entitled to American diplomatic protection. In the 1840s, the U.S. Minister at Berlin (and later famed international jurist) Henry Wheaton told Prussian-born Johann Knocke that, despite many years in the United States as a naturalized citizen, once back in Prussia, "your native domicile and natural character revert, . . . and you are bound in all respects to obey the laws exactly as if you had never emigrated."[23] A few years later, H. V. de Sandt—who had only declared his intention to become a naturalized American—was harassed upon his return to Prussia. A new U.S. minister in Berlin, Thomas Bayard, insisted that naturalized Americans owing no military service to Prussia and, having violated no local laws, had the right to visit and reside there without molestation.[24]

The Civil War and After

In the Anglo-American experience, according to John Kettner, "concepts of allegiance at any given time consisted of clusters of theory, practice, law, and tradition, which often coalesced suddenly under the pressure of events that thrust individuals and the state into new and ill-defined relationships."[25] As the 1790s had been one of those generative decades, so too did Civil War and Reconstruction transform not only domestic citizenship, but also the meaning of American nationality beyond U.S. territorial limits.

To begin with, Civil War conscription convinced some naturalized Americans to return to their native lands; they then used distance to avoid one call to arms, and their U.S. citizenship another, i.e., the military service demands of their birth country. The U.S. minister to Prussia reported in 1865 at least five hundred of these cases. Decades later, in the 1920s, the leading expert on the subject speculated that from this Civil War conscription experience sprang "a prejudice . . . in the State Department and in our whole government against the American citizen who was abroad."[26] Earlier federal zeal to shelter naturalized Americans sojourning abroad from the military reclamation efforts of their native countries waned, according to an 1873 report, "when it was seen that worthless naturalized citizens fled before the requirements of military service by their adopted Government here, and not only took refuge from such service in their native land, but impertinently demanded that the United States should interpose to procure their exemption from military service exacted here."[27]

Second, Reconstruction brought the 14th Amendment (1868), which declared, inter alia, that the citizen—whether native or naturalized—had the right to be protected by the federal government when in a foreign territory or on the high seas.[28] The practical implications of this for those then sojourning abroad might have been diluted by popular and official frustration over the Civil War conscription battle, but for the eruption that year of an Anglo-American imbroglio over the trial in Ireland of two naturalized Irish-Americans. The two men (Warren and Costello) had joined an expedition during the Fenian uprising in Ireland; when brought up under local law for treason-felony, they invoked their status as aliens. As aliens they claimed a right to be tried by a "jury de medietate linguae," composed of equal parts British and foreign elements. The British invoked "perpetual allegiance," and tried the prisoners as British subjects, causing what the Secretary of State described as an outcry "throughout the whole country, from Portland to San Francisco and from St. Paul to Pensacola."[29]

Almost one hundred memorials from across the country prompted the Committee on Foreign Affairs to submit a bill declaring expatriation as an absolute and natural right, and calling for presidential action on behalf of Americans—native or naturalized—who might find themselves in trouble abroad. Both parties held their conventions around this time, and adopted platforms supporting the bill.[30] The result was the 1868 Act, which instructed the President, upon learning "that any citizen of the United States has been unjustly deprived of his liberty by or under the authority of any foreign government," to employ all means short of war to effect the release of that individual.

When Reconstruction amendments and constitutional case law, such as the *Slaughter House Cases*, construed diplomatic protection as an inherent right of citizenship, this predictably exacerbated the "free rider" phenomenon. One contemporary looking back in 1905 upon this post-Civil War era complained that "hordes of foreigners" had "come to this country to become naturalized with the intent to return" home to live under the great boon of American protection. "The naturalization of such persons in no wise adds to the strength or greatness of this country, and their presence in the country of their origin is undesirable and irritating."[31]

Consular reports from Costa Rica in the late 1860s told of young men going to the United States obtaining letters of naturalization, and returning home after a short stay to use their adopted citizenship as a bar against obligations.[32] In the 1870s, officials complained of "a large number of people floating through the Spanish-American Republics, claiming the protection of the American flag, a majority of whom, perhaps, are not entitled to the protection they demand." Some were bona fide native American citizens, who had left the United States at early age, were engaged in permanent business in their adopted country, had married there, owned property, participated in internal affairs—both social and political—and evidenced no expectation of ever returning to the birthplace.[33] Others had been naturalized, legitimately or through fraud, and seemed to see nationality as a mere convenience.[34]

Diplomatic Protection and Constitutionality

The predictable response among federal officials was to seek limits "to the right and duty of a government to interfere in behalf of persons born or naturalized within its jurisdiction," who had then left the United

States with no obvious intent of ever returning.[35] The challenge was to establish and control the criteria by which sojourners could be sorted into citizens and pretenders. Protection was to be reserved for the individual who is "ready to support the government with his services, his fortune, and his life even, should the public exigencies be such as to require them."[36] When questions arose in 1873 about an American-born individual who had moved to Fiji and now wanted a passport, for example, the test applied was this: had his protracted absence deprived the United States of his services and resources at a time when they were most needed (i.e., the Civil War)? Ultimately, the State Department recognized this individual as a citizen upon learning that he had served in the Mexican War, and had become disabled, moving then to the South Seas on medical advice.[37]

In contrast to the 1790s legal issues in *Henfield's Case* and *Talbot v. Janson*, the question became not whether an individual could freely expatriate himself under any circumstances, but whether a government could assume (and thus formalize) expatriation from an individual's actions and circumstances. The most obvious precedent in automatic expatriation was the 1855 Nationality Act, which embraced the principle of female derivative nationality, by which a foreign woman assumed the nationality of her American husband.[38] For Congress, at least in the late 1860s and with regard to males, the inherent right of expatriation belonged to the individual, not the government. Capitol Hill repeatedly rejected bills calling for involuntary expatriation of citizens who had committed certain acts, such as establishing domicile abroad with no evident intent to return.[39]

However, presumed expatriation was the preference for federal officials. "Citizenship involves duties and obligations, as well as rights. The correlative right of protection by the Government may be waived or lost by long-continued avoidance and silent withdrawal from the performance of the duties of citizenship as well as by open renunciation."[40] In a revival of the principles enunciated in the 1790s, the individual himself could not unilaterally throw off allegiance, but required the government's consent as expressed through legislation.

Highlighting the growing abuse of diplomatic protection and acquired nationality, President Ulysses Grant used his annual address to instruct the State Department to exercise cautious scrutiny in reviewing claims from U.S. citizens abroad.[41] Thus emerged a growing list of actions and circumstances that could be taken to signify a sojourner's abandonment of U.S. citizenship. First and foremost, was prolonged absence from the country with no evident intention of returning to America. There were exceptions and ambiguities, however. Merchants and businessmen who established domiciles abroad for commercial purposes only did not lose their American nationality.[42] Harkening back to the precedents of the 1790s, protracted absence did not bring expatriation unless the individual had since acquired a new nationality: the "man without a country" was intolerable.[43]

Other actions raising the presumption of American citizenship abandoned included naturalization or preparation for such abroad, voluntary entrance into the civil or military service of another government express renunciation, concealing naturalization when convenient, purchasing or cultivating land abroad, nonpayment of the income and excise tax imposed on sojourners after 1861.[44] In short, if the sojourner permanently withdrew himself and his property, and placed both "where neither can be made to contribute to the national necessities," acquired a political domicile in a foreign country, and avowed his purpose not to return, his country has the right to presume that he has made his election of expatriation."[45] Automatic expatriation was also effected through bilateral treaties. For example, an agreement between the United States and the North German Confederation in 1868 stipulated that German subjects naturalized in the United States and residing there five years would be treated as American; they could not be prosecuted for any criminal offense, except those committed prior to expatriation; naturalized subjects who returned to their native country and resided for two years would be considered reverted.

Thus, the executive branch sought to do through administrative procedure what Congress would not allow it to do legislatively. Case by case, the State Department constructed a citizenship regime for sojourners, a bureaucratic rationale for the dispensation or withholding of diplomatic protection and recognition of status. Underlying these various efforts was the drive by federal officials to make diplomatic protection the government's discretionary right, not the individual's legal entitlement. "The duty of protection depends much on the conduct of the citizen abroad" was the argument put forth in the early 1870s by the Secretary of the Navy. "If he manifests a contempt or hostility to his own Government or country, and avoids every duty of a citizen, the Government is

not bound to protect such person. The Government is left to its own discretion in such cases, and must act, under its responsibility, in each particular case." Yes, all pleas for diplomatic protection merited attention, he
conceded, but could justifiably be denied to the citizen who, "by his conduct, has forfeited clearly his claim to it."[46]

BETWEEN THEORY AND PRACTICE

There was a distinct geographical and cultural dimension in the evolution of American diplomatic protection and extraterritorial jurisdiction.
Nineteenth-century U.S. doctrine and practice on sojourner questions
developed on three different tiers. The first comprised relations with perceived legal and cultural equals, Western Europe in particular; the second, interactions with Latin America, the Pacific islands, and certain
African areas; the third, dealings with non-Western sovereigns who had
ceded resident foreigners varying degrees of self-governance.

In both the first and second spheres, resolution of conflicts over
sojourning nationals occurred through invocation of international law,
arbitration, bilateral treaties, and power politics. The defining difference
between the two realms lay less in the exercise of formal diplomacy than
in the impact of U.S. attitudes and decisions on the less powerful, underdeveloped countries of Latin America, the Pacific, and Africa. What
occurred as "comity" in U.S.–European relations, translated into "hegemony" in the second realm, most especially in Central America.

As suggested by earlier remarks, U.S.–European conflicts typically
centered on the latters' efforts to lay claim to the military services of their
nationals who had become naturalized U.S. citizens. After decades of
periodic incidents and imbroglios, the United States and Western European powers reached a modus vivendi, settling competing claims on the
basis of "comity," meaning a broad agreement among perceived legal and
cultural equals about the rules of the game. While adhering to different
membership models, Western governments concluded bilateral treaties
by way of preempting mutual conflict over the actions, circumstances, or
fate of particular individuals. In terms of criminal jurisdiction, similar
notions of "due process," concern for reciprocity, and relative social and
political stability, allowed U.S. officials to pursue what has since been
termed the "global due process" approach to diplomatic protection and

extraterritorial interventions. As described by Gerald Neuman, sub-scribers to this model sought a balance between the rights and needs of sojourners, on the one hand, and the "national interest" on the other. They reasoned that as absent citizens have fewer obligations, and live beyond the government's effective reach, they might, in exchange, be called upon to settle for less than the full panoply of individual rights. Private interests must be balanced against national interests.[47]

In practice, this meant that an American citizen abroad charged with a crime was turned over to local authorities, with the proviso that the individual would be treated humanely and get what most would con-sidered a "fair" trial; official American responsibility was to obtain basic due process for an individual, less because of U.S. citizenship, more because common humanity demanded it. The approach was succinctly expressed by President Grover Cleveland in his 1886 annual message: "When citizens of the United States voluntarily go into a foreign coun-try they must abide by the laws there in force, and will not be protected by their own Government from the consequences of an offense against those laws committed in such foreign country." The government would demonstrate "watchful care and interest," though, and demand "a fair and open trial" for U.S. nationals charged with crimes committed abroad.[48]

In the second tier, territoriality and limited government translated into hegemony and exploitation. Successive waves of American "oppor-tunists, filibusters, and mercenaries," arrived in Central America and the Caribbean beginning in the 1850s. The most notorious example, of course, was the filibustering William Walker, who died before a firing squad in Honduras only after invading Central America three times, and trying to induce Southern slaveholders to annex the area.[49] In the 1850s the independent republics of Nicaragua, Costa Rica, Honduras, Guatemala, and El Salvador opened their markets and resources to for-eign investment, in an effort to put their economies on the path of lib-eral development. The encouragement of foreign capital produced "iso-lated centers of extraction, exploitation, and production," built upon "bananas, coffee, and minerals." Traditionally weak central control over coastal areas encouraged and enabled foreigners to establish autonomous enclaves. Indigenous efforts to impose fiscal exactions or political control in these areas prompted outside intervention, in the name of diplomatic protection and the "rule of law."[50]

The general policy of the United States, and other Western nations, was to let loose their sojourners in underdeveloped areas, and then capitalize on their predations by aggressive diplomatic protection and unwavering defense of foreign-owned property. In this setting, with a power ratio shifting decisively in America's favor, U.S. insistence that beyond American territory its citizens came under local authority gave free rein to soldiers of fortune, entrepreneurs, and would-be despots. Anti-imperialist attitudes at home facilitated imperialism beyond national boundaries. While deploring the lawless behavior of individuals such as William Walker, the U.S. government seized on any pretext to protect property and concessions thereby gained, engaging in what was in effect "a form of official filibustering."[51]

While federal officials tended to defer to local authority in Latin America in cases involving an individual brought up on criminal charges, they energetically defended the physical safety and property rights of sojourners. Because mercenaries and filibusters tended to get rewarded by indigenous politicos through land grants and concessions, interventions undertaken for principles—the sanctity of property, for example—typically served the exploitative agenda of expatriate U.S. nationals. After 1892, sections of Honduras become refuges for about 2,000 Americans; concession holders took virtual control of the Mosquito Coast. When their interests were threatened, these sojourners called on the United States for "civilized authority."[52]

By the 1890s, such activities had generated a wave of anti-Americanism in Central America and the Caribbean, reinforcing ongoing efforts in those areas to rationalize citizenship, to sort out foreigners from citizens. Guatemala, for instance, issued a decree in the early 1890s stipulating that in exchange for equal access to property and protection, foreigners could not claim diplomatic protection from outside governments.[53] Haitian authorities tried to expel foreigners and, in later years, broadened efforts to expel "foreigners who are prejudicial."[54]

As regards Africa, the most visible activities of antebellum Americans there centered on first, contributing to the slave trade; then, working with Britain to shut it down; missionary work; experiments with the "repatriation" to Africa of American blacks; coastal trade in East, West, and South Africa; and, finally, a rush of fortune hunters to diamond and gold mines.[55] There were few notable incidents involving American diplomatic protection over sojourners in African areas below the northern bloc of countries (Morocco, Algeria, Tunis, Tripoli, and Egypt) where the United States had extraterritorial rights. The most important arose out of local American involvement in the protracted and brutal conflict between Dutch Boers and the British in Southern Africa. By 1870, the United States had official ties with both the British South African Republic and the Boers' Orange Free State; American interest in South African markets continued to expand, leading to a concerted effort by traders, consuls, and publicists to build up relations. Heightened involvement in the area led in the mid-1890s to the entanglement of sojourning Americans in what ultimately became the Boer War. Wavering between official neutrality and support for the British, the U.S. government did no more than complain when a group of U.S. nationals were arrested by Boer leader Paul Kruger and tried for treason.[56]

The Asia-Pacific Tier

It was in the Asia-Pacific region that the second tier blended into the third, that is, into the realm of non-Western sovereigns who had (often involuntarily) ceded resident foreigners varying degrees of self-governance. The Pacific was for late eighteenth- and early nineteenth-century Americans a maritime extension of westward expansion, rich in fur, sea commodities, exotic woods, and convertible "heathens." Penetration of this amorphous frontier turned upon a characteristically American "combination of private and public initiatives." Fur trappers, whalers, miners, missionaries, planters, merchants, and sea traders ventured forth into the Pacific marketplace; their private endeavors then supported by treaties, naval patrols, preferential tariffs, consuls, government sponsored expeditions, indemnities, and emergency assistance. Successive "integrating impulses sent out by the national government to protect its adventuring citizens and nourish their interests gave official character to private actions and legitimated trespass and territorial appropriation."[57]

However, support from national authorities in Washington, D.C., for extra-continental expansion was "often reluctant, uneven, and never as prompt as in the case of response to the more immediate continental frontier demands."[58] The consular service established by President George Washington grew up hostage to patronage politics and congressional miserliness. The East Indies Squadron was created in 1835 (renamed the Asiatic Squadron in 1866), and American warships maintained a steady regional presence, although the American projection of power was weak as compared to Great Britain's eleven-ship China Squadron. "American policy was so passive that the navy was less an instrument of coercion than a benign presence that smoothed away obstacles to reasonable intercourse."[59]

AMERICAN EXTRALITY IN NINETEENTH-CENTURY CHINA

China was the most distant and most promising outpost on this Pacific frontier. The "China market" took on mythic proportions as one of few opportunities not foreclosed by European trading monopolies.[60] Before the Opium Wars of the 1840s, the few Americans who found their way to China were subject to local jurisdiction and assumed the risks involved as a trade-off, part of the costs of doing their own, or their god's, business. As underscored by the Terranova case discussed in chapter 1, their ostensible attitude was that: "The American Government requires of us to submit peaceably to the laws of the country we may visit; hence we consider ourselves bound to obey the laws of China."[61]

Their small numbers dictated American compliance: figures for 1830 show only 19 Americans, as compared to 59 Englishmen; by 1842, there were 49 male Americans, some of whom had families, residing in Canton, Macao, or Hong Kong.[62] Making a virtue of necessity, Americans even sought to use Ch'ing authority to counter British impressment of American sailors off the China coast just prior to the War of 1812.[63] Further, submission was part of a strategy to distinguish themselves from the more resistant British in the eyes of Chinese officials. Meanwhile, Ch'ing strategists sought to keep the dominant British in check in part through favorable treatment of lesser foreign powers on the scene, a move that reinforced the American tactic of claiming a "special friendship" with China.[64] Among themselves, Ch'ing officials characterized the British as "overbearing and tyrannical," the Russians as "crafty," the French as mercenaries and missionaries; Americans, though adjudged more trustworthy than Russians, were deemed obstinate, suspect, and more talk than deed.[65]

Yet, as was the case in U.S. dealings with Latin America, Pacific islands, and African areas, there was a fundamental divergence between official policy and the activities of Americans on the scene. The discrepancy was most glaring with respect to the opium trade. Prior to 1820, American involvement was minor, with one or two ships participating in the annual India-China trade; although Americans opened up traffic to China from Turkey, this was slow to take hold. However, by 1820, Americans controlled about one-third of the trade, with particular dominance in Persian and Turkish opium. Official interference seemed only to push out the petty dealers, giving full sway to the larger firms, such as the House of Perkins and Astor & Company.[66]

Americans in Coastal Ch'ing China

Jacques Downes has illuminated the phenomenon of otherwise respectable business houses trafficking in opium, arguing that: "Opium traders were not importantly different from other merchants of their time. They generally acted in accordance with received standards of mercantile conduct, standards which were interestingly similar to norms found in medieval folklore and chivalry." They were often model citizens back home.[67] Yet, they were savvy enough to appreciate that the U.S. government would not publicly support any American involvement in the trade. Thus, when China merchants asked for help from back home, they deliberately misstated the facts.[68] Domestic political opinions mattered, as they had found in the 1820s, when free trade groups and cotton interests successfully lobbied against Congress's "paternal care" for China traders.[69] Playing to Anglo-American rivalry, petitions from Canton to Congress pleading for help and official backing routinely condemned British "base cupidity and violence, and high-handed infraction of all law, human and divine."[70]

By 1840 Americans merchants and missionaries in South China had shifted more toward the hard-line British position, and no longer felt it necessary to submit to Ch'ing territorial sovereignty. Their lobbying efforts in Washington were made easier by the fact that a decade before, the United States had signed a treaty with the Sublime Porte, giving Americans extraterritorial immunities from local authority in Turkey and Egypt. The departure from territoriality had been driven primarily by commercial motives, as Americans hoped to challenge British and French dominance. The treaty allowed American navigation in the Mediterranean and through the Dardanelles and the Bosporus Straits; it also gave access to the Black Sea and markets of southern Russia. Extraterritorial rights over sojourning U.S. nationals came by virtue of the "most-favored-nation" clause, which gave America all the gains won by other nations, such as Britain and France. American goals were to get out from under the British Levant Trading Company, to which they had been forced to pay "consular protection" fees.[71]

When the Opium War broke out, local Americans memorialized Congress for naval support and a treaty, promising to end the dealings in opium they had consistently denied existed.[72] They stressed the commercial possibilities made possible by formal relations, as well as the need to get out from under British dominance. Extraterritoriality was required, they argued, because Ch'ing authorities were no less arbitrary and predatory than the Barbary States. In the wake of British victory in the first Opium War, the United States negotiated its first treaty with China, affording Americans all of the concessions forced upon the Chinese by the powerful British.[73] It provided that Americans charged with a crime in China would be tried and punished only by U.S. officials; "mixed" cases involving Chinese complainants should be resolved by American and Chinese authorities, "acting in conjunction"; finally, all legal questions involving only Americans were wholly under U.S. jurisdiction. Consistent with Jacksonian attitudes toward indigenous groups standing in the way of "manifest destiny," China became "a nation to be exploited rather than" esteemed.[74] For Americans, Ch'ing defeat at the hands of the British relegated China to that third realm of bilateral relations, reserved for countries considered legally and culturally outside the "family of nations," and thus not entitled to govern sojourning foreigners.

These same provisions and perceptions served as the model for subsequent similar arrangements in Siam (Thailand) in 1856, Japan (1858), and Korea (1856). The United States exercised extrality in varying degrees in these colonial areas, and for the most part followed the European lead. In the Ottoman empire, American extrality was shaped largely by preexisting Ottoman-Western arrangements. For example, in Turkey and Egypt the United States went along with standard practice in providing that native courts took jurisdiction over criminal cases, but foreign defendants were assured immediate consular notice of their arrest, the presence of a "dragoman" (typically an educated native Christian or Jew of high standing), and execution of the penalty under supervision of the national authorities of the convicted. In Egypt, the venue for mixed cases was the International Mixed Court, to which the United States had the right to appoint judicial representatives. According to one contemporary expert, foreign powers could decisively influence the resolution of key cases, so that "the main benefit of extraterritoriality was thus kept." In civil cases, Americans consuls used an assessor system, calling upon local U.S. nationals for advice, but not a verdict; supplementing these arrangements were infrastructural agreements, such as an extradition treaty (1874), and a protocol on real estate and property questions. In areas quite distant from consular posts, foreigners were tried by local councils of elders.[75]

EARLY AMERICAN "JUSTICE" IN CHINA

American extraterritorial jurisdiction ultimately reached its most extensive and elaborate form in treaty port China. At the start, the federal presence was distinct, but notably weak. Federal representatives consistently articulated and idealized version of U.S. policy that led Americans at home to believe that they had a "special relationship" with China. This began during the Opium War, when Washington sent Admiral Stephen Kearny to Canton on board the warship *Constellation*, with orders to assess the military situation, to protect Americans, and to reassure the Chinese government of American good will and willingness to stay away from drug trafficking. Writing to Chinese officials, Kearny asserted that unlike the British, Americans were "not begging any favors," but simply seeking "peace and quiet for . . . [those] trading here legally." U.S. citizens smuggling opium could be left to the mercy of Native courts, as such individuals, "grasping for gain, and [working] to benefit themselves alone, never regard the national honor . . . scheme for profit, and in all ways transgress laws, trampling down all obstacles in their path."[76]

In the early days of the treaty port system, Commissioner Humphrey Marshall drew a distinction between "obligations of duty to the government of the United States, which require me to keep primarily in view the *national*" interest, and the various "*individual* interests" of local Americans. Invoking Vattel, he condemned the effort among American and British merchants to take advantage of internal rebellion to make Shanghai a free port, exempt from duties: "a government which permits

its citizens to injure a foreign nation in its body or members, does no less injury to that nation than if the government itself inflicted the injury." Long-term U.S. national interests meant scrupulous adherence to treaties: "You must accept the treaty altogether, or reject it altogether." American authorities would "not permit the weak or vicious of their own countrymen to imperil the safety of all." Stated policy was that sojourners had a "duty . . . to respect the imperial government, under which, in concert and co-operation with the authorities of the United States, they are protected and defended, and permitted to resort to China for the purposes of commerce."[77]

Despite obtaining the privileges there in 1844, Congress neglected to pass enabling legislation for consular courts until 1848, leaving only Secretary of State Buchanan's instructions to consuls to urge upon "Americans in China the importance of making a good impression" and observing treaty restrictions. Consuls could not try, or punish, a U.S. citizen in these early years; a presidential order enabled them, in serious cases, to send the accused home. In 1860, partly in response to continued judicial challenges and continuing petitions from missionaries and businessmen, Congress enacted new arrangements for American consular courts abroad. These broadened consuls' ability to handle contract, debt, and replevin cases. In addition, a statute of limitations was put in place, stipulating six years for noncapital heinous cases, and civil causes based on written instruments; two years for lesser civil actions, and one year for minor criminal offenses.[78]

Even after consuls were vested with the necessary powers (in these 1848 and 1860 Acts), the State Department continued to caution that this authority was more "mediatory" than authoritative, urging arbitration and summary proceedings over trials. In the criminal sphere, the system was ineffectual, to say the least. U.S. consuls lacked adequate power over their wards: they had no right to deport repeat offenders, no ability to make shipmasters liable for debt, and no capacity to regulate the use of the American flag.[79] Consuls, merchants, and missionaries sought funds for prisons and marshals, while showing a reluctance to accept intrusive federal attention. Believing that ineffective self-policing fueled Chinese reluctance to welcome foreign trade, American merchants expressed a willingness to erect a U.S. prison in 1860, but only if they could be assured an extended lease.[80] The U.S. Attorney General ruled in 1875 that consular courts convicts had to be jailed within the jurisdiction of the trial, and could not be sent elsewhere without congressional sanction.[81] In 1892, this was expanded to allow sentences in China to be served in any consular district there.[82]

The 1860s

The 1860s brought stronger federalist voices in the person of Minister Anson Burlingame and his successor, George F. Seward (nephew of William Seward), both of whom pushed constantly for a greater fiscal, institutional, and political commitment to extraterritorial jurisdiction.[83] In 1864, in a privately published letter to the State Department, Seward argued that "We should seek to strengthen the Chinese administration in the direction of order. . . . [W]e seek to do justice that we may have justice and thus co-operation becomes the rule in carrying out these relations."[84] Characteristically, this federalist critique of extrality took a hard line toward Ch'ing authority, but portrayed "the Chinese people" as victims of foreign predations. Consuls, echoing their long-ago EIC counterparts, consistently pleaded with Washington for more power, more legitimacy, and more respect. "Our ex-territoriality now operates as a shield between the felon and the laws of China, and as she cannot, and the United States does not punish these wrongdoers, the consequence is abounding and unrebuked crime."[85]

Federal and local interests coalesced in three death penalty cases arising in 1863/64, the only capital cases in nineteenth-century American consular courts in China. In 1863, George Seward, newly appointed U.S. Shanghai consul general, sentenced three men to death by hanging. David Williams was found guilty of robbing and killing three Chinese on a river vessel. He claimed British nationality to no avail; his appeal to the U.S. minister in Peking was rejected; he committed suicide on the eve of execution. James White, was found guilty of killing another foreigner in an argument over money; White escaped before his sentence was carried out. John Buckley killed another foreigner in a fight over the Civil War back home. He was executed 1 April 1864, the only U.S. national to suffer that penalty in the one hundred years of American extraterritoriality in China. Initially, Buckley escaped to Nagasaki under an alias, but was lured back to Shanghai by an official ruse.[86]

Each of the men was tried by Consul Seward, sitting with four assessors, selected from a preapproved list of Americans in the district; defendants were permitted to reject candidates. Each had an appointed defense attorney. The consul himself did not prosecute; instead an outside attorney was called in for these extraordinary cases. Buckley's British attorney appealed without success to the U.S. President, citing the lack of a grand jury indictment, the deprivation of a jury trial, and various technical issues. There is no question but that the trials and sentences were meant to send a message not only to wayward Americans, but to Chinese officials. In the words of Minister Anson Burlingame: "Such men as Williams, White, and Buckley had so long escaped punishment that they had come to believe that they could take life with impunity. The United States authority was laughed at, and our flag made the cover for the villains in China. I felt that any relaxation of our purpose to punish the guilty would only aggravate the evils of our situation." Early on, Minister Burlingame instructed Consul Seward to forward information about the Buckley case to Chinese officials, "that they may understand the case as well as learn our determination to carry our laws into effect."[87]

Seward's Folly

Seward's energetic efforts to federalize extrality and improve its efficiency ultimately cost him his job, career, and reputation. Congressional propensity to politicize even the search for markets became clear in 1879, when House Democrats led by William Springer (D-Ill.), chairman of the Committee on State Department Expenditures, ordered Seward's forcible arraignment before the House.[88] Seward's appearance before the bar of the House was, according to the *New York Times*, "of great confusion and uproar."[89] Seward was brought into the House in the custody of the sergeant-at-arms to answer contempt charges for refusing to turn over certain records of the U.S. consulate in Shanghai, records which particular House members believed would prove him guilty of "injustice, tyranny, extortion, and bribery in his official capacity as judge of the [Shanghai] consular court."[90]

Contemporary headlines such as "Minister Seward's Arrest Ordered By the House—The Charges Which the Democrats are Trying to Prove," indicate the extent to which the Seward investigation was propelled by a partisan effort to embarrass the Republican Hayes administration. George Seward must have seemed a tempting target: his appointment to China had been obtained by his uncle, Secretary of State William Seward (1861–69), and charges of corruption against him thus stoked the Democrats' most potent issues—nepotism, the spoils system, and political scandals. The investigation had been undertaken because of charges of perjury, extortion, and malfeasance brought by Seward's successor in Shanghai. The three key areas of alleged wrongdoing were consular dealings toward Chinese officials and Chinese residents of the area, corrupt and arbitrary behavior toward Americans in the Shanghai consular court, and systematic corruption in all areas of consular finances. As to wrongdoing in the U.S. consular court at Shanghai, Consul General John Myers charged that Seward had arbitrarily and corruptly exercised his judicial powers and had mishandled tens of thousands of dollars in court fees. The execution of Buckley was prominently cited as representative of judicial arbitrariness.[91]

Seward's claim, echoed by his representatives and supporters in the committee hearings, was that during his time in China he had been forced by miserly congressional appropriations and by the handicaps of the patronage system, to navigate a thin line between pragmatism and criminal wrongdoing: if Oliver Bradford, as consular clerk and acting consul, had abused his powers and engaged in corrupt practices, these were not to be confused with Seward's sometimes questionable ad hoc measures to establish and maintain an official American presence in Shanghai. Indeed, Seward asserted, he had kept the Department appraised of his practical solutions to matters unforeseen by consular regulations. The Republican minority agreed, arguing that the "multifarious and difficult" duties and authority of U.S. consuls in China, coupled with inadequate resources, had forced Seward to undertake a questionable course of action, one which had been tacitly approved by his Departmental supervisors.[92]

The State Department agreed, and protected Seward from congressional impeachment efforts. However, Seward's effectiveness as minister had been greatly undermined by the experience, and he resigned in early 1880. The unfortunate Bradford found himself idling in the Shanghai consular jail during most of the congressional hearings, having pled "technically guilty" before Judge G. Wiley Wells to charges of embezzling funds of the U.S. government and tampering with U.S. mail. Bradford was removed from office and returned home after a short stay in the Shanghai consular jail; Seward returned to New York to become a prominent insurance salesman.[93]

Anti-Imperialist Imperialism

The great paradox of American extrality was that staunch anti-imperialism at home produced stark imperialist consequences abroad. Having accepted consular jurisdiction in principle, and convinced of the commercial potential of undeveloped markets, Congress nonetheless remained reluctant to fund projects and institutions viewed as imperialist, such as a full-dress extraterritorial judicial system. Although approving sporadic improvements, until 1906 Congress consistently rejected more systemic legislation; even at a time of general civil service reform, there was insufficient support for successive bills drafted by the State Department for the establishment of a superior court in Shanghai. While domestic courts endorsed extrality, Congress found State Department consular jurisdiction unconstitutional, philosophically anathema, and fiscally unwarranted. Hard-line opponents agreed: "If we are too mean as a nation to pay the expense of observing the Constitution in China, then let us give up our concessions in China and come back to as much of the Constitution as we can afford to carry out."

This attitude led to perpetual underfunding of consular courts, inattention to diplomatic problems resulting from the inadequacy of these courts, and the general willingness of Congress to entertain attacks by Americans abroad on the excesses and alleged corruption of these same courts. In response to this lack of support from home, consuls themselves became ever more the legal tyrants congressional opponents painted them to be, taking legal shortcuts to meet the exigencies of the moment and meting out summary justice more concerned with preemptive social control than civil liberties. Conscientious consuls, if not cowed by the fate of George Seward, were thwarted by the constitutional and fiscal shakiness of the system. Reliance on federal law, the common law, and ministerial regulations, did not meet daily needs as regards probate, divorce, injunctions, mechanics liens, rape, and various other crimes and misdemeanors.[94] (In the United States, all of these areas came within state, not federal, jurisdiction.) Thus, for example, Americans in Japan in 1881 petitioned Congress for legislation modifying the antiquated rules of the common law, writing: "For us there is no statute of frauds; there is no insolvency legislation . . . imprisonment for debt has not been abolished; the disabilities of woman at the common law have remained unaltered; we have no statute of limitations and none providing for conditional bills of sale or chattel mortgages."[95]

CONSULAR JUSTICE AND EXTERNAL CITIZENSHIP

Surviving records indicate that outside of Shanghai, most legal conflicts were settled by arbitration and out of court, with the advantage generally accruing to privileged foreigners. In the Shanghai consular district (Chiang-su, Che-chiang, An-hui, comprising today's Jiangsu, Zhejiang, and Anhui provinces), the consular court handled about 250 complaints a year, the majority of which involved criminal allegations.[96] Only one-fourth of the total directly involved Chinese complainants. Consuls emulated their British counterparts in dispensing with the majority of complaints through a summary magistrate's court; only a small percentage of the total were remitted for further consideration at a more serious level, with assessors in some instances. At the summary level, most criminal complaints were intra-foreign, and involved charges of assault, desertion, disorderly conduct, drunkenness, and theft. Punishments included fines and jail sentences, although inadequate jail facilities tended to favor the former; consuls were not permitted to deport "undesirables."[97]

Getting Down to Cases

Several overarching conclusions emerge from the details and early court dockets. First, extrality's most important contribution to the American presence in China was that it preempted native elites from using indigenous institutions to control or extirpate the foreign presence. It is the absence or paucity of litigation, rather than particular precedents or codes, that most eloquently attests to this preemptive impact. When there was litigation with broad implications for the treaty system itself, involving the legality of the British-dominated Customs Service for example, these cases were typically taken out of court and turned over to diplomat-arbiters.[98]

Second, American companies sought to use extrality to discipline their native employees and compradors, as in the two cases brought in 1862–63 by Frazar and Company against two clerks for robbery and bribery. Consuls, on shaky constitutional ground as it was, resisted the impulse and generally turned over Chinese nationals to Ch'ing authorities.[99] The flip side was the extension of extraterritorial privileges to employees, associates, and native converts. Missionary efforts to extend their protection to native converts was also problematic, and the legation court docket at the capital was consistently dominated by such cases.[100] That converts received exemptions from certain local taxes and duties, and tended toward the opportunistic use of their affiliation, remained a constant source of antiforeignism in interior villages; in some cases, local leaders posted rewards for killing particularly interfering missionaries.[101]

The State Department (backed up by successive attorneys general) consistently pushed to limit consular jurisdiction to U.S. nationals only.[102] However, protégé coverage—as with extrality more generally—tended to work through preemption and intimidation. This is well illustrated by a story related during the congressional investigation of Seward regarding a prominent Shanghai investor who, upon the arrest of his comprador by the local taotai, "jumped up and . . . overtook Feng [Taotai] with his party carrying off my compadore with four soldiers on each side. . . . He had no right to arrest the man without proper authority from Mr. Seward, so I took my man away from them, and took Feng by his cue and brought him back to my place. I was exceedingly angry at the time, so, when I got him there I tied him up and took off his jacket and cowhided him until I was tired."[103]

Concomitantly, after having demanded the protective cover of their home government, American Canton interests sought to avoid federal interference. Although ostensibly beneficiaries of the merchant-consul system, trading houses objected to being bound by the arbitrary, sometimes self-serving decisions of a "brother merchant." This became clear in the 1840s in the first reported civil case, *Shing Ho v. Wetmore*.[104] Wetmore refused to pay judgment, saying: "not now, or at any time hereafter, will we receive as a final decision of our right the judgment of any one individual in China." Commissioner Biddle, lacking statutory power, had to rely on arbitration. Wetmore and other American houses turned to Congress only when local British urged their countrymen to refuse credit to Americans and declined to assist U.S. nationals in collecting debts from Englishmen.[105]

Some leading Western business houses, while skeptical of the durability of U.S. consular jurisdiction, did bring their contract and debt disputes to the Shanghai consular court, as in *Augustine Heard v. Olyphant*, brought in 1861 for fulfillment of contract. American reliance upon merchants to perform consular duties continued to be problematic, as businessmen—both American and not—occasionally took up the post to obtain legal advantages over their compradors and competitors, in the form of power over transit passes, arrest power, and control of the consular courts.[106] However, though they complained about the merchant-consul system, the number of civil complaints brought to the consular court by American merchants paradoxically decreased with the professionalization of the consular service. In part, this owed to the fact that nonmerchant consuls frequently lacked legal knowledge. More generally, like sojourning U.S. and British traders elsewhere, there was a tendency to avoid formal legal system entirely, and settle commercial conflicts among themselves according to basic common law precepts well known to them.[107]

In the civil sphere, there was in fact an approximation of equity, primarily because of the ability of Chinese merchants and creditors to threaten to opt out of business with Americans if they were not treated fairly. Anxious for immediate satisfaction and consistency, rather than concerned about abstract notions of "justice," treaty port Chinese compradors and vendors made frequent use of both American and British judicial venues. Chinese plaintiffs came to the Shanghai consular court to collect debts large and small, as in *Chaio Van Sing v. Mason* brought for a $20 claim, and *Wang King Kee v. Bull & Company* (1860), for $12,790. U.S. officials, even those who favored hard-line gunboat treaty enforcement, urged consuls to keep their courts visibly open to Chinese civil litigants.

Extrality as a Boon

The third general conclusion suggested by consular court records is that nonmissionary women and American-born blacks in China availed themselves of the extraterritorial system. Little has been written about either group, although the consular court docket reveals their distinct presence, particularly in Shanghai.[108] As to the first, some Chinese and foreign-born women were able to benefit from the shift in U.S. law to marital derivative citizenship after 1855.[109] Until the Cable Act (1922), marriage to a sojourning American male brought U.S. nationality benefits, which could be held on to even after divorce. Some Asian women used this as an avenue of mobility and improved circumstances: between 1879 and 1909, 34 out of 221 registered American marriages involved Chinese or Japanese wives; the number of unregistered marriages was substantial, but unknown.[110] Until well after 1900 there were no cases of American woman marrying Asian men.[111] Chinese and Japanese women married to U.S. citizens could not be naturalized, as was the case for Chinese in America more generally. However, in the China district of U.S. extraterritoriality, they enjoyed virtual American citizenship; in other words, ineligibility for naturalization was irrelevant so long as the couple remained in China.

Until after the turn of the century, consular courts adhered to the common law rule that a married woman's property belongs to her husband.[112] Married couples could not contract with each other, as they were one person in law.[113] However, several factors intervened in women's favor. Consuls were particularly concerned to keep women solvent, not public charges or vulnerable to disreputable behavior.[114] Thus, the courts were liberal. Illustrative is the case of Bridget Williams and her sometimes-husband John: married in Yokohama, they opened the Commercial Hotel in Shanghai in the early 1870s, and she obtained a written agreement from him to hand the hotel over to her for $1.00; they separated, but could not seem to stay apart for long. In 1876, Bridget Williams brought suit against John, seeking a court order to keep him away from her and the hotel; though witnesses testified that she had invited him back, the court ruled in her favor, finding that in view of their contract, he was "only a tenant at will," at the hotel on her "sufferance."[115]

Further, Western women engaged in prostitution in Shanghai—about 250 from 1865 to 1900 were able to draw simultaneously the benefits of marriage and the ability to contract by assuming a working name. Such was the case of Jennie Grant, a.k.a. Ada L. Nesbit, who divorced her husband, Frank Nesbit, a theatrical agent who deserted her in 1888. (Concomitantly, as the following chapter explains in more detail, the laxity of American consular justice made U.S. nationality particularly desirable among non-Asian prostitutes.) In the 1870s and 1880s, approximately 30 to 40 of these women appeared in the Shanghai consular court docket, as both defendants and plaintiffs in civil cases. (Until 1900, there were no criminal prosecutions for prostitution among U.S. nationals.) As American consuls still depended heavily upon judicial fees to fill out their meager stipends, they welcomed all paying customers. Thus, in 1874, for example, of the 72 civil cases heard by the American consular court, 32 involved prostitutes (and 14 of those 32 cases were brought by Chinese plaintiffs). Lawyers, all British at that time, were available if not affordable; however, so open was the American consular court in the 1870s and 1880s that women represented themselves with good result.[116]

As to American-born blacks, they were a distinct minority in treaty port China but present nonetheless.[117] The status of American-born black sojourners abroad had been settled in several cases arising in Latin America; after initially refusing recognition to their claims for property damage, the State Department agreed to issue certificates attesting that an individual had been born free in the United States.[118] In treaty port China, the same question was resolved in the early 1880s, when an individual filed charges against a U.S. consul who refused to recognize him, despite the fact that he was the legal off-spring of an American-born black.[119] Civil and criminal cases in the Shanghai consular court indicate that local American blacks arrived as seamen or—in the case of women—as ships stewards, and became innkeepers, saloon owners, and more rarely, traders.[120]

Between Extrality and the Deep Blue Sea

Fourth, criminal court proceedings indicate that one crucial function of the Shanghai consular court was to augment and reinforce labor discipline on board American vessels. After 1851, between 85 to 100 American ships a year passed through the port, and the consular court processed about 150 cases a year against sailors for insubordination, desertion, mutiny, vagrancy, public disturbance, and assault; so too, a few such cases were brought on behalf of crewmen against excessively abusive masters.

Labor discipline cases typically favored complainants, overriding even the Sino-foreign divide, as in the 1854 case of *Chinese Officer v. Eaton and Gilfillin*, when the defendants were found guilty of refusing to obey a Chinese officer. The widespread practice of "running out a shop" cut labor costs by forcing the original crew to desert after arrival in an Asian port, and enlisting Chinese or Malays at lower wages. A federal inspector found in the 1860s, that "as a general rule, 'Jack' looks upon the consul, the shipping-master, and the boarding-house keeper, as a trio of 'sharks,' . . . who are in constant conspiracy against his liberty and his wages."[121] Typically, fines against "sailor stealers" hovered around $200, or one month imprisonment; often the latter option was taken, and escape was easily effected.[122]

As underscored in Briton Busch's 1994 work on nineteenth-century American whalemen, consuls were a vital link in the interaction between seamen, employers, and financiers. The consul enforced protective legislation on behalf of crew members, with specific attention to the effort of masters to discharge crewmen abroad without pay. Over the course of the century, various congressional acts shifted the balance of power in this relationship back and forth, from labor to management. For example, an 1840 act allowed consuls to waive the requirement on masters to pay out three months wages before letting crewmen go; and limited a consul's duty toward deserters to reclaiming them and discouraging insubordination by all available means, including reliance on local authorities. On the other hand, in 1872 masters became subject to a $100 fine for failing to allow crewmen to complain to the local consul.[123] Busch concludes that in the absence of firm statistical evidence, whalemen probably believed they suffered more than they gained at the hands of American consuls abroad.[124]

In China, U.S. officials tried preemptive measures, taking British policy as a model.[125] Shipmasters and officers were enjoined "to use due vigilance to preserve the peace, and prevent difficulties between all seamen and subjects of China." Captains were pushed to assume responsibility for crewmen's debts ashore, for example, and were advised to use due diligence in issuing passes.[126] An 1858 memorial by a group of shipmasters in Shanghai sought: a consular prison; harsher punishments; and a man-of-war always in port to enforce the law. They pointed out that consular preference for fines over imprisonment placed masters—who could pay—at a disadvantage to crewmen—who generally pleaded poverty.[127] They rightly feared the rough justice of sailors. For example, in the 1850s eight seamen from the American barque *Science* took their first mate to a boardinghouse on shore, where they met up with about 30 armed men, and marched him through the streets to a paddy field, where he was beaten. The original eight crewmen were punished only by being placed on board another ship. The coincidence of interest in shipboard discipline and treaty port policing centered on the predatory activities of deserters. According to one consul in 1853, "They roam about the suburbs of the Chinese city, getting into constant brawls with the natives, in which both sides use weapons, and dangerous wounds and even death are the consequence."[128]

Infrastructural Crime

Fifth, and finally, crimes such as trafficking in "coolie" labor, opium, and weapons—were beyond the capacity of consular courts to handle. After the Opium War, the trade in that drug "became more obscure and . . . larger."[129] It was fully legalized and regulated by the 1858 Treaty of Tientsin. By then, American officials had come came to see the trade as inevitable, and something the United States should not concede to others: "From what I can see you might as well keep back the waves of the sea," as to stop opium, U.S. Minister William Reed reported in 1858. Reed noted that "at every port, I found Americans dealing in opium freely and unreservedly," often in combination with British nationals.[130] The early Sino-American treaties identified the drug as contraband; those dealing in contraband were to be left to the mercies of native officials. The false notion grew up because of these provisions the United States had prohibited its nationals from opium trafficking.[131]

When, finally, a law was enacted in 1887 making participating in opium trade illegal for Americans, the penalties were a minuscule fine of $50–$250, imprisonment from 30 days to six months or both, and confiscation. In later years, because of a clerical error, the imprisonment provisions were omitted, leaving only inadequate fines.[132] And there is only one known criminal prosecution in the Shanghai consular court involving opium, *U.S. (a Ship Captain) v. Chinese Crewman of "Shantung"* (1872), for the theft of opium. (This was remitted to the Mixed Court, which dealt with Chinese defendants.) Likewise, Americans in China were told that they would forfeit protection if found to be participating in the "coolie" trade in Chinese labor.[133] However, such an outcome never occurred. The loophole that insured no convictions, and no abandonment of nationals to Ch'ing justice, was the distinction between "assisted emigration," and trafficking.

Preventing the involvement of U.S. nationals in Chinese internal rebellion as arms traders or mercenaries was also continuing problem. American citizens doing so were told that they would "be deemed guilty of high misdemeanor, fined not more than 10,000 and imprisoned not more than 3 yrs."[134] In 1854, Commissioner Robert McLane instructed his countrymen: "It is the duty of citizens of the United States residing and sojourning in China to respect the imperial government.[135] Although there were criminal prosecutions, there were no convictions. Probably the best-known case was that of Frederick Jenkins, accused of conspiring to sell guns to the Taiping rebels, and traveling to Korea to exhume the body of a king for sale to a museum at home. This raised the question of "whether the American system of consular jurisdiction was capable of preventing the use of China as a place of refuge for adventurers who might involve the United States in embarrassing, if not dangerous, international complications." Lack of evidence on the arms charge, and the fact that exhuming bodies was not against the law, led to a consular verdict of "simple acquittal."[136]

Continuing difficulties in China with extrality made American officials less enthusiastic about obtaining and expanding similar rights in Japan. Townsend Harris, who negotiated the first U.S. treaties there, said privately that demanding extrality was "against his conscience." Similarly, Secretary of State Marcy underscored that the provisions for extraterritoriality were meant only to bridge gaps and reconcile discrepancies in a very limited class of cases on behalf of host countries.

These sentiments, and the greater control Japanese governing elites were able to wield over foreign privileges, made for a more rigorously run system. U.S. consuls in Japan, as in China, could not expel an American; however, they could legitimately abstain when Japanese officials undertook that task.[137] American consuls in Japan operated under similar fiscal constraints as in China; in general, though, the United States was much more conciliatory toward Japanese efforts to contain extraterritorial privileges.[138] For example, the 1858 treaty sanctioned travel restrictions on individual U.S. nationals convicted of a felony or multiple misdemeanors. By 1872, Meiji officials succeeded in establishing a general court in Kanagawa to take over all judicial matters involving nationals of nontreaty powers, something Chinese did not accomplish until the late 1920s.

As chapter 3 illuminates, post-Reconstruction federal efforts to impose a new citizenship regime ran aground most particularly in this third realm of foreign relations, the "anomalous zone" of colonial areas where sojourning Americans came under direct U.S. jurisdiction.[139] The "free rider" challenge was particularly intractable in this realm, because the benefits package of transported membership and lax jurisdiction was so rich, in relative terms. Much of the resistance predictably came from entrenched local interests, long accustomed to Washington's benign neglect. Not unlike the American colonies facing the "Intolerable Acts" by a British Crown in search of revenue, established groups of native and naturalized U.S. nationals in China, Japan, Turkey, and other colonial and semicolonial enclaves resented metropolitan efforts to dictate the terms of the allegiance-for-protection bargain.

CHAPTER THREE

COLONIZING THE COLONIZERS

Sojourning Americans, both native and naturalized, were targets of the ethno-centrism pervading the United States in the 1890s.[1] One contemporary despaired: "When the phrase 'Americans residing abroad' is uttered, several groups form themselves before the mental kodak," most prominently well-born women in search of titled, but likely impoverished, European males.[2] In general, the European air was fine for a brief time, but enervates the American spirit, thought Theodore Roosevelt. The Europeanized American was no traitor, but constituted "a silly and undesirable citizen," "a noxious element in our body politic," "over-civilized, over-sensitive, over-refined."[3] One congressional critic lamented how easy it had become for American women to travel abroad, and "coin American citizenship into gold which they may use to purchase some Count-No-Account, some degenerate from overseas."[4]

The U.S. government's push to make diplomatic protection a privilege bestowed on condition, not an entitlement given on demand, set in motion a complex negotiation between colonial sojourners and State Department officials over the terms of this allegiance-for-protection exchange. Though not yet the empire it would become, nonetheless the

United States had imperial problems by 1890. Heightened federal scrutiny was evident in court decisions regarding the portability of constitutional due process rights, changing residency requirements to retain nationality, amended passport regulations, and—ultimately—in the creation of the U.S. Court for China in Shanghai.

Although overdetermined by the expansion of the federal government, changes in business and commerce, and the rise of "Progressivism," understanding these changes in the federal-sojourner relationship also requires the larger context of imperial politics in the closing decade of the century. Expansionist powers across the board undertook to tighten control of their sojourning nationals and to "make empire respectable." Competitive nationalism abroad, and support back home for costly foreign ventures, required colonial sojourners to be something more than merchant princes and beachcombing adventurers.

Chapter 3 examines these developments, turning particular attention on four topics: the changing relationship between U.S. federal authorities and extraterritorial Americans, the multinational campaign to colonize the colonizers, the crisis of imperialism in China around the Boxer Rebellion, and events leading up to the creation of the U.S. Court for China in 1906.

BENEFICIARIES OF EMPIRE

The 1890s intensified the struggle between federal officials and colonial sojourners, largely because the political and economic stakes involved became critical both at home and abroad. The "search for markets" so remarked upon by historians did not necessarily favor sojourners, particularly those long in place in colonial areas now identified by American-based businesses as lucrative targets. Increased trade—with Japan, the Ottoman empire, and China—seemed to be hindered, rather than facilitated, by the presence of missionaries and locally driven businesses.

The choice between markets and sojourners was clearest in Japan, where the United States and other great powers yielded to Japanese pressure to abrogate the unequal treaties and end extrality by 1899. Although groups of privileged foreigners resisted the course of events there, the prevailing view among import-export firms, banks, and—less predictably—missionaries, was that the country would be fully opened if local officials did not fear the "Midas touch" impact of extrality in the interior. Indeed, American investment did greatly expand after this treaty revision, driving home the lesson.[5] By 1907, the United States had relinquished extrality in Algiers, Tunis, Servia, Madagascar, Japan, and portions of Samoa; the privilege was greatly circumscribed in Egypt, and leased areas of China, Zanzibar, Borneo and Tonga, Morocco, and Tripoli. After 1910, it remained only in Turkey, Bulgaria, China, Persia, Siam, and Maskat.[6]

At the same time, the closing decade of the nineteenth century brought an unprecedented expansion of the federal government and of national administrative capacities in general.[7] Most historians agree with Robert Wiebe's description of this process as "a search for order" amid industrialization, immigration, and international competition. The post-Reconstruction emergence of a nationally based market, the rise of organized labor, and the organization of trusts and oligopolies, placed unprecedented demands upon the state as broker.[8] Reform efforts aimed at national administrative development were entangled in a protracted contest over the redefinition of power relationship and official prerogatives.[9]

If Progressives sought foreign markets for a surfeit of domestic energies and goods, they first had to bring American foreign policy fully under the control of the state. Just as the massive corporations around them undertook horizontal and vertical integration to bring under one auspice the entire system of production and distribution, Progressives sought to rationalize the foreign policy process through centralization, hierarchy, and homogenization. This meant wresting power across institutional lines of authority, evidenced in, for example, the executive branch's appropriation of consular and foreign service patronage rights from Congress beginning in the 1890s. It also necessitated reining in individuals and groups, such as overseas missionaries and treaty port Americans, long accustomed to bullying and bribing their consular officials, and predisposed to view as private resources the instrumentalities of their home government—gunboats, indemnities, treaties and, indeed, diplomacy itself.

By way of example, American missionary groups in Turkey were advised: "The application of extraordinary means for individual protection, especially if the assertion of the individual's rights be demonstratively aggressive, and calculated from the nature of things in the locality to lead to conflict, is hardly to be expected."[10] In the case at hand, then, they were to use discretion, and accept simply that: "the United States Government was not willing to make the right to use church bells on private dwellings a diplomatic question with Turkey." They should seek "the avoidance of opportunities of giving offense to the people among whom their lot was cast."[11]

Commodification of Imperial Gleanings

The dilemmas of diplomatic protection and its extreme form, extrality, prompted congressional and State Department efforts to establish procedures that would identify "what individuals" were "deserving of American protection," and facilitate the "detection" of those intending to use the power and prestige of the United States merely as a shield for nefarious practices." According to the leading work on the subject at the time:

> The right to be acknowledged as a citizen of the United States must be held as a high privilege and a precious right. When the person who possesses it is untainted by crime, or by the suspicion of expatriation, or by the non-fulfillment of the duties which accompany it, it entitles him abroad to the recognition and protection of a power which is not the least among the powers of the earth, while at home, under general regulations of law, he may participate in the distribution of political rights and privileges.[12]

For federal officials, "rationalizing" the constitutional right to diplomatic protection meant maximizing control over the dispensation of benefits and guaranteeing the extraction of duties. The new concentration of foreign policy power in the executive branch, and a general retreat of Congress before the "imperial presidency," facilitated the subordination of diplomatic protection and intervention to the imperial agenda.[13] Protection could be extended, but only in response to domestic pressures and the "national interest." For example, although holding political office abroad was among the criteria for presumed expatriation, exceptions could be made when doing so helped American interests. In an 1894 case of a U.S. citizen serving in the Blue Fields region of Nicaragua, the State Department agreed with arguments presented that the arrangement kept radicals and corrupt locals out of office; "good government" in turn improved the value of local American property.[14]

The problem in extraterritorial zones, as officials saw it, was that indigenous subjects acquired American nationality, but not "American habits of thought." Protégés or virtual dual citizens were able to pass along their status to their progeny, who then gained access to membership benefits without visible costs or negotiation.[15] This not only created complications for U.S. foreign policy, but fueled domestic nativism. The goal was not necessarily to end the extension of benefits, but to bring it firmly under federal monopoly and exact something in return. For example, the United States extended protection to Moroccan Jews, but toward the goal of placating American Jewish groups rather than simply making life that much easier for savvy foreigners.

When Washington attempted to apply the new residency criteria for presumed expatriation, Americans—naturalized and native—living in Turkey and Japan objected. A U.S. consul explained to Washington that among his wards in Turkey, only missionaries were "American in every sense—birth, feelings, habits of living, thought, national pride in holidays." The remaining citizens were as a rule "intermixed with other nationalities by marriage and family ties; and . . . American only when in trouble."

Retreating from an earlier (1887) decision to apply the standards rigorously, the State Department maintained in 1889 that native or naturalized Americans would not lose their citizenship regardless of protracted absence from the United States if they were identifiable as "members in Turkey of a community of citizens of the United States. . . . who avail themselves of the extraterritorial rights given by Turkey to such communities and not merging themselves in any way in Turkish domicile or nationality."[16]

Exceptions could be made for those engaged in the "active representation of American business interests abroad, and identification with affairs in this country." Agents of American commercial establishments in foreign country who were "useful in promoting our mercantile relations, in spite of long-continued absence from the United States," merited special consideration. Seeking clarification, a group of naturalized Americans in Turkey wondered whether they qualified, given that "they, as private citizens [were] pursuing their own business and not in any particular manner subserving American interests or [being] identified therewithin."[17] The resulting definition was less subjective, but equally emphatic that "Americanism" was the federal government's to define: U.S. citizens in Turkey were "all non-Mohametans descended from citizens of the United States . . . whose parents or prior ancestors settled in Turkey for religious or business purposes, and who themselves remain non-Mohametans, retain and proclaim their American nationality, and are recognized by Turkish authorities as citizens of the United States."[18]

Americans in Japan similarly pleaded their case to Washington via the U.S. minister in Tokyo, who explained that quite a number of local U.S. nationals, including merchants, technical advisers, and missionaries, would suffer if protracted absence from the United States meant automatic expatriation. These Americans, each and all, were "exercising an influence on civilization and giving strength to the position of our country." "Our institutions" were being upheld, our flag honored, and the national character exalted"; the withdrawal of diplomatic protection guarantees would undermine their influence, leaving national rivals to step in. "These men exert as much good for their country as they could if they were within its territory." Further, they performed civic duties, such as being assessors in the consular courts, and were amenable to those courts. So, to "suspend their rights means to destroy one of the great national influences of our people in the East."[19]

Thus, extraterritorial U.S. nationals ultimately won exemption from the new residency requirements in expatriation laws. However, the asking price of the concession was that the individual's "Americanism" must be apparent through lifestyle, associations, language, and so on. A continuing connection with legitimate business interests having their roots in the United States would be given weight; but other corroborative tests included continued "identification with affairs in this country," evincing "a bona fide conservation of the American character," and making "an effort to uphold the good repute of our country abroad."

These added criteria undermined the intended objectivity of the new regulations and invited abuse, conceded the State Department. Yet, "common sense," and a careful assessment of an applicant's appearance and demeanor, would be sufficient "to distinguish between *merely selfish residence abroad*, under circumstances which involve a practical renunciation of all home ties and the adoption of a course which essentially requires the individual's nationality to be asserted."[20] Heightened scrutiny of individual diplomatic protection cases, as well as a more general federal effort to exact a full measure of allegiance from recipients, forced sojourning nationals to demonstrate their worth as citizens, to identify themselves and their work as integral to and consistent with U.S. policy more generally.

The Ross Regime

The chief accomplishment of late nineteenth-century federal policy in the extraterritorial zone was to unbundle the panoply of rights and responsibilities embedded in domestic citizenship. The compromise solution arrived at to deal with the "bargaining risks" associated with protecting Americans under extrality was to insist that the price of heightened protection was abbreviated due process.[21] These terms of exchange were, in effect, ratified in the 1891 landmark Supreme Court case, *Ross v. United States*. The precedent arose from an intra-foreign murder case first decided in 1880 by a U.S. State Department consular court in Yokohama; although John Ross was a British subject, the U.S. consul assumed jurisdiction because Ross was employed on an American ship. Ross was sentenced to death; his sentence commuted by President Rutherford Hayes on condition he serve a life term in the Albany penitentiary.[22]

The Supreme Court held on appeal in 1891 that the Constitution had no application beyond the territory of the United States; sojourning U.S. nationals were entitled only to "fundamental rights," which did not necessarily include trial by jury. Although deprived of certain constitutional guarantees in consular court hearings, in fair exchange American defendants were protected from "often arbitrary and oppressive" foreign tribunals. This principle was expanded at the turn of the century by the high court's ruling in the "insular cases": "the Constitution does not follow the flag."[23] Successive decisions reaffirmed the precedent up through the mid-1950s.[24]

Ross created a new category of "federal citizenship" for dealing with American sojourners abroad either in territories directly under U.S. sovereignty or in countries where foreign nationals had extraterritorial status. Allegiance and protection were reciprocal in the government-citizen relationship; however, not every citizen was entitled to every privilege and immunity.[25] Sojourners challenged this regime at every turn, through Congress, the press, and appellate courts in the continental United States. Those targeted for integration into American national interests found themselves, to paraphrase legal historian David Bederman, "American" enough to come under U.S. authority but not "American" enough to enjoy the Constitution in all respects.[26] As subsequent sections make clear, the Supreme Court's decision was not the final word, as treaty port Americans challenged this regime of abbreviated due process in both judicial and political venues for the next three decades.

RENEGOTIATING IMPERIAL CITIZENSHIP

The 1890s saw a general crisis throughout extraterritorial enclaves, as instability on the colonial periphery and changing domestic sentiments about empire pushed metropolitan governments to undertake a more rigorous subordination of their sojourning citizens to the "national interest." The campaign to colonize the colonizers, evident in the politics of America, Europe, and Japan, relied on reformed overseas judicial procedures, more demanding qualifications for access to diplomatic protection, and a morally infused, intensely patriotic discourse about citizenship and its obligations.

Ongoing support for imperial projects among domestic constituencies pushed colonial authorities "to make empire respectable," in the apt phrase of Ann Stoler. This project was manifest not only in programs of "native uplift," but also in tightening supervision over colonial sojourners themselves, particularly those straddling and blurring racial and cultural boundaries.[27] Colonial prostitution became a volatile issue in domestic British politics in the 1890s.[28] British Shanghailanders worried that if they did not stem the "profusion of facilities for vice," Chinese groups would surely petition London, and "[p]ublic opinion at home . . . will side with the Chinese, and we shall be bidden to put our house in order."[29] Mark Peattie has found that sojourning Japanese included a significant element of "adventurers, opportunists, and even ruffians," although the majority comprised petty traders, shopkeepers, and commercial servants.[30] Fearful of the damage to the country's international reputation, the Foreign Ministry instructed consuls in 1897 to report regularly on the numbers and lifestyle of Japanese migratory prostitutes in their district.[31] In the U.S. presidential campaign of 1900, Prohibition Party supporters trumpeted allegations that the incumbent Republican administration was "laying the foundation of its new oriental empire" in the Philippines "in rankest debauchery and foulest vice," allowing "swarms of loose [American and European] women...[to] prowl about the streets" of Manila.[32]

To a great extent, the push from the center was facilitated by a pull from the periphery. Within Asian and African extraterritorial enclaves, established colonial communities themselves experienced a collective alarm about the influx all around them of impoverished whites, both male and female, who preyed upon the locals and debased the racial, cultural, and national constructs legitimizing foreign privilege. Race exerted an ambiguous influence. Articulating a widely held sentiment, an 1898 editorial in the local Shanghai English-language newspaper lamented that "just as a Senator from the Southern American States once declared that most of the pleasure of his trip to Europe was spoiled by the sight of white men doing menial labour, so we wince at the sight of a destitute foreigner."[33] However, racial solidarity also promoted the campaign toward more restrictive privilege and a more rigorous surveillance over "whiteness."

Some colonials reacted to increased antiforeign violence by trying to establish complete independence and autonomy, as in the early 1890s proposals among Shanghai English merchants "for forming an independent republic of an area of 100 square miles, thus inclosing all the business centres of foreign merchants and many of the mission establishments in this vicinity and on the Woosung and Tang-tse Rivers."[34] Almost as a rule, though, colonial elites—often a de facto mix of foreign and native elements—reacted to this influx of poorer whites by soliciting help from home governments in the form of increased spending, more elaborate overseas legal systems, and more rigorously defined criteria for the extension of diplomatic protection. The challenge for those who sought such help then became to use the new resources without sacrificing any of their own autonomy vis-à-vis their home officials.

The Vagrant "Other"

Central to this reinvigoration project was the emergence in extraterritorial jurisprudence and discourse of a "vagrant Other," white, but of uncertain nationality, wandering through the structures of imperialism, a free rider in the system of colonial privilege, and a threat to the legitimizing myths of Western superiority. This was the imperial counterpart of the dangerously idle and nomadic vagrant Other generated a half-century earlier by social control efforts in metropolitan societies undergoing industrialization.[35] In both instances, the image of the predatory, rootless nomad, though not without some basis in empirical reality, served as a totemic device that put certain behaviors beyond the pale of norms and values buttressing new relations of production, property, and power. There had always been itinerant, impoverished types in European expansion; now, however, the imperial loiterer emerged as an unpatriotic, self-seeking and dangerous individual.

There was an element of reality in the discourse; vagrancy, like prostitution, is both a metaphor and reality in human experience. In China's treaty ports, newcomers overwhelmed those coastal enclaves. Treaty port communities became more heterogeneous, in terms of class, race, gender, and nationality. Between 1895 and 1905, Japanese in China surged into the thousands, overtaking the British by 1915.[36] This led not only to competition among various nationalities, but also to racial, sexual, and class tensions, as indigenous "opportunists" and "riffraff" threatened the hegemony of colonial elites, and brought into question the legitimizing rationale of foreign legal privilege. There was a sizable influx of foreign (Western and Japanese) prostitutes into the region from Manchuria (fleeing the chaos of the Russo-Japanese War), from South Africa (fleeing a clean-up campaign there), and from the United States and Western Europe (in search of opportunities opened by the American occupation of the Philippines and the multinational suppression of the Boxer Rebellion in North China).[37] Ch'ing diplomatic officials complained of the proliferation of foreign vice in North China, identifying in Peking alone four foreign casinos and eighteen brothels with foreign women or Chinese prostitutes catering to foreign males.[38]

The arrival of a large number of "respectable" white women at the same time fueled efforts to expel disreputable foreigners in the colonies. In Shanghai, a group of American missionary wives calling themselves the "Executive Committee of the Shanghai Missionary Association" petitioned the White House in 1900 to end the parade of prostitutes from the United States into Chinese treaty ports. Though sympathetic toward indigenous prostitutes, these Western women sought expulsion, rather than redemption, of their fallen sisters. Reporting that bawdy houses brazenly claimed U.S. nationality—issuing invitations embossed with the Stars and Stripes, for example—the letter writers saw all about them "vice from America flaunt[ing] itself in the face of the heathen."[39] In the American-occupied Philippines, to take another example, missionary groups focused their energies toward not only uplifting Filipinos, but also "elevat[ing] the spiritual and moral qualities of the American population of the islands" by way of preserving them "from that colonial degeneration which belies religion and contaminates the bewildered native."[40]

Colonial elites sought metropolitan intervention to combat these changing dynamics, but struggled to insure that the infusion of power did not eradicate their own autonomy. Thus, the push from the center was both solicited and feared. Colonial notables resented "being called upon to support" disreputables and tramps, but not being given sufficient authority from home governments to control these marginals. By the 1890s, there was clear class agenda in the campaign to reform colonial privilege. Unclaimed foreigners, that is those of no clear nationality, were identified as the central problem in extrality. This evidences the dynamic Stoler describes as the "grid of transgressions which tapped into metropolitan and colonial politics at the same time."[41] Whereas the essential unity of interests between governments and treaty port nationals was evident in the demand for and continued insistence upon the privilege of extrality, what some have called "the tensions of empire" were manifest in periodic efforts to reform extrality through a refinement and redefinition of the criteria used to bestow colonial privilege.

THE BOXER REBELLION AND AFTER

These tectonic shifts in great power imperialism and colonial nationalism found a vortex in China. The Boxer Rebellion (1900), together with the rout of Ch'ing westernizers by dynastic conservatives two years earlier, made manifest the inability of the post-Opium War, British-run unequal treaty system to manage one of the central contradictions of the process of penetration and incorporation, that is, the need to harness indigenous elites while also shoring them up long enough for that process to become self-generating. The massing of foreign troops and gunboats to force an end to the Boxer crisis in and of itself also served as a challenge to the nature of the Western presence up to that moment.

First, Japan and Russia in particular sought to take advantage of the crisis to bring in a permanent military and formal colonial presence, something quite contrary to the spirit of informal imperialism. Occupying armies and continued strife were not cheap, whether one was talking about the drain on coffers or the strain upon public opinion back home.[42]

The Ch'ing "self-strengtheners" of the 1860s had sought in vain to use westernization to preserve Confucianism against foreign penetration, i.e., to use "Chinese culture as the essence," and "Western technology as the means" by which to save Chinese society from external penetration.[43] Decades later, court conservatives effectively crushed the 1898 reform movement, again illuminating the difficulties facing any would-be collaborative elite. For those bent on opening China, the Boxers' siege of the foreign legations in Peking and the eruption of antiforeign violence elsewhere in China, primarily against foreign missionaries and their indigenous converts, made it starkly clear that central authorities were unwilling and unable to deal with the crisis.

The Role of the United States

Although the United States was by no means a major player in the "great game" of East Asian politics at the time of the Boxer crisis, it was ultimately the American-inspired, British-run, Open-Door system that emerged to fill the void. America's preferred strategy for keeping the open door open, from the outside against the predations of other foreign powers, and from the inside against antiforeignism and social disintegration, was evident in the approach U.S. officials took to the post-Boxer foreign occupation of Peking and other coastal areas. The United States sought a rapid withdrawal of foreign troops from China, and the reestablishment of central authority and order, in large part because there was little domestic support in America for long-term costly involvement abroad. Within their own sphere of supervision, U.S. officials worked with local collaborative elites against disruptive locals and foreign soldiers (including Americans) who looted and broke into homes.[44]

Presidents William McKinley and Theodore Roosevelt recognized that America's strategic interests in China were minimal. However, the Republican Party relied upon the "open-door constituency" of outward-looking commercial and secular reform groups interested in a "large policy" generally and, more particularly, in the pursuit of China as a market for surplus production and redemptive Progressivism.[45] Actual American investment in China was, from the perspective of this constituency, disappointingly low, but its members were vocal advocates of preserving a long-term option on the China market, in the main by preventing any one nation or combination of powers from closing the open door.

However, anti-immigration and anti-imperialism groups could not be ignored, and each concession to market expansionist required similar placation of their opponents. Thus, America's turn-of-the-century island-hopping campaign from Hawaii to Manila brought the China market much closer; yet, in order to gain domestic support for Pacific expansionism from organized labor and other anti-Oriental groups, discriminatory immigration laws and quotas were extended to Hawaii and the Philippines, thereby virtually closing these territories off to most Chinese and Japanese.[46] In direct response, the Ch'ing government refused to renew the 1894 immigration treaty, due to expire in 1904. Continued U.S. intransigence on the issue led to a 1905 anti-American boycott in the treaty ports, as well as in communities of overseas Chinese in Japan, the Philippines, and Hawaii. Generally speaking, the object of the boycott organizers was to demonstrate support for the Ch'ing government's efforts to stand up to foreign powers, most particularly the United States on the issue of immigration. The boycott thus raised the question as to whether domestic racist nativism would prevail over, or at least curtail, the search for foreign markets, in the main because discrimination and brutality toward Chinese in America galvanized anti-imperialist Chinese nationalism in a way few other issues at the time could.[47]

THE PUSH FOR "REFORM"

The American Vagrant "Other"

When Progressives looked about for the source of this Chinese anti-Americanism, the chief culprits seemed to be wayward treaty port Americans, unrestrained opportunists who had given the United States a "bad name" in Asia. For them, the dilemma harkened back to the great era of western expansion, when Congress and federal officials sought to keep back the human "torrent" of idle poor, squatters, and speculators. Contemporary essayists such as "Lycurgus," who wrote in the *Connecticut Magazine* in 1786, had warned that without government measures, the frontier would become "an asylum for decayed patriots" and asylum-seekers "running away from publick taxes, and private debts." Open, unregulated expansion would bring "[t]he poor, the oppressed, and the persecuted. . . . This Western-World will be the dernier resort, the last refuge, and asylum for afflicted merit." As in the western lands, even more so in treaty port China and the new Philippine colony, congressional initiative was needed to prevent "semi-savage predator[y]" whites who prospered by encouraging "uneasiness" and hostility among the original inhabitants.[48]

State Department reports indicate that by the early years of the new century American extrality in China had come to include an ever-widening array of individuals and enterprises. In the aftermath of the Spanish-American War, the U.S. takeover of the Philippines, and the multinational military suppression of the antiforeign Boxer Rebellion in Peking, hundreds of these beachcombers, campfollowers, China coasters, and adventurers straggled into Shanghai, Tientsin, Canton, and Amoy. United States sovereignty over Guam, Puerto Rico, Hawaii, and the Philippines created the situation where individuals from those countries came under American extrality when in China.

The increasing variety of individuals coming under U.S. nationality, and thus under State Department protection, exacerbated the problems faced by an already overwhelmed consular service. Consular records document the phenomenon, for example, of Chinese born in America, Hawaii, or the Philippines moving to China and operating on the margin of the two societies, not only culturally, but also legally through a sort of dual citizenship resting on the confusion of indigenous and American authorities as to who had jurisdiction.

With the advent of Good Government in the American-occupied Philippines under Governor General William Taft, who undertook the purification of Manila as a personal project, the situation in China's treaty ports worsened: "The Chinese ports and especially Shanghai are burdened with [American] indigents who have come from Manila," a U.S. consular official reported in 1906.[49] Their habit was "to commence at the beginning of a certain street, and visit every house and to continue their [begging] canvass until [all the] streets have been covered and until sufficient funds have been obtained to provide the wherewithal for a long continued spree of elaborate dimensions."[50] The city was "becoming the favorite rendezvous of a class which, under the stress of circumstances, can easily overstep all bounds and become criminal," according to the consul, who "doubt[ed]" at the time if his superiors had "anything approximating an understanding as to the character of some of the American population of Shanghai."[51]

Police, consular court, and probate records indicate, not surprisingly, that most of these "birds of passage" lived life on the margin, pushed from one port to another, with frequent stays in consular jails, often falling victim to cholera, dysentery, alcoholism, starvation, or the brutality of street life. Together with the structural barrier in the treaty port labor market, the inability and unwillingness of their wealthier fellow countrymen in China to subsidize them kept these newcomers far afield from the material rewards being white in the colonies had led them to expect. If these indigents came "to the consulate and . . . appear[ed] to be Americans and . . . sober," all they could expect is that their applications for relief would be noted, and they would receive "a ticket entitling them to one meal and a bed at some cheap hotel. If they prove[d] troublesome and persistent beggars," though, every effort was made to "get them out of town," the Shanghai consulate reported. Self-described "respectable" treaty port Americans would "do [this much] for the beachcomber class who appear[ed] to be worthy."[52]

Beyond providing opportunities in vice-based enterprises, the extraterritorial system also generated a black market in foreign privilege. Newer arrivals commodified the protégé system of the nineteenth century that had been built upon the extension of immunities to native employees, compradors, and converts.[53] By making commodified foreign privilege more widely available to interested Chinese on a simple cash-and-carry basis, "adventurers" and "beachcombers" stretched this protégé system beyond the realm of a face-to-face, patron-client network. Chinese seeking to collect real or fictitious debts from one another sold promissory notes to U.S. nationals like Harriet Falconer, who shuttled back and forth from Hong Kong to Canton buying up discounted Chinese debts and forcing payment from Chinese debtors through the good offices of U.S. consuls who, after all, were responsible for representing

"American interests" in such controversies.[54] Struggling entrepreneurs established bogus partnerships, which—according to both U.S. and Chinese officials—specialized in the sale of foreign transit passes (affording exemption from internal Chinese taxes) to indigenous merchants, mainly those trafficking in guns and opium.[55]

The "American Girl"

By 1907, the inroads made by early twentieth-century U.S. nationals in prostitution enterprises prompted then Secretary of War Taft to observe that: "Americans had rushed through the [open] door [to China] fast enough that in Shanghai 'American woman meant prostitute,' and in going to visit the red light district one said he was 'going to America.' "[56] There were an estimated forty "American" prostitutes in Shanghai claiming U.S. citizenship, according to Consul General James Rodgers, or approximately 13 percent of the total 317 female U.S. nationals reported in the port's annual official census.[57]

Some came to the business directly from the United States by way of established procurement rings linking leading American cities (such as Chicago and San Francisco) with the Asian prostitution market.[58] The ranks of self-described "American" prostitutes in Shanghai was further swelled when policy changes issued by Parliament apparently allowed British consuls to deport alleged prostitutes, causing many sex workers to claim U.S. citizenship instead. Up the coast in Tientsin, the situation was not very different, according to U.S. Vice-Consul General Albert Pontius. On 22 September 1906 he reported that "the gambling houses and houses of prostitution conducted under American auspices in China, and especially at Tientsin, have become so numerous and are conducted so openly and shamelessly that the situation has become intolerable."[59]

Many of the women coming down to Shanghai from Manchuria had American passports and, indeed, a brothel locally known as the "American Legation" in Port Arthur had come by its name because the Russian and Austrian inmates all had such documentation. This situation raised the vexing policy question as to whether the Secretary of State should deny or void passports on the basis of illegal, immoral, or undesirable conduct. The judicially sanctioned State Department position had long been that the Secretary had full discretion to deny a passport to a citizen;

possession of such a document was a privilege, not a right.[60] In 1905, the Secretary reversed a decision made in 1900 to deny passports on moral grounds.[61]

However, when presented with the case of J. H. "Tientsin" Brown, a Russian-born naturalized American operating casinos and brothels in Peking, Tientsin, and Shanghai, policy shifted again. Brown had repeatedly denied his U.S. citizenship to avoid consular jurisdiction. So long as the document was simply useful but not required for travel, a consul could deny one to an applicant clearly engaged in criminal activities.[62] Until World War I, when a passport became mandatory in many countries, the Supreme Court supported this position that no law or precedent obligated the secretary to provide applicants with a U.S. passport.[63]

From the Ranks of "Respectables"

Leading treaty port Americans, including missionary-reformer the Reverend Gilbert Reid, businessman Murray Warner, and representatives of corporations such as Standard Oil, argued that the continued influx of itinerant poor and the rise of gambling and prostitution interests under American auspices would undermine U.S.–China relations more generally. Reid, for example, who in 1901 had penned "The Ethics of Loot" in defense of forcible missionary appropriations of Chinese property and of exaggerated Boxer indemnity claims, by 1905 had come to see the wisdom of cooperation across the cultural divide.[64] Not only were he and his like-minded peers concerned about what they alleged was a debasement of American nationality in general, but they also predicted that the Chinese government could take the presence of penniless transients and dubious characters in the treaty ports as the occasion for duplicating the intrusive and degrading procedures used to restrict Chinese entry and internal travel within the United States.[65]

The threat of reprisal and reciprocal mistreatment was fueled by contemporary perceptions in the treaty ports that a "now powerful [Chinese] student class, which under the teachings of foreign educated Chinese, and perhaps others not friendly to American interests where they conflict with their own, has developed an influence recognized by officials, guilds, merchants and laborers." Both the anti-American boycott of 1905, and the December 1905 riots against certain procedural changes enacted by the British-run Mixed Court, filled Shanghai with "nervous tension."[66] By late March, 1906, Consul General James Rodgers discerned an "entire change of attitude on the part of the officials and gentry in dealing with matters connected with foreign interests. There is obstruction of one kind or another in nearly every thing, and an independence which goes farther to demonstrate the transition than any other factor." He cautioned that "the [Chinese common] people, unable to distinguish between issues, will seize upon the opportunity to retaliate and thus follow the advice of those who are now proclaiming principally that China is for the Chinese."[67] Their long-held monopoly on extraterritorial privilege challenged by the influx of new groups, leading Americans in China called upon Washington to establish a nonconsular judicial court, presided over by a trained judge, to adjudicate cases involving U.S. nationals as defendants. It was something of a "Terranova solution" to the contradictions of imperialism requiring the American colonial elite in China to jettison some its most expendable countrymen in a defensive, preemptive move to preserve privilege. As one leading Shanghai American observed: "Foreign privilege [was] on the defensive," required to "prove its right to exist . . . by recognizing that rights carry with them corresponding duties." "Every denial or postponement of justice, every judgment given against a Chinese plaintiff when that plaintiff knows his cause is just, every escape of an American criminal when the facts are clear but legal technicalities get him off, every such decision is felt to be an outrage by the whole Chinese people and its consequences fall . . . upon the law-abiding and reputable Americans."[68]

The Peirce Report

The battle to reform American extrality crystallized between 1904 and 1906 in a controversial State Department investigation of the China consulates. In 1904, Third Secretary of State H. H. D. Peirce went to China, not only as part of his worldwide inspection tour, but also with specific instructions to investigate charges and rumors of misconduct on the part of various U.S. consuls there. His confidential inspection report, a sanitized no-names-named version of which was released late that year, led to the wholesale removal of incumbents in the Shanghai and Canton consulates. (Although suspicions were raised about the integrity of U.S. officials in Amoy, the consulate suspiciously burned to the ground in the midst of Peirce's investigations, hindering a conclusive assessment.)[69]

Shanghai Consul General John Goodnow was charged with looting the estates of Americans who had died in China, accepting payoffs to transfer the China Steamship and Navigation Company's vessels fraudulently to American ownership, selling U.S. passports to non-Americans, and extorting money for his judicial services. Canton Consul General Robert McWade was charged with gross drunkenness upon a public occasion, employment of a convicted felon in the consulate, selling fraudulent certificates to Chinese "coolie" laborers seeking admission into the United States and the Philippines under the guise of merchants, illegally extending consular protection to Chinese subjects, interference with the affairs of the government of China, persecution of an American citizen for purposes of revenge, and general corruption in office. Consuls in Canton and Amoy were unable or unwilling to uphold the rigorous enforcement of visa certification procedures for would-be Chinese immigrants, which in turn exacerbated the tension at home between the open-door constituency and groups hostile to Chinese immigration, such as organized labor. More generally, according to Peirce, consular extraterritoriality was sorely compromised by the drinking, womanizing, and pilferous habits of State Department field officers.[70]

The American consular service in China had proven itself unable to manage the two primary issues hindering the emergence of a westernizing collaborative elite, i.e., immigration and the curtailment of treaty port Americans' visibly predatory behavior. State Department consuls at the time had neither the financial nor legal wherewithal to control and discipline those under their jurisdiction, in contrast to Great Britain, which devoted more resources to its colonial infrastructures. Forced to rely on a hodgepodge of outdated common law, federal statutes, and ministerial decrees, and without the power of extradition, U.S. officials on the scene could not effectively fulfill America's treaty obligation to China to exercise jurisdiction over U.S. nationals. This, in turn, made U.S. nationality the citizenship of choice for opportunists and lawbreakers from other treaty port powers in China, further compounding the problem.

Peirce and other consular inspectors him found a sizable gap between what formal agreements and regulations called for and what actually went on from one day to the next. Not unexpectedly, when State Department inspectors uncovered illicit dealings on the part of field officers, they generally attributed the incongruity between theory and practice to individual moral lapses on the part of spoils system appointees and—more systemically—to continued congressional resistance to civil service reform. Taking a more historical perspective, Samuel Hays's analysis of early twentieth-century Progressivism suggests that, although submerged in moralizing rhetoric, the real "drama of reform lay in the competition for supremacy between two systems of decision-making," one local, the other centralized, and at the core was a "debate over who should be represented, over whose views of public policy should prevail." The power of local interests over U.S. China policy at the point of impact, that is in the treaty ports themselves, was crystallized by various consular inspection reports. Consular courts, like antebellum federal district courts within the U.S., were embedded "in the local constituencies they served, . . .as potentially responsible to local interests as to the dictates of national authority." In both instances, "reform" meant nationalizing and federalizing local judiciaries.[71]

Reform's Unexpected Allies

Among the strongest supporters for consular and judicial "reform" were leading American entrepreneurs in treaty port vice. It would be wrong to assume that the relationship of ostensibly marginal treaty port Americans to the legal process was unambiguous, such that any "reforms" in the extraterritorial system would be harmful to their survival and prosperity. True, for impoverished itinerants pushed from port to port, known to contemporaries as "beachcombers," the law was to be feared and hated. For their more monied counterparts, though, "justice" was as necessary as it was arbitrary.

Western prostitutes operating under U.S. nationality required access and recourse to the legal process for credit relations, mutual misunderstandings, and physical safety. Early twentieth-century American female brothel inmates and managers in Shanghai were often prosperous businesswomen. Probate records, a reliable source for relative degrees of wealth (though not exact figures, given the high incidence of estate looting by American consuls in China) suggests that some among these women did quite well.[72] A known courtesan, Cosette Denvers (alias Laura Leslig, alias Belle Wheeler), died at the early age of thirty, having accumulated about $7,000 worth of furniture, $4,000 in cash, and about $1,200 in IOUs.[73] In the cash-poor economy of Shanghai this woman had money and in fact was the financial backer of and "silent partner" in at least one American enterprise in China, the China Pipe and Tile Company, formed by a somewhat dubious character himself, L. C. Passano.[74] Barbara Beatrice Foster, co-owner with Maxine Livingstone of the brothel at 52 Kiangse Road, died in 1905 at age thirty-two, having accumulated in six or seven years an estate of about $25,000, more than half of which she bequeathed to the poor.[75]

These women were a vital part of the local economy, as conspicuous consumers, creditors, debtors, stockholders and, not to be overlooked, well-paying clients of the small circle of Shanghai American lawyers. Female brothel owners registered as U.S. nationals in Shanghai at the time likely wished that each arm of the U.S. government in China, the diplomatic and the judicial, would operate in isolation from the other. In particular, wayward treaty port Americans sought a court concerned only with technical questions of legal guilt and responsibility in each case as it arose, rather than one overly curious about the social standing and source of income of litigants and their lawyers.

Consuls acting judicially took the position articulated by Consul General James Rodgers when asked to hear a case involving a contract dispute between two brothel keepers: "I have made a practice never to allow the affairs of women of the character" of these litigants "to appear in my Court."[76] This blend of judicial and political authority in the hands of a single official—the consul general—was thus something of a disadvantage to treaty port Americans on the fringes of legality, and made highly desirable to them the prospect of consulates without judges, and courts without consuls.

The Case of J. H. "Tientsin" Brown

The suggestion that American gambling and prostitution interests in China shared the desire of open-door Progressives for extraterritorial reform is incontrovertibly supported by the activities of treaty port American and "bawdy house" keeper extraordinaire, J. H. "Tientsin" Brown, mentioned above in connection with the passport issue. From humble beginnings as a Tientsin saloon keeper and semi-legal procurement contractor for foreign military forces in China, Brown diversified into real estate speculation and underwriting houses of prostitution, opening in 1903 the Shanghai Alhambra "house of amusement."[77]

When on 5 October 1904, Shanghai U.S. Consul General John Good-now brought Brown before the consular court on the basis of Brown's sworn affidavit in an earlier case that he had been naturalized in 1888 by a Chicago judge, the Alhambra owner repudiated that affidavit—through his attorney—and rejected the consul's jurisdiction over him. Goodnow's actions were part of a joint effort by the foreign consular body in Shanghai to "corral" Brown, who had eluded municipal law (International Settlement regulations) by locating the Alhambra just outside of city limits, and consular jurisdiction by repeatedly claiming some nationality other than the one of the magistrate he stood before in any given instance. German officials ultimately convicted him in 1904, but Brown then fled to Manila, where he obtained an American passport from U.S. officials, returning then to Shanghai and his niche in the China market.[78]

Not long after his ordeal in the U.S. Shanghai consular court, though, Brown apparently capitalized on political connections in Oregon and obtained an invitation to the White House and there, on 4 December 1905, he chatted with President Roosevelt about the crying need for American consular reform in China. "J. H. Brown . . . who for many years has been engaged in business in Shanghai and Tientsin. . . . urged the President to use his influence to have established in Shanghai an American court . . . to adjudicate cases now handled in consular courts," the *Washington Evening Star* reported.[79] Roosevelt was suffi-ciently impressed by Brown's various arguments that the Chinese had lost confidence in the consular system, that British dominance in Shanghai was hindering U.S. business, and that the U.S. consul general in Shanghai (John Goodnow) had "incited" the 1905 anti-American boycott, to ask his guest to follow up their wide-ranging discussions with a written statement of "his views on the situation in China as it affects Americans and American interests," and suggested further that he meet with Secretary of State Elihu Root about matters of national concern.[80]

Historians may wonder, as did Consul General John Goodnow, "[h]ow such a man gets the ear of the President" of the United States, and why he then used that audience to advocate a more rigorous adjudi-cation of American extraterritoriality in China.[81] First, through a strat-egy of subversive alignment Brown successfully represented himself to be just the sort of American businessman in the "China market" Roosevelt and his like-minded colleagues were looking for by way of increasing America's material stake, and thereby its leverage, in the "great game" of East Asian power politics. Brown first appears in the record, for instance, in January of 1902, when he joined the small group of American missionaries and businessmen petitioning the U.S. government to establish an American concession or settlement at the port (Tientsin).[82] At the time, the main obstacle to an increased American role in that city and in north China more generally was a lack of interested U.S. nationals to hold ground gained: it might "be advantageous to us in many ways to have an American concession at Tientsin," Minister Edwin Conger had written to Secretary John Hay on 31 December 1900, "but we have learned by experience that it takes both money and citizens to own and operate a concession. We have not enough there of either."[83] It is little wonder, then, that a prosperous and self-described U.S. national like Brown found shelter in the American fold.

When he expanded and diversified into the more cosmopolitan, less frontier-like, British-dominated International Settlement at Shanghai, however, Brown found the going more difficult, as suggested by the 1904 multinational consular campaign against him. Although using nationalities of convenience helped him to evade prosecution for a time, that strategy also hindered his recourse to the consulates and consular courts for the conduct of day-to-day business, whether that meant notarizing documents, storing valuable property and cash, registering land deeds and mortgages, collecting debts, or protecting his business more generally. We know this situation troubled Brown, because on 28 January 1904 he wrote a letter to Theodore Roosevelt—in the form of an affidavit signed before the U.S. Consul at Tientsin and forwarded to Washington by Minister Edwin Conger—expressing outrage that he, one of the most prosperous and prominent American businessman in China, would be kept waiting at the Shanghai consulate by an official "known far and wide as a grafter" (Consul General John Goodnow). He offered to pay the costs of an investigation of the consul, arguing that Goodnow's removal was in the interests of all Americans in China.

Why this letter was not just tossed in the circular file of the White House, or any other such bin along the way, highlights a second point about Brown's odyssey, i.e., his ability to thrive within the ambiguities, generalities, inconsistencies, and institutional and partisan rivalries inherent in U.S. China policy. Brown's desire to be rid of a particularly

troublesome consul dovetailed not only with the hostility other Shanghai Americans felt toward Goodnow for personal and political reasons,
but also with the grander vision among outward-looking Progressives of
a nonpartisan, merit-based consular service. So too, Brown's desire to
have judicially impotent consuls and politically impotent judges coincided, paradoxically, with the campaign to rationalize and invigorate
China policy, in part, through the divorce of consular from judicial functions.

The "open door constituency's" reform agenda both at home and
abroad provided Brown with the means to undercut Consul General
Goodnow. Brown's letter/affidavit formed part of the evidence used by
Third Secretary Peirce when he sat down in late 1904 to write his report
on the alleged misconduct of State Department personnel in both
Shanghai and Canton. That the Alhambra owner was left out of the final
confidential version released to the House of Representatives a year and
a half later seems due only to a 9 March 1906 memo to Peirce from the
State Department Solicitor's Office, to the effect that: "In view of Brown's
claim to protection as an Argentine and Spanish subject," as well as his
"repeated denials of American nationality, and refusal to recognize the
jurisdiction of our consular court," the actions of Goodnow and his suc-
cessors "in declining to assume jurisdiction over him as an American citizen [were] entirely justified."[84]

In fact, the primary charges against Goodnow came from affidavits
from treaty port Americans like Brown, that is, individuals who were
unhappy with the consul's judicial decisions against them in particular
cases and, more generally, by the system of consular jurisprudence that
decided their litigation with an eye toward maintaining good state-to-
state Sino-American relations. Initially, after a brief trip to the "Orient,"
Peirce cleared Goodnow on various counts of misconduct, according to
a *New York Times* report of 29 September 1904, but even while he was
completing his report, Shanghai American attorney George F. Curtis,
who had run afoul of Goodnow in a number of Chinese debt and
indemnity collection cases, had assembled further charges and evidence
and presented it to the State Department by way of the office of President Roosevelt.[85] Curtis's debt collection efforts on behalf of Chinese
clothiers and craftsmen put him in a constant battle with U.S. consuls
about the procedures of settling estates of Americans dying in China,
particularly those of conspicuously consuming brothel owners and

inmates. Curtis pointed out to Congress in his testimony against Good-now that, as American prostitutes in China often died without wills, under aliases, and with few known relatives willing to come forth, their estates were tempting sources of graft and malfeasance on the part of State Department field officers. Although damning on the face of things, the lawyer's case was more circumstantial than conclusive, as Peirce him-self conceded "the almost inextricable confusion brought into the affair by George F. Curtis."[86]

As Minister George Seward had learned to his great misfortune in the 1870s, local Americans had a powerful, albeit covert, source of leverage over China policy in the demonstrated ability to wreak havoc in the relationship between the U.S. government and its appointed consuls and ministers in China, typically—and ironically—in the name of good government and consular reform. It is not that Brown or even Lawyer Curtis alone brought down the consular service, but rather that the Alhambra owner and others like him were able to use the fault lines of the American political system, and of the consular service itself, to undermine the authority and continuity of U.S. policy in China.

CREATION OF THE U.S. COURT FOR CHINA

In direct response to the Peirce Report, the Roosevelt administration pushed through the 59th Congress, the Consular Reform and the U.S. Court for China Acts of 1906.[87] The first, supplemented by Executive Orders on 27 June 1906, classified American consulates abroad into grades with prescribed salaries, abolished the corruption-prone office of commercial agent, created an inspector corps of five super-consuls, increased salaries across the board, ended the fee system of official emol-ument, and required that all posts be filled by American citizens. Together with Executive Orders issued on 27 June 1906, which placed entry into and promotion within the Consular Service on the basis of examination and merit, this 1906 Act provided the opening wedge of professionalism and nonpartisanship in the day-to-day conduct of U.S. foreign policy.[88]

Signed into law by Roosevelt the same day as the Consular Reform Act, 30 June 1906, the U.S. Court for China Act dramatically truncated the judicial powers of U.S. consuls in China, and established an extra-territorial court in Shanghai with jurisdiction over all Americans in China.[89] The Court, eventually abolished after 1943 when the United States ceded its extraterritorial rights in China, was granted original jurisdiction in most civil and criminal cases where Americans were defendants, and appellate jurisdiction over cases decided first in the now greatly circumscribed U.S. consular courts in China's treaty ports.[90]

Most Americans at the time hardly noticed the establishment of an extraterritorial court in China. The passage of the bill received only brief mention in leading newspapers, and Congress had to be reminded many times over in subsequent years that it had in fact created such a Court. The years 1905–1906 were, historian Richard McCormick has noted, a time when Americans experienced "wrenching moments of discovery" that "business corrupts politics," as muckraking exposés and official investigations in cities and states across the country revealed egregious outrages in the insurance, meatpacking, railroad, and banking indus-tries.[91] Thus, the news that the political spoils system was corrupting American business abroad was merely a variation on an increasingly familiar theme.

The prevailing trope of corruption has obscured the intimate con-nection between consular and extraterritorial reform and the Expatri-ation and Naturalization Act of 1907. Codifying preceding decades of State Department precedents and federal court decisions, this Act put the United States in line with other Western powers in tightening and clarifying the laws of naturalization, expatriation, and diplomatic pro-tection.[92] Certain actions were now, by law, to be taken as evidence of voluntary expatriation: naturalization elsewhere, marriage by an American woman to a foreigner, an oath of allegiance made to another nation, and protracted residence abroad with no evident intent to return to the United States. Expatriation was prohibited in times of war.[93]

The Act and conventions signed at the same time were most specifi-cally directed against large groups of naturalized Americans living in their native land, enjoying virtual dual citizenship. As Elihu Root explained a few years later, for example, the State Department found seven or eight thousand native Turks capitalizing on this borrowed nationality; an investigation proceeding the Algeciras Conference (1906) showed that one-half of all American nationals in Morocco had left the United States within three months of their naturalization.[94]

Whether "Americans" sojourning in the anomalous zones of colonial privilege could now be brought into conformity with the comprehensive citizenship regime of imperial progressivism was as yet unknown.

CHAPTER FOUR

PROGRESSIVISM SHANGHAIED

This chapter examines American official responses to intersecting domestic and international developments in extraterritorial enclaves at the turn of the century. The focus turns upon the early operations of the U.S. Court for China by way of illustrating the competing pulls on extra-territorial justice systems. The discussion details how Court officers tried to rein in their troublesome treaty port wards, hoping thereby to gain Chinese cooperation and commercial openness. These efforts brought the Court into conflict with a shifting coalition of powerful treaty port Americans, including Catholic missionaries, local (i.e. Anglo-American) real estate companies, attorneys at law, and American gambling and prostitution interests. The friends of the Court included, at first, groups and individuals hoping to use it and extrality more generally as a ful-crum for the Americanization of China.

The originating purpose of the United States Court for China was to subordinate treaty port Americans to the "national interests," and harness them to an expanding imperial state. As the Court bill moved through a reluctant Congress, and then the Court itself opened for business in late 1906, its mission became a threefold one: a) disciplinary—to bring treaty port Americans to heel in the service of Open Door expansionism; b) protective—to buffer and enhance America's "stake" in China, securing the lives and property of U.S. nationals, and enabling Americans to compete in the China market; c) tutelary—to provide late Ch'ing constitutional and legal reformers with an object lesson in American-style jurisprudence.

The Court's early years revealed, though, that while complementary in the abstract, these aspirations were ultimately contradictory and unattainable. Those whom Washington sought to embrace had many resources at their disposal to resist their government's embrace, not the least of which were the very legal procedures and moral principles the Court itself brought to China. The constraints and imperatives inherent in law as an instrument of power and hindered its capacity for reining in treaty port Americans. In turn, American Progressives' failure to legitimize extrality as a "square deal" for Chinese contributed to indigenous hostility to transplanted courts, and to Western jurisprudence more generally.

Part one of the discussion below presents the intra-American political struggle over extrality initiated by the Court's arrival in Shanghai in late 1906. In getting the Court bill through Congress, architects Roosevelt, Root, Taft, and Representative Edwin Denby (R-MI) had been deliberately vague on the details. Left unclear, for example, was the precise relationship between the State Department and the Court. This situation, combined with the Progressivist vision of the Court's first officials, generated a high-stakes contest over American extrality, stretching from Shanghai to Washington, leading eventually to the forced resignation of Judge Lebbeus Wilfley. Part two of the chapter begins with the Court's shift in 1909 away from zealous Progressivism under Wilfley's successor, Rufus Thayer. Though short lived, the modus vivendi between the USC-C and Shanghai Americans, provides an opportunity to look beyond high-profile cases to the broader efforts of the Court to systematize and federalize "law and order" among Americans in the anomalous zone of treaty port China. The chapter concludes with an overall analysis of the Court's civil and criminal case load from 1907 to Judge Thayer's (forced) resignation in 1913.

THE FIRST U.S. COURT FOR CHINA (USC-C)

The man sent by the Theodore Roosevelt administration in 1906 to rein in treaty port Americans was Lebbeus Redman Wilfley. A Missouri-born,

Yale-trained lawyer, Wilfley had served five years as attorney general in Manila under Governor General William Howard Taft.[1] He had been schooled there in Taft's "little brown brother" approach to empire, formulated on the profound, though from the Filipino perspective somewhat belated, insight that the most effective route to pacification and reconstruction was not the costly and politically suicidal war of attrition then being waged by U.S. forces against inhabitants, but rather a cooptive "policy of attraction" designed to give amenable indigenous groups a stake in the process, as well as a sense that American suzereignty promised a "square deal" for locals.[2]

Amid virulent opposition from Americans in the Philippines, Taft crafted a criminal justice system there that included among its judges, police, and attorneys, both U.S. nationals and Filipinos, drawn together in the unequal partnership of informal imperialism.[3] Under Wilfley's direction, the attorney general's office in Manila had been instrumental in cementing the ties between the American colonial administration and the educated, urban *ilustrado* elite. It was an alliance forged in the interest of authority and property against "outlaws" and "bandits" on both sides, whether Filipinos resisting "assimilation," or indigenous and American "birds of prey" operating houses of prostitution, hawking "common bawdy," and otherwise doing visible, unauthorized violence to those around them.

The "militant decency," moral zeal, confident Americanism, and commercial tenor of the Judge's conception of his duties placed him squarely in the ranks of outward-looking Progressives who saw in their country's culture and commerce a transforming force in world affairs.[4] That Wilfley turned his energies to China put him in the "open-door constituency" that emerged at the turn of the century, as the forward agents of free trade expansionism and of a more energetic American presence in East Asia.[5] So too, Wilfley's belief that he and his Shanghai-based Court could teach Chinese the difference between "a government of men" and a "government of laws," enlisted him in the legion of activists who saw in China a "tabula rasa," a laboratory for every garden-variety of reform that crossed the Progressive imagination.[6]

A man of his time, Judge Wilfley was all of these things: a "big policy" expansionist, supremely convinced that what was good for his country was good for all. In the broader scheme of things though, that is, in terms of the history of the rise and fall of empires, the task that fell to Lebbeus

Wilfley was not so very different than that which had challenged George Grenville, or Thomas Hutchinson, or any other of the late eighteenth-century English ministers charged with bringing rogue colonists—too long allowed to roam—under the authority of the imperial state.

The struggle between center and periphery took on a moral tone, and a "Wild West" flavor, as the most "insolent" among those whom he was sent to bring under federal control were the gambling and prostitution interests reportedly giving America a "bad name" in Asia and hindering U.S. progress in the China market. As the Judge wrote to his mentor and patron Taft in June of 1907: "You have no idea the extent to which corrupt officials and renegade Americans have hurt the American name and American business interests in China. . . . The bad feeling engendered by the unscrupulous and contemptuous treatment of the Chinese by American swindlers and sharks, has made it hard for respectable American merchants to do business in China."[7]

Given the tendency of "Orientals . . . [to be] impressed by what they see rather than by what they hear and read" about America's intentions in China, the Judge concluded, it was no wonder that U.S. "prestige and . . . trade interests" had suffered in the region. There was no doubt in his mind "that the restoration of national [i.e., American] decency in China" had to precede "the establishment of solid trade relations between the two countries," because "in order to trade with people you must first secure their confidence and good-will."[8]

The new Court and its blustering judge thus brought to Americans in China two seemingly contradictory lessons. The first pertained to the long-held fantasy among U.S. officials about a "special relationship" with China, and said to sojourners, in effect, that they owed their survival and prosperity to Chinese sufferance, reinforced by American power. Thus, sojourners should be on their best behavior. This normative view recalled a commonplace nineteenth-century belief that: "as a good family takes care that its children, when on a visit, behave themselves, so a state is bound by honor and self-respect, to provide that its subjects, when abroad, don't commit an act that would be indictable, when committed at home."[9]

The second lesson was borrowed from what one historian describes as the primer of "capitalist morality," and pertained to the much sought after expansion of American business in China.[10] This lesson said to entrepreneurs, in effect, that participation in the marketplace did not recognize racial, ethnic and national distinctions: the same ethical standards (ideally) in play at home, obtained while doing business abroad under the American flag. This was a major assault against the double standard, or double-think, that had given rise to the phenomenon (described in chapter 2) of American businessmen well respected in the U.S. knowingly engaging in the China opium trade.

On the receiving end of this tutorial, though, one Shanghai American newspaper editor wondered:

> Is it possible that American interests in Shanghai are to have such an experience as Hawaii did following the organization of the Territory? That the establishment of a new court here, with a new judge is to be interpreted . . . as the opportunity for the new judge to claim the distinction of introducing 'Americanism' there, and to do it by ruthless attacks on the Americans and Americanisms he finds there; by attempting to destroy the means of livelihood of Americans who came there before he did, and of the American interests he find there?[11]

Opening Salvos in the Battle Over "Americanism"

Upon his arrival in Shanghai from Manila in late 1906, Judge Wilfley made immediately clear his intent to bring to heel treaty port Americans, using the second-class federal citizenship category devised under the *Ross* precedent. "It must not be inferred . . . that the rights and privileges guaranteed by the Constitution extend to American citizens in China. . . . [I]n a foreign country, the Constitution can have no operation," he told a banquet audience convened to greet the new Court. As Americans were in China at Chinese "sufferance," they must "establish and maintain an orderly rule" among themselves.[12]

The orientation of the new U.S. Court toward a "policy of attraction" in the China setting was further reinforced by the State Department's candidate for court clerk, Dr. Frank Erasmus Hinckley. A graduate of Columbia University, and student of famed international jurist John Bassett Moore, Hinckley's published dissertation on American extraterritoriality in China (1906) long remained the standard work on the subject.[13] In broad historical terms, both Hinckley and Wilfley attest to the rise of "committing elites" in early twentieth-century America, groups whose material interests and worldviews became intertwined with the imperatives of expansionism. Imperialism, informal and otherwise, became a "regenerative principle" within expanding societies in large part by the reorientation of cultural norms, public discourse, and internal structures—such as leading universities—around the philosophical and personnel requirements of empire.[14]

The court clerk was well suited by training and disposition for the task of assisting in the formation of a collaborative alliance, or a "community of understanding" between right-thinking Americans and open-minded Chinese, based upon the rule of law. Addressing his sojourning countrymen during the banquet at the Astor House in Shanghai welcoming the Court, Clerk Hinckley succinctly articulated the essence of the post-Boxer, post-Boycott "bargain" between the U.S. government and Chinese elites: "this new Court is a Court for China. I would emphasize the word 'for.' It is a United States Court for China," charged with "assisting the Chinese Government in one of the chief prerogatives of its national sovereignty. It is our duty to use this privilege aright." This was a clear endorsement of a view floated by jurists since the 1890s, that extraterritorial consular courts were properly agents of indigenous governments which, temporarily unable to exercise full sovereignty, consented to the arrangement.[15]

Accustomed to the luxury of exclusive American suzerainty in the Philippines, and convinced (quite wrongly) that the Court's sponsors in Washington were as committed to the task as he, Judge Wilfley moved quickly and without compromise. His clean-up campaign began with an attack on local American attorneys known to solicit and rely upon "disreputable clients." Breaking with custom, and borrowing Taft's Philippine policies, Wilfley restricted the right to practice before the Court to those who presented "a certificate of good moral character satisfactory to the Court," and passed an examination given by the Judge.[16] The combination disqualified all but two of the nine American attorneys in the city.

Denying certification from the U.S. Court simultaneously jeopardized lawyers' access to other foreign and mixed treaty port courts, as the latter required the former; at the same time, having no jurisdiction over non-Americans, Wilfley's new policy did not apply to foreign attorneys, who would be permitted to practice before the U.S. Court simply by presenting proof of membership in their own extraterritorial courts.[17] Wilfley wrote privately to Root, local American lawyers were abetting American criminals, undermining Chinese faith in American extrality; through "boisterous and unscrupulous methods," these lawyers had "succeeded in confusing and bulldozing the community in general and the Consular Court in particular, and [had] aided the criminal and vicious classes in defying law and decency."[18]

Having decimated the bar, Wilfley moved on to its clientele, working hand-in-glove with District Attorney Arthur Bassett to bring before the bench *U.S. v. Price* and *U.S. v. Biddle.* Both cases were fashioned by the Court to try to bring down reputed kingpins of the gambling and prostitution trade in Shanghai. Charles Biddle was joint owner and manager of the Metropole Hotel, which Wilfley had learned was "little more than a large house of prostitution," and was also the lessee of the Alcazar, an entertainment house similar to the Alhambra. Biddle was convicted of fraud and sentenced to 12 months, on evidence originating in a civil suit (*Woo Ah-Sung et al. v. Biddle*) heard by the Court brought against Biddle by a group of Shanghai Chinese who had entered into an agreement with him to lease various premises to run gambling operations during "race week" in Shanghai.[19]

Stuart Price had been prosecuted by then Attorney General Wilfley in Manila for keeping a gambling house, but the case had been dismissed. Price had then moved on to Shanghai, and took up the lease on the Alhambra resort and other such "bawdy houses." He was sentenced by the new Court for six months for assault with a deadly weapon (an unloaded pistol) upon local (Norwegian) innkeeper; Price was also denied bail pending appeal, as Wilfley felt that the defendant's guilt was obvious, and "it was better for justice to have the punishment follow swiftly on the heels of the commission of the crime."[20]

"Wilfley's Purge" continued when, in late January 1907, Bassett filed charges against eight of the most "celebrated [female] American bawdy house keepers in Shanghai" on common law misdemeanor charges. These were the elite "Water Tower" women who ran the stately brothels on Kiangse and Soochow Roads. A few immediately claimed alternate nationalities; most were found guilty under common law, promised to leave the city "in a reasonable time" and never return again, and so were let off with $1,000 (Mex) fine. Wilfley then secured a Vagrancy Decree from the U.S. minister that would have enabled the Court to target practically any U.S. citizen leading an idle, immoral life, with no visible legitimate income.

The direction of the new legal regime was clear within weeks of the Court's arrival, then, its Judge having moved with exhilarating speed. "The atmosphere is clearing up in Shanghai rapidly," Wilfley wrote home in late January 1907. "All the bad lawyers are out of business and the law breakers are receiving their just dues." The city was "on its head." The imagined Chinese audience was "enthusiastic," Wilfley insisted with characteristic hyperbole, as the Court's "work is known and thoroughly appreciated by the Chinese people throughout the Empire," and leading Chinese report that it has "meant the beginning of a better understanding between the Chinese and Americans."[21]

Resistance to the New Regime

As the English Crown came to realize in the late eighteenth century, though, a decision by the home government to diminish the status of its settlers on the periphery, and to reharness colonial outposts to the changing needs of the imperial state, does not take force by simple fiat but, rather, is the subject of some controversy and resistance.[22] Almost immediately upon the Court's opening, the battle among Americans over extrality began, continuing for about two years. It spread from Shanghai to Manila, where Judge Wilfley's old enemies took up the cause against him; thence to San Francisco, where the 9th Circuit Court of Appeals overturned his anti-vice decisions; and finally to Washington itself, where those he had tried to run out of Shanghai brought their complaints to the U.S. Congress.

The first phase of struggle, spanning the Court's inauguration in December 1906 to May of the following year, was led by attorney Lorrin Andrews, whom Wilfley had refused license to practice before the Court. Speaking on behalf of his colleagues, and on retainer from clients including Stuart Price, the bawdy house keeper convicted by Wilfley in early 1907, Andrews took on the Court, deftly using reform rhetoric and the "rule of law" ideology to break the Court and run its Judge out of town. On 14 January 1907, a "Committee" from Shanghai, led by Andrews and comprising mostly other rejected lawyers, telegraphed their plight to Theodore Roosevelt, pleading "for protection from gross injustice." When the White House failed to respond to the desperate pleas from Shanghai, Andrews then traveled to the United States to gain redress. On his own behalf, and as counsel for those whom Wilfley had targeted, Andrews pursued a two-pronged strategy to neutralize the Judge and his Court.[23]

First, he stopped in San Francisco and succeeded in getting the 9th Circuit Court, which Congress had designated as the appellate court for American cases heard first in Shanghai, to issue an injunction ordering Wilfley to release Price on bail pending his appeal. Then, in a political version of the same process, he proceeded on to Washington, where he managed, through his close contacts in the New York Republican Party, to get a bill through the Senate that would have allowed attorneys qualified in higher state or federal courts in the United States to be admitted pro forma into the bar of the Court for China. Congressmen Edwin Denby, who had almost single-handedly shepherded the Court creation act through the maze of dockets and hearings, blocked Andrews' bill in the House on behalf of the State Department, although the attorney was permitted to air his complaints before a subcommittee headed by Denby.[24]

Fault Lines in the USC-C

The struggle between Wilfley and his treaty port wards revealed several of the Court's major institutional and political fault lines, and portended the nature of future struggle. First, the subordination of the Shanghai Court to an appellate court six thousand miles away in a city not noted for its solicitude toward Chinese enabled defense attorneys to present the *Price* and *Biddle* cases outside of their original and highly political context. Far removed from Shanghai, and absent a driving concern to redeem America's good name in the Far East, both cases seemed nothing less than miscarriages of justice to the appellate bench, and were each reversed on various grounds. As Wilfley told Taft, the appellate reversals were disastrous, as "[t]he convictions of these two men [had done] more to establish the Court in the confidence of the Chinese people than anything the Court has done."[25]

The appellate process highlighted a second fault line in the Court's foundation and structure, i.e., its Judge lacked a specific, detailed, comprehensive, and internally consistent body of laws upon which to decide cases. The 1906 creation act prescribed that the Court would adjudicate cases according to U.S. federal statutes, common law, and decrees issued by the U.S. minister in Peking, all of which could be supplemented and amended by the Judge as required by circumstances. In the United

States, criminal law has traditionally been largely within the purview of individual states, and federal statutes at the time did not speak to the daily needs of Shanghai. Similarly, the Court could not draw selectively from one or another state's body of law, but was instead held to earlier, largely anachronistic, common law precepts dating from the era of British America. Thus, in order to break the power of American gambling and prostitution interests in the treaty ports, Wilfley was forced to stretch eighteenth-century common law, as in *Biddle*, and to rely on decrees from Minister William Rockhill that were not fully binding until approval by Congress. These factors made him particularly vulnerable to charges that he dispensed arbitrary and vindictive justice.

Of course, rivalries within Congress and between the White House and Capitol Hill provided a receptive venue for the case against Wilfley. At the time, the Roosevelt administration was in bitter conflict with a Congress feeling bullied and strong-armed by a domestic version of the "big stick." Within the Republican Party, a widening divide between "stalwarts," such as Speaker of the House Joseph Cannon, and Roosevelt's reform-minded "insurgents," weakened party solidarity, making the U.S. Court for China "fair game." Attorney Lorrin Andrews, one-time attorney general in Hawaii, had little trouble convincing sympathetic congressmen that Wilfley's bar admissions policy was wholly arbitrary, as it permitted foreign attorneys of questionable qualifications to practice, while excluding lawyers who had presented cases before the Supreme Court of the United States.

This vulnerability to politicization was accentuated by a third distinct fault line in the Court's foundation and structure, a vulnerability symbolically expressed by the fact that the Court was forced to operate out of borrowed second-floor rooms in the Shanghai Consulate General. Although fiscal limits played a role here, the larger reason was the State Department's sense that Sino-American treaties permitted only consular courts, and so the new Court should be within the consulate. It was, though, exceedingly difficult for the Roosevelt administration to present and treat the Court as an independent judiciary, protected from State Department interference by the constitutional separation of the executive and judicial branches, at the very same time that Root and his ally Representative Denby were beseeching Congress to pass a special bill allocating Court operating funds for the current fiscal year. Root's dilemma is evident in a 16 February 1907 telegram to Wilfley, in which he underscored the difficulties of getting congressional funding given the prevailing impression in Washington that Wilfley had excluded able attorneys simply to allow his own district attorney to solicit their clientele.[26]

The natural inclination Root might have felt to resolve the dilemma by ordering Wilfley onto a less controversial tack, at least until the appropriations had been obtained, was tempered by a genuine uncertainty about the status of the Court in the departmental hierarchy. That this uncertainty was pervasive is reflected in internal correspondence on matters ranging from the mundane—whom to notify about Court Clerk Hinckley's delayed arrival in Shanghai in 1906—to the more urgent matters—such as Root's question to Departmental Solicitor James Scott as to the propriety of recommending to Wilfley a less stringent bar admissions policy.[27]

From the State Department's perspective, the very reason for establishing a nonconsular extraterritorial court in China had been to erect a cordon sanitaire around the myriad legal imbroglios treaty port Americans found themselves in from time to time, and thereby prevent those conflicts from muddying the waters of state-to-state diplomacy. However, the department could not at once present the Court as a diplomatically neutral sanctuary for the resolution of conflicts strictly according to an abstract and universally binding "rule of law," if at the same time the Wilfley's policies and decisions were subject to revocation or dilution by political authorities. Tempting though it might have been to dictate a more politically expedient course to Wilfley, Root must have seen that if once the State Department stepped in on behalf of a disappointed litigant, there would be no end to demands from Americans and Chinese alike to do so again in other instances of apparent inequity.

The larger question of the Court's status within the departmental hierarchy remained a source of discord and misunderstanding. More substantively, Judge Wilfley and Consul General Charles Denby Jr. split irrevocably on the question of the Court's proper place in official hierarchy, and on the political wisdom of Wilfley's all-out assault on treaty port vice. "Mr. Denby and I no longer agree upon the policy to be pursued out here, and this difference is fatal to the successful performance of our official duties," the first Judge had complained to Washington officials in the fall of 1908.

Denby, son of one-time U.S. Minister to China Charles Denby, brother of Rep. Edwin Denby (R-MI), and long-time China hand himself, believed that both the Court and the consulates were "commercial institutions created solely for the purpose of subserving our business interests in China, and that they should not engage in so-called 'reform' work." Similarly, Chefoo Consul John Fowler kept up a steady barrage of anti-Wilfley dispatches, complaining: "Judge Wilfley was not sent to China to revolutionize the lives, commerce or habits of Americans, but to administer the law, as he found it. . . . [H]e is not empowered to decide what is, or what is not American."[28]

Denby had balked at Wilfley's directives and allowed lawyers Wilfley disbarred from the U.S. Court to appear before the lower-level consular court, which in turn made them eligible to practice before all other extraterritorial courts in China except for Wilfley's own. This same consular court provided a venue for an attack on USDA Bassett as the defendant in a case brought by a Chinese woman accusing Bassett of double-dealing in an insurance case he took on for her in his private capacity.[29] Most notably, Denby also used his consular court to undermine Wilfley's crusade against the American-run bawdy houses, refusing to prosecute as vagrants the employees of these casinos and brothels.[30]

Concomitantly, although missionary organizations and various other "respectable" treaty port Americans supported in principle the new Court's attack on vice, they resisted the dramatic federal intervention into their own affairs. They sought, above all, a court imbued with federal power but amenable to their own guidance. This was to be achieved, they argued, through the use of a modified jury system. This was, in fact, the way that His Britannic Majesty's Supreme Court in Shanghai worked, with the general result, according to one American observer, that jury sympathy made for lenient justice, but when a British national was jailed, he (or she) rarely challenged the system, juridically or otherwise. A few leading Americans feared, though, that Filipinos and other U.S. subject-citizens under American extrality in China would find their way onto juries. They thus floated the alternative proposal to revive the nineteenth-century American custom of civilian assessors, whereby the consul sat in consultation with leading citizens, who then brought to bear on the process their own concerns as an elite and their own sense of values appropriate to the treaty port context.[31]

Second Phase of Wilfley v. Shanghai Americans

By May 1907, a stalemate had set in, as both Wilfley and the lawyers claimed victory. The impasse was broken, and the second phase of struggle over the Court initiated, when American attorney George Curtis, the man most responsible for unseating Shanghai Consul General John Goodnow in 1904, seized upon what appeared to be anti-Catholic statements contained in a legal opinion issued by Wilfley, and charged publicly that the Judge had refused to admit him to practice because he, Curtis, was a Catholic. Wilfley's opinion in the case quoted classical English legal sources describing how "the popish clergy" had historically abused their power over probate affairs, leading to "legislative interposition" by secular authorities.

Somewhat the wiser after the Andrews affair a few months earlier, but characteristically myopic, Wilfley wrote to Secretary Root in June 1907, passing along the information that Curtis had been "stirring up a few of the Catholics here," but "[n]othing was thought of this at the time, and nothing is thought of it now, except by a few Catholic brethren who have been stirred up by Curtis and other rejected Lawyers here." Nine months later, though, the Judge was still trying to extricate himself from the imbroglio, as the story of his anti-Catholic remarks had found its way into leading papers in urban America, and the religious storm in Shanghai had been roiled by waves of criticism from his old foes in Manila.[32]

In the late summer of 1907, Wilfley turned the full machinery of the Court against the "renegade" attorneys, and launched his own public relations campaign. Having admitted Lorrin Andrews under pressure from Washington, and allegedly upon the attorney's promise to break his ties with the other rejected lawyers, Wilfley and Bassett reversed course and initiated charges of misconduct against Andrews, and of contempt against Curtis. On September 5, the judge traveled to Yokohama to meet Secretary Taft, then on the eve of a Shanghai stopover during his Far Eastern tour. He accompanied Taft into the city, as if to underscore his own political capital, and convinced Taft to speak, somewhat obliquely, in support of the Court and its Judge.

On 8 November 1907, though, Wilfley closed the Court (for what ultimately became almost a full year) to travel to San Francisco to answer criminal charges against him there leveled by Attorney Lorrin Andrews. The Shanghai attorney alleged that Wilfley was guilty of "oppression and a gross misuse of his powers as judge" of the U.S Court for China, and had brought the Court and the United States into odium and contempt among not only all right-thinking Americans, but all people of standing of every nationality in China. That still unresolved, he went on to Washington to lobby Congress for legislation embodying his landmark *Price* and *Biddle* decisions, but in early January 1908 was forced to put all business aside to defend himself on allegations against him which Lorrin Andrews presented to Roosevelt.

Root's defense of Wilfley, prepared by the State Department Solicitor's Office in concert with the Judge and USDA Bassett, characterized Andrew's charges—quite correctly—as "an effort . . . to subject the judge to a trial by the executive branch of the Government." There was, said the Secretary of State, "a broader view to be taken of this petition as a whole and of the proceedings of the United States Court for China," i.e., "the existence of conditions in Shanghai, and, to a less degree, in other treaty ports of China, discreditable to the United States and humiliating to American self-respect." Essentially, Root's position was, then, that exigencies in U.S. China policy justified the Court's emphasis on crime control over due process.[33]

Congress saw the issue differently. On 24 February 1908, a subcommittee of the Committee on the House Judiciary began hearings to decide whether Judge Lebbeus Wilfley should be brought up on charges of impeachment. Although the subcommittee ultimately declined that option, the publication of the congressional transcripts in the local Shanghai papers galvanized public opinion against the Court, and unleashed a torrent of vituperative attacks on its Judge. Upon his return to the treaty port and reopening of the Court—after a nine-month suspension of business—Wilfley put himself and the Court into British hands, asking HBM Supreme Court for China to bring libel charges against one of their nationals for publishing accusations that Wilfley, "a coarse, unscrupulous and ignorant and vulgar mountebank," was guilty of "indecency, mendacity and a contempt for truth."[34]

It was perhaps inevitable that Great Britain, the dominant power in the treaty ports, would have to sanction and modify decisions emanating from America with implications for the entire edifice of unequal privilege in China. Although, fortunately for Anglo-American harmony and the Western enterprise in China, HBM Supreme Court found for Wilfley in the libel case (*Rex v. O'Shea*), the British Chief Justice—"with the greatest reluctance"—noted that the new U.S. Judge "need not have been in such a hurry," that "if he had settled down quietly and without any question of lawyers," he could have avoided the acrimony of scandal and the embarrassment of treaty port foreigners fighting amongst themselves over the meaning of their privileges.[35]

Wilfley's Demise

"The general sentiment here is that he must be got rid of, but I wonder how it can be done," U.S. Court Marshal Hugh O'Brien wrote to friend and one-time law partner Representative Denby in late October 1908. The Judge seemed "possessed of the idea to *down* everybody who fails to agree with him.... The general English and ... foreign sentiment on the subject" was, reported O'Brien, that the new judicial regime in China had been "an exceedingly unfortunate incident." In the end, Wilfley himself provided the government of men who had appointed him two years before the means by which to be "rid" of him.[36]

On 14 November, Root cabled Wilfley, advising him to come to an accommodation with treaty port Americans, as, "[t]he President and the State Department have been much disturbed by the strife and recrimination which have attended the conduct of affairs in Shanghai since you returned." For Root, the lesson of the Court's congressional ordeal was clear: Wilfley should do what was necessary to avoid controversy. However, Wilfley continued, and even expanded, his crusade to bring treaty port Americans under the legal and moral authority of the Court. When, in exasperation, Wilfley told the secretary that he would resign whenever the President felt it necessary, Root seized the moment and accepted this rhetorical flourish as a resignation.[37]

Root and Representative Edwin Denby, the Court's principal patron in Congress, had been in correspondence about the situation in Shanghai, and had jointly concluded that the survival of the Court—and the domestic tranquility of the Republican Party—required Wilfley's removal. Denby had originally hoped that the Judge of the Court would serve as "an ancillary, unofficial ambassador of the United States," who could "exercise in an entirely unofficial way a considerable influence in matters affecting foreign relations." By 3 October 1908, he was fully convinced that Wilfley was not up to the task, and wrote a personal note to Secretary Root to say that "the situation at Shanghai is bad, if not critical. We provided an excellent machine to do the work that needed to be done, but the engineer has almost wrecked it," by his refusal to "conciliate the Americans at Shanghai."

In the face of this receding support, Wilfley resigned effective 1 January 1909, but apparently continued to lobby for rehabilitation through his various supporters. His patron, President-elect William H. Taft, telegraphed Root from Hot Springs, Virginia, asking "Is there no way possible to save Wilfley? Has he committed the unpardonable sin? I am afraid that his enforced resignation will gratify the wicked and unregenerate and not help us in the Orient." Root's decision in the matter prevailed though, which Wilfley saw as "a *brutal* act and a *crime* against the cause of *Decency* and *Good Government* in the *Far East*." His removal from the bench was, the former Judge argued, "*the most colossal blunder our nation has ever made in the Far East*." The man sent to bring the "rule of law" to the far reaches of America's Pacific frontier had been utterly routed, left by the ordeal, in his words, like "a homeless dog . . . seek[ing] shelter."[38]

WASHINGTON'S RETREAT: THE SECOND USC-C

Anxious to control the perceived damage to American prestige stemming from the rout of the new U.S. Court and its first Judge, Secretary of State Elihu Root issued a public statement through the Shanghai consulate that the Court itself, though closed until a successor could be found, would "continue to have the full support of the Government," and that "the forces of disorder" among U.S. nationals in China would "have no reason to rejoice" at the turn of events.[39] Still, treaty port Americans had made their point, and the conservative shift that accompanied the transition in the White House from Roosevelt to Taft after the 1908 election more generally was evident in the Court's affairs as well.

Appointed to fill Wilfley's place was Rufus Hildreth Thayer, a 68-year-old Washington attorney who had spent his entire professional life shuttling between a small private practice centered around the federal government and various low-level official postings, such as law clerk in the Treasury Department, assistant to the Librarian of Congress, and most recently, judge advocate general of the National Guard of the District of Columbia.[40] After several leading judges from the federal courts of New Mexico, Arizona, and Puerto Rico turned down the Shanghai post, Secretary Root—then one month away from assuming his new duties as U.S. senator from New York—turned to Thayer, whose name had been urged upon him by William Barnes Jr., head of the New York Republican Party and Thayer's brother-in-law.[41]

The second Judge of the U.S. Court for China arrived at his post on 24 February 1909 and, to his credit, managed to serve almost five years before hastily retiring on 15 September 1913, the day the House of Representatives opened its investigation of him on charges of corruption and abuse of authority.[42] The end was sudden, not at all portended by Thayer's politically uneventful, though brief, tenure.

In place of Wilfley's polarizing and aggressive "exact justice," Judge Thayer dispensed "substantial justice," a conciliatory brand of adjudication evidently aimed at keeping the Court's, and the Judge's, enemies at a minimum. It was a strategy that turned on issuing judicially defensible precedents, on the one hand, and using a full measure of judicial discretion to spare defendants—especially the more powerful among them— the full brunt of his rulings, on the other.[43] Whereas Wilfley's decisions had sent litigants hurrying to the 9th Circuit Court of Appeals in California for a second hearing, and to Capitol Hill, for political remedies, there were virtually no complaints against Thayer until 1913, and only two of his verdicts were reviewed at the higher appellate level, as compared to six of Wilfley's.[44]

Thayer was pragmatic and accommodating where Wilfley had been dogmatically inflexible. He came to his post having been advised by State Department officials to proceed gradually, through accommodation and consensus.[45] Wilfley had taken a hard-line approach to the question of treaty port Americans' rights and juridical status, believing that in exchange for the prestige and protection of their home government these Americans ought to be willing to conform to "simple, old-fashioned" justice where troublemakers got their just dues with little heed to the finer distinctions of civil liberty. Wilfley's fate forced Thayer and later judges to be more deferential to concepts such as "reasonable doubt" and the "presumption of innocence."

The post-mortem on "Wilfley's Purge" on the part of American officials clearly urged caution and nonconfrontation in dealings with their wayward countrymen in the treaty port. It was a game not worth the candle; indeed, the lesson distilled from the anti-prostitution campaign by British officials in Shanghai and Hong Kong was that Wilfley had only made the situation worse, as it encouraged marriages of convenience and protective alliances between foreign prostitutes and lower-class, criminally minded white males. Further, airing American "dirty linen" only gave Chinese nationalists ammunition against the unequal treaties.[46]

So successful was Thayer at stilling the controversy and factionalism among his treaty port wards that not long into his tenure all efforts ceased in the State Department and Congress to remedy the institutional and structural deficiencies that had left the Court and its first Judge politically vulnerable. Thus, when in Thayer's fifth year disgruntled litigants found no redress from what seemed to them arbitrary, inconsistent, or—at the very least—inconvenient rulings, they were able to take on the Court using the same tactics as had Wilfley's adversaries. Like the accusations against consular personnel in 1904–1906, and those against Lebbeus Wilfley in 1908, details of Thayer's alleged "high crimes and misdemeanors" originated from particular treaty port Americans determined to make extrality work more for them than against them. In Thayer's case, a House committee was induced to hear testimony against him under pressure from a politically well-connected Shanghai American attorney unhappy with the his rulings in particular cases before the Court. That the prime mover behind the effort to undermine, disgrace, and remove Thayer was none other than George Curtis—who had been instrumental in the consular purges of 1904–1906 and in Wilfley's demise—gave a certain continuity to the process. Thayer's treaty port enemies were few, but in the end they were able to drive him from Shanghai just as they had driven other troublesome and uncooperative federal officials—through the simple but historically subversive insistence that those whom Washington sent to govern them, do so perfectly.

In the political sphere, the federalization of American extrality in China had thus run aground by 1913. By the end of its first six-odd years in operation, the U.S. Court had shown itself incapable of subordinating treaty port Americans to the short-term requirements of the "special relationship." So too, the spectacle of two federal judges run out of town by lawyers representing casino owners, brothel managers, real estate speculators, and itinerant vagabonds was not the object lesson Progressives had intended for a Chinese audience. Notwithstanding the efforts of the Court's first officers to make that tribunal an exemplary one, a testament to the presumed fundamental affinity between U.S. and Chinese interests, recurring farewell "tiffins" for Court officials had demonstrated that the extraterritorial rule of law could not be coerced or imposed from Washington, but instead required the sanction and tacit consent of powerful groups deeply entrenched within the treaty port system.

Winners and Losers

When announcing its establishment to Ch'ing officials in 1906, the U.S. government had been optimistic that the Court would "not only inspire American citizens in China with . . . confidence in the judicial administration under which they live," while at the same time convey to Chinese "the solicitude of this Government for the worthy and impartial exercise of the judicial functions which are reserved to it under the extraterritorial provisions of our treaty."[47]

How close did the Court come to this Progressive vision of equal justice under unequal treaties? From 1907 through 1913, the USC-C heard approximately 102 criminal cases, 76 of which arose in Shanghai; the remainder, in Tientsin, Nanking, Chefoo, Chungking, and Hankow.*

Of the 102 cases, 43 were crimes of property (e.g., false pretenses, larceny, arson, libel), 13 of violence (e.g., assault, rape, murder, manslaughter, threats to kill), and 36 of morals (e.g., bawdy house, lewdness, white slavery, gambling). Eighty-five defendants were male, 17 female. Only 52 of the total 102 cases resulted in convictions, with the remaining defendants found not guilty or pleaded out. Ten defendants were never apprehended; seven were convicted.[48]

In a continuation of the pattern in nineteenth-century consular courts, the overwhelming majority of criminal cases brought before the USC-C did not directly involve Chinese litigants, but were instead between and among treaty port foreigners. This dearth of "mixed" criminal cases owed to a combination of factors. The local U.S. consul remained the primary gatekeeper in American treaty port justice, determining on a day-to-day basis which complaints merited judicial consideration. First, the USC-C was only infrequently away from Shanghai traveling—not always on schedule—to Hankow, Canton, and Tientsin on annual circuit. Outside of Shanghai, then, consuls tended to resolve complaints informally—a letter to an American debtor on behalf of a

* There were 14 U.S. consular districts at this time: Amoy, Antung, Canton, Chefoo, Chungkung, Foochow, Hankow, Harbin, Hukden, Nanking, Newchuang, Shanghai, Swatow, Tientsin.

Chinese vendor, for example—or push Chinese complainants to reduce their claims such that the case could be tried in the consular court.*

Surviving consular court records are incomplete, but a report for the fiscal year 1913–14 is suggestive: of a total 163 complaints of criminal offenses, 116 involved males; 47, females. Shanghai accounted for 118; Tientsin, 17; and Hankow, 14. Of the total, 70 were handled by the consulates and 93 by the office of the District Attorney (USDA). Of the 163 initial complaints, 40 complaints went on to either the consular courts or to the USC-C, resulting in 14 convictions. Of 106 defendants in all the courts (with some cases having multiple defendants), 37 were in military service (coming under the concurrent military and USC-C jurisdiction); 27 were transients (defined as under six-months time China); 14 were repeat offenders.[49]

In Shanghai itself, where most of the Court's business was conducted, local Chinese continued to seek out the consul first, virtually ignoring the USC-C. A brief 1909 exchange between the consul and the USDA-China conveys something of the dynamics by which some mixed cases and not others moved beyond the initial complaint. Writing to USDA Bassett, Consul Denby explained that a Chinese individual had come to the consulate to complain about having been slapped by an American national, Carl Gunther.[50] Denby urged the adoption of the British system of a scale of fees "to prevent the Chinese occupying the time of the Court with trivial action." Bassett responded that justice required that all complaints, large and small, should be sent to his own office for determination.[51]

The reality was that the early USC-C did little better than predecessor consular courts in curbing the endemic daily violence dosed out by treaty port Americans upon Chinese, high and low. The truth of this is especially evident in instances of chronic offenders, such as Joseph Munz. Arriving on the USS *Princeton* in 1901, Munz became a river policeman, and prone to beat his way through Chinese in his way. In 1904, the Shanghai consular court sentenced Munz to 18 months for beating a Chinese boatman to death; the two assessors hearing the case with the consul dissented and forwarded their petition for a pardon to

---

* As noted earlier, after 1906, consular courts were limited to civil cases involving less that $500, and criminal cases involving potential sentences of less than 6 months, or fines less than $100.

President Roosevelt, saying that the Chinese "water population" were "extremely ignorant, stupid, obstinate and averse to any interference and control." Consul Goodnow endorsed the request, but suggested that Munz, "a man of most excellent character," ought not be permitted to return to China until expiration of his sentence lest Chinese be provoked. By 1909, Munz was evidently back, as the USDA initiated a preliminary hearing in the consular court against him for wounding Sun Kau-sz by striking her over the head, and wounding her male companion. Although the case was sent on to the higher USC-C, months later charges were dropped for unstated reasons.[52]

From 1906 to 1913, then, there were seven criminal prosecutions in the USC-C involving Chinese complainants: *U.S. v. Biddle*, the false pretenses case discussed earlier; *U.S. v. McCord* (false pretenses); *U.S. v. Torres* (rape); *U.S. v. Demenil* (manslaughter); *U.S. v. Lunt* (manslaughter); *U.S. v. Gery* (manslaughter); and *U.S. v. Jones*, the manslaughter case also discussed earlier.

Victorino Torres, a Filipino under American extraterritorial protection, was sentenced to three years for the rape of a Chinese woman. Robert McCord was sentenced to two years for obtaining about $30 from a Chinese comprador under false pretenses, the harsh sentence owed to McCord's long consular court record as a debtor, con-man, and small-time predator along the China coast. While waiting sentencing after the guilty verdict, McCord escaped from the flimsy "Jail for American Convicts" located in the consulate. In *U.S. v. Lunt* and *U.S. v. Gery*, the two defendants were found not guilty on the basis of reasonable doubt.[53]

For Sino-American relations more broadly, perhaps the most important of these cases was *U.S. v. Demenil*, heard in December 1907 and the source of discord between the United States and the Chinese governments for nearly two years following. In May 1907, traveler-explorer Henry Demenil killed a Tibetan Buddhist lama during an altercation with his Chinese guides while passing through a village in Yunnan province, a prohibited area under the terms of his travel visa. Angry with one of his slow-moving Chinese escorts, Demenil fired a revolver twice at the man, allegedly hoping only to intimidate rather than kill him; one of the shots hit the priest. Brought to the U.S. Court in Shanghai, Demenil was tried in the presence of the local district magistrate, and was acquitted on the basis of entries in his diary describing the incident as unintentional.

Judge Wilfley determined that the killing was due to the defendant's "nervous condition" and physical debilitation, brought on by "the rarefied mountain air of the locality, the loneliness of the place, and the wilderness of his surroundings." So too, Demenil had "hitherto borne a good name" as "a peaceable law-abiding citizen," and in fact was an established physician who came from the Judge's own home state of Missouri. Taken together, these factors left little doubt in the mind of the Court that the affair, though unfortunate, was wholly accidental, and as the doctor had already "suffered much inconvenience and pain. . . . the ends of justice would [not] be served by imposing further punishment" upon him.[54]

Ch'ing officials in Shanghai and Peking objected, asking how a man who took another human life was "not convicted of any crime" or "even fined." Indeed, from an official Chinese perspective, the U.S. Court's promise for a new era in extrality was even less satisfactory than that of the British Supreme Court in Shanghai; in a similar murder case around the same time, that latter court—sitting with 12 jurors—sentenced the defendant to one year, leading to similar Chinese objections.[55] After studying the records of the Demenil proceedings, Ch'ing foreign affairs authorities concluded that, although the American had not killed the man he aimed at, "he had murder in his heart." Thus, U.S. Minister Rockhill was requested by the government in Peking to "straighten this affair out . . . so that angry passions may be calmed and justice displayed."

The State Department's response was to forward the text of the 1906 act creating the Court, underscoring in a cover letter the constitutional separation between executive and judicial branches in the American system. The correspondence between Peking and Washington reflects the view of these Ch'ing officials that "[the] so-called judge [of the United States Court for China] is only an executive officer" serving at "the pleasure of the President." Although "the term 'judge' is employed it is evident that he is only an official of the executive department appointed for the conduct of foreign relations." Finding the State Department unreceptive, though, the recently created Ministry of Foreign Affairs (Wai-wu-pu) then retreated to the position that Demenil ought to be made to pay restitution to his victim's family. In response, U.S. representatives offered only a law school lesson: punitive damages could be recovered only if the family of the deceased were to bring civil suit against Demenil for negligence, and if the doctor was still to be found within the jurisdiction of the United States Court for China.

Ultimately, the U.S. government insisted, quite apart from its long history of indemnity collecting in China, that it could "not be held responsible" for damages resulting from the "act of a private [U.S.] citizen traveling in China," and "there is no way under the laws of the United States whereby this Government can compel a private citizen to fulfill a promise [of restitution] to the subjects of a foreign nation."[56] The assertion had grounds in (Western) international practice. As one well-known expert of the time argued: "The weaker the control of the police, or the local safeguards for the protection of foreigners and the proper administration of justice, the greater and more rigorous becomes the diplomatic protection exerted by foreign governments and the harsher the demand for prompt satisfaction for violation of the rights of person or property of an alien." Injuries to Chinese in the United States did not merit government indemnities because Chinese there could use local courts and—theoretically—be assured of "justice."[57]

Given that Chinese officials ceased attending mixed cases in the U.S. Court following the Demenil trial, the unsatisfactory outcome seems to have caused an irrevocable break with those whom Roosevelt and Root had hoped to win over.[58] The backstage bargaining that went on *U.S. v. Jones* (1909), discussed in the introduction, where the Judge and defense attorney privately requested a presidential pardon for the convicted man, thus seemed the wiser course for both Court officials and local Americans. In *Jones*, where Thayer handed down a three-year sentence for the murder of a Chinese, the Judge prevented the case from becoming a diplomatic controversy or a rallying point for anti-foreign demonstrations. Indeed, Thayer conceded that his goal had been to use the trial to curb the tendency of Americans to treat lower-class Chinese badly at a time of great anti-foreign ferment. On the other hand, quiet bargaining among Americans outside of Chinese view satisfied treaty port prejudices without apparent cost to the Sino-American "special relationship."[59]

Although U.S. officials continued to resist the lesson, it was simply not possible to secure "due process" for the accused while at the same time appeasing Chinese sensibilities; this was as much the case in the early 1900s as it had been in the 1820s, when Francisco "Frank" Terranova was turned over by local Americans and strangled under Ch'ing law. As in racially polarized democratic societies, so too in the colonial setting: each "mixed" case became a lightning rod for mutual grievances and prejudices. Nothing but acquittal on one side, or severe punishment on the other, appeared to serve "justice."

Ultimately, though, "the Chinese" were an abstraction in the justice of the U.S. Court in these early years, with concrete contacts limited to the few mixed cases, the four or five low-level Chinese employees of the Court, minimal (and generally unsatisfactory) dealings with Ch'ing officials, and sporadic exchanges with Western-oriented treaty port Chinese. They served primarily as an imagined audience for the USC-C, supposedly just waiting to be shown that U.S. officials were determined to bring their own nationals under control, and bring the "square deal" to the unequal treaty system. Particularly for Wilfley, "the Chinese" were a foreign analog to "the People" in Progressive rhetoric.

Casting the Chinese masses as essentially "kindly, timid and capable ... law-abiding and contented," and identifying predators and agitators on both sides of the Sino-foreign divide as the common enemy of stability and prosperity, was a characteristically American coalition-building strategy for empire.[60] Wilfley and his reform-minded contemporaries had believed that "good" Chinese could be won over to Western ways, both commercially and culturally; attacking "whores, gamblers and sharks" as the reason why the unequal treaties were unequal, and why foreigners were disliked by Chinese, was the core of this strategy. The political and legal obstacles to its success became clear in the failure of "Wilfley's Purge" and that judge's own ignominious fate.

Purity and Reform Abandoned

The bulk of the USC-C's criminal docket under Wilfley thus comprised vice cases brought against U.S. nationals. However, the Shanghai madams targeted by the Court were neither redeemed nor repentant; indeed, the Court's efforts had simply pushed them into closer consort with male protectors, contributing to the very "organized vice" Wilfley had been sent to combat. The women who in 1907 had been effectively deported from Shanghai had nearly all returned; one in particular— Emily Moore—emerged in the 1920s as one of the leading American madams of the port. U.S. officials claimed to be satisfied with the fact that few still claimed American nationality.[61] The publicity generated by American anti-vice efforts convinced British officials in Shanghai and Hong Kong to avoid similar efforts.

Under Thayer, Court and district attorney began operating separately, rather than hand-in-glove. For example, Thayer overturned the consular court conviction by Amos Wilder (Denby's successor) of casino manager Robert Sexton in 1909 on charges of vagrancy based upon his exclusive employment as a manager at the Alhambra roadhouse. Thayer's decision in the case set out several important legal principles constraining the rights of Americans in China; yet at the same time he set Sexton free.

First, responding to Sexton's plea of immunity from American jurisdiction on the grounds that he had renounced his allegiance to the U.S. government in 1900 when forced to do so to avoid prosecution as a saloon keeper in Johannesburg (South Africa), Thayer ruled that nationality was not a matter of convenience. Expatriation requires clear and convincing proof. The U.S. government could legally deny protection to Sexton, based on his self-described actions; however, these same facts did not justify allowing him to escape jurisdiction.

Second, *U.S. v. Sexton* confirmed that the USC-C could apply the laws established by Congress over certain federally governed territories, such as the District of Columbia and Alaska, which specifically outlawed gambling. Henceforth, Thayer declared, "vagrancy" was reserved for "the idle or dissolute wandering about . . . [with] no fixed place of abode of a sane, healthy, adult person, who has no obvious means of honest livelihood . . . unwilling to work and who is, or is likely to become, a public charge, or who is the inmate of a house of ill-fame or is engaged in soliciting for prostitution"—in other words, impoverished itinerants and brothel inmates, rather than well-off managers and owners of gambling casinos and brothels.[62]

In 1910, the District Attorney's office brought charges against six U.S. nationals alleged operating or abetting gambling casinos. Two of the six were well-known Shanghai residents, including Robert Sexton, alleged manager of the Alhambra. Four of the other individuals charged with gambling were centered in Nanking, and their activities had been the subject of complaint to U.S. authorities by the Chinese Foreign Ministry and the Shanghai Municipal Council, both to the effect that "certain undesirable characters of American nationality" had organized gambling houses to pursue various "disorderly callings" to the detriment of legitimate business interests.[63]

The penalties imposed on these individuals ranged from fines of $100 to 60-day sentences. To Chinese officials, this seemed lenient, and records indicate that several of the defendants went on to more significant crimes, such as embezzlement, fraud, and assault with intent to kill.[64] However, the Court's response seemed rigorous as compared to British reactions when Chinese police arrested British gamblers, turning them over to the local consuls in Peking and Tientsin. Acknowledging that gambling houses were a nuisance, British officials nonetheless felt it necessary to "draw the line" against what they saw, characteristically, as Chinese overstepping the treaties.[65]

Thayer's general leniency deprived powerful defendants of the motivation, and the legal grounds, to challenge the Court either in the 9th Circuit Court in San Francisco or that appellate court of politics, the U.S. Congress. At the same time, the Judge's clear unwillingness to go beyond the evidence at hand, or use his power to punish particular individuals rather than proven crimes, gave the Court greater legitimacy in their eyes, demonstrating—according to the *North China Daily News*—that "the most useful Judge in Shanghai must be one who is not intimately connected with local life."[66] "Light sentences were no doubt more effective under the circumstances than severe sentences," conceded Court Clerk Frank Hinckley, evidently thinking back to his and Wilfley's battles with Stuart Price and Charles Biddle. No less important, in his estimation, "the entire separation of the Judge of the Court from the interests of the prosecution, and the strength of the former decisions of the Court [under Thayer] had satisfied all classes of people that absolute fairness in trial and fairness in applying the law would be had."[67]

In 1911, Hinckley was appointed USDA. He and the abstemious Consul General Amos Wilder (who threatened several times to resign over U.S. failures to curb American involvement in the "liquor traffic" in China) worked together energetically to continue Wilfley's work, though with hard-learned subtlety. Hinckley cooperated with consular officials to shut down American-owned brothels and casinos, exchanging information with the consulate about U.S. nationals applying to the Shanghai Municipal Council for tavern licenses.[68] So too, he used U.S. consuls elsewhere in the region, namely Japan and the Philippines, to work around the problems created by the absence of an extradition treaty between the United States and China, by putting in place informal arrangements to apprehend individuals wanted by the Court who had fled the jurisdiction.[69] Working with Wilder, the district attorney also offered the full assistance of the Court to Chinese officials seeking to close down American-run casinos and brothels which, although located in the Chinese part of Shanghai, were on a street owned by the Shanghai

Municipal Council, and therefore in something of a jurisdictional netherworld. This zealous prosecution fizzled before Thayer's caution and his effort to build good relations with local attorneys by combining controversial precedents with leniency toward particular defendants.

What of the notorious J. H. "Tientsin" Brown, the nemesis of earlier consular court judges? Initially, Brown was able to use the new Court to protect his questionable business interests; he evaded USC-C criminal jurisdiction by putting the properties in his wife Laura's name (and on occasion relying upon Fanny Beck, Laura's mother). Thus, the Browns moved against Stuart Price, and later Robert Sexton, for recovery of loans to these new owners of the Alhambra.[70] Brown endeavored to use the USC-C to force American consular officials to recognize him as a U.S. citizen, then subsequently tried to evade the Court's jurisdiction by claiming repatriation to Russia.[71] In 1912, Judge Thayer overruled Brown's plea against the jurisdiction of the Court, asserting that Brown had repeatedly importuned U.S. officials to protect his personal and property rights in China—and therefore could not abandon the responsibilities of citizenship for the sake of convenience.[72] He was supported in this by the Solicitor's Office in the State Department.[73]

However, Brown was ultimately driven from China in 1913 by mounting legal difficulties, which resulted primarily from his continuing efforts to use the Court without becoming its target.[74] Between May and December of that year, Brown was up before the Tientsin consular court and the U.S. Court on circuit to defend himself on a variety of charges, including: larceny and forcible entry (stealing his appropriated property from storage); swindling (assisting in an effort to steal money from Chinese bank employees); arson (assisting several other bawdy house keepers destroy a property to collect the insurance); and keeping a bawdy house.

The latter charge was dropped, and Brown was found not guilty beyond a reasonable doubt by Thayer in the swindling case, with the Judge calling into question the motives of witnesses against the defendant. Brown broke bail on the other charges, though, forfeiting the property put up as bond collateral, in time provoking Laura Brown—upon her return to Chicago—to issue demands for relief addressed to Secretary of State William J. Bryan and various lesser officials.[75] (J. H. Brown eventually found his way back to Washington, D.C., forming a partnership with C. P. Holcomb, third USC-C district attorney, forced to resign because of allegations of official misconduct; they did business as lobby-ists representing various American businesses registered in China.)[76]

Civil Cases

Of the approximate 131 civil cases heard by the first two judges, 29 explic-itly involved Chinese plaintiffs.[77] These litigants were generally com-pradors seeking loan repayments, or local treaty port contractors in Shanghai and Tientsin demanding payment for goods and services from local businesses or shipping agencies, typically claiming amounts rang-ing from $1,500 to $15,000.[78] The lone exception was *Leu Ching-tsau et al. v. Methodist Episcopal Church* (1908), where the plaintiffs represented "the local officials, literati and people of Huchow." Here, the parties were able to work out a settlement over a disputed piece of public land, which the Church had bought in good faith. The USC-C's role was to sanction the settlement as a legally binding judgment.[79]

By and large, Chinese plaintiffs won their suits and were awarded approximately what they had asked for. Compradors and Chinese busi-nessmen were well equipped to deal with foreign courts; they relied on British and American attorneys, who had little difficulty translating complicated and often idiosyncratic treaty port practices into Western legal concepts. Rare was a case along the lines of *Foh Chang (aka Woo Yung-kwang) v. Fraser and Co.* (1911), where the defendant successfully argued that Woo had mistaken a verbal exchange for a contract.[80]

Whether successful Chinese plaintiffs collected their awards cannot be said, although it is known that several losing defendants subsequently declared bankruptcy or fled the jurisdiction.[81] The USDA had recourse only to informal methods of tracking chronic debtors from one port to another.[82] This was not just an American phenomenon. Chinese debtors were known to "go down to Ningpo," i.e., to flee creditors and Mixed Court judgments. In addition, the widespread practice among Chinese of veiling their ownership and interests behind foreign registration com-plicated matters greatly for both courts and creditors.[83]

More generally, two themes emerged in the USC-C's handling of "mixed" civil cases. First, the ostensibly simple task of restricting juris-diction to "American" defendants proved quite complicated. For exam-ple, U.S. defendants often sought to use the opportunity of a case against them to countersue plaintiffs of other nationalities, thinking their

chances better before an American judge. The USC-C thus quickly limited countersuits to the amount of the original claim.[84]

Often, causes with no apparent Chinese interest turned out to be
quite the opposite. *In re Stephen Barchet's Estate* well illustrates the point.
Chinese were not permitted to own land in the International Settlement;
thus evolved the practice of foreigners renting out their names and
nationalities to wealthy Chinese. While settling the estate of Stephen
Barchet, one-time consular interpreter, the Court refused to entertain
contending Chinese title claims to land Barchet had registered in his own
name. Indeed, Judge Thayer ruled that land title controversies between
Chinese came under Ch'ing authority and could not be decided by the
USC-C or the International Mixed Court in Shanghai. If an American
became involved in such controversies, resolution fell to diplomats, not
judges.[85]

In addition, corporations and partnerships doing business in China
were only "American" by virtue of registration in one of the forty-eight
states back home; often, though, actual ownership was not in the hands
of U.S. nationals. Initially, Judge Wilfley refused to assume jurisdiction
in questionable cases, such as *In re China Metal & Commercial Co., insolvent*. However, by 1910 the State Department ruled that the Secretary had
full discretion, and could extend protection and jurisdiction to such corporations when in "the commercial and other advantage of the United
States."[86]

Second, the Progressives' distinction between "legitimate" and
"shady" American businesses in the China market was, in practical
terms, nearly impossible to police. In *Zun Hoong-sun et al. v. J. S. Dooly
& H. J. Black et al.* (1909), the defendants were well-known lottery entrepreneurs who had been pushed out of both the Philippines and Hong
Kong. However, USDA Arthur Bassett and Vice Consul Frederick Cloud
were invested and publicly associated with an alleged pyramid scheme
known as the China Investment Corporation.[87]

Like the American opium traders of the nineteenth century, who easily shifted from legitimate to dubious business activities, so too in the
early twentieth-century China market. Sammuel Zimmerman, for
example, was before the early USC-C quite frequently as plaintiff and
defendant in contract and debt disputes arising from his import-export
transport business. However, he also attempted to evade a debt of
$38,980M incurred when he chartered a vessel to ship "coolies" from

Vladivostok to Mexico; Judge Thayer rejected the defendant's argument that the charter contract was void because of its illegal object.[88]

LOOKING AHEAD

The Court's decisions under Wilfley and Thayer, taken together with various State Department policy changes regarding sojourning Americans, offered the potential for a tighter rein, given both a unwavering show of political will from Washington, and a change in the circumstances of those just beyond effective federal reach. The *Biddle* precedent made accessible federal territorial codes, equipping the Court to bring vice crimes within its purview, as well as to assume jurisdiction over divorce and bankruptcy. In *U.S. v. Grimsinger* (1912), the Court also declared that whatever the source of borrowed laws, the Judge had full discretion on determining penalties. In *U.S. v. Engelbracht* (1909), Thayer reaffirmed the doctrine established by the U.S. Supreme Court in the 1891 appeals case, *Ross v. United States*, to the effect that extraterritorial judicial officers are granted larger powers than their domestic counterparts, and therefore did not have to afford litigants before them basic constitutional rights, such as trial by jury.

On the eve of World War I, though, the only group of treaty port Americans truly under firm U.S. federal jurisdiction were deceased U.S. nationals, as Wilfley's concept of American "extraterritorial domicile" in China insured clear, uncontested jurisdiction in probate matters.[89] The jurisdictional netherworld of extrality, continued fiscal constraints, and the anomalies of America's "China District" gave sojourners the upper hand in the allegiance-for-protection bargain. Even while resisting the disciplinary edge of the "special relationship," sojourning U.S. nationals remained confident of continued privileges. The future seemed presaged in the USC-C's decision in *U.S. v. Jordan* (1912), that although the 1911 Revolution ended the Ch'ing dynasty and brought the birth of the Chinese republic, it had not voided the unequal treaties of the previous century. For the defendant, an alleged gun-runner, the point was moot; by then, Jordan had broken bail and was well beyond the Court's reach.[90]

CHAPTER FIVE

WILSONIANISM AND AMERICAN
IMPERIAL CITIZENSHIP

The intensification of international competition for markets during the Wilson era made the U.S. government highly responsive to the needs of American business throughout Latin America and Asia. There was a tremendous expansion in what Emily Rosenberg has called the "promotional state," as seen in the multiplication of government bureaus directed to collect information on trade, the passage of legislation designed to give companies every advantage in foreign markets, and the general celebration of commerce as a vehicle for advancing the American vision.[1] The issue of diplomatic protection came to the fore not only because of Woodrow Wilson's efforts to maintain U.S. neutrality in the European war, but also because of the great increase in trade and travel.[2]

This chapter presents a history of the USC-C and American extrality in China from about 1914 to the early post-World War I era, a period coincident with the tenure of the Court's third and most illustrious Judge, Charles S. Lobingier. Having greater philosophical and political backing from the Wilson administration back home, Lobingier made the Court more the disciplinary and tutelary instrument its founders had envisaged, greatly increasing its case load and its openness to Chinese litigants. The relative stability of the Court from 1914 to 1922 permits a fuller examination of how contemporaries negotiated individually and collectively within the extraterritorial legal regime.

The overthrow of the Ch'ing dynasty in 1911–12, and establishment of a republican government under Sun Yat-sen, reinvigorated Progressive ambitions for a new China in the American image. The U.S. Court in Shanghai gained new energy and importance in this project when the departure of Rufus Thayer in late 1913 provided the Woodrow Wilson administration with the opportunity to use extraterritoriality to bring to China the guiding "modern trinity" of "democracy, the rule of law, and Christianity."[3] The Court's accomplishments and shortcomings in this endeavor, as well as the compromises it made along the way, leave little doubt that the issue for U.S. China policy came down to an incongruity of ends and means or, more specifically, to the insolvable paradoxes of transcendent participation. As Woodrow Wilson's own battle for the League of Nations raised the question of how the United States could be "*in* but yet not completely *of*" a rivalrous, almost Darwinian, international system of exploitative great powers, so too, the U.S. Court for China's struggles under its third and most eminent Judge underscored America's inability to be at once "*in* but yet not completely *of*" unequal treaty imperialism in China.[4]

FROM PROGRESSIVISM TO WILSONIANISM

In early 1914, President Wilson and Secretary of State William Jennings Bryan found just the right man for the Shanghai bench, though more precisely, he found them. Thayer's successor, Dr. Charles Sumner Lobingier, was confirmed by the Senate on 8 February 1914. He was a prolific legal scholar, a prominent judge in the American-run Philippine Judiciary since 1904, and a practicing Methodist—all three of which helped him meet the requirements set by Wilson for the "new men" to be sent to the Far East, i.e., a broad international vision, with "Christian service and university connections."[5] When hints of his availability had gone unheeded by his primary patron, William Taft, Lobingier took leave from the Philippines and, possibly through (fellow Nebraskan) Secretary Bryan, arranged a private meeting with Wilson, during which the Judge secured the Shanghai post.[6]

Lobingier was, according to the widely read *Review of Reviews*, "an admirable representative of the spirit of American helpfulness and good-will in the Orient."[7] The Judge's sense of his country's "mission" in China had been forged in the crucible of the American-occupied Philippines. His ten years on the Philippine bench (1904–14), his work on the law codification committee there, and his teaching stints at the University of the Philippines—all of these things gave him a sophisticated understanding of America's "civilizing mission" in East Asia. As Lobingier himself argued, although Americans wanted most immediately "a larger share in the trade of China and [were] sometimes impatient that the increase [was] not more rapid," if the United States became the "teacher of Asia," especially in the areas of jurisprudence, economics, and governance, "material things" would naturally follow. So too, the Judge added, "is it not a higher honor to enlighten a people than to conquer it or even to supply its imports?"[8]

For Lebbeus Wilfley, the first Judge of the Court, and for the President who had appointed him, bringing the "rule of law" to late Ch'ing China meant most of all taming the "criminal and vicious" elements among treaty port Americans, so as to win the good will of prospective Chinese customers and clients of U.S. business. Lobingier, and the President who sent him to Shanghai, shared this Progressive distinction between "good" businessmen who spread wealth and the American way of life abroad, and "bad" ones who incited indigenous antiforeign violence by their exploitative and fraudulent tactics.[9]

Although Taft-era "dollar diplomacy" seemed more congenial to Americans abroad, and the interventionist impulse stronger, the situation from the perspective of sojourners was more ambiguous. Views Taft acquired in Manila and Shanghai permeated his administration, prompting some to reassure him "that whatever may have been the fact in years past," Americans abroad were "NOT ticket-of-leave men, fly-by-nights, criminals and scapegoats." Instead, they "comprise among their numbers men in every profession, trade and line of industry, to claim fellow-citizenship with whom would confer an honor on the best citizens who remain within the geographical confines of their country."[10]

Under Taft, presidential proclamations in 1911 and 1913 directed the 40,000-plus American citizens living in Mexico to return home, as the United States could not protect them in the current revolutionary chaos. When some among this number asked to testify before congressional committees deliberating American intervention in Mexico, they were asked individually whether they had material interests involved, and if they did, they were disqualified.[11] One contemporary specialist argued that federal officials seemed to believe that sojourners were solely concerned with their own "selfish interests," could not be trusted to report their situation accurately, and refused to accept that having left their homeland, they had "waived all claim for consideration and protection as" American citizens.[12]

For Wilsonians too, the embrace of commerce was leavened by a "deep-seated suspicion of any business that violated [the] notion of an open, liberal order."[13] In Mexico, China, and Costa Rica, for example, President Wilson withheld support from particular firms and banks; he initially refused to endorse an international banking consortium in China, changing his mind only with assurances of broader participation.[14] In short, "Wilson drew a sharp distinction between advancing the *nation's* economic interests and advancing *particular* businesses."[15]

The general policy of the Wilson administration and State Department was that sojourning U.S. nationals should get only a "fair field and no favor." Popular hostility arose around reports that about one-million naturalized Americans evaded the wartime draft by returning to their birthplaces, there continuing to invoke their constitutional right to diplomatic protection.[16] Passport regulations in 1915 required American nationals residing abroad for protracted periods to furnish affidavits explaining the cause of their absence; identifying their current family, property, and business ties with the United States; showing their payment of income taxes; and demonstrating their ultimate intention to return.[17]

Washington now targeted for elimination sojourners' "special privileges," supporting only equality of treatment toward Americans and America through "most-favored-nation" provisions in treaties. This attitude came through in the State Department's response to insistent demands for protection among missionaries in Turkey, for example, refusing them special exemptions from tax and local registration requirements.[18] Citizens, naturalized or native, had no "absolute and inherent right (that is, a right that is enforceable in the courts) either to the protection or the intervention of this Government." Indeed, to the extent some sojourners were more equal than others, the advantage fell to those temporarily residing in areas near the United States, including Canada, the Caribbean, and Central America.[19]

In China, resident Americans fell into an anomalous category, because "most-favored-nation" benefits actually included full extraterritorial jurisdiction. There was, though, a decided philosophical shift in Washington on the most profitable interpretation of the privileges. Most policy makers agreed with Charles Denby, former U.S. consul in Shanghai, who argued in 1918 that extrality had become a "handicap." It should not be abrogated entirely, he believed, but should be modified and rationalized; for example, an international tribunal should replace all of the various consular courts.[20] It had become clear even to a strong treaty port apologist "that extraterritoriality, as at present administered, is a barrier to our relations with China, and is a handicap to the Chinese themselves in their attempt to establish autonomous government free from control." Given the clear inevitable end of extrality, Denby suggested, the race was to the swift: if the United States pushed ahead, China would more likely turn to Anglo-American common law, and give special considerations to American interests.[21]

THE BURDEN OF INFORMAL EMPIRE

By 1914, the tasks of "spreading the American dream" were more subtle and complex than simply reining in its most visibly predatory advance agents. The sine qua non of Wilsonian open door internationalism was the fundamental reorientation of indigenous legal, economic, and political structures in less developed countries, such as Mexico, China, and the Philippines, toward the capitalist world market and Western-dominated "family of nations."[22] Exporting the "rule of law" thus meant, inter alia, putting in place in target areas systems of law, adjudication, and enforcement making their resources fully available to more developed nations, propping open their markets to Western exports, and guaranteeing the order and stability required to protect Western investments and interests.[23] The burden of empire shouldered by individuals like Charles Lobingier was, then, to "teach people order and self-control in the midst of change" (in the words of Woodrow Wilson), and more generally to assist in laying and protecting the institutional buttresses of the "open door."[24] As Lobingier himself argued, although Americans wanted most immediately "a larger share in the trade of China and [were] sometimes impatient that the increase [was] not more rapid," if the United States became the "teacher of Asia," especially in the areas of jurisprudence, economics, and governance, "material things" would naturally follow.[25]

There was in these myriad goals, a characteristically Progressive assumption about the essential affinity between American and Chinese interests. The notion was well expressed by Minister Paul Reinsch when he suggested in 1916 that the U.S. Court in Shanghai itself would "disappear" as China made further progress in achieving "the universal reign of law and justice" which that Court supposedly stood for. All "[w]ell-wishers of China," being "enlightened men," Reinsch asserted, truly appreciated that "this very Court, itself the fruit of . . . extraterritoriality, may through the excellence and soundness of its work contribute to . . . the development of judicial efficiency in China," and by implication, to the obsolescence and dismantling of the unequal treaty structure as a whole.[26]

The dilemma of the U.S. Court for China, though, was how to survive in the treaty port setting long enough to bring an end to treaty ports and the Old World imperialism they symbolized. The demise of its first two judges had revealed just how little political capital the Court had in Washington, D.C., as federal officials were less concerned about moral absolutes and long-term consequences than that there be peace and quiet on their "watch." Above all, this meant that the Court's ability to fulfill its Wilsonian tasks in China, or even to endure as an institution at all, depended upon the willingness of its presiding judge to come to a modus vivendi with Americans in China and, indeed, with the treaty port system itself.

TOWARD THE TRIUMPH OF COMMERCE

Lobingier's arrival coincided with a great surge of competitive nationalism sweeping through China's treaty ports. Where historically cooperation had generally prevailed among the unequal treaty powers by virtue of their stark and shared recognition that if divided they might be thwarted, the economic reverberations of war in Europe pitted them against one another in the high-stakes rivalry for the China market.[27] The outbreak of war initially precipitated a commercial crisis in Shanghai, a major entrepôt of international trade. Disruptions in shipping led to an increase in import prices, a prohibitive growth in insurance rates and transports costs for exports. The Shanghai stock exchange shut down, money and credit became ever more scarce, and unemployment spread, particularly among Chinese laborers in the port. Over the long term, however, the diversion of European imports, the more general curtailment of Western European economic ties to China, and the increased worldwide demand for raw materials, cumulatively heralded a "golden age" of wealth and expansion for China's native industries and nascent bourgeoisie, and an era of internecine warfare among treaty port nationals hoping to capitalize on these developments.[28]

The impact of these developments upon U.S. interests in China was a mixed one. Despite the efforts by U.S. officials to draw American companies and investors into China, particularly in the area of loans, mining, and oil, most business concerns wisely focused on the more certain markets of the Western Hemisphere, ultimately displacing European powers from Latin America and Canada. To the extent that Asian markets did attract American investors, their focus was on Japan, and on what is now Malaysia and Indonesia.[29] However, there was an observable American financial penetration of the China market in the period, as Marie-Claire Bergére has noted. At the transnational level, for example, the Asia Banking Corporation, organized as the agent of various American trusts, gained controlling shares in many of China's burgeoning native industries.[30] Similarly, in 1915 National City Bank president Frank Vanderlip purchased the International Banking Corporation, with its worldwide branches. At the same time Vanderlip created the American International Corporation, a $50 million venture, which by the end of the war had a sizable stake in shipping, trade, rubber plantations, and meat canning throughout East Asia. So successful was AIC both at home and abroad, that the corporation was able to finance unilaterally the Grand Canal Project for China.[31]

Federal assistance came in a number of different forms. In China, U.S. officials dealt directly with Chinese authorities on behalf of specific American firms, as seen in, for example, negotiations for the second International Financial Consortium and related loans, or in direct governmental aid to the Federal Telegraph Company in its efforts to begin operations in China.[32] There was also the active defense of treaty port foreign nationals and their privileges, employing in each case a blend of military power, punitive indemnities, and diplomatic pressure against Chinese authorities.[33] Congressional support was manifest in the Webb-

Pomerene Act (1918), the Edge Act (1919), and the China Trade Act (1922/1925), the cumulative effect of which was to make it easier for bankers, exporters, and producers to operate in China (and elsewhere) through preferential tax policies, as well as exemption from domestic antitrust and financial securities restrictions.[34]

WITHIN THE TREATY PORTS

At the local treaty port level, Americans moved to take advantage of the opportunities created by British and German distractedness, as well as the boom in native (Chinese) industries; both increased demand in the areas of shipping, insurance, financing, and legal services. The U.S. Court's utility to business was most evident in the establishment of a large body of American extraterritorial case law supporting the sanctity of contract, the primacy of property, and other basic principles of free market capitalism. Lobingier drafted an extraterritorial remedial code, the goal of which was to provide uniformity, simplicity, and clarity in the conduct of American business in China. In Wilsonian fashion, he argued: "If American business is ever to extend abroad as its promoters hope, the law which accompanies it must be administered with due regard to those who are outside its pale and, if possible, so as not to conflict with established commercial usage."

Lobingier and the USC-C

The fortunes of the U.S. Court for China prospered greatly not only because competitive nationalism discouraged the internal factionalism among Americans that had fed the attacks against earlier judges, but also because—under Lobingier's skillful direction—the Court demonstrated its usefulness in the ever fiercer battle for the China market. Lobingier did much to continue the work begun by Judge Thayer in extending to China the "contract regime" of free market capitalism. The bulk of the approximately 2,000 cases heard by the Court under Lobingier involved the application of basic principles of contract law, such as the stipulation that there must be a "meeting of minds" between contracting parties. This "contract regime" was reinforced by the adjudication of criminal cases in such a way as to uphold the sanctity of property, reward respect for hierarchies of authority and employment, and endorse the trust of fiduciary relationships, such as that between investor and client. In the criminal law realm, the contract regime was manifest in charges against defendants for theft, fraud, property damage, and vagrancy.[35]

The Civil Docket

In the hundreds of civil cases Lobingier decided, there was neither an obvious bias in favor of U.S. nationals, nor a clear, consistent prejudice against Chinese plaintiffs, underscoring the function of the Court as a defender of the ideology of capitalism, rather than the agent for particular capitalists. In the 1920 case, *Lung Chu v. Sino-American Trading Corp.*, for example, Lobingier rejected the Chinese plaintiff's claim for 6,233 taels, reasoning the alleged breach of contract on the part of the U.S. company arose from an initial misunderstanding between the two parties concerning the precise terms of their agreement. In *Luk Hop Co. v. American Express Co.* (1923), Lobingier attempted to apply the "meeting of the minds" principle to a comprador agreement. Plaintiff had pledged a tract of land in the International Settlement to secure faithful performance of an agreement by which two members of his company became the defendant's compradors. The latter argued that they had completed performance, thus terminating the contract, while the defendant company argued that the two men had made themselves liable for all debts incurred by individuals guaranteed by them as compradors. Declaring that all instruments should receive a sensible and reasonable construction, Lobingier found for the compradors. However, underscoring the ability of litigants to "shop around" for justice, the American company successfully countersued its compradors in the Mixed Court, prompting the U.S. Court to defer to its "sister" court.[36]

Lobingier's court was pro-business, but not necessarily pro-businessman. Historically, in serving the changing needs of capitalism, law courts did not reflexively find for employers or commercial elites. Law seemed to function in ways that helped these elites in spite of themselves, sometimes sacrificing individual interests for the sake of establishing hegemonic legitimacy among the lower and middling order. In industrializing Western societies, legal systems facilitated the gradual "shift...from the production of absolute surplus value based on plunder and coercion to that of relative surplus value based on the systematic operation of a labour market and the cash nexus, and the proletarianization of labor."[37] There was a criminalization of worker mobility and "idleness," and punishment for breach of contract in employer-employee relations.[38] Perhaps most important, courts taught and enforced democratic capitalism's "subliminal curriculum," i.e. contractualism, a cultural and cognitive style, the morality of free agency, and the boundary between the market and a "private sphere."[39]

Illustrations of this dynamic in the civil case law built up by the U.S. Court for China include decisions that upheld the sanctity of contract over customary concerns for equity, and that used due process concepts to support an understanding of the "wage bargain" that ignored the disparity of power and resources between the two parties to the contract. Similarly, the "fellow servant" and "contributory negligence" rules, which freed employers from liability in damages resulting from the negligence or misdeeds of employees and their coworkers, also found a place in U.S. extraterritorial law. Other examples of common law in the service of commerce included: courts cannot make contracts for parties nor inquire into the wisdom or advisability of their undertakings;[40] a meeting of the minds is essential to the existence of a contract, and there must be something gained by both parties, though such reciprocity does not have to be equitable or reasonable;[41] an offer must be accepted absolutely and in identical terms between parties to constitute a contract;[42] failure to read a contract before signing is not grounds for avoiding its terms;[43] not every departure from terms of contract is actionable, only actual or compensatory damage is recoverable in absence of malice or gross negligence;[44] loss of profits is a proper item of damage for breach of contract only so far as it could be reasonably foreseen by contracting parties;[45] a wrongfully discharged employee must seek and accept other employment so as to mitigate damages, but may stop short of efforts that would endanger his professional standing;[46] contributory negligence bars recovery.[47]

Judge Lobingier's decision in *Raven v. McRae* (1917) enabled Americans to incorporate locally, i.e., in China itself, which made the Corporation Act of Congress of 2 March 1903 (for Alaska) available to Americans in China.[48] The *Raven* precedent did help to increase the number of American firms in China, as seen in the growth of the U.S. Chamber of Commerce there from 48 in 1915 to 313 in 1920.[49] The prime beneficiaries of the process, however, were local American attorneys, who became major stockholders in (and sometimes principal organizers of) many of these new China Court companies, and profited by fees derived from the proliferation of legal suits against such companies as well. As of 31 December 1920, the *Raven* precedent had produced 58 locally incorporated American companies. None of these were multinational or large-scale national corporations. Rather, those who availed themselves of the changes were generally individuals, who together with their spouses, siblings, minor children, and friends, would incorporate themselves, so as to avoid personal liability for their business debts. The State Department refused to make a uniform ruling on the question of what constituted a "substantial American financial interest" in corporations set up under the *Raven* ruling, preferring instead a case-by-case approach.[50]

As a U.S. consular inspector concluded, the *Raven* ruling had encouraged the very thing the U.S. Court for China had been created to curtail, i.e., the "alliance of the Chinese business man," typically anxious to put his capital out of the hands of predatory officials, and "the American adventurer, assisted by an American attorney."[51] When coupled with a weak judiciary and extrality, local incorporation opportunities simply invited abuse. Prior to the decision, State Department consulates had been responsible for certifying companies as legitimately American, and part of their task was to investigate informally how the individuals involved had conducted business in the past, whether they had previously been in trouble with the law, and so on. In contrast, the *Raven* ruling required the court clerk to accept properly executed articles of incorporation, without undertaking any prior or subsequent investigation of those involved. Consular officials had not always been thorough or honest when looking into the affairs of allegedly American businesses, but with the new procedures, there was virtually no oversight.

Illustrative of the abuses this generated was the Yangtze Transport and Supply Company, set up in 1919, primarily to front for Chinese-owned vessels, some of which were involved in the opium trade. Company president and holder of one share, Seeley Donohoe, had been brought before the U.S. Court in Shanghai 1914 for mail fraud.[52] Corporate attorney R. S. Haskell, a Shanghai attorney, was given 767 shares, probably in exchange for his services in connection with the incorporation. The Chinese secretary and treasurer together accounted for 734 shares. The firm was subsequently reorganized first as the Asia Trading Corporation, and then as the West China Navigation Company, the director of which was William S. Fleming, the attorney who would lead the attack upon the Lobingier Court beginning in 1921.[53] Similarly, the "American Chinese Steamship Company" was nothing more than a cover for the well-known Chinese-owned China Merchants Steam Navigation Company, which in this particular instance sought to use American registration to protect its vessels on the pirate-ridden Yangtze River.[54] Lobbying efforts by local Americans led to the 1922 passage of the China Trade Act. The State Department was energetic in shaping the bill to insure that the Secretary of State retained a large measure of discretion in extending diplomatic protection to ostensibly American firms.[55]

Impact of Extrality

What difference did extrality make in the ability of Chinese and American individuals and companies to operate in the colonial context? Again, as argued earlier, matters of equity and justice cannot be assessed by trial transcripts and verdicts. Ostensibly, Chinese high and low had access to a fair hearing, with their claims determined on their merits.[56] The docket offers up cases such as *Chang Quai Ching et al. v. Dodge and Seymour*, a successful appeal from consular court brought by four Chinese mechanic fitters to recover accrued wages denied them after they quit without notice.[57] Or, *Ling Ah Choy et al. v. Standard Oil* (1916), an unsuccessful claim pursued by a lowly Chinese contractor to recover his costs and wages for building a (defective) oil tank.[58]

However, extrality facilitated external business penetration less by acting as local businessmen's handmaiden, and more by preemption, i.e. by keeping likely Chinese complainants out of court. This is clear in a case such as *Hsu Wen Hwa Tang v. Standard Oil* (1922), where the plaintiffs were denied "standing," and their property claim in Chinkiang dismissed, when the Court found that: "In an action to recover the possession of real property an averment that 'the plaintiffs are a Chinese family' is insufficient to show capacity to [sue]."[59] Added to this, foreign plaintiffs not permitted to sue in *forma pauperis*; American citizens could, by virtue of an 1892 Act for the District of Columbia.[60] The hurdles presented to a Chinese plaintiffs to appeal USC-C decisions in California's 9th Circuit practically closed that avenue to native litigants as well; from 1914 to 1942, only 6 of the 31 appealed cases involved Chinese litigants.[61]

Criminality

On the criminal side, the thousand-plus cases processed by the Lobingier court suggest three general conclusions. First, as in the civil sphere, the aggregate injustice of extrality was structural more than individual. There was a two-track justice system in China's relations with the United States (and with the foreign powers more generally). In terms of Sino-American affairs, one track comprised the United States Court for China in Shanghai, and various subordinate State Department consular courts in each treaty port, both of which types adjudicated civil and criminal cases involving U.S. nationals as defendants. However, the other track, where Sino-foreign disputes involving Chinese defendants were resolved, comprised not only various "mixed courts" generally presided over jointly by indigenous and foreign officials, but also all of the political, economic, and military force at the collective disposal of the unequal treaty powers. In other words, Chinese with grievances against Americans were asked to accept resolutions of the U.S. Court in Shanghai as justice, whereas for treaty port Americans with a grievance against Chinese, court litigation was only one of many avenues of recourse.

The results were mixed. In 1920, for example, when American seaman Homer Darke killed a Chinese cobbler who had come to collect a debt from him, the venue for redress available to interested Chinese was the U.S. Court in Shanghai. Lobingier ultimately found that the failure to recover the body of the deceased from the river where Darke threw him mandated a reduction in charges from murder to assault with intent to harm, resulting in a two-year sentence and a $500 fine. (In the event of future similar cases, the precedent established was that: "Where a Chinese is thrown overboard in the Yangtse [sic] River at Hankow less than 150 feet from the river bank in the midst of about 50 sampans, and with a chance of swimming ashore notwithstanding rough weather, such circumstances alone will not justify a finding that the victim was drowned.")[62]

Similarly, in *U.S. v. Welch* (1920), where the defendant "playfully" shot to death a Chinese prostitute at point-blank range in her bedroom, the sentence was two years and a $500 fine for involuntary manslaughter. Here, the Court went out of its way to insure that the sentence given would be no less and no more onerous than punishments called for in contemporary Chinese criminal codes, in this instance two years and

3,000 yuan.[63] In another case (*U.S. v. Rohrer*), where the defendant, a U.S. Army deserter, received a life sentence for killing a Chinese police-man, the American Court felt obligated to insure that this crime by an American in China would be punished just as if it had been committed by an American in, say, New York. Rohrer's accomplice, Hilton A. Williams, alias James Carter, was sentenced to three years for robberies committed during the flight of the two men from the Army, a punish-ment mitigated by Williams' help in the case against Rohrer.[64] Only after years of Chinese petitions did Congress voted a $1,500 reparation for the victim's family.[65]

Order versus Opportunity

Second, its strong anti-vice impulses notwithstanding, the overall record of the USC-C, even under its strongest judge, attests to the accuracy of Walter LaFeber's argument that historically Americans were far more interested in the "search for opportunity" than a "search for order." Americans, according to LaFeber, have "willingly sacrificed order for the sake of opportunity," in the process spawning revolution abroad and an imperial presidency at home.[66] During the Lobingier era, the U.S. Court had numerous opportunities to contribute to "law and order" in China by rigorously trying to police the opportunism of American nationals in the new Republic of China. Trafficking in opium and in arms, for exam-ple, were two activities specifically identified as inimical to the possibil-ities of stability in China. Yet, in these instances, leniency was the order of the day, particularly when dealing with longer-term American resi-dents of China (as opposed to beachcombing transients).

On the opium question, for example, while the U.S. featured promi-nently in international efforts to end the trade, penalties on American in China found to be engaged in the trade were comparatively light. British extraterritorial courts in China held their nationals there liable to the Chinese government's own punitive laws against narcotics dealing. However, the U.S. Court insisted that Americans in China should answer only to American laws.[67] In *U.S. v. Beeks* (1915), *U.S. v. Biddle* (1916), and *U.S. v. Woodward* (1918) for instance, the defendants were fined $500, a small sum even then (especially given the profits of opium dealing), but one which, because of an error on the part of some unknown Washing-ton clerk omitting certain phrases in the relevant statutes, constituted the maximum penalty then available to the U.S. Court in Shanghai.[68] Though the Court pointed out the clerical omission on each such occasion, it went uncorrected, and so at the time a U.S. national in China guilty of adultery or vagrancy could expect to receive a harsher sentence than might his opium-smuggling compatriot.

On 5 May 1919 the leading foreign powers signed an Arms Embargo Agreement, by which they consented to "restrain their subjects and citizens from" engaging in the arms trade; yet scholars have concluded that none of the signatories were especially energetic in their enforcement of those provisions, that, in fact, there was "widespread infringement of the embargo by almost all the Western countries as well as Japan."[69] This laxity seemed to begin at the water's edge, as gunrunning and drug-trafficking activities that directly impinged upon law and order within the domestic societies of the unequal treaty powers themselves were met with harsh penalties, as witness the punitive response by California authorities to defendants on the San Francisco side of a Shanghai-linked arms-smuggling operation uncovered in the early 1920s.[70] Within Chinese waters, U.S. officials refused to let native officials search American vessels for suspected drug shipments, even in instances where suspected crewmen were Chinese nationals.[71] So too, the United States rejected League of Nations urging to treaty powers that they deport from extraterritorial jurisdictions nationals convicted of trafficking in narcotics.[72]

The two major arms-dealing cases during Lobingier's tenure were *U.S. v. Kearny* (1923) and *U.S. v. Slevin* (1923). In the first, Lawrence D. Kearny, formerly of the U.S. Army, was charged for conspiring with at least five others, including Chinese, to buy and sell a large quantity of weapons and ammunition. Kearny had seized on the opportunity for profits arising when Russian ships fleeing the new Bolshevik regime arrived in port with weapons. Though acquitted on several of the charges, he was found guilty on others, and fined $2,500. The maximum possible penalty available to the Court was a two-year jail term and/or a $10,000 fine; because arms-trafficking could be construed as participating in rebellion against the Chinese state, Sino-American treaties also afforded the Court the option of simply turning Kearny over to Chinese authorities for trial. Judge Lobingier weighed the two conflicting imperatives in the balance, i.e., the public good and "menace to life and property in China," versus the fairness of rigorously enforcing against the defendant prohibitions that earlier American officials had virtually ignored.[73] Ultimately, the latter won out, as Kearny was spared the harsher penalties of Chinese jurisdiction.[74]

In the *Slevin* case, the defendant was charged with importing airplanes under license for commercial use but redirecting them for shipment to Warlord Wu Pei-fu. As the relevant U.S. regulations prohibited "exportation to China" and this deal involved shipment *within* China, there could be no violation, the Court found. Slevin was acquitted, as Judge Lobingier concluded that he could not "penalize the sale of articles designed primarily for commercial purposes merely because they might fall into the hands of the military." Further, the defendant was entitled to the presumption of innocence, such that the case against him had to be established beyond a reasonable doubt, which it apparently had not been.[75]

In addition to these two high-profile cases, there were numerous instances of Americans or U.S. companies violating the Embargo Agreement. The American representative on the Inter-Allied Technical Railway Committee reportedly diverted machine guns, rifles, and ammunition from Vladivostok to Warlord Wu Pei-fu. American companies Arnhold Karberg and Co., and Carlowitz and Co., were instrumental in stocking one of Wu's principal arsenal. Anderson Meyer and Co. of Shanghai sold machinery for production of cartridges and uniform accoutrements; a Tientsin U.S. national brought in significant quantities of armored cars; while another American sold bulletproof breast plates.[76] Also, it was generally believed that of the three or four large international arms rings, one was centered in North America. Reports of large seizures in Seattle, Washington, in early 1923 of weapons headed for China confirmed such suspicions. Americans in Manila were found engaged in a plot to export arms to China through local (Philippines) Chinese. As guns became more profitable than opium, a number of U.S. military personnel visiting Chinese ports sold whatever miscellaneous weapons they could get hold of.[77]

Power versus Authority

Third, the Court endeavored to bring treaty port Americans under tighter rein but—as before—ambition far outran accomplishment. Lobingier undoubtedly had some successes in subordinating treaty port Americans to the extraterritorial rule of law. He "streamlined" due process by refusing to apply various procedural protections given defendants back home. For example, in *U.S. v. Pablo Sonico* (1918), Lobingier ruled that rules excluding evidence to avoid misleading the jury were not relevant to the nonjury-based system in China. The defendant was a Filipino on trial for the manslaughter of Loh Yuen Zien in an argument over money.[78] In *U.S. v. Furbush* (1921), the defendant received a life sentence for murder (of another foreigner); Lobingier used the case to condemn the jury system, and condemned the jury acquittal of a British national for the murder of a rickshaw coolie.[79] *U.S. v. Charles Carberry* (1923) set the rule allowing into court confidence "freely and voluntarily made," even if the accused was not warned that his statements could be used against him.[80] Lobingier extended the USC-C's jurisdiction, largely by assuming functions usually reserved to state courts including probate, divorce, adoptions, juvenile offenses.[81] His definition of "improper acts," a term used in Sino-American treaty provisions on extrality, was given in *U.S. v. Allen* (1914) as follows: it would "be a reproach to America" if what was viewed as improper elsewhere in the U.S. domain was permitted in China.[82]

Under Lobingier the Court's most punitive justice was directed toward individuals on the margins—transients living on public charity, petty hustlers, and violence-prone sailors darkening America's "good name" in China. Using laws borrowed from the District of Columbia Code, Lobingier forced vagrants to purchase a $100 bond, or spend time in prison, for example. Not long after his arrival in 1914, the Judge obtained permission from the U.S. attorney general to use Bilibid Prison in the Philippines to house those sentenced by the Court for over three months. From there, the prisoners were often shipped back to the United States on a timetable such that their sentence expired just as they arrived home.[83]

During World War I and after, the Court's concerns broadened to include the political scrutiny of sojourners. The continuing extraterritorial function of maintaining ship discipline took on political overtones, as malcontented crew members brought to Court were on occasion identified as organized radicals and party members.[84] However, Court officials' resistance to being made political lackeys was clearest in their refusal to prosecute Gilbert Reid, the well-known enterprising missionary-turned-entrepreneur. Minister Paul Reinsch petitioned the Shanghai district attorney to prosecute Reid for "seditious libel." Reid then in Peking, was running a newspaper (*The Peking Post*) "whose sole purpose seemed to be to justify German aggression in China and elsewhere, and to lambaste U.S. officials for not seeing things quite his way."[85]

In an article "Are China's Loans Made in the Open?" Reid had accused the U.S. legation with improper involvement in loan negotiations on behalf of American bankers. In a second article, he charged the Wilson administration of pro-British neutrality. When brought before the Tientsin consul, Reid pleaded guilty to defamation charges, but was spared sentencing by an apology. When he continued along the same editorial lines, the USDA drew up an indictment, but then declined to prosecute, a decision supported by Lobingier in *U.S. v. Gilbert Reid* (1917). Continued agitation by Minister Reinsch forced Reid to retreat to Manila. The Reverend no doubt wondered how he had become nothing more than an undesirable beachcomber in the eyes of American officials. He was widely condemned by local Americans, anxious to demonstrate their patriotism from afar: "The few men and women. . . . who have come under German influence, and who while claiming American citizenship, are half-hearted in their allegiance and in their private speech belittle the American flag . . . had better take warning from the fate of Gilbert Reid. There is no halfway mark, they are either for or against their country."[86]

CORPORATIONS AS "GOOD CITIZENS"

There was a characteristically Wilsonian effort to hold American businesses to a higher standard, in exchange for extraterritorial protection. In *U.S. v. Sin Wan Pao Co.* (1920), Lobingier fined the defendant $250, while also insisting upon "The special duty of corporations enjoying the extraterritorial privilege to avoid all violation of law." This Delaware corporation's publication of pornography advertisement in Chinese-language newspapers had larger implications for Sino-American trade, said the Court: "If the increase of American corporations in China is to continue, and is to receive official encouragement, it is only on the condition that they conform to our best national standards. And especially in a matter like this, where the morals of the Chinese public are so gravely affected, the standards can be none too high and the care exercised none too sedulous."[87]

However, the tendency to depart from conservative jurisprudence was discouraged by fiscal constraints, the need to work with other foreign courts, the ability of defendants to shift nationalities and corporate registration to friendlier courts, the political vulnerability of judges, and the likelihood of appeal against particularly egregious decisions.[88] Extrality did not function in a vacuum. If facilitating the penetration of China by American capitalism were all that Charles Lobingier had to do, he might have done more and better on that score. However, as the ordeal of earlier judges suggests, for the Court the overwhelming imperative was survival within the treaty port setting. This meant many different things over time, but most of all, that the Judge of the Court, if he wanted to remain on the bench, had to use the enormous discretion at his disposal to garner, solidify, and sustain the support of Americans in his jurisdiction.

THE COURT AND THE BAR

In fact, the key to the success of the Lobingier Court during the Wilson era was the Judge's tacit compact with local American lawyers, through such things as local incorporation procedures, which proved an enormous bonanza for them in many respects. In late 1914, Lobingier had organized the lawyers under the auspices of the Far Eastern American Bar Association, which he presided over until 1922. Originally comprised of eighteen attorneys, twelve of whom practiced in Shanghai, the organization grew to forty-seven by 1916, and in 1922 the total stood at seventy-one, with about half centered in Shanghai.[89] In 1919, Lobingier wrested all remaining consular judicial powers from the Shanghai Consulate, shepherding through Congress an act investing these powers in a U.S. Commissioner's Court, over which Lobingier appointed a member of the local (American) bar, further cementing his ties to that association and effectively subordinating the lower court under his patronage. Lobingier drafted the bill that became the Act of 4 June 1920 creating the Commissioner's Court, having brought that Court to life using the case *Barkley Co., Inc. v. William E. Maloney* (1919).[90] Lobingier argued that the earliest treaties between the United States and China made Court commissioners a part of the judicial machinery in China, and that subsequent treaties had never abrogated those provisions.

Court and bar members were prominent members of various civil, professional, and social clubs and organizations, and were on retainer from most American businesses in Shanghai, as well as from well-to-do urban Chinese. Through these connections, the Court was thereby drawn into, and anchored within, the treaty port's interlocking web of relationships. The U.S. Court's most direct avenue of access into the Chinese dimension of this treaty port relational web was the Soochow School of Comparative Law, established on 3 September 1915 by the Southern Methodist Mission Board, with Judge Lobingier's help.[91] Typifying the Progressive blend of missionary zeal and pragmatic tutelage, the school was the object of great personal interest and professional involvement on the part of the Judge, other members of the Far Eastern American Bar Association, and powerful, prominent Chinese who shifted in and out of public and private life during the period. Its graduates tended to go on to advanced study in the United States, and thence take their place in Republican China as judges, diplomats, government officials, bankers, and merchants.

One of Soochow's most eminent graduates, for example, was Wu Ching-hsiung, known more popularly as John C. H. Wu, born in 1899 at Ningpo, trained at Soochow and then at the University of Michigan (1921). He became a legal scholar of international reputation, presided over the Shanghai Provisional Court, served as principal of Soochow Law School, was appointed Chinese adviser to the Shanghai Municipal Council from 1931 to 1933, and joined the Drafting Committee of the Legislative Yuan beginning in 1933. Illustrative as well is the career of Liang Yuen-li (Liang Yuanli), born in 1903, who received an LL.B. in 1926 from Soochow, and an advanced law degree in 1930 from Harvard University. In 1928, he became judge of the Shanghai Provisional Court; the following year he served at the Chinese Legation in Washington D.C.; went on to the League of Nations from 1930 to 1932, and in 1933 joined the Ministry of Foreign Affairs as senior secretary, thereafter appointed professor of law at his alma mater, and managing editor of its journal, *The China Law Review*. More generally, the American University Club of Shanghai, to which Court personnel belonged, boasted a sizable number of the city's leading Chinese attorneys, doctors, bankers, businessmen, officials, and academics.[92]

Court-related functions, such as the gala tribute to Lobingier in 1922, had in attendance a small contingent of Shanghai's leading, generally Western-educated, Chinese.[93] Through these professional and social contacts, Lobingier gained the good will of individuals such as Wang Chung-hui, China's most eminent contemporary jurist: one-time chief justice of his country's Supreme Court, Chinese representative on the Court of International Justice at the Hague, and a leading figure in KMT officialdom, both on the Mainland and—after 1949—on Taiwan. Wang indicated in a letter to Washington officials endorsing Lobingier in 1921 that Chinese "have learned to repose entire confidence in that [the U.S.] court and they have come to regard him [Lobingier] as a high example of judicial probity and trustworthiness."[94]

A large dose of caution is necessary in assessing the impact of these private Sino-American contacts on formal diplomacy, and on the course of events more generally. The endemic political turmoil of the era meant that Chinese officials among the friends of the Court had only ephemeral influence on the ultimate direction of the country. The disorder of post-Revolutionary China, especially after the 1916 death of Sun Yatsen's strongman successor Yuan Shih-k'ai, further undermined the collaborative mechanisms of informal imperialism; the absence of a strong center to enforce the unequal treaties, and the volatile flux of internal politics, meant that "friendly," i.e. pro-Western, Chinese were of little use beyond positive public relations.[95]

China's (sometimes) premier, Li Yuan-hung (Li Yuanhong), also wrote—no doubt at the request of Lobingier—a supportive letter to President Calvin Coolidge endorsing the Judge for reappointment in 1923. Chinese "feel that before him [Lobingier] they are on a footing equal with . . . [all] others," Li noted. "No Court in China stands higher today in the estimation of all nationalities than the United States court under the administration of Judge Lobingier." Quite a testimonial, but Li wrote it just a few days after he had been ousted as premier, and from that date to his death in 1928, he did not wield power or influence over his country's fate (nor, it will be seen, over Washington's decisions concerning the Court).[96] In other instances, the connection Chinese may have felt to the Court or its Judge was just one among many, usually more compelling, loyalties, and their transactions with American judicial officials were purely opportunistic, as were the Court's dealings with them.

LOBINGIER'S DEMISE

In early 1921, the Lobingier Court's modus vivendi with local treaty port Americans began to unravel. That year was a time of great economic distress in Shanghai, as the end of the war saw exports decline, silver prices fall, and imports stagnate, leading to a wave of unbridled speculation and bank failures.[97] The ever-fiercer competition for clients within the Far Eastern American Bar Association—the Court's primary base of support—and the increasingly bitter personal animosities among members, tore that organization apart, once again setting the Court adrift, vulnerable from all sides. Further, alienation from the U.S. consulate had resulted from Lobingier's refusal in 1917 to cooperate with Minister Paul Reinsch's efforts to expel Gilbert Reid.

Leading the attack was local attorney William Fleming, attorney for various China-incorporated companies, agent of real estate interests, and opportunist linked to gambling casino interests.[98] Fleming was endorsed and supported by consular personnel, whom Lobingier had antagonized the past six or seven years through his efforts to solidify the Court's monopoly over American extrality in China. Further, Fleming's membership in the Far Eastern Bar Association—an organization created by Lobingier himself—meant a great deal in Washington, D.C., as it gave the attorney professional standing and credibility. The attack took the form of a well-documented, well-reasoned critique of the Court itself as an unconstitutional concentration of power in a single man.[99]

The Justice Department investigated the charges against Lobingier.[100] Thus began a year-long ordeal, during which the Court was closed, as witnesses from Shanghai and elsewhere made their way to Washington to testify on one side or the other. The long closure of the Court in Shanghai became the subject of complaints to President Warren Harding and his various Cabinet officials. Secretary of Commerce Herbert Hoover notified Attorney General Harry Daugherty in early 1922 that "the China merchants" were complaining that without a court fully empowered to adjudicate commercial disputes, force payment of debts and so on, American businesses could not compete with their foreign rivals.[101] Representative Leonidas Dyer, the congressional sponsor of various China Trade bills from 1919 to 1922, informed Harding that he was under pressure from Americans in China, embarrassed by the Court scandal, to send Lobingier back at least to fill out his ten-year term, scheduled to end in February of 1924.[102] By far the most serious possible implication was that Chinese officials would take advantage of the moment and demand an end to extraterritoriality. Chinese representatives at the Washington Conference in 1921 had successfully forced the great powers to pledge an eventual end to extrality, and to establish an independent commission to investigate the current system and formulate a blueprint for gradual abolition. The turn of the tide meant a closer Chinese scrutiny of treaty violations, such as not having on hand a suitably empowered American official to oversee extraterritorial cases.[103]

As in the Wilfley case, the persistence, visibility, and volubility of the Judge's critics won out over long-range considerations about the course of American justice in China and the state of Sino-American relations. The Justice Department ultimately concluded that, whatever the merit of the charges against Lobingier, he had "lost his usefulness in China and [was] not conducting his office to the best interests of the Government." The Judge's handling of a case involving his own clerk's theft of a client's assets had created an "unfortunate situation which . . . weakened the prestige" of the Court and undermined the Judge's efficacy.[104]

The Justice Department wrote to Lobingier in early April (1922) with Harding's endorsement that the Judge should be permitted to resign "for the good of the service in China and in order to establish that atmosphere which is so essential to a Federal Court, especially in a foreign country." However, that decision was never made public, and some three months later, on 23 June 1922, Lobingier was exonerated and ordered back to the bench by an Executive Order. The President's ultimate decision came in the wake of a 21 June 1922 visit to the White House by Lobingier, during which, later correspondence between them would indicate, Lobingier assured Harding that if sent back he would make peace with Fleming and once again there would be peace and quiet.[105]

However, the Judge's pledges notwithstanding, the Fleming-Lobingier feud continued, factionalizing the entire American treaty port community. Complaints that the Court was favoring its supporters in particular litigation before it continued to reach Washington. In the meanwhile, the 9th Circuit Court upheld Lobingier's verdict in the contempt case, *Fleming v. U.S.*, prompting Fleming to appeal to the U.S. Supreme Court. Then under the direction of Chief Justice William Taft, one of the founding fathers of the U.S. Court for China, the high Court declined to hear the case, thereby upholding the appellate decision and Lobingier's original decision. Under pressure from Washington, Lobingier remitted Fleming's remaining jail sentence (of about five and a half months), but not without forcing the attorney to admit publicly the criminal and vindictive nature of his attack upon the Court.[106]

Over the next year, Lobingier set about orchestrating a campaign for his reappointment for another term, as his first was scheduled to end in February 1924. This, in turn, led to another flurry of complaints to officials in the White House, the State Department, and the Attorney General's Office, to the effect that the Judge was deciding cases toward the goal of shoring up his support. His critics succeeded in stripping his pronouncements from the bench of any pretensions higher than rank ambition and pandering for office and power, as the Court's decisions clearly favored the attorneys who had supported the Judge in his ordeal with Fleming.

The Harding administration, by general agreement one of the most corrupt Cabinets in modern American history, was somewhat preoccupied with its own domestic troubles during these years. Attorney General Daugherty himself, for example, eluded prosecution for bribery and fraud in one particular scandal only by invoking his constitutional privilege against self-incrimination. In 1923–24 the Secretaries of the Interior (Albert Fall) and of the Navy (Edwin Denby—another USC-C founding father) were forced from office in the well-known "Teapot Dome" affair. Still, the President and his Cabinet took seriously the complaints of Shanghai Americans about the continuing Fleming-Lobingier feud, and they continually urged the Judge to "keep the peace" and reach an accommodation with his foes, neither of which he did to their satisfaction. Thus, when the Judge's ten-year term came up for renewal, Calvin Coolidge (who had assumed the presidency after Harding's death on 2 August 1923) consulted with State and Justice Department officials, and ultimately opted to find another, less controversial man for the Shanghai bench.

CHAPTER SIX

INTERWAR DEMISE OF
CONSULAR JURISDICTION

In the interwar period, the conditions that had buttressed great power agreements on colonial empires dramatically changed, leading ultimately to war in Europe and in the Pacific. The end of formal empires, though, was not the end of imperialism, but rather one signpost of a new stage in that unfolding process. The era, traditionally seen as a time when overidealistic statesmen belatedly realized their inattention to the dictates of realism, was more in fact one "long transitional crisis that led ultimately to a basic restructuring of the global order," principally involving a shift "from imperial systems . . . to corporate forms" of capitalist expansion and penetration.[1] The forward movement in the colonies was from treaty ports, gunboats, indemnities, foreign-run customs, and legal privileges to more subtle instruments of domination, such as world monetary organizations and international courts of justice. In this setting, "[m]ilitary threat and coercion were increasingly unsuitable means for defending imperial interests."[2]

This chapter covers changes in the American federal-sojourner relationship in the interwar era, particularly in areas where extraterritoriality applied. It tracks the operation of the U.S. Court for China in its final two decades (1924–43) as a generally passive and reactive institution, living out its own contradictions, its fortunes shaped less by the contest of wills with its turbulent wards than by the disintegration and dismantling of the unequal treaty system around it. The Court did not guide, but was instead guided by, larger developments around it, in particular by the confluence of events that led to sharply conflicting perceptions among Americans as to just what their "stake" in China comprised. The Court functioned as a collector of rents, enforcer of contracts, assessor of debts, and custodian of impoverished riff raff. How defendants came before it was a matter determined for the most part by the social, economic and political forces at work around it. The justice it dispensed in criminal cases was largely a system-sustaining effort to find a place for the human refuse produced by those forces.

AFTER THE GREAT WAR

Following World War I, the end of the extraterritorial enclave became imminent. Although unable to block the great powers from turning over Germany's China possessions to Japan, Chinese representatives at Versailles did get a pledge for a commission of inquiry into extrality. Turkey notified parties to the long-standing "capitulations" that consular courts had until 1923 to wrap up pending cases. The 1924 Lausanne Convention embraced the principle of territorial sovereignty, enunciating a code of conduct for sojourners and businesses operating abroad.[3] At the same time, world organizations, such as the International Labour Organisation, pushed for the application in extraterritorial areas of regulatory standards widely applicable elsewhere.[4]

In China, the essential unity among privileged foreign interests unraveled after 1920, as a defeated Germany and Austria were punitively deprived of their privileges, and Bolshevik Russia revoked its unequal treaties with China in the name of anti-imperialist revolutionary diplomacy. Japan indicated a willingness to give up extrality in return for recognition of its Manchurian claims. The treaty ports saw a simultaneous breakdown in foreign ranks. By the mid-1920s, approximately 254,006 individuals and 6,473 firms in China enjoyed extrality; at the same time, 83,235 foreigners and 1,270 foreign firms did not. Of the former group, 87 percent were Japanese, 3.8 were American, with the remainder comprising French, British, and Portuguese; the changing composition of extrality's beneficiaries added to its vulnerability in Sino-foreign diplomacy. Most among the officially unprotected group became something of free riders in the system, enjoying the perquisites of foreign nationality without the onus. Non-treaty foreign nationals were, as one observer put it at the time, "weeds in the shadow of the big trees, not getting as much sun as they, but enjoying more the fertility of the ground."

Chinese nationalism became practically synonymous with anti-imperialism. With the inauguration of the May Fourth Movement (1919), and the outbreak of the anti-foreign May 30th Incident (1925), the legitimacy of aspiring indigenous elites came to depend upon their commitment to overturning the unequal treaties and recovering foreign territorial enclaves. Combined with the disintegration of foreign unity, these internal forces raised the political and fiscal costs of informal imperialism in China to metropolitan governments and their domestic constituencies. In the end, neither the United States nor Great Britain was willing to foot the bill of continuing the unequal treaties against Chinese resistance, and both adopted a policy of gradual acquiescence, culminating in the 1943 abrogation of the unequal treaties.[5]

International legal scholars, diplomats, and philanthropic groups proved ever more receptive to Chinese appeals for an end to the unequal treaties and restoration of complete sovereignty. Western-trained Chinese jurists made effective use of forums such as the League of Nations to argue that the unequal treaties hindered China's ability to combat problems with international implications, including trafficking in narcotics, arms, and prostitution. Missionary groups became more clearly convinced that terminating extrality was an essential condition for lowering Chinese resistance to proselytization. Indeed, in the mid-1920s, the American Board of Commissioners for Foreign Missions (ABC-FM) petitioned the State Department for permission to "vacate" their members' extraterritorial privileges; however, they were informed from Washington that "a citizen cannot by his independent act control the right of his government to intervene or afford protection." Extrality belonged to the government, not to individual citizens. Chinese officials made it clear to business interests that movement into hinterland markets was contingent upon an end to extrality and related privileges.[6] U.S. and British multinationals—Standard Oil, the Texas Company, and British American Tobacco, for example—each negotiated a pragmatic modus vivendi with warring indigenous factions, giving way on issues of taxation and jurisdiction.[7]

When Nationalist and communist factions re-took successive foreign territorial enclaves, such as Hankow, the British did not act to regain them by force or duress; by 1927 twenty out of thirty-three Concessions had been reclaimed. In addition, following upon the May 30th Incident (1925), Chinese demands for the rendition of the International Mixed Court in Shanghai to native control were eventually acceded to, and that imperial landmark was ultimately supplanted by a Chinese-run district court and a higher appellate provincial court. Chinese formal representation on the Shanghai Municipal Council (SMC) was increased from zero to three, and then to five, the same number as allotted to the British community there. The Nationalist government unilaterally abolished extrality in 1930, though subsequently retreated to a more gradualist position.[8]

The unequal treaty powers' concessions to the Nationalists during the interwar period came largely in response to the rising costs of defending the unequal treaty system. Increases in the cost of imperialism, stemming from indigenous resistance movements and international economic dislocations, undercut the support of groups within the metropolitan powers for financing and defending such things as treaty ports and special privileges. This, in turn, meant greater reliance on indigenous collaborators to insure continued market access and containment of anti-foreign violence. As Ronald Robinson has noted, in the imperialist matrix, "accommodations at various levels [were] interdependent, and an alteration of terms at one level involve[d] an alteration of contracts on the others."

As earlier chapters have underscored, indigenous collaborators had to move powerfully in their own society if they were to be of any utility to the imperialist enterprise. As numerous historical examples prove, the transition "from imperial systems . . . to corporate forms" of capitalist expansion and penetration could not happen in target areas unless collaborators survived the crisis of legitimacy they faced in their own society, something imperialist powers therefore helped them to do. The struggle for potency and legitimacy by these collaborative westernizers involved attaining a monopoly over coercive force, exercising effective legal and financial authority over those within their territorial jurisdiction, and gaining credibility as an autonomous, patriotic government rather than a rapacious clique of imperialist lackeys.

The emergence of radical nationalists to the left and right meant that in order for westernizing elites to hold the middle against both ends, they had to bring about the formal retreat of imperialism. Ideally, from the perspective of imperialists, this retreat would come at a time when there was already in place the self-regenerating infrastructure of westernization (e.g., Western-style criminal and civil law codes, open markets, a standard and stable currency, a liberalized civil sphere founded on the urban middle class, and a democratic party system that could resolve political differences by means short of civil war). In the China setting, this meant that those who hoped to make of the Kuomintang (KMT) a westernizing, collaborative elite had to give way on issues such as tariffs, gunboats, treaty ports, and extrality. As a contemporary magazine noted, this situation "impaled" the treaty port denizen "on the horns of a dilemma": "if the Nanking government fails, the Communist movement . . . may succeed, and would doubtless sweep him and his gunboats and all his works from their precarious perch along the Bund; whereas should the bankers and Nanking succeed, their intensely nationalistic followers may drive him out just the same. The only difference being that in one case he would probably be killed; in the other he would doubtless be given the opportunity to buy a ticket home."[9]

The KMT was not the ideal indigenous collaborator, as numerous historians have made clear, but it seemed then the only available alternative to Japanese puppet regimes or communist adversaries.[10] In the interwar period, the KMT's crisis of legitimacy was manifest most particularly in three areas of Sino-foreign relations: first, Nationalists' broad demands for the end of extrality itself, a continuing theme in the period; second, their efforts to bring foreigners in China under indigenous authority (through taxation, registration, licensing, and so on); and, third, their endeavor to force foreign governments to prevent the use of extrality as a shelter for anti-Kuomintang groups. The fundamental challenge for the KMT was "to displace the local elite's control over the police, militia, taxation, and other matters of local government," including the control over lucrative treaty ports by local Sino-foreign elites.[11]

THE UNITED STATES IN EAST ASIA

Ever more focused on European affairs, reluctant to antagonize Japan, and without robust domestic support for colonial wars, Great Britain pressured the United States to take over its leadership role in East Asia.[12] The architects of U.S. China policy between 1925 (the May Thirtieth Incident) and 1943 (the end of the unequal treaties) generally favored accommodating KMT needs and demands. For example, Secretary of State Frank Kellogg, acting largely on the advice of Nelson Johnson, later U.S. minister in Peking, acquiesced to Chinese tariff autonomy in 1928, and worked toward a mutually acceptable resolution of the "Nanking Incident" (March 1927), involving anti-foreign violence on the part of Nationalist soldiers.[13] The outer limits of support for China and the Nationalists, though, were made clear by U.S. reluctance to restrain in any material way Japanese territorial incursions. As is well known, when Japan seized Manchuria in 1931, and established Manchukuo in 1932, Secretary of State Henry Stimson limited U.S. reaction to outrage and nonrecognition. The Japanese attack on Shanghai earlier that same year, and its continuing buildup of forces and munitions in that port throughout the 1930s, was only rhetorically challenged by the U.S. government.[14]

Bounded by these two objectives—shoring up the Nationalists and trying not to antagonize the Japanese—U.S. policy makers generally yielded to Nationalist demands regarding extrality, albeit with no small amount of foot-dragging. Pressed by the KMT's campaign to abrogate— unilaterally if necessary—all foreign privileges as violations of Chinese sovereignty, the United States made gradual concessions regarding its unlimited access to China's sea lanes and waterways; the de facto immunity of its nationals and their property from both taxation and regulation by Chinese officials; the abuse of American extrality by Chinese themselves as a shelter for anti-KMT dissent; and, finally, the historic autonomy of U.S. missionaries vis-à-vis indigenous authorities, laws, and mores.[15] U.S. China policy was, like American interwar foreign policy more generally, "a kind of semi-internationalism; a half-way house between isolationism . . . and full-blown, consistent internationalism."[16]

Treaty Ports as Bargaining Chips

Among the most visible casualties of these turbulent events in East Asia was the foreign treaty port elite in China and the century-old edifice of privilege it had constructed on the foundations of extrality. Western liberal observers in the 1930s likened the treaty ports to a "parasite fungus-growth," a "little colony of white mold on the edge of a gelatine culture," that lives believing that its host exists for it.[17] What had once been seen as the "bridgehead" of the Western enterprise in China was for U.S. officials by 1940, "a card" to be "played" in international affairs, though only for the maximum possible quid pro quo.

Washington's marked tendency to see the treaty ports as an expendable asset, rather than as an indispensable precondition to Sino-foreign trade, accurately reflected America's changing portfolio abroad. By 1920, the United States was a major international creditor and investor, with an interest in stable world finances and the post-World War I status quo. In terms of protecting American nationals and property abroad, this translated into an ambitious approach remarkable in that it simultaneously insulted foreign governments and American sojourners. "The person and property of a citizen are a part of the general domain of the nation, even when abroad," declared President Calvin Coolidge in 1927, and thus must be defended. On the other hand, the "operations" of Americans developing resources abroad "must be carried on with justice and humanity. They must not be permitted to sink to the level of mere exploitation."[18]

In China during the interwar era, America's stake was more political than material, that is, it rested more on China's survival as an entity than on the defense of treaty port vested interests. In 1938, the official position of the U.S. government was that American interests in Asia were

> not measured by the number of American citizens residing in a particular country at a particular moment nor by the amount of investment of American citizens therein or by the volume of trade. There is broader and much more fundamental interest—which is that orderly processes in international relationships be maintained. . . . This interest far transcends in importance the value of American trade with China or American investments in China; it transcends even the question of safeguarding the immediate welfare of American citizens in China.[19]

Shanghai Americans well understood from 1925 on that they were being abandoned by their home authorities and found no allies among powerful domestic constituencies willing to pay for gunboat diplomacy and far-off privileges. Prominent American, and "Lord Mayor" of Shanghai, Stirling Fessenden was apparently informed during a 1929 private conversation at the White House that he and his countrymen should make their peace with their own inevitable demise, as the U.S. government had no intention of trying to push back the tides of history by deploying military force against Chinese reclaiming their sovereign rights. Domestic groups such as the National Council for Prevention of War lobbied vociferously for acquiescence to indigenous and Japanese pressures in China, arguing that it would cost the United States about $40 billion to protect what the group estimated was an American investment in China of only $130 million. What public money was spent on the China market in the interwar period tended to be directed toward the interests of U.S. manufacturers and raw material suppliers, rather than American middlemen growing rich on Shanghai's position as "the neck of the bottle through which most of China's commerce" traveled.[20]

Earlier works have noted that Americans in China in this period became more "American," that is, they moved to establish a separate national identity within the cosmopolitan treaty port; this was manifest in, for example, the creation of an independent national Chamber of Commerce in Shanghai, with branches throughout coastal China. Fed by the growth in their numbers from about 1,900 in 1914 to 3,075 in 1919, Americans established identifiable neighborhoods, schools, churches, civic clubs, local branches of the Boy Scouts and the Rotary Club—in general, all of the trappings of home. The Committee on Public Information, set up in the U.S. during World War I, opened a China branch in 1918, to spread the good word about America.[21]

By the mid-1920s, contemporaries spoke, with mixed opinions, about the "Americanization of Shanghai."[22] In part, local American boosterism came in reaction to doubts on the home front as to sojourners' citizenship credentials. In pleading for exemption from domestic income tax laws, for example, Shanghai Americans felt it necessary to reassure Capitol Hill that "The 8,000 Americans [or so] in China are staunch, loyal American citizens and in no sense wish to evade any responsibilities or duties as American citizens."[23]

Although there was a strong contingent of Americans in Shanghai who found common cause with Western-educated urban Chinese in the campaign to abrogate the unequal treaties, paradoxically this period of U.S. acquiescence also witnessed the height of American influence in the "die-hard" councils of treaty port municipal government.[24] U.S. nationals, including real estate magnate Frank Jay Raven, and his attorney Cornell Franklin, as well as the well-known Stirling Fessenden, were all prominent members of the SMC during these years.[25] Raven and his clique had come to the fore as staunch conservatives willing to take a stand against the post-May 30th Incident surge of Chinese nationalism, and by 1927, they had taken control of the American Chamber of Commerce.[26]

The SMC, and the real estate and development interests it represented, exerted continuous expansionist pressure on the contiguous areas outside the Settlement, inasmuch as that is where their continued prosperity lay.[27] They were emblematic of what, in the 1930s, was widely described as the "Shanghai mind," denoting the reactionary, racist, exploitative imperialist unwilling to let go of the "good old days" predating the rise of Chinese urban nationalism.[28] In 1932, unidentified members of this coalition, in collusion with Japanese agents, called—in vain—upon the League of Nations to sponsor the demilitarization of Shanghai, and the creation around it of a "free city state" to include the core city and all of the land within a twenty-mile perimeter. This autonomous municipality would be off-limits to Chinese officials, and be overseen by a governor general appointed by the League, assisted by a seven-member senate with one Chinese member.[29]

Fortunes of the USC-C

As for the U.S. Court in Shanghai, Judge Lobingier had been forced out in 1924, denied a second term by the State Department, under pressure by Shanghai Americans. As in Wilfley's ordeal, the persistence, visibility, and volubility of the Judge's critics won out over long-range considerations about the course of American justice in China and the state of Sino-American relations. Thus marked the end of the Progressive vision of extrality embraced first by the Theodore Roosevelt administration, then by Wilsonians. To both groups, the USC-C had seemed a promising and relatively inexpensive way to advance American commercial, cultural, and political interests in that country. In the wake of the Boxer Rebellion (1900), the anti-American boycott (1905–1906), and—later— the Chinese Revolution (1911–1912), the reform of extrality seemed essential to the preservation of internal authority in China, to the survival of nascent, Western-oriented elites, and to America's ability to play a significant, nonentangling, role in the "great game" of East Asian power politics.

The original function of the U.S. Court had been a threefold one, embracing tutelary, disciplinary, and protective tasks. The first involved providing Chinese with a visible, day-to-day object lesson in modern Anglo-American jurisprudence, such that their transition to Western mores would be that much easier. The second required reining in the most visibly predatory U.S. nationals in China (those whom Judge Lebbeus Wilfley had called "whores, gamblers, sharks and buccaneers") in the interests of a Sino-American "special relationship." Finally, extraterritorial tribunals, including the U.S. Court, were part of a larger treaty port edifice built upon tariffs, gunboats, indemnities, territorial concessions, loans, and the like, all of which enabled foreign nationals to thrive and prosper amid the tumultuous consequences of their own collective demands upon Chinese society.

By 1924, the Court's most pressing challenge gravitated around the third function, that of protecting Americans and American interests in China. Neither Milton Purdy (1924–34) nor Milton Helmick (1934–43) were visibly targeted by disgruntled litigants or local interests. To a great extent, this quietude signaled the Court's domestication within the treaty port setting, most especially its solicitude toward groups that had unseated previous judges.

Three events help to illustrate this tacit rapprochement. First, in 1927 U.S. District Attorney Leonard Husar was (justifiably) indicted for extorting money from Shanghai-American brothel owners and, most infamously, from a U.S. national deeply complicit in the opium trade whom Husar threatened to prosecute unless he was paid some $25,000.[30] (Husar's defense was that unexplained deposits in his bank account were payoffs from Chinese warlords for brokering arms deals.)[31] Second, the State Department sternly reprimanded the Court in 1926 for being too closely identified with the campaign of the Far Eastern American Bar Association to block the rendition of the British-run International Mixed Court to Chinese control and to thwart the prohibition of foreign lawyers from that venue.[32] Finally, upon his (voluntary) retirement from the USC-C bench in 1934, Judge Purdy remained in Shanghai as an attorney and president of a local finance company, evidently quite at home among his former wards.[33]

WINNERS AND LOSERS IN THE USC-C

In their cumulative twenty years on the bench, Milton Purdy and Milton Helmick heard about 630 cases, as compared to the 2,000 or so adjudicated by Lobingier from 1914 to 1924. Two-thirds of the later cases were civil or administrative matters covering contract disputes, unpaid debts, estate settlements, divorces, and the like. As in the earlier period, cases involving Chinese plaintiffs were but a small percentage of the total, and were brought primarily by local treaty port businessmen and compradores seeking to recover damages, claim commissions, collect debts, enforce contracts, or redeem insurance policies.[34] Approximately one third, or about 210 cases, involved criminal charges, and ranged from opium trafficking and grand larceny, to petty theft and vagrancy.[35] The Court's diminishing case load and a lower political profile was a manifestation of a more general Chinese withdrawal from the formal legal system in treaty port society, as extrality was discredited and the "politics of gangsterism" penetrated the treaty port setting.[36]

The USC-C's docket in this period is interesting in a number of respects. First, it provides evidence that women of various nationalities, including Chinese, were more active and visible in treaty port affairs, both legitimate and illicit. Second, it reflects the emergence of American-born Chinese as a distinct treaty port constituency able to benefit more than suffer from their de facto dual nationality.

Female Litigants

As to the first, the post-World War I influx of American working women into Shanghai is reflected in cases such as *Lucille Russell Georges v. E. Georges* (1926). The petitioner had been born in Atlanta, Georgia, and gone to Washington, D.C., as a wartime stenographer in the Justice Department; there she met the man she married in early 1919. After the war, they went to Manila, where he filled a civilian post in the Quartermaster's Department and she edited a women's page in the Manila *Bulletin*. He lost his job, they went to Shanghai, where she supported him through her job as a stenographer in the Pacific Mail Company. After his desertion in 1925, she sought and obtained a divorce.[37] Similarly, there was Ruth Sullivan, who married an American attorney in Honolulu in

1921; they came to Shanghai, where she worked in the British American Tobacco (BAT) Company. She sought a divorce when he failed to return from Manila after many years. These working women were not the likely audience for pleas in the English-language press that newly arrived women take up social redemption work among the Chinese and the expatriate riffraff.[38]

More generally, beginning in the early 1920s—when Judge Lobingier was still on the bench—women began appearing with greater frequency in the USC-C as plaintiffs and defendants in civil suits.[39] They sued and were sued, as customers, creditors, victims, employees, and—more unusually—as employers.[40] They used the USC-C to negotiate their relationships with men, suing seducers for breach of promise, as in *Henrietta Weil v. J. Thomas Wright* (1921). Weil, a stenographer living with her widowed mother, had been seduced by a U.S. Navy yeoman on promise of marriage, had gotten pregnant and obtained a abortion from a local Japanese practitioner, damaging her health; she was awarded US$5,500, payable in monthly installments.[41]

The Married Women's Nationality (Cable) Act in 1922 stipulated that marriage did not affect a woman's nationality status.[42] This left many women in the United States stateless, as they lost their nationality because of the marriage laws of their country of origin and now could not take on U.S. nationality by marriage.[43] However, within the treaty port setting the implications were unique, as suggested by the case of Madame Isis (a.k.a. Emma Wallace), whom the USC-C tried to prosecute (under a 1736 act) for telling fortunes in Shanghai. She was the wife of a U.S. national but claimed immunity from the Court's jurisdiction, reassured by the unlikelihood of prosecution by officials of other nationalities. The district attorney feared then that alien women would marry Americans to evade crime, and he warned (without credibility) that he would prosecute husbands in such instances.[44]

Marriage to an American insured stateless women were not turned over to Chinese courts, but did not bind them to unwanted jurisdiction. This seemed to be the incentive for the noticeable number of Russian women who married U.S. nationals. Stateless after the Soviet abrogation of colonial privileges in China after 1919, they became Americans when married to U.S. nationals, because U.S. practice was to extend nationality to wives of Americans if they would otherwise be stateless. American officials were also loath to turn over individuals to the now Chinese-run

174

Mixed Court, which dealt with unrecognized foreigners. Even after divorce, they could call upon the USC-C to grant child support, enforce judgments with contempt of court hearings, collect alimony, and prosecute spousal abuse.[45] The proportion of divorce petitions to the total case load increased; to some extent, this owed to the greater percentage of married couples within an increased postwar population, but it also reflected the delinking of marriage and acquired nationality.[46]

Although in prior years, Chinese females had appeared as complainants in criminal suits (rape, assault, property damage), in the 1920s and 1930s they were also plaintiffs in civil suits. Illustrative of the trend is *Lily Thomas v. James Ching*. This was a successful appeal by the defendant from a $25 fine imposed by the Commissioner's Court, which had found him guilty of using vile and abusive language. Ching (an American-born Chinese) had contracted with Thomas (a native Chinese) to be an assistant in his medical office; she was to receive 20 percent of the proceeds, suggesting that she had agreed to bring in new Chinese patients to the practice.[47] Most cases involving Chinese female plaintiffs were personal injury cases, ultimately decided against the plaintiff.[48] Without understating the advances made by women in the Nationalist era, their higher profile in the USC-C is more likely due to greater competition among Western lawyers to find paying cases.[49] More solicitous attorneys helped bring to court cases such as *Mrs. Kwong Leong-kwok v. R. W. Squires* (1929), a mother suing for US$10,000 and 2,000 taels on behalf of her daughter, who had been struck by Squires's car and died a few days later from complications arising because of the door handle lodged between two ribs. Judge Purdy, though lamenting the loss of a "girl . . . educated, above the average, bright, cultured, and of a superior type," found the victim negligent.[50]

In *Kung Yoeh-tsing v. Asia Life Insurance* (1933), the female plaintiffs sued for $20,000 (Mex) on behalf of a husband/father, the financial controller of the YMCA, who had been found drowned in the Whangpoo with a wound in his neck. The insurance company won, citing a clause in the policy exempting wound or death by suicide, bandits, robbers, kidnappers, highwaymen; further, plaintiffs had not submitted to arbitration as required by their contract.[51] *Woo Lan-ying Estate v. Drs. Mourer & Dale* (1940) was a malpractice suit brought by the estate of a Chinese woman who died of an overdose of a drug sold to her as a cure for opium addiction.[52] Again, the plaintiff lost, in part because estate representatives refused to allow their American lawyer to present any witnesses or evidence that would have brought disgrace upon the family. In *Mrs. Chen Wong-shih v. Chas Raven,* a wife sued for US$10,000 when the defendant's car killed her husband, a "wheelbarrow coolie" whose job was to transport female workers to and from cotton mills. Raven, brother of leading treaty port entrepreneur Frank Raven, was found liable only for about $2,000 (Mex) in damages.[53]

"WAYWARD" FEMALE LITIGANTS

There were, to be sure, American women engaged in legitimate enterprises, such as Mrs. A. A. Clement, 28 years in China and creator of the Sino-Belge Tientsin Carpet Factory.[54] However, predictably, those who came before the USC-C were less mainstream. One of the longest prison terms handed down by the U.S. Court during the period, for example, was the four-year sentence of Margaret Enders, a 48-year-old American woman who in 1938 evidently tried to supplement her income as a tutor by transporting seventeen 25-ounce tins of high-grade heroin.[55] The earlier phenomenon of "American Girl" prostitution dissipated after a brief revival in the 1920s, less because of judicial activism, than changing economics and Japanese territorial incursions into China.[56] Large numbers of impoverished White Russian women forced into the trade, and an increasing regional population of Eurasian women, fed a vast proliferation in commercial vice in the late 1920s and 1930s in Shanghai, as "love became less segregated—and cheaper," to quote one contemporary.[57]

Women operating in business outside of Shanghai and alone, i.e., not in partnership with their husbands, were suspect in the eyes of U.S. officials. Such was the case of Nelle Devin, who arrived in Hankow in 1918 from Shanghai, "without any particular object or attachments," and with no evidence beyond her own statements as to "her antecedents." The local U.S. consul kept her under scrutiny, reporting in 1921 that she was by then involved personally and professionally with a Greek national, doing shady business selling transit passes to Chinese seeking to evade internal taxes. She had claimed a dubious $16,000 indemnity for losses from looting by Chinese soldiers. Lacking funds to investigate reports that "Devin Inc." was engaged in gun running and drug trafficking in Hunan, the consul turned to the manager of Standard Oil in the vicinity for verification. Devin was kept under consular scrutiny, but not prosecuted.[58]

In some instances, women became involved in illicit dealings through men, primarily as wives or mothers.[59] This was the story of Mrs. Dorothy Underwood, a twenty-year resident of China and the owner of a newsletter ("Peking at Play"), who was arrested in Tientsin in 1926 for helping her husband defraud a Chinese warlord of $42,000 for bogus arms sales. James Underwood, an Army deserter, received 30 months at McNeil's Island in the United States; Mrs. Underwood, though found guilty, had her sentence suspended on condition of reporting to the USC-C once every three months for one year.[60]

In other instances, women pursued criminal enterprise using the advantage of their virtual dual nationality, as in the case of American-born Chinese women. Maria Wen[dt], a former nurse at Paulun Hospital (local-foreign hospital), was arrested at the port of Los Angeles with US$50,000 worth of heroin in her trunk. Wen, a.k.a. "Molly," was found guilty in California. Her accomplices, both German nationals, committed suicide; she initially escaped custody, flew to New York, and was eventually recaptured on board a German liner.[61]

Chinese-Americans

For Chinese-Americans, both men and women, their anomalous situation could be profitable and dangerous; for U.S. officials, it was inevitably problematic. In *U.S. v. Seu Kee Mau* (1934), a young Chinese-American student at St. Johns University, was given a 30-day suspended sentence after assaulting a Chinese watchman in the municipal park, who refused him passage when Seu could not produce his pass.[62] Nick Wai-yuen Char, a Hawaiian-born Chinese, who practiced law in Shanghai, was the object of punitive energies by both U.S. and Chinese authorities. Both governments claimed jurisdiction over him following his involvement in a public fracas. Of Cantonese parents, Char had served in World War I, been admitted to the Nebraska Supreme Court (1922), and was a legal adviser to various Nationalist government agencies. Eventually, Char was handed over to the U.S. consul when his father, a member of a KMT committee in Hawaii, traveled to Shanghai to plead to Chiang Kai-shek personally.[63]

Both Seu and Char were able to claim U.S. nationality on the basis of their births in Hawaii; in other cases, the 1899 Supreme Court decision in *Wong Kim Ark* obtained, such that American-born Chinese were considered U.S. citizens. However, until the 1940s, Chinese could not be naturalized as U.S. citizens. These considerations arose most particularly around probate and adoption cases, as in the estate of Robert E. Lee, born in St. Louis in 1868, of a Chinese father (Alla Lee) and an American woman (Sarah Lee). Father and son returned to China, without Sarah, in 1880; Robert married Daisy Chang in 1889, and they raised four European-educated children. A real estate commission agent, Lee left an estate worth $10,000 gold. He had earlier claimed that his protracted residence in China should not expatriate him, because he was "advancing American interests" by brokering deals between Chinese and Americans.[64] In adoption cases, U.S. courts including the USC-C ruled that Chinese children could be adopted and brought to the United States, but would remained aliens.[65]

"Dangerous Persons" in the Treaty Port Context

Most of the criminal cases the Court heard involved nonmilitary personnel, originated in Shanghai rather than in the other treaty ports it visited on annual circuit, and were brought to its attention by local authorities, namely the Shanghai Municipal Council, French Concession officials, and the Chinese police. (Americans lived throughout in what was called "Greater Shanghai," i.e., the British-run International Settlement, the French Concession, and the Chinese district, and were subject to arrest by authorities within these sectors.)[66] The initiation of criminal charges against Americans by local (both foreign and Chinese) municipal bodies, though perhaps not so unusual in and of itself, had a very particular meaning in interwar Shanghai where, according to recent scholarship, "local government depended upon organized crime as an instrument for social control," and municipal government was "part of a global colonial network of imperial control."[67]

In the British-run International Settlement, where a sizable number of Americans lived and many American-owned businesses operated, foreign and indigenous brothels were "at the very heart of the city's commerce," as witness the Shanghai Municipal Council's half-hearted and unsuccessful efforts to phase out prostitution under pressure from moral reform groups.[68] Brothel license fees supplied a hefty portion of municipal revenues, their profits strengthened the hand of investors, and their myriad needs supplied income to real estate brokers, craftsmen, tailors, lawyers, and the like. One of the most eminent of the city's British firms, Atkinson and Dallas, established by the scion of a former Jardine Matheson and Company agent, was the leading landlord of saloon, brothel, and casino tenants. So too, various members of the SMC were investors in gambling operations like "Luna Park," a dog-racing stadium that took in over a million dollars per annum.[69]

In the neighboring French Concession, where a large percentage of Shanghai Americans also lived and worked during this interwar period, "law and order" was a contract negotiated between French officials and various Chinese gangs, most especially the "Green Gang" (Ch'ing pang). Illustrative of the blend of underworld and mainstream was Tu Yuesheng, one of what historian Brian Martin has called Chinese "compradores of violence," who rose to the fore to organize and mediate crime in the hybrid treaty port world.[70] In addition to his leading role in the Green Gang, Tu was at various times director of the Shanghai Stock Exchange, on the board of the Shanghai Bankers Association and the Bank of China, member of the Shanghai Chamber of Commerce and the French Municipal Council, as well as a philanthropist to many charities, including the Chinese branch of the Red Cross.[71] (Beginning in the early 1940s, Tu worked with American military and intelligence forces through the Sino-American Cooperation Organization (SACO) and the Office of Strategic Services (OSS), an arrangement calling for tacit U.S. protection of Tu's criminal activities in exchange for information.)[72]

So too, during these years, the Nationalist government, under the leadership of Chiang Kai-shek, also came to rely heavily on the proceeds of opium, prostitution, gambling, and arms trafficking. Through overlapping personal and political ties to the Green Gang, the Nationalists profited from Shanghai's role as a hub in worldwide narcotics traffic, a nexus which connected them indirectly to organized crime in the United States. The revenues from this trade allowed Kuomintang leaders "to wage war," and to "buy organization and influence."[73] Nationalist opium suppression efforts were largely an outgrowth of KMT leaders' own participation in the trade, and involved the manipulation of legal institutions and police power to undercut rivals, while imposing the harshest penalties on independent operators and poverty-stricken offenders.[74]

This, then, is the context required to understand cases such as *U.S. v. Edward Allen Carter*, where the impoverished vagabond son of an African-American missionary and a German mother was sentenced to ten months for stealing a bicycle worth about US$17.[75] The criminal docket of America's extraterritorial court in China must be studied within this larger setting of a semicolonial society oriented toward the world markets for narcotics and weapons.

Those who found themselves before the U.S. Court were generally not "kingpins," or the real movers and shakers in the world of commodified vice, but were instead typically freelance entrepreneurs operating unprotected by patrons in the underworld, the municipal government, or the local (foreign and Chinese) police. Those prosecuted for arms trafficking, for example, tended to be amateurs, such as John "Mal" Maloney, fined $50 for buying a few revolvers from a police informant.[76] Or, they were failed arms traffickers, such as Bert Hall, who participated in Nationalist bombing operations in the civil war, and received 2.5 years at McNeil's Island—not for that service but for obtaining about $10,000 by false presences in an arms deal with Northern warlord General Ho Chukuo. (Upon his return to California, Hall sued Douglas Aircraft Company for money owed him for facilitating the sale of 20 airplanes to the Nationalist government.)[77]

Imperial Loitering

By and large, adjudicating criminal cases in the USC-C meant dealing with those Americans who, for one reason or another, could not find a secure place in the treaty port socioeconomic complex. In other words, the very fact that they ended up at the mercy of the Court indicates not that they were the most egregious violators of law and morality, but that they were the most vulnerable.

Numerous Americans were brought before the Court by French, British, or Chinese municipal authorities on charges of operating gambling establishments, to take another example. These were typically fringe elements, unable to afford protection from police raids. Of course, this sort of selective prosecution was precisely what the casino operators who drove out the first Judge of the U.S. Court, Lebbeus Wilfley, had sought, i.e., the definition of "crime" as illegal activities undertaken outside of, and therefore not adding to the prosperity of, established channels and networks, themselves built upon narcotics, gambling, graft, influence-peddling, and malfeasance.

Beyond freelance entrepreneurs in vice and crime targeted by the justice system largely because they lacked powerful patrons, the U.S. Court's criminal docket gravitated around the usual pool of unfortunates and miscreants who tend to find themselves before the bench of any court as debtors, forgers, thieves, itinerant beggars, bar brawlers, murderers, or candidates for the asylum.[78] In the treaty port context, individuals tended to arrive at these destinations by one of two routes. Either they were on a downward spiral, if not from respectability, then at least from economic sufficiency; or, they were caught in a cycle of impoverishment, violence, and criminality that pushed them from one port to the next across America's Far Eastern frontier.

In the first instance, those on their way down tended to come from the lowest fringes of the professional and semiprofessional classes in the treaty ports who had lost their balance through a combination of circumstances. Some were doing well but sought to do better. ("Respectability" in Shanghai required, according to U.S. consular reports on the subject, membership in at least one club, a couple of Chinese servants ("boys"), a high entertainment budget, well-tailored clothes, and a commodious, advantageously situated living space.)[79] Representatives of this latter type included Eugene Hickey, a former employee of China Transport and Storage Company, and Harry Walsh, a one-time employee of the China National Air Service. The two were sentenced to just over one year in 1932 to McNeil's Island for a failed attempt to steal and sell $6,000 worth of famine-relief wheat destined for Hankow.[80]

Other treaty port Americans who fell into the criminal justice system as debtors, forgers, brawlers, and the like, typically had lost the job they had when they came out to East Asia, gone through a succession of positions, each more temporary and ill-paying than the last, used up their credit in the "chit"-based local economy, and finally turned to gambling, theft, check forging, or relatively small-scale arms and drug sales in hopes of recovering their status. In a society run by "the politics of gangsterism," they were well-suited grist for the wheels of justice, inasmuch as their lack of highly placed patrons made them noticeably and uniquely vulnerable. A typical example was Samuel Fair, repeatedly brought before the Court on vagrancy charges in the mid-1920s.[81] The offspring of an American soldier and a Romanian refugee, Fair spent fifteen years in China, and ended up a vagrant, deserted by his wife and children. First convicted in 1925, he spent time in jail, was returned to the United States, but was refused entry by immigration authorities and returned to Shanghai.

The structure of the treaty port labor market was such that there was no room for foreign nationals as artisans and craftsmen. The possibilities of low-paying manual work were practically precluded by the abundance of indigenous "coolies" and the pervasive racialized disdain for physical labor. To the extent that the foreign community had a middle class, it was dominated by Portuguese nationals, who had by the 1920s "become a race apart, with their own clubs and entertainments," comprising "Shanghai's bookkeepers, clerks, typists, cashiers, and secretaries, paid less than another white man but more than a Chinese."[82] The influx into China of Filipino nationals under U.S. auspices further narrowed opportunities for semiskilled foreign males in slots such as barkeepers, small import-export provenders, and so on.[83]

The lower ranks of the white-collar classes—bank tellers, clerks, semiprofessionals, and the like—were dominated by Chinese, either Western-educated or products of the compradorial apprentice system. Anti-imperialist urban nationalism was, in part, the upward pressure of these Chinese upon professions and positions of power long dominated by foreign nationals, such as lawyers, educators, and customs officials. In general, most foreign businesses relied primarily on Chinese personnel, who provided a cheaper source of labor, and were more adept in treaty port concepts and complexities. So too, unlike treaty port foreigners, Chinese employees were less likely to use extraterritorial courts to seek punitive damages and redress against their (foreign) employers for unpaid wages, excessive work demands, or wrongful discharge. These factors together created something of a structural siphon within treaty port society which carried individuals, in particular lower to lower-middle-class white males, from relative security into one of informal imperialism's various holding pens—jails, poorhouses, and pauper's cemeteries.

The other route to these same destinations was carved out by those who started out at the bottom and could never quite manage to break into the higher ranks. African-American William Fondell, before the Court uncountable times on charges of vagrancy and disorderly conduct, was one such individual, as was C. S. Sully, "Vagabond King of the Pacific," an educated man from Pittsburgh condemned to wandering by drug addiction.[84] Typically, vagrancy escalated to petty theft, and then to assault, and more serious crimes, as in the instance of Ray Pietzold, persistent beggar and loiterer, eventually jailed for killing a Chinese rickshaw puller.[85]

A sizable number of these migratory empire-builders were successful in the treaty ports as brothel, saloon, and restaurant keepers, lawyers, and real estate speculators. Typical in many respects was the multimillionaire Frank Jay Raven, who came to Shanghai in 1904 as a penniless engineer, and found prosperity through a silent partnership in a British real estate firm, and an advantageous marriage into a wealthy American missionary family. In early 1935, Raven was featured by *Fortune* magazine as a "modern American taipan" with the "Midas touch," by then worth about $70 million, and the prime mover of Asia Realty, the American Oriental Banking Corporation, and the Raven Trust, all companies with a substantial missionary, professional, and Chinese clientele. (Raven's point man in Washington, D.C., was J. H. "Tientsin" Brown, one-time owner of the Alhambra resort, who had since gone into partnership with former U.S. Court for China District Attorney C. P. Holcomb, doing business as "China Trade Act Services.")[86] Less fabulously wealthy than Raven, but illustratively successful in their own right, were Edith Wolfe and Dorothy Grant, Shanghai American prostitutes, who had arrived in the port around 1905, been temporarily inconvenienced by "Wilfley's Purge" in 1907, and by 1930 had become brothel owner-managers on the Kiangse Road "line."[87]

In general, then, many of Shanghai's most prosperous Americans in the 1930s had come to that status via shady pasts in Hawaii, Manila, and China itself, and a good number of them had been the principal targets of first Judge of the Court Lebbeus Wilfley's campaign against vice. It was primarily in the interest of these now affluent and, in some cases "respectable," treaty port Americans that the U.S. Court functioned during most of its last two decades, as a collector of rents, enforcer of contracts, assessor of debts, and custodian of impoverished riffraff. As the mundaneness of most of its cases suggest, the Court enabled mainstream treaty port Americans to live ordinary lives in extraordinary circumstances.

STRUCTURAL AND PHILOSOPHICAL SHIFTS

Judge Lobingier's indefatigable efforts from 1914 to 1924 to give law its due majesty—to fuse authority, power, and pomp into an amalgam of legitimacy—had paradoxically made the U.S. Court ever more "a rich man's court," as a leading local American attorney observed. High fees, large deposit requirements in civil suits, the near absolute necessity for an attorney to help one through the maze, and the unlikelihood of collecting full judgments from savvy defendants—all of these things limited Chinese access to and participation in the U.S. Court.[88] As the Peking Legation reported home in 1924, ordinary Chinese by and large continued to prefer the rough justice of consular executive action over the formal, public, costly, and disembodied justice of the Court.[89] Proposals to make the Court more accessible to ordinary Chinese—a 1928 bill that would have required a Chinese representative to sit with the Judge of the U.S. Court in all matters involving Chinese parties, for example—were firmly rejected by the State Department as unlikely to convince Chinese that the Court was any less "the agent of oppressive imperialism than it now appears to [them to] be," given that "the real root of opposition is the existence of [such] courts at all."[90]

Ultimately, though, the Progressivist vision of the Court was dealt its fatal blow in 1933, when an Executive Order transferred the Court from State to Justice Department auspices. The shift to Justice Department purview ended the Court's role as—in State Department language—"a part of the machinery for conducting the foreign relations of the United States," and "indirectly an agency of the Government of China." The treaty ports became simply a distant hinterland of the American criminal justice system, to be tended only insofar as its denizens posed a threat to the domestic peace and security of the continental United States.

Concomitantly, the U.S. Justice Department became part of Shanghai colonial police surveillance efforts in the areas of political subversion, arms dealing, the "white slave trade," and opium trafficking; U.S. Court officials both tapped into, and added to, the growing data base on "suspicious" individuals and groups. Court and consular officials were both alert to political "undesirables," but the USC-C was effectively constrained from using "justice" as a State Department cipher. Although it has been said that "The law is simply expediency wearing a long white dress," human experience suggests something more complicated.[91]

The Court's dilemma was demonstrated most clearly in the widely covered story of two Americans, Carl Lemcke and Eugene Brinson, brought before Judge Helmick for helping to rescue a communist spy (Mr. X) from a 15-year sentence in an Wuchang prison. Lemcke was acquitted; Brinson was fined $500, and given a suspended six-month sentence. Both were subjected to a (toothless) lecture from the bench:

> It must be thoroughly understood that American citizens in China
> are to engage in legitimate occupations and pursuits, and no one
> must be allowed to think that China is a fair field for American
> ventures, or that Americans can with impunity concern them-
> selves—in an illegitimate fashion—with the affairs of the Chinese
> government or any other government.[92]

In the late 1920s and early 1930s, the issue arose as to whether the USC-C could be used to discipline or silence anti-KMT sentiment and activities among Americans. When the U.S. Legation explained to the Nationalist government that it could not deport American journalists for critical coverage, the former discussed bringing libel charges against American employees of the *North China Daily News*, the *New York Times*, and other papers. The *Times* threatened to fight any such case, and when Chinese authorities moved further to refuse postal service to the foreign press in China, the State Department rediscovered the First Amendment. When Chinese officials in Shanghai asked the district attorney to pursue Harold Isaacs and the *China Forum* for allegedly pro-communist activities, he declined; but, agreeing that Isaacs's activities tended to "embarrass our Government," he seconded the consulate's plan "to inform Isaacs that our Government would not accord him protection should the Chinese authorities take steps to curtail his activities."

The 1904 Supreme Court precedent *Dorr and O'Brien v. U.S.*, one of the "insular cases" discussed earlier, had held that the First Amendment did not apply to Americans in the Philippines, sanctioning the conviction of two U.S. newspaper men on charges of libel against a member of the Philippine Commission.[93] In 1917, the State Department had been able to intimidate Gilbert Reid, the reverend-turned-journalist accused of seditious libel, into leaving China. However, by this later date, such censorship was less easily accomplished. The *New York Times* told its readers that "for the first time in the history of Sino-American relations the United States Government is threatening to withdraw the protection of extraterritorial rights from an American citizen, leaving him to trial in the Chinese courts."[94]

Although forced to retreat, the Shanghai Consulate and Peking Legation henceforth remained watchful toward the operations of "anti-KMT" journals and groups using American extrality as a shield. The State Department staked out "a distinction between diplomatic protection which may be granted or withheld at the discretion of the President and the treaty rights of extraterritoriality to which American nationals have a legal claim."[95] The Shanghai Consulate thus acquiesced to Nationalist moves to shut down pesky newspapers through postal regulations. The Eastern Publishing Company had its consular registration yanked on the ground that its operations were not "in any way . . . advancing American interests or prestige in China," and seemed "calculated to foment discord and to disseminate propaganda prejudicial to peace and good order and to friendly relations between peoples and governments with which the American Government and people are at peace."[96]

POLITICS, PENNY-PINCHING, AND "GOVERNMENTALITY"

For Americans, bureaucratic ambitions toward far-reaching control and discipline were consistently thwarted, not merely by constitutional and philosophical considerations, but by competing priorities over limited resources. For example, in the early 1930s the American jail in Shanghai was closed down as part of a larger financial retrenchment of U.S. offices overseas, thereby further contributing to the Court's general leniency toward criminals it could not afford to send home and could not accommodate locally. The most concrete constraint on the official impulse to use the extraterritorial legal system punitively was a financial one. The decision to incarcerate, deport, or institutionalize an individual typically came down to a question of how best to allocate persistently inadequate official funds and private charity.[97] The legal system among Americans in China, though an extension of the U.S. federal judiciary, did not have ready and unlimited access to the larger infrastructure of the home society, which by the 1930s came to include a minimum wage, workmen's compensation, state hospitals and asylums, social security, and so on. In Shanghai, there was an American community chest contributed to by subscription, and the U.S. Shipping Board helped to find outbound passage for vagrants and petty criminals.

The swift finality of justice was slowed in the treaty port setting, as a combination of forces edged penalties in the direction of leniency and laxity toward the lower ranks. First, there was a solidarity among all foreigners vis-à-vis Chinese, generally expressed in racialized terms. As a contemporary American magazine observed in the early 1930s: "Shanghailanders' incomes vary from the hundreds down to stenographic salaries, but . . . the distinction between taipan and wage earner, old family and upstart, is lost in the glaring fact of their common race."[98] As indicated in earlier chapters, this apparent racial solidarity was in constant tension with class ties, and required constant behavioral policing. This policing was not uniformly translated into harsh justice, as in the 1926 insanity inquest before the U.S. Court of one William Fondell, an African-American vagrant long resident in East Asia. Fondell was adjudged sane when the Court was convinced by his lawyer's argument that "Fondell was typical of those found in the Southern sections of the United states."[99]

THE RAVEN CLIQUE

Early in the summer of 1935, the multimillionaire Frank Jay Raven became part of the treaty port flotsam that moved through the U.S. Court. As the "American Girl" was the totemic device generated at the turn of the century to federalize extrality, Raven came to signify the end of an era in Sino-American relations. In late May of that year, Raven closed the American Oriental Banking Corporation (AOBC), the American Oriental Finance Corporation (AOFC), and Raven Trust, claiming that to continue operations in the midst of the worldwide depression would lead inevitably to total bankruptcy. Although at the time Raven assured the public that the demands of creditors and stockholders could still be fully met, several weeks later court-appointed liquidators announced that the "Raven Group," purportedly worth $70 million, had only about $17,500 in redeemable assets. Over the course of the next eight months, it was revealed in lurid detail that all of the companies had been bankrupt since at least 1932, and that Raven had first looted them, and then lost every dollar subsequently entrusted to those various firms gambling on the New York Stock Exchange.[100]

For those who knew him or of him, whether or not they were among the thousands of his now pauperized treaty port clients, the question of the day was how this church-going, teetotaling pillar of the community and one-time member of the Shanghai Municipal Council could have been so duplicitous. For historians, though, the more urgent question is how Raven ended up before the U.S. Court on felony charges, given that in the treaty port setting, it was political, economic, and social vulnerability, rather than criminality alone, that put an individual on the wrong side of the law.

The creation and continued survival of Frank Raven's multicorporation empire had depended upon the structures, privileges, and mores of unequal treaty imperialism in China, as well as upon America's continued support of that system. Raven and his various enterprises had emerged, thrived, and prospered by virtue of the unique benefits afforded by Shanghai's advantageous location in the intersection of world, regional and national trade routes, as well as by the legal loopholes opened up by extrality. The venture capital for the Raven Group came from the Shanghai real estate market, as did a large percentage of its later profits (through Asia Realty).[101] This market was built largely upon the past and current proceeds of imperialism, opium, gambling, prostitution, and more legitimate endeavors. Inflated land prices, in turn, depended upon the physical and legal security afforded residents by extraterritoriality and foreign gunboats, a security which increased in value with each new wave of violence and chaos in China at large.[102]

Though a partner in the treaty port system from the start, the United States historically held itself up as a "special friend" of China. Many Americans in China clung to the belief that their missions, schools, hospitals, and cultural institutes there somehow transcended imperialism, and stood apart from the unequal treaties, warships, and usurious loans that underwrote the creation and continued survival of these various eleemosynary enterprises. Throughout the 1930s, as noted earlier, missionary groups urged an end to extrality and the revision of U.S.-China treaties, realizing as they did that their good works would be for naught in the post-May Fourth era so long as these legacies of an earlier century's diplomacy held.

Yet, while they were waiting for their officials in Washington to do right by the Chinese, these missionaries and their secular counterparts invested much of their own and their organizations' funds with those like Frank Jay Raven. This prominent treaty port "die-hard" was entrenched in the much condemned "Shanghai mind" that could not imagine life without treaty-sanctioned privileges.[103] Raven's marriage to the daughter of a missionary, and the fact that his second-in-command had first come to China (in 1918) as an auditor for the Presbyterian Mission in South China, brought the Raven Group a sizable missionary clientele, and a number of missionaries were on the boards of Raven companies. The collapse of Raven enterprises thus meant an estimated $5 million loss to missionary corporate interests, including $1,200,000 in now worthless IOU's issued to such groups by Asia Realty. Contemporary reports compared the impact on missionary assets to that of the Japanese occupation of Manchuria a few years earlier.[104]

Though there were reputable and disreputable denizens of "Greater Shanghai," there was, then, no tenable moral distinction between one dollar and the next in the treaty port economy. Shanghai had become a boom town at the turn of the century as those grown rich on the opium trade bought up land there, and in turn invested their profits as landlords and speculators in banks, which then loaned that money to local businessmen, both foreign and indigenous, who then paid employees, suppliers, and so on, and so on.[105] The implications of this process became clear to liquidators when they began collecting from companies and individuals in debt to the AOBC, AOFC, or Asia Realty. Given the inextricable entanglements of the treaty port socioeconomic complex, pressing (commercial) debtors to pay (missionary) creditors began to bring down carpet factories, auto dealers, silk markets, Chinese banks, and so on, and so on.

The ambivalence, inconsistencies, and contradictions of U.S. policy in China had long provided fertile ground for Raven and his investments, many of which had always straddled the margins of legality. Thwarted in 1917 by Judge Charles Lobingier's rigorous enforcement of a U.S. law forbidding American banks with no offices in the continental United States from operating abroad, Raven had then turned to a Connecticut incorporation law with a loophole large enough to enable him to establish the American Oriental Banking Corporation, headquartered in Shanghai and operating solely outside of U.S. territorial limits but under American extraterritoriality in China.[106]

The possibility that the U.S. Court might exercise a restraining influence on his subsequent illegal diversification into stock speculation was preempted by the successful crusade, led by Raven's attorney, to drive Judge Lobingier from the bench. In this sense, Raven benefited from the persistent unwillingness of State Department officials and their executive branch superiors to spend political capital protecting the U.S. Court for China from its treaty port foes. Practically abandoned by Washington, the Court had been forced to reach an accommodation with Shanghai Americans, and ally with local vested interests. (One visible measure of the extent to which this had occurred by the 1930s was the fact that, upon his retirement from the bench in 1934, fourth Judge of the Court Milton Purdy did not simply remain in Shanghai, as noted earlier, but also accepted a seat on the board of directors of a Raven-owned concern.)[107]

So too, although several of the corporate components of the Raven Group were China Trade Act companies, and thus open to inspection by a federal agent resident in Shanghai, close scrutiny was evidently lacking. It did not take the liquidators long to discover what any rigorous inspector could have found years earlier, i.e., that most of the "assets" listed in various annual reports were nothing more than unsecured loans made to other Raven-owned enterprises, to Raven himself, and to other corporate officers along with their wives and close friends.

The shift to Justice Department auspices in 1933–1934 meant that when Raven asked the U.S. Court to liquidate his financial empire in late May 1935, the presiding Judge stood apart from State Department formal and informal controls.[108] Though U.S. Minister to China Nelson Johnson met with Helmick about the case, ultimately the Judge was responsible to an entirely different arm of the federal government, and could proceed without fear of the diplomatic repercussions of justice. This latitude may help to explain how Helmick was able to withstand what contemporary accounts described as the enormous pressure exerted on him by Raven and other unnamed locals to appoint a Raven crony as liquidator, who could then be trusted to cover up corporate misdeeds. Instead, refusing to be bulldozed, Helmick appointed Frank Hough, of R.C.A. Victor Company, who had only recently returned to China after a decade in South America. Still, Chinese scholars have subsequently argued that the delay in the process was deliberate, that it enabled Raven to hide his remaining wealth, and that Raven's brief prison sentence in the United States sheltered the banker from Chinese litigants.[109]

In terms of Sino-American relations, the Raven collapse and subsequent revelations about his long abuse of extrality virtually guaranteed "impaired" commercial ties between the two countries, concluded the *New York Times*, adding on a more positive note that the debacle also "mark[ed] the end of careless, unsupervised and unscrupulous American business methods in China."[110] Net Chinese losses were estimated at $6 million, with over one thousand individuals and firms affected.[111] The AOBC's collapse ignited a run on local Chinese banks, in turn leading to the closure, in June 1935, of the National Industrial Bank of China, the Ningpo Commercial and Savings Bank, and the Commercial Bank of China. Nationalist officials met with U.S. Minister Johnson, appointed a prominent Shanghai Chinese attorney to represent Chinese interests, demanded that foreign banks be made liable to newly enacted regulations for their indigenous counterparts, and undertook a series of moves bringing Chinese-owned banks more firmly under the authority of the central government.[112]

Raven as an Object Lesson

The whole affair was, contemporary financial analysts concluded, "the most severe blow to American business prestige in the Far East since the beginning of Chinese-American business relations."[113] And yet, scandal aside, Raven's demise was a boon to both the United States and China, that is to say, to certain groups within those larger aggregates. Just as the rise of the Raven empire came by virtue of the expansion of foreign privilege and power in China, so too did its collapse mark a dramatic signpost in the shift within informal imperialism to more subtle forms of domination in the face of Chinese nationalism and the KMT's continuing crisis of legitimacy. Just as the Progressive "open-door constituency" and late Ch'ing officials had shared overlapping interests in the taming of American treaty port predators at the turn of the century, so too did the agendas of the "New Deal coalition" and the Kuomintang intersect in the liquidation of the Sino-foreign capitalist oligarchy entrenched in the structures of unequal treaty imperialism. Both governments sought to "officialize" all Sino-American relations, bringing the treaty port "frontier" under central, bureaucratic control.[114]

On the Chinese side, the Raven banking crisis abetted the KMT's campaign to gain control of the anomalous, energetic treaty ports, and assert effective "state authority over 'foreign relations,' in both the international and domestic sense of the term." The real battle centered in Shanghai, some 280 kilometers from the nationalist capital of Nanking. "Shanghai. . . was the place where the separation of state and society in China had gone furthest, where society was best secured against the state's onslaught." It "thus became a pole, even a vital nerve center," for contending visions of China's modernity.[115]

The collapse of the Raven Group and affiliated concerns provided the Kuomintang a convenient pretext for escalating their already ongoing effort to bring Shanghai capitalists, and their myriad assets, under government control. The government takeover of various banks in June, just weeks after the Raven collapse, followed upon "the banking coup of March 1935" by top Nationalist officials (led by H. H. Kung and T. V. Soong), seeking to subordinate the treaty ports' financial infrastructure to their personal and political needs.[116] The three banks affected in June had already been targeted for government takeover but were able to resist those pressures, that is, until the collapse of the American Oriental Banking Corporation precipitated a run on them, in turn leaving them insolvent and unable to redeem the enormous quantity of stockpiled creditor's notes suddenly presented to them by several Shanghai banks already controlled by Nanking.[117]

While the KMT had to take an activist approach, and readily turned to extortion, kidnapping, assassination and organized crime, for the U.S. government the process was less conscious and less explicit. It was more a matter of *not* doing certain things on behalf of the approximately 10,500 (known) Americans in China, or—and this was more often the case—of simply putting other constituencies in line ahead of treaty port Americans in the policy process. In fact, what made well-off treaty port Americans so vulnerable in the late 1930s was the priority in American politics of internal needs over the livelihood of distant countrymen. This hierarchy of needs was especially clear in the 1934 U.S. Silver Purchase Act. It pleased certain domestic pressure groups, but drew world silver supplies into the United States by draining places such as Shanghai, bringing higher interests rates there, lower exchange rates, the collapse of the local Shanghai real estate market, the undoing of Frank Jay Raven's paper empire, and the demise of America's treaty port taipans.[118]

In Shanghai, although treaty port locals suffered mightily from

Raven's demise, having staked their fortunes on the perpetuation of nineteenth-century imperialism, the toppling of America's own treaty port "taipans" within the Sino-foreign oligarchy ruling Shanghai cleared the way for U.S. financial syndicates, multinational corporations and export manufacturers more interested in doing business *with* China than *in* China.[119] The Court-appointed liquidator found ultimately that "there was little about the American Oriental Banking Corporation that was *American* except the name and the fact that Raven happened to be an American citizen.[120] Further, as one astute contemporary observed: "It has only been in the fields of strictly 'local' enterprises that disaster has come," inasmuch as the interests of treaty port middlemen were not synonymous with those of American domestic producers and investors, and U.S. China policy was not equivalent to the property interests of Shanghai Americans.[121]

Individual ethical lapses aside, what transformed Frank Raven into an undesirable beachcombing adventurer in the eyes of his government were the continuing, though not always intentional, efforts by his home government to jettison him and what he represented from America's international portfolio. As President Franklin Delano Roosevelt warned so succinctly in 1937, after the Japanese takeover of Shanghai, Americans who opted to stay in China did so at their own risk.[122] A mass evacuation of Westerners from Shanghai, and from China more generally, occurred over the period 1937–41, with Japan's assault on, and occupation of, coastal China. The Nationalists' flight inland (eventually to Chungking [Chongqing]) paved the way for a Japanese puppet regime in Nanking. Extrality, and the non-Japanese controlled areas of Shanghai, gave shelter to anti-Japanese Chinese resistance groups, and war profiteers of various nationalities; at the same time; Japanese and their collaborators profited from the revenues of vice in the "badlands," a zone of unclear jurisdiction between the International Settlement, the Chinese sector, and the French Concession.[123]

The U.S. Court for China was effectively shut down on 8 December 1941. In the aftermath of the bombing of Pearl Harbor, Japanese forces took control of Shanghai; they closed the USC-C and temporarily interned Judge Milton Helmick. Not long after Helmick's safe return to the U.S., the Justice Department was asked to handle an extraterritorial case in China involving an American Army sergeant charged with killing a fellow serviceman over a poker game. Unwilling to send the Judge back in the China theater, and more generally finding extrality a bureaucratic nightmare, the Justice Department pushed President Roosevelt to abolish "extraterritorial jurisdiction rather promptly."[124]

In 1943, after a decade and a half of piecemeal concessions, and looking for a low-cost, low-risk way of boosting the morale of Chiang Kai-shek's Nationalist government, then in a two-front war against Japanese aggression and indigenous communism, the U.S. and Great Britain abrogated their unequal treaty privileges, ending a century of American extraterritoriality in China. Indeed, by that late date, very little beyond vacated extraterritorial courts remained of the multi-national informal empire staked out in late imperial China.

E P I L O G U E

SOJOURNING AMERICANS IN
THE AGE OF EMPIRE

*In former daies we were under the pleasing sound of
priviledges and Immunities. . . . Now those things are
vanish and forgotten. All the care now is, to pare us
close, and keep us low.*   Edward Littleton, 1689[1]

Americans returned to post-World War II China in significant numbers, bringing political, cultural, and commercial expectations not so
different from turn-of-the-century Progressives. By 1947, there were
about 152 American business concerns and 4,000 U.S. nationals centered in Shanghai. The Chamber of Commerce, as well as American
clubs and schools, were reestablished with surprising speed, and the
effort to propagate the American vision was facilitated by the arrival of
the U.S. Information Service.

These Americans expected to assume the preeminent position long
held by Great Britain, but to supplant treaty port imperialism with a
"cosmopolitan, 'Open Door' community" fully embracing like-minded
Chinese. In this respect, they echoed the hopes of post-World War I
American newcomers to urban China, described in earlier chapters.[2]

In place of extrality were various status-of-forces agreements remov-
ing U.S. military personnel from native jurisdiction. Thus, repeated
clashes—ranging from auto accidents to rape—between military personnel and locals kept alive Chinese bitterness over extrality. By 1948,
U.S. officials were advising evacuation by local Americans. Chiang Kai-
shek's Nationalist regime provided further incentives to leave when it

enacted import and currency requirements as well as subsidies to firms owned by KMT officials and supporters.

After the Nationalist retreat to Taiwan in 1949, remaining American companies—including Shanghai Telephone, Standard Vacuum Oil, Chase National Bank, and Shanghai Power—were caught in the Truman administration's shifting and inconsistent policies toward the victorious Chinese Communist Party (CCP). Shanghai Power, vital to local survival, was initially given a U.S. government promise of support, protection, and a workable evacuation plan, provided it continued its operations. Washington hoped the firm would serve as a "toehold" and diplomatic lever in the Communist-dominated city.[3] However, with the withdrawal of the U.S. Navy, and continued bombing by Nationalist forces from Taiwan, Shanghai Power fell under CCP control, as did all American properties.[4]

Collective memories of colonial legal privileges and resultant injustices continued to roil U.S. relations with Asian allies, Japan and Taiwan in particular. Status-of-forces agreements had to be defended and amended in response to explosive incidents involving American military personnel accused of crimes against locals. In 1957, a mob of 6,000 attacked and destroyed the U.S. Embassy and U.S. Information Agency in Taipei after a military tribunal acquitted an American sergeant of manslaughter in the death of a Chinese "peeping Tom." That same year, the U.S. Supreme Court approved the turnover to Japanese jurisdiction of an American soldier accused of killing a local woman who was scavenging metal on the firing range.[5]

Officials understood the galvanizing role of history in these incidents, acknowledging that when the military tried its own, this was "a procedure reminiscent of the hated extraterritoriality of the past." Cases could be "exploited by hostile groups to arouse opposition both at home and abroad against" alliance with the United States.[6] As late as 1979, U.S. sources noted that the Iranian clergy had persuasively portrayed certain provisions of a 1964 agreement between the shah and America as no different than the "capitulations" so long enjoyed by colonial oppressors.[7]

A NEW IMPERIAL CITIZENSHIP

As the United States took on the characteristics, burdens, and benefits of a superpower, questions about the status of sojourning citizens came ever more to the fore. Congress and the executive branch moved full force to limit individual freedoms in the interest of national security. In contrast, the Supreme Court's cold war stance was, as Louis Henkin observes, to favor "national security" when adjudicating relations among federal government branches, but to construe "national security" narrowly when adjudicating relations between the individual citizen and the central government.[8]

For example, the State Department moved in the 1950s to deny passports to members or supporters of "the Communist movement." Refusal followed when the Secretary judged that an applicant's activities abroad would violate U.S. law, prejudice American interests, or disrupt the orderly conduct of foreign relations.[9] These executive branch initiatives were thwarted by the Supreme Court, which ruled in 1958 that travel was a constitutionally protected right, not to be limited without due process. There might, the Court thought, be valid reasons for denial, but the applicant must be told what they were and be permitted a defense. In 1965, the Justices determined that the only restrictions permitted were those due to "foreign policy considerations affecting all citizens."[10]

Further, in the late 1950s, the Court narrowed military jurisdiction over dependents and civilians on U.S. bases abroad, in the companion decisions *Reid v. Covert* and *Kinsella v. Krueger*. Both cases involved wives of U.S. servicemen found guilty by courts martial of killing their husbands, one in Japan, the other in England. Reversing a decision made a year earlier in these same cases, the Court's majority held that "When the Government reaches out to punish a citizen who is abroad, the shield which the Bill of Rights and other parts of the Constitution provided to protect his life and liberty should not be stripped away just because he happens to be in another land." The Court ruled further that the benefits received by the wives of servicemen, such as quarters, food subsidies, and protection, could not exact as their price the loss of basic rights guaranteed by the Constitution.[11]

The 1955 decision in *Toth v. Quarles* stipulated that ex-servicemen could not be tried by court martial for crimes committed while in the armed forces, at home or abroad.[12] A 1960 decision extended *Covert* to noncapital crimes (in this instance, unpremeditated murder).[13] That year the Court also imposed the same due process requirements in the prosecution of civilian employees of the armed forces abroad. Predictably, the Defense Department was fearful about the implications of these decisions for policing the approximately 265,000 dependents and 142,000 civilian employees then comprising the U.S. military establishment abroad.

The principal casualty of *Covert* was the 1891 Court decision in *U.S. v. Ross*, that the Constitution did not follow the flag, the precedent that had served as the linchpin of American consular jurisdiction in China. The Warren Court now condemned as a "dangerous doctrine" the position that foreign policy exigencies justified abbreviated due process. Indeed, the Court's liberal individualism echoed the rhetoric of pre-World War II treaty port sojourners. "The consular power approved in the *Ross* case was about as extreme and absolute as that of the potentates of the 'non-Christian' countries to which the statutes applied," noted one Justice. Paraphrasing Gilded Age congressional opponents of extraterritoriality, the Court argued: "If our foreign commitments become of such nature that the Government can no longer satisfactorily operate within the bounds laid down by the Constitution," it becomes time to rethink those commitments.

The United States now uniformly uses a "global due process" approach, or the "reasonableness doctrine," to cases of sojourning U.S. nationals caught up in criminal justice systems abroad.[14] According to the authoritative *Restatement (Third) of Foreign Relations Law* (1986): although "[t]erritoriality and nationality remain the principal bases of jurisdiction to prescribe," in dealing with individual cases "rigid concepts have been replaced by broader criteria embracing principles of reasonableness and fairness to accommodate overlapping or conflicting interests of states, and affected private interests." Increasingly, it is a "search for the 'center of gravity' of a given situation" that courts and decision makers seek, endeavoring to balance competing interests and claims.[15]

EXTRALITY REVISITED

"Extraterritoriality" has remained a problematic jurisdictional space in the American polity in two distinct areas. In the first, the courts have consistently rejected plaintiffs' efforts to apply domestic legislation, such as environmental standards and worker protections, to the operations of American companies abroad. In the second, high court decisions now bind the U.S. government to full constitutional due process restrictions whenever and wherever it acts against U.S. nationals.[16] Indeed, in a 1990 case involving "search and seizure" violations by American officials in Mexico against a Mexican national who is also a U.S. registered alien, the Court applied the logic of *Reid v. Covert*: the "government may act only as the Constitution authorizes, whether the actions in questions are foreign or domestic."[17] The rejection of *Ross* by the Warren Court has thus culminated in a rough consensus, not without critics, that in criminal cases it is not the nationality of the target that triggers constitutional safeguards; it is the status of those in pursuit as U.S. government and police personnel.

Reid v. Covert, and later cases expanding the liberal Warren Court's doctrine of sojourners' rights, resonates with the view espoused by many Shanghai Americans—respectable and riff raff alike. Those on the receiving end of the state's embrace expressed—with varying levels of eloquence—the view that the State Department had failed to master what constitutional scholars term the "paradox of unconstitutional conditions": the U.S. government may confer or withhold rights and benefits, but may not stipulate conditions in the transaction that waive or void constitutional rights.[18] The overthrow of the *Ross* regime, and the demise of the nineteenth-century world of the territorial nation state, illuminate an era in the genealogy of the American federal state. Extrality considered as a citizenship regime reveals that state as an "open-ended constellation of authoritative exercises of jurisdiction over individuals and institutions across the world."[19]

In the international system more generally, in the last several decades many governments have reached into alien settings to lay hold of alleged terrorists and drug traffickers. The justification used for transgressions of sovereignty is the nationality, not of the offenders, but of the victims.[20] Governments' assertion of legal authority over their own nationals for acts committed abroad has come in response to the post-cold war rise of "sex tourism" in Asia. In 1995, Great Britain joined the United States, Australia, Germany, Sweden, France, Belgium, Norway, Canada, and New Zealand, by enacting an extraterritorial "sexual offenses" act to allow prosecution of pedophiles who travel abroad and systematically victimize children.[21] The justification in such instances is not the alleged incompetence of courts in the country where offenses occur, but the very likely probability that offenders will, to quote the nineteenth-century voices heard in chapter 1, "escape every responsibility for foul deeds committed abroad."

EPILOGUE

Dual Nationality and Changing Citizenship Regimes

America's two-hundred-year-long prohibition against dual nationality
was also a victim of 1960s liberalism, and has been given what seems the
deathblow by post-cold war developments. As late as 1958, the Supreme
Court affirmed earlier precedents calling for automatic expatriation in
instances where a U.S. citizen swore allegiance to a foreign sovereign,
served in a foreign military, or voted abroad. In 1967, the shift began.[22]
Since that time, all Americans have had the right to claim nationality in
a foreign country without jeopardizing their U.S. citizenship if the laws
of that country permit it and they qualify.[23]

Supreme Court decisions since the 1960s have gradually blocked the
power of the federal government to expatriate any citizen on the basis of
the latter's actions, behavior, or circumstances—at home or abroad. The
burden of proof is now on the government to prove clear intent on the
part of an individual to leave off his or her U.S. nationality.[24] Naturalization regulations still require applicants to forswear allegiance to all
other sovereigns; this has been so since 1795. However, it is not now
enforced. Fiscal and practical constraints help to explain this laxity.
Added to this, there is also substantial support for these developments
among liberal activists and Democratic Party leaders in search of likely
votes. U.S. relations with allies have been complicated in recent years by
controversies over dual nationality and extradition. Several native U.S.
citizens have found sanctuary from the legal process by claiming Israeli
citizenship through one or both parents.[25]

Dual nationality has emerged as a potent economic development
strategy for certain "sender" countries in Latin America, Asia, and
Africa.[26] These states seek the money and skills of expatriates, as well as
the electoral power of overseas communities in "host" areas such as the
United States. Dual nationality, by which individuals retain all rights of
their original birth except suffrage, provides a formula for tapping into
the wealth and know-how of expatriates, while at the same time limit-
ing their ability to exercise unwelcome control in the political system
back home. Vietnam has offered inducements to the approximately 2.5
million Vietnamese living in Thailand, Laos, Cambodia, China, and the
United States, in the form of allowing them to pay local prices for rail,
road, river, or air transport.[27] In 1991, Colombia passed laws giving emigrants the right to retain their nationality even if they acquired citizen-

ship elsewhere; this contributed to a doubling in the number of Colombians who became U.S. citizens.[28]

The end of the East-West bipolarity of the cold war era has occasioned an even more wide-ranging rethinking of the allegiance-for-protection exchange animating citizenship.[29] Successive waves of regime collapse, state implosion, and territorial realignment have left in their wake large groups of individuals with unclear citizenship and contested nationality. For example, the reunification of East and West Germany inflamed simmering issues about the status of long-term resident aliens, particularly Turkish "guest workers." The sheer magnitude of the problem was unprecedented, owing to the country's policy of taking in large numbers of refugees from the former Soviet bloc (an effort to make amends for Nazi-era atrocities), and the economic distress of the reincorporated population. Individuals able to document even a drop of "German blood" qualified for full citizenship, while resident aliens born in Germany found only locked doors.[30]

Ongoing shifts in internal citizenship contracts have, in turn, begun to force nations to rewrite the rules of the game as regards dual citizenship, expatriation, extraterritorial jurisdiction, comity, extradition, and diplomatic protection. For example, certainly by World War II contemporaries believed they had laid to rest the vexing issue of whether emigrants who take on a new citizenship abroad still owe civic obligations—such as military service—to the country of origin. The first run at the question came in the American Revolution, and the second, in the Anglo-American War of 1812. In the 1860s, the "Bancroft Treaties" eased the problem by providing for mutual acceptance of naturalization after a certain period of residence. Renewed conflict came from German and Italian efforts in the 1920s and 1930s to lay claim to the military services of "their" original nationals wherever they may have roamed. World War II having mooted the issue, it is now a telling sign of the times to see headlines in the late 1990s such as: "Tourist Hoping Holiday Won't Include Army Duty" or "French Relent Over Briton Seized for National Service."[31]

Concurrent globalization, regionalization, and fragmentation bring into doubt the long-term survival of the nation-state itself as the primary organizing unit of world affairs and individual identity. Although the end of the nation-state is projected, there is broad agreement among observers that it will not wither away with any great haste. Still, states—

like everybody else in the New World Order—must prove their worth and compete in the much-heralded global marketplace, with "multiple subnational and cross-national group loyalties."[32] As Jean-Marie Guehenno remarks in his *The End of the Nation State* (1995), "sovereignty and territory ... remain key features of the international system. But they have been reconstituted and partly displaced onto other institutional arenas outside the state and outside the framework of nationalized territory."[33]

As the day-to-day implications are still not immediately apparent, commentators continue to struggle with the question, "Is dual citizenship bad?"[34] In the United States., where size and diversity will give dual citizenship or denationalized citizenship greatest impact, reactions have generally been fearful.[35] To paraphrase popular columnist Georgie Anne Geyer: By clarifying loyalty, citizenship gives "isolated human beings the knowledge of where they belong—and why." Dual nationality, being a "breakdown of fealty," introduces into the lifeblood of the nation "a kind of dangerous civic polygamy."[36] The "death of citizenship" in the United States has, Geyer adds, "fostered the idea that America is no more than one big job market and shopping mall."[37]

Proponents of rigorous immigration control and revitalized civic obligations warn: "At some point, you start looking like Rome, with an influx of alien hordes who never get on board."[38] Even those to the left of this position are not ready to let go of nation-based citizenship, in some instances for the very good reason that, to quote Michael Walzer: "To tear down the walls of the state is not ... to create a world without walls, but rather to create a thousand petty fortresses."[39]

The speed and magnitude of change rightly inspire fear and excitement that the world could be remade on new specifications and improved sensibilities. Yasmin Soysal has invoked the image of a "postnational" model in which rights are no longer dependent on citizenship status.[40] New York City Councilman Guillermo Linares, the first Dominican American elected to political office in the United States, has been quoted as saying that the demand for dual citizenship "reflects a universal blurring of boundaries that is new and unique to this era, a prelude to a world of regions as well as nations, 'a transition to something else that we can't begin to define.' "[41] Still others have characterized the increase in dual citizenship as the "vanguard of ... new notions of community and society." Less effusively, Ronald Steel has wondered whether the "world of the twenty-first century [is] one without borders, without flags and heroes, and without loyalties."[42]

Individuals are increasingly linked by connections that transcend the nation and, in fact, run counter to national citizenship. To quote Saskia Sassen, "The relationship of the citizens to the body politic is in competition with the infinity of connections they establish outside it."[43] The significance of territory and geography in the allegiance-for-protection bargain between state and citizen is in flux, irrevocably altered by post-cold war developments. We now speak of sojourner "cybervillages."[44] Quite fittingly, several legal scholars in search of a historical precedent for government jurisdiction in cyberspace have settled upon Judge Lebbeus Wilfley's 1904 decision in *In re: Young John Allen*, establishing the juridical concept of "extraterritorial domicile" by way of holding sojourning Shanghai Americans liable to all U.S. laws.[45] The past world of extraterritorial citizenship is indeed an apposite model for current developments.

Finally, it is worth noting that at least one among the reprobate notorious American "sharks, gamblers, and prostitutes" that had brought the U.S. Court to Shanghai in 1906 lived on beyond all probability and expectation. In 1981, the Secretary of State took the politically controversial measure of revoking the passport of Philip Agee, a former Central Intelligence Agency employee who had begun publishing detailed information about American operatives abroad.[46] Here, a now more conservative Supreme Court supported the primacy of "national security" over individual rights. The man the Secretary had turned to in seeking a way to thwart Agee was none other than J. H. "Tientsin" Brown, as the latter's struggle with the State Department seventy-five years earlier was (Agee's attorney noted dryly) the pivotal precedent cited in the government's brief.[47] For Justice William Brennan, dissenting, both cases— Agee's and Brown's—underscored that the judicial branch should not mistake national security with diplomatic embarrassment. He could not have known how little difference between the two there had been for American citizens in treaty port China.

NOTES

INTRODUCTION AND OVERVIEW

1. Rogers Smith, *Civic Ideals: Conflicting Visions of Citizenship in U.S. History* (New Haven: Yale University Press, 1997); Gerald Neuman, *Strangers to the Constitution: Immigrants, Borders, and Fundamental Law* (Princeton: Princeton University Press, 1996); Richard Epstein, *Bargaining with the State* (Princeton: Princeton University Press, 1993).

2. On the distinctions between functional and affective citizenship, see: "The Functionality of Citizenship," *Harvard Law Review* (June 1997), 110:1814–1831. This work employs standard citation format for court cases and legal opinions, i.e., volume number, case/decision/opinion, first page number, page cited. In the instance of law review articles, however, conventional humanities citation format is used, i.e. author, article title, journal title (date), volume/number: page.

3. C. A. Logan, U.S. Legation, Guatemala City, to Secretary of State Evarts, 20 August 1879, *Foreign Relations of the United States* (Washington, D.C.: GPO, 1879), 143–45. [Hereafter, *FRUS*, an annual State Department publication since the 1860s containing significant correspondence between the United States and other governments]. In the early 1990s, when various organizations representing the 2.6 million or so U.S. nationals on foreign shores appealed for a non-vot-

ing representative in Congress and an easier tax burden, the response of one leading Senator was to dismiss these "moans of the mink-swathed Americans abroad." Myra MacPherson, "Mink Coats or Roaches for Americans Abroad?," *Washington Post*, 13 April 1978, B-1; U.S. Congress, House Committee on Foreign Affairs, "U.S. Citizens Overseas," 102 Cong., 1st sess. (Washington, D.C.: GPO, 1991), SUDOC Y4.F76/1:C49/2.

4. Charles Tilly, "Citizenship, Identity and Social History," in Charles Tilly, ed., *Citizenship, Identity and Social History* (Cambridge: Cambridge University Press, *International Review of Social History Supplement 3*, 1996), 5–6.

5. Epstein, *Bargaining with the State*, 5. While my understanding of constitutional "bargaining" comes from Epstein, my characterization of sojourning Americans as parties at the negotiating table was inspired by Neuman's *Strangers to the Constitution*.

6. The concept "anomalous zone" is adapted from Gerald L. Neuman, "Surveying Law and Borders: Anomalous Zones," *Stanford Law Review* (May 1996) 48:1197–1234. Neuman defines the term as territorially limited enclaves in which government suspends fundamental norms; examples include red light districts, the District of Columbia, Guantanamo Bay refugee processing center.

7. R. Malley et al. "Constructing the State Extraterritorially," *Harvard Law Review* (April 1990), 103:1286.

8. Edwin Borchard, *The Diplomatic Protection of Citizens Abroad* (New York: Banks Law Publishing, 1916), vi.

9. H. W. Brands, "The Idea of the National Interests," *Diplomatic History* (Spring 1999), 23:239–261.

10. Nicholas R. Clifford, *Spoilt Children of Empire. Westerners in Shanghai and the Chinese Revolution of the 1920s* (Hanover: University Press of New England, 1991).

11. Geoffrey R. Watson, "Offenders Abroad; the Case for Nationality-Based Criminal Jurisdiction," *Yale Journal of International Law* (Winter 1992), 17:48–49.

12. Borchard, *Diplomatic Protection of Citizens Abroad*, 432–33.

13. Edwin Smith, "The End of the Consular Courts," *Foreign Service Journal* (January 1960), 37:44–49.

14. For detailed descriptions of the system, see Frank E. Hinckley, *American Consular Jurisdiction in the Orient* (Washington, D.C.: W. H. Lowdermilk, 1906); George Keeton, *The Development of Extraterritoriality in China* (London: Longmans, Green, 1928); Anatol Kotonev, *Shanghai: Its Courts and Council* (Shanghai: North China Daily News and Herald, 1927); Westel W. Willoughby, *Foreign Rights and Interests in China* (Baltimore: Johns Hopkins University Press, 1927 [1920]).

15. For concision and clarity, the best work on the treaty port infrastructure is still Albert Feuerwerker, *The Foreign Establishment in China in the Early Twen-*

tieth Century (Ann Arbor: University of Michigan Press, 1976). A more analytical discussion can be found in Jürgen Osterhammel, "Semi-Colonialism and Informal Empire in Twentieth-Century China. . .," Wolfgang J. Mommsen and Jürgen Osterhammel, eds., *Imperialism and After: Continuities and Discontinuities* (London: Allen and Unwin, 1986).

16. The United States operated non-consular courts in its insular possessions, such as Guam, Panama and the Philippines. The U.S. Court for China was unique in that it originated out of Sino-American treaties, rather than out of American territorial suzerainty, as was so in the other instances. Further, until transferred to the Department of Justice in 1933–34, the U.S. Court for China was directly under State Department auspices, whereas the others fell within the purview of the War Department and/or the Justice Department. After World War Two, America operated various "occupation courts" in Japan and Germany, including the U.S. Court for Berlin, extant until the reunification of Germany. C. M. A. McCauliff, "The Reach of the Constitution: American Peace-time Court in West Berlin," *Notre Dame Law Review* (1980), 55:682–707.

17. American extraterritorial jurisdiction in China covered native-born and naturalized U.S. citizens, as well as residents of Guam, Puerto Rico, Hawaii, and the Philippines, whenever such individuals entered Chinese territory.

18. British extrality, in particular, evidenced intricate racial and class issues because of the wide array of non-English born individuals covered as subjects and nationals. See, for example, *Rex v. Keechill*, involving the intentional murder of a Cantonese girl by a Malayan British subject. *North China Herald*, 30 April 1870, 311; 19 May 1870, 358–9; 28 May 1870, 391.

19. Extrality and intra-foreign tensions are briefly discussed in Sally Engle Merry, "Law and Colonialism," *Law and Society Review* (Winter 1991), 25:891.

20. Joseph Levenson, "Western Powers and Chinese Revolutions: The Pattern of Intervention," *Pacific Affairs* (September 1953), 26:231.

21. For "imperialism on the cheap," see Ronald Robinson, "The Eccentric Idea of Imperialism, with or without Empire," in Wolfgang Mommsen and Jürgen Osterhammel, eds. *Imperialism and After: Continuities and Discontinuities* (London: Allen and Unwin, 1986), 271. On the symmetry of interests, see Johan Galtung, "A Structural Theory of Imperialism," *Journal of Peace Research*, 2 (1971), 83.

22. Jack P. Greene, *Negotiated Authorities: Essays in Colonial Political and Constitutional History* (Charlottesville: University of Virginia, 1994), 1–4.

23. Peter Burroughs, "The Law, the Citizen, and the State in Nineteenth-Century Australia," *Journal of Imperial and Commonwealth History* (September 1994), 22:542–554.

24. "Tensions of Empire," *American Ethnologist* (November 1989), 16:609–765.

207

Quotations are taken from the introduction to this symposium, authored by Frederic Cooper and Ann L. Stoler, pp. 610, 613, 614.

25. Mary Wilkie, "Colonials, Marginals and Immigrants: Contributions to a Theory of Ethnic Stratification," *Comparative Studies in Society and History* (January 1977), 19:67–95.

26. Patrick Wolfe, "Review Essay. History and Imperialism: A Century of Theory, from Marx to Postcolonialism," *American Historical Review* (April 1997) 102: 402, discussing Ronald Robinson's work on the subject.

27. "Tensions of Empire," supra; David Arnold, "European Orphans and Vagrants in India in the Nineteenth Century," *The Journal of Imperial and Commonwealth History* (January 1979), 7:104–127; Ann Stoler, "Rethinking Colonial Categories: European Communities and the Boundaries of Rule," *Comparative Studies in Society and History* (January 1989), 13:134–61.

28. "A British Blue's View of Shanghai," *North China Herald*, 1 September 1893, 351, emphasis in original; hereafter, *NCH*.

29. See, for example: June Starr and Jane F. Collier, eds., *History and Power in the Study of Law: New Directions in Legal Anthropology* (Ithaca: Cornell University Press, 1989).

30. Consul General Edwin Cunningham to Minister Nelson Johnson, 7 August 1931, RG 59, 893.5034/279; U.S. Legation to Secretary of State, 23 July 1931, Ibid., 893.5034/278; "Lax Municipal Factory Inspection," *China Weekly Review*, 13 July 1935, 209; "15 Die, 75 Injured As Toy Factory Destroyed in Western District," *China Press*, 29 June 1935, 1; Cunningham to Secretary, 15 July 1935, RG 59, 893.5034/308.

31. Dietmar Rothermund, "The Legacy of the British-Indian Empire in Independent India," in Mommsen and Osterhammel, *Imperialism and After*, 139–53, especially 143–45.

32. Jerome Cohen and Hungdah Chiu, eds., *People's China and International Law. A Documentary Study* (Princeton: Princeton University Press, 1974), 615–638.

33. When three American Marines stationed in Okinawa were accused in 1995 of kidnapping and raping a 12-year-old local girl, the United States made much of its acquiescence to local jurisdiction; after the guilty verdict, the American embassy in Tokyo formally apologized and declared confidence in the soundness of the Japanese judicial system; the Defense Department followed with a reaffirmation of its commitment in Japan to the watchwords "good manners . . . good neighbors and good discipline." See: "3 GIs Convicted in Okinawa Rape; Japanese Court Sentences Each to at Least 6 ´ Years," *Chicago Tribune*, 7 March 1996, 8; "U.S. Concerned over Okinawa Sexual Assault by Serviceman," *Japan Policy and Politics*, 28 April 1997.

34. See, for example: Wu Meng-hsüeh, *Mei-kuo tsai Hua ling-shih ts'ai-p'an*

ch'üan pai-nien shih [One Hundred Years of American Consular Jurisdiction in China] (Beijing: She-hui ko-hsüeh wen hsien chu-p'an she, 1992); Ch'en Kuo-huang. *Ling-shih ts'ai-p'an ch'üan tsai Chung-kuo chih hsing-ch'eng yü fei-ch'u* [The Formation and Abrogation of Extraterritoriality in China] (Taipei: China hsin shui ni kung ssu wen hua chi chin hui, 1971), especially 41–46, 71–77; Hao Li-yu. *Ling-shih ts'ai-p'an ch'üan wen-t'i* [The Problem of Consular Jurisdiction] (Shanghai: Shang wu yin shu kuan), 1930, 69–74.

35. The contrast between China and the West, and China and the United States more particularly, in terms of the cultural understanding of "justice," is succinctly laid out in: Richard M. Pfeffer, "Crime and Punishment: China and the United States," in Jerome A Cohen, ed., *Contemporary Chinese Law: Research Problems and Perspectives* (Cambridge: Harvard University Press, 1970). On the theoretical point more generally, see also: Herbert L. Packer, "Two Models of the Criminal Process," *University of Pennsylvania Law Review* (1964) 113:1–5.

36. Frederic Wakeman, Jr., "Policing Modern Shanghai," *China Quarterly* (September 1988), 115:408–440; Gail Hershatter, "Regulating Sex in Shanghai: The Reform of Prostitution in 1920 and 1951," and Brian Martin, " 'The Pact with the Devil':The Relationship between the Green Gang and the French Concession Authorities, 1925–1935," both in Wakeman and Yeh Wen-hsin, eds., *Shanghai Sojourners* (Berkeley: University of California, 1992), 145–185, and 266–304, respectively.

37. Thomas B. Stephens, *Order and Discipline in China. The Shanghai Mixed Court, 1911–27* (Seattle and London: University of Washington Press, 1992), 116. Stephens notes a 1967 unpublished study of the British Supreme Court for China and Japan in the nineteenth century as additional support for this same portrait of surprisingly equitable foreign justice for indigenous plaintiffs, Stephens 140*n*7.

38. Stephens, *Order and Discipline*, 103.

39. Richard Chang, *The Justice of the Western Consular Courts in Nineteenth-Century Japan* (Westport: Greenwood Press, 1984), xii.

40. *United States v. Jones*, 4 May 1909. Charles S. Lobingier, comp., *Extraterritorial Cases* (Manila: Bureau of Printing, 1920, 1928), volume 1, 161. Lobingier was the third Judge of the U.S. Court. His two-volume work, *Extraterritorial Cases*, is a compilation of most of the Court's decisions from 1906 to 1924. From its first case in early 1907 to 8 December 1941, the day Japanese forces in Shanghai shut down its offices, the U.S. Court for China heard approximately 4,000 cases. Figures are approximate because, particularly in the early years, cases were haphazardly numbered. Brief case reports are available for all years in *The North China Herald, Supreme Court and Consular Gazette*, which published decisions from all extraterritorial and mixed courts in Shanghai every week. In addition, information about cases from 1910–1929 can be found in State Department

records at the National Archives (Record Group 59, Decimal file 172.00; and, Record Group 84, Records of the Shanghai Consulate). In 1933–34, the Court was transferred to Justice Department auspices, and the records of the Court from 1934–41 are located in Record Group 118, Records of U.S. Attorneys and Marshals, District of China. I found no relevant material on the Court in the Shanghai Municipal Archives, or in the Tsungli-yamen archives at the Academia Sinica in Taipei, Taiwan.

41. Huntington Wilson, Acting Secretary, to Attorney General, with enclosures, 2 May 1910. Record Group 59, Records of the State Department, 172.6J71/ii, National Archives Records Administration, College Park Maryland. (Hereafter RG 59, decimal #, NARA).

42. Many of those convicted by the U.S. Court of robbery and embezzlement, for example, and sentenced to serve time in American domestic prisons were paroled well before the end of their terms. For letters back and forth from the Superintendent of Prisons, Department of Justice, to the U.S. Court in Shanghai during the late 1920s, see RG 59 172.6/386+, Box 3056, NARA.

43. Charles Lilley and Michael Hunt, "On Social History, the State, and Foreign Relations: Commentary on [James Huskey's] 'The Cosmopolitan Connection,'" *Diplomatic History* (Summer 1987), 11:246.

44. Richard W. Flournoy, Jr., "International Problems in Respect to Nationality by Birth," *ASIL Proceedings* (1926), 82.

45. Daniel M. Crane and Thomas A. Breslin, *An Ordinary Relationship. American Opposition to Republican Revolution in China* (Gainesville: Florida International University Press, 1986).

46. Michael Hunt, *The Making of a Special Relationship; The United States and China to 1914* (New York: Columbia University Press, 1983).

I. EXTRATERRITORIALITY IN THE CHANGING WORLD OF THE NINETEENTH CENTURY

1. Borchard, *The Diplomatic Protection of Citizens Abroad*, 5.

2. The eighteenth-century quote is borrowed from Jack Greene, "Competing Authorities: The Debate Over Parliamentary Imperial Jurisdiction, 1763–1776," in Philip Lawson, ed., *Parliament and the Atlantic Empire* (Edinburgh: Edinburgh University Press, 1995), 47–63.

3. Resat Kasaba, "Treaties and Friendships: British Imperialism, the Ottoman Empire, and China in the Nineteenth Century," *Journal of World History* (Fall 1993), 4:216–17.

4. Joseph Ratner, ed., *Intelligence in the Modern World: John Dewey's Philosophy* (New York: Modern Library, 1939), 471.

5. Adda Bozeman, *Politics and Culture in International History* (New Brunswick: Transaction, 1994 [1960]), 74.

6. Coleman Phillipson, *The International Law and Custom of Ancient Greece and Rome* (London: Macmillan, 1911), vol. 2, 192, paraphrased.

7. M. H. van der Valk, "Le Statut des Etrangers en Chine," in John Gilissen, ed., *L'Etranger* (Brussels: Librairie Encyclopèdique, 1958), vol. 11, 267–303.

8. Shalom Kassan, "Extraterritorial Jurisdiction in the Ancient World," *The American Journal of International Law* (April 1935), 29: 240–42, paraphrased.

9. Susan Treggiari, "Social Status and Social Legislation," *Cambridge Ancient History* (New York: Macmillan, 1996), vol. 10, 873–904, 874; H. Galsterer, "The Administration of Justice," Ibid., 397–413.

10. Hugh Last, "Gaius Gracchus," *Cambridge Ancient History* (New York: Macmillan, 1932), vol. 9, 45–47.

11. J. Balsdon, *Romans and Aliens* (Chapel Hill: University of North Carolina Press), ch. 5.

12. Phillipson, *The International Law and Custom of Ancient Greece and Rome*, vol. 2, 124–25.

13. G. H. Stevenson, "The Provinces and their Government," *Cambridge Ancient History*, vol. 9, 472–73.

14. This discussion of the Ottoman capitulations is drawn from J. Wansbrough and Inalcik Halil, "Imtiyazat," *Encyclopaedia of Islam* (Leiden: E. J. Brill, 1971), vol. 3, 1178–95; "The Development of Western Judicial Privileges," in Majid Khadduri and Herbert J. Liebesny, eds., *Law and the Middle East* (Washington, D.C.: Middle East Institute, 1955), chs. 1 and 8; James B. Angell, The Turkish Capitulations," *American Historical Review* (January 1901), 6:254–59.

15. N. Steensgaard, "Consuls and Nations in the Levant from 1570 to 1650," *The Scandinavian Economic History Review* (1967), 15:19.

16. Thomas Naff, "The Ottoman Empire and the European States System," in Hedley Bull, ed., *The Expansion of International Society* (Oxford: Clarendon Press, 1984), 133–69.

17. Emmeric de Vattel, *The Law of Nations*, Joseph Chitty, ed. (London: Johnson, 1861), 250, 261, 266, quoted and paraphrased.

18. Borchard, *The Diplomatic Protection of Citizens Abroad*, 6, paraphrased.

19. Gerrit Gong, *The Standard of "Civilization" in International Society* (Oxford: Clarendon Press, 1984).

20. Bull, "Introduction," *The Expansion of International Society*, 2.

21. Antony Anghie, "Finding the Peripheries: Sovereignty and Colonialism in Nineteenth-Century International Law," *Harvard International Law Journal* (Winter 1999), 40:4.

22. Ibid., 22, 35–36.

23. Borchard, *The Diplomatic Protection of Citizens Abroad*, 6, paraphrased.

24. Vattel, *Law of Nations*, 246, paraphrased.

25. Peter Spiro, "Dual Nationality and the Meaning of Citizenship," *Emory Law Journal* (Fall 1997) 46:1418–20.

26. Tomas Hammar, "State, Nation, and Dual Citizenship," in William R. Brubaker, ed., *Immigration and the Politics of Citizenship in Europe and North America* (Lanham: University Press of America, 1989), 46, 47.

27. Ibid., 48.

28. Paul Vinogradoff, "Foundations of Society (Origins of Feudalism)," *Cambridge Medieval History* (New York: Macmillan, 1964), vol. 2, 631–55.

29. David Kennedy, "International law and the Nineteenth Century: History of an Illusion," *Quinnipiac Law Review* (Spring 1997), 17:122, 128; Daniel Philpott, "Sovereignty: An Introduction and Brief History," *Journal of International Affairs* (1995), 48:353.

30. Candice Bredbenner, "Toward Independent Citizenship: Married Women's Nationality in the United States: 1855–1937." Ph.D. Dissertation, University of Virginia, History, 1990. (Ann Arbor: University Microfilms, 1997), 16.

31. Eric Hobsbawm, *Nations and Nationalism since 1780: Programme, Myth, Reality* (Cambridge: Cambridge University Press, 1990), 83.

32. Ibid., 82–83.

33. John Bassett Moore, *A Digest of International Law* (Washington, D.C.: GPO, 1906), vol. 2, 811.

34. Spiro, "Dual Nationality," 1418.

35. Borchard, *The Diplomatic Protection of Citizens Abroad*, 503.

36. The discussion here of dual nationality and statelessness, as well as the quotation, are from Spiro, "Dual Nationality," 1418, 1430–31.

37. Adolph Hepner, *Extraterritorial Criminal Jurisdiction and Its Effects on American Citizens* (Washington, D.C.: GPO, 1890), 18–19.

38. John Torpey, *The Invention of the Passport. Surveillance, Citizenship and the State* (Cambridge: Cambridge University Press, 2000), 2.

39. Ibid., 1–3.

40. "Passport," in *Encyclopedia of the Social Sciences* (New York: Macmillan, 1936), vol. 12, 14. On the sixteenth-century rise of restrictions against alien vagabonds, see John Gilissen, "Le statut des Etrangers en Belgique du XIIIe au Xxe siecle," and Hans Thieme, "Die Rechtsstellung der Fremden in Deutschland Bis zum 18. Jahrhundert," both in *L'Etranger*, vol. 11.

41. Hepner, *Extraterritorial Criminal Jurisdiction*, 20.

42. Ibid.

43. George Lewis, *On Foreign Jurisdiction and the Extradition of Criminals* (London and New York: Parker, 1859), 29.

44. Westel W. Willoughby, "Citizenship and Allegiance in Constitutional and International Law," *American Journal of International Law* (1907), 1:914.

45. Moore, *Digest of International Law*, 2:256.

46. Ibid., 925.

47. Greene, *Negotiated Authorities*, 15, quoting Charles Tilly, *Coercion, Capital, and European States, A.D. 990–1990* (1990).

48. Jurgen Osterhammel, "Britain and China, 1842–1914," in *The Oxford History of the British Empire* (Oxford and New York: Oxford University Press, 1999), vol. 3, 154.

49. "Memorial: Mu-chang-a and the Other Grand Councillors Present Their Critique of the Treaty of Wang-hsia (August 15, 1844)," in Earl Swisher, *China's Management of the American Barbarians: A Study of Sino-American Relations, 1841–1861, with Documents* (New Haven: Yale University Press, 1972), Document 93.

50. Keeton, *Extraterritoriality in China*, vol. 1, 36.

51. Reproduced in Hosea Morse, *The International Relations of the Chinese Empire* (London: Longmans, Green, 1918), vol. 2, Appendix A, 157.

52. Keeton, *Extraterritoriality in China*, vol. 1, 31.

53. The English East India Company was chartered in 1600; the (English) Levant Company, in 1581. Responding to continuing complaints among anti-monopoly and rival merchants, Parliament reconstituted the EIC in 1709 into the form it sustained until its demise in the 1830s. P. J. Marshall, "The English in Asia to 1700," in *The Oxford History of the British Empire* (Oxford and New York: Oxford University Press, 1998), vol. 1, 281–83.

54. For insight into Ch'ing officials' understanding of extraterritorial jurisdiction, see R. Randle Edwards, "Ch'ing Legal Jurisdiction Over Foreigners," in Jerome Alan Cohen et al., eds., *Essays on China's Legal Tradition* (New York: Columbia University Press, 1980), 241.

55. Marshall, "The English in Asia to 1700," 276–77; Michael J. Braddick, "The English Government War, Trade, and Settlement, 1625–1688," in *The Oxford History of the British Empire* (Oxford and New York: Oxford University Press, 1998), vol. 1, 286–308.

56. H. J. Leue, "Legal Expansion in the Age of the Companies: Aspects of the Administration of Justice in the English and Dutch Settlements of Maritime Asia, c. 1600–1750," in Wolfgang Mommsen, and J. A. De Moor, eds., *European Expansion and Law: The Encounter of European and Indigenous Law in 19th- and 20th-Century Africa and Asia* (New York: Berg, 1992), 141.

57. Jorg Fisch, "Law as a Means and as an End: Some Remarks on the Function of European and Non-European Law in the Process of European Expansion," in Mommsen and De Moor, *European Expansion*, 15–38.

58. Steensgaard, "Consuls and Nations in the Levant."

59. P. J. Marshall, "The Whites of British India, 1780–1830: A Failed Colonial Society?" in *International History Review* (February 1990), 12:28–29.

60. Leue, "Legal Expansion," 129–30. On the "dramatic transformation of the East India Company from trader to sovereign during the mid-1760s," see H. V. Bowen, "British India, 1765–1813: The Metropolitan Context," *The Oxford History of the British Empire* (Oxford and New York: Oxford University Press, 1998), vol. 2, 530.

61. Marshall, "The English in Asia to 1700," 266.

62. Nicholas Canny, "The Permissive Frontier: The Problem of Social Control in English Settlements in Ireland and Virginia, 1550–1650," in K. R. Andrews et al., eds., *The Westward Enterprise: English Activities in Ireland, the Atlantic, and America, 1480–1650* (Detroit: Wayne State University Press, 1979), 919–23.

63. Edwards, "Ch'ing Legal Jurisdiction," 237; Keeton, *Extraterritoriality in China*, vol. 1, 8–9.

64. Keeton, vol. 1, 88–95.

65. Lo-shu Fu, ed. *A Documentary Chronicle of Sino-Western Relations (1644–1820)* (Tucson: University of Arizona Press, 1966), document 8:10:14 (29 November 1743), discussing a case of two Russian soldiers put to death for fatally beating two Chinese merchants; ibid., document 13:10:3 (23 November 1748); ibid., 14:3:6 (22 April 1749), 187.

66. Edwards, "Ch'ing Legal Jurisdiction," 235, 255.

67. Sir George Robinson to Viscount Palmerston, 1 December 1835, "Papers Relative to the Establishment of a British Court of Judicature," *British Parliamentary Papers*, China-26 (Shannon: Irish University Press, 1974), vol. China–2, 2–3

68. Quoted in Edwards, "Ch'ing Legal Jurisdiction," 232.

69. Morse, *The International Relations of the Chinese Empire*, vol. 2, 106; *North American Review* (October 1834), 39:327. Indeed, it was "quite customary," according to one contemporary, to rely on substitute culprits when exigency or social sensibilities required. Substitution was done openly in cases where expected penalties were light or only financial compensation was at issue, less openly when the stakes were higher. In a 1754 case, for instance, when an English sailor was killed by a French officer and Chinese took jurisdiction at British request, it was widely believed that in place of the officer a "renegado" was hired to take the anticipated punishment of short imprisonment to spare his social better. Sources: Morse, *International Relations of the Chinese Empire*, vol. 2, 100; Keeton, *Extraterritoriality in China*, vol. 1, 34.

70. Keeton, *Extraterritoriality in China*, vol. 1, 39, 48–49; Morse, *International Relations of the Chinese Empire*, vol. 1, 101; Keeton, "The International Status of Macao Before 1887," *The Chinese Social and Political Science Review* (1927), 11:404–13.

71. Morse, *International Relations of the Chinese Empire*, vol. 1, 104.

72. U.S. House, "Political Relations Between the United States and China,"

26th Cong., 2d sess. (1840, Exec. Doc. 71, 9–52); Wu Meng-hsüeh, *Mei-kuo tsai Hua ling-shih . . .* , 23. The most detailed secondary account of the Terranova case is William J. Donahue, "The Francis Terranova Case," *The Historian* (February 1981), 43:211–24. For the place of the Terranova case in the history of Sino-American diplomacy, see Michael Hunt, *The Making of a Special Relationship: The United States and China to 1914* (New York: Columbia University Press, 1983), 1–2.

73. Ch'ing-tai wai-chiao shih-liao, *Tao-kuang chao* (Historical Materials on Ch'ing Dynasty Foreign Relations, Tao-kuang reign), no. 7, 8–11. A summary of contemporary commentary and translations of Ch'ing documents may be found in Keeton, *Extraterritoriality in China*, vol. 2, appendixes 4 and 5, pp. 130–201.

74. Keeton, vol. 1, 184.

75. Ibid., 57–59. In the solicitude of Ch'ing officials for an outcaste boat-woman, we may see a state-making claim by central authorities over a traditional out-group. Prasenjit Duara, "Transnationalism and the Predicament of Sovereignty: China, 1900–1945," *American Historical Review* (October 1997) 102:1030–1051.

76. Quoted in Donahue, "The Francis Terranova Case," 223*n*55.

77. Morse, *International Relations of the Chinese Empire*, vol. 1, 194.

78. Morse, vol. 2, 146–47.

79. A. J. R. Russell-Wood, "Seamen Ashore and Afloat: The Social Environment of the *Carreira da India*, 1550–1750," in Ursula Lamb, ed., *The Globe Encircled and the World Revealed* (Brookfield: Variorum, 1995), 99, 105.

80. Morse, *International Relations of the Chinese Empire*, vol. 2, 16.

81. John Brewer and John Styles, eds., *An Ungovernable People: The English and Their Law in the Seventeenth and Eighteenth Centuries* (New Brunswick: Rutgers University Press, 1980), 17.

82. Michael Greenberg, *British Trade and the Opening of China, 1800–42* (Cambridge: Cambridge University Press, 1951), 53.

83. Morse, *International Relations of the Chinese Empire*, vol. 2, 105.

84. P. J. Marshall, "The British in Asia: Trade to Dominion, 1700–1765," *The Oxford History of the British Empire* (Oxford and New York: Oxford University Press, 1998), vol. 2, 493–94.

85. Phillipson, *The International Law and Custom of Ancient Greece and Rome*, 268.

86. Keeton, *Extraterritoriality in China*, vol. 1, 142.

87. Edwards, "Ch'ing Legal Jurisdiction," 250.

88. *Law Officers' Opinions to the Foreign Office 1793–1860* (Westmead: Gregg International, 1970–73), vol. 19, no. 22, 66.

89. Edwards, "Ch'ing Legal Jurisdiction," 251.

90. Keeton, *Extraterritoriality in China*, vol. 1, 166–72, passim.

91. U.S. House, "Trade with China," 26th Cong., 1st sess. (1840), H. Doc. 119, 2.

92. Keeton, *Extraterritoriality in China*, vol. 1, 162–63.

93. Cheng Tsuan, "Shang-hai tsu-chieh hsing wang lun" (A Discussion of the Rise and Fall of the Concessions in Shanghai), *Shang-hai she-hui k'e-hsüeh yuan-hsüeh shu chi-k'an* (Quarterly Journal of the Shanghai Academy of Social Sciences) (1988), 4:66–76; Paul Ch'en, "The Treaty System and European Law in China: A Study of the Exercise of British Jurisdiction in Late Imperial China," in Mommsen and De Moor, *European Expansion*, 83–100; Britten Dean, "British Informal Empire: The Case of China," *Journal of Commonwealth and Comparative Politics* (March 1976), 14:64–81; Tan Chung, "The Unequal Treaty System: Infrastructure of Irresponsible Imperialism," *China Report* (September/October 1981), 17:3–34.

94. Osterhammel, "Britain and China," 148.

95. Ibid., 154.

96. Ibid., 149.

97. Jules Davids, ed., *American Diplomatic and Public Papers: The United States and China* (Delaware: Scholarly Resources, 1979), series 1, vol. 11.

98. Albert Feuerwerker, "The Foreign Presence in China," *The Cambridge History of China* (Cambridge: Cambridge University Press, 1983), vol. 12, pt. 1, 129, 150.

99. "Complaints of the Tsungli Yamen respecting lending of names by British subjects to Chinese in Canton," Foreign Office (FO) 656/68, 28 November 1885; "Correspondence respecting British Protection to Anglo-Chinese in China, 1886–1898," FO 405/81.

100. "Surrender of Extraterritorial Jurisdiction in China," 15 May 1929, Central Records of the Department of State, 1910–1943, NARA, RG 59, 711.933/48.

101. The theoretical point is from Wilkie, "Colonials, Marginals, and Immigrants. . ."

102. Secret memorial from Kiying, 16 February 1843. Translated and discussed in T. F. Tsiang, "Difficulties of Reconstruction After the Treaty of Nanking," *Chinese Social and Political Science Review* (July 1932), 16:319–27. According to this memorial, on the one hand, British "secretly told those inhuman, lacking in self-respect colored barbarians to rape and plunder," while on the other, "they permitted the victims to report such crimes to them, which once found true upon investigation were immediately punished with death." The identity of "colored barbarians" is derived from Russell-Wood, "Seamen Ashore and Afloat."

103. D. B. M. McCartee, vice consul, Ningpo, to Peter Parker, commissioner of the United States in China, 19 February 1855, in "Report of the Late Commissioner in China," 842.

104. *Law Officers' Opinions* (1860), vol. 22, no. 605: 54, 56.

105. Shanghai Consulate to State Department, 1 December 1851, no number, M118.

106. Prince Kung (chief secretary of state for Foreign Affairs) to U.S. chargé d'affaires ad interim (S. Wells Williams), *FRUS* (1869), 559.

107. "Members of the Foreign Office to S. Wells Williams," *FRUS* (1869), 472–73.

108. "The Hansa," *Cambridge Medieval History* (New York: Macmillan, 1932), vol. 7, 216–47; Bozeman, *Politics and Culture*, 506–12.

109. Anghie, "Finding the Peripheries," 37.

110. *NCH*, 12 February 1892, 149.

111. T. F. Tsiang, "The Extension of Equal Commercial Privileges to Other Nations than the British After the Treaty of Nanking," *The Chinese Social and Political Science Review* (1931), 15:422–44; Thomas Kearny, "Tsiang Documents: Elipoo, Ke-ying, Pottinger, and Kearny and the Most-Favored-Nation and Open Door Policy in China in 1842–44," *Chinese Social and Political Science Review* (1932), 16:73–104.

112. Japanese in China's treaty ports tended largely to fall within the lower middle class, in direct contrast to European populations there. Together with Western racism, this class difference contributed to the lack of integration of Japanese within the social life of the treaty ports. Mark R. Peattie, "Japanese Treaty Port Settlements in China, 1895–1937," in Peter Duus et al., *The Japanese Informal Empire in China, 1895–1937* (Princeton: Princeton University Press, 1989), 166–209.

113. Quoted in Douglas Greenberg, "Crime, Law Enforcement, and Social Control in Colonial America," *The American Journal of Legal History* (1982), 26:321.

114. Ronald Robinson, "Non-European Foundations of European Imperialism: Sketch for a Theory of Collaboration," in Roger Owen and Bob Sutcliffe, eds., *Studies in the Theory of Imperialism* (London: Longman Group, 1972). For a critical discussion of the concept of "informal imperialism," see: C. M. Turnbull, "Formal and Informal Empire in East Asia," *The Oxford History of the British Empire* (Oxford and New York: Oxford University Press, 1999), vol. 5, 379–402.

115. Jurgen Osterhammel, "Britain and China, 1842–1914," *The Oxford History of the British Empire* (Oxford and New York: Oxford University Press, 1999), vol. 3, 157–58.

116. Westel W. Willoughby, *Foreign Rights and Interests in China*, 107–8.

117. *FRUS* (1871), 99–110.

118. Knight Biggerstaff, "The Secret Correspondence of 1867–1868: Views of Leading Chinese Statesmen Regarding the Further Opening of China to Western Influence," *Journal of Modern History* (June 1950), 22:122–36.

119. Yen-p'ing Hao and Erh-min Wang, "Chinese Views of Western Relations, 1840–95," *Cambridge History of China* (Cambridge: Cambridge University Press, 1980), vol. 11, pt. 2, 142–201.

120. U.S. Minister Frederick Low to Secretary of State, *FRUS* (1875), 332–36.

121. Mary Wright, *The Last Stand of Chinese Conservatism: The T'ung-Chih Restoration, 1862–1874* (Stanford: Stanford University Press, 1967), 21; emphasis in original.

122. Nathan Pelcovits, *Old China Hands and the Foreign Office* (New York: Kings Crown Press, 1978), 300, 302, 2, 6.

2. EXTRATERRITORIAL AMERICANS, BEFORE THE RUSH TO EMPIRE

1. Neuman, "Anomalous Zones."

2. Nancy F. Cott, "Marriage and Women's Citizenship in the United States, 1830–1934," *American Historical Review* (December 1998), 103:1446.

3. Peter Onuf, "A Declaration of Independence for Diplomatic Historians," *Diplomatic History* (Winter 1998), 22:82.

4. Cott, "Marriage and Women's Citizenship," 1444.

5. *Holmes v. Jennison*, 39 *U.S. Reports* 540 (1840); "Passports," 10 *Opinions of the Attorneys General* 517 (1863). The *United States Reports* and Opinions of the Attorneys General are both available in most libraries, and on-line through Lexis-Nexis.

6. Neuman, *Strangers*, 9, 12; Frederick Dunn, *The Protection of Nationals* (Baltimore: Johns Hopkins University Press, 1932), 48.

7. Moore, *Digest of International Law*, vol. 2, 225.

8. Watson, "Offenders Abroad," 41.

9. Moore, *Digest of International Law*, vol. 2, 263. An 1835 revision of the 1790 Act further restricted this maritime criminal jurisdiction to acts committed by one or more of the crew of any American ship or vessel. Treaties typically gave consuls full authority to settle disputes involving only crew members of U.S. vessels.

10. James Sofka, "The Jeffersonian Idea of National Security: Commerce, the Atlantic Balance of Power, and the Barbary War, 1786–1805," *Diplomatic History* (Fall 1997), 21:519–44. Another interesting exception was the Franco-American Convention of 1788 giving each government consular jurisdiction over its own nationals in the other's territory. This was revised 1800 to limit extraterritorial authority to police power on ships, arrests of deserters from ships, and arbitration of civil disputes between French nationals in the United States. E. Wilson Lyon, "The Franco-American Convention of 1800," *Journal of Modern History* (1940), 12:305–33.

11. Sofka, "The Jeffersonian Idea," 520. Further, extraterritorial jurisdiction was limited: in Algiers (now Algeria), for example, U.S. consuls heard only civil suits between Americans, while in mixed civil and in criminal cases, American defendants went to a Mixed Court.

12. This paragraph drawn from Rogers Smith, *Civic Ideals*, 159–64, 196.

13. In keeping with their pro-immigration sentiments, Jeffersonians emphasized the individual's right to expatriate himself from his native land, to throw off one nationality and adopt another. Naturally, they resisted Federalist efforts to narrow this right of expatriation through heightened government scrutiny of immigrants and increased residency requirements for naturalization. So too, they feared the partisan abuse of expanded federal powers over individuals and states in the name of collective security.

14. Kevin Kearney, "Private Citizens in Foreign Affairs: A Constitutional Analysis," *Emory Law Journal* (1987), 36:294. This federal criminal statute, still in force, prohibits private citizens from interacting with foreign governments in order to influence the conduct of U.S. foreign policy in general or in specific instances. The act has always been more preemptive than punitive; there have been no reported prosecutions, and only one indictment.

15. Rogers Smith, *Civic Ideals*, 156.

16. Ibid., 156, 157. Gideon Henfield had joined a French privateer and been made the "prize-master" in charge of captured English vessels. President Washington declared official U.S. neutrality between England and France; Henfield was accused of violating this proclamation, and he offered the defense that his own actions left little doubt that he had relinquished U.S. citizenship and so was not subject to American authority.

17. *Henfield's Case*, Case No. 6360, *Circuit Court, D. Pennsylvania*, 11 *Federal Cases* 1099; 1793 *U.S. App. LEXIS* 16, page 5 of 34 in Lexis version (5/34).

18. *Talbot v. Janson*, 3 *U.S.* 133; 1795 *U.S. LEXIS* 331, 13/25.

19. *Talbot v. Janson*, 6/25.

20. Ibid., 8 and 13/25.

21. Thomas Franck, "Legitimacy in the International System," *American Journal of International Law* (October 1988), 82:705–59.

22. John Adams, Letter to the *Boston Patriot*, 9 January 1809, in C. F. Adams, ed., *Works of John Adams* (Boston: Little, Brown, 1854), vol. 9, 315.

23. *FRUS* (1873), 1293.

24. Ibid.

25. Robert Calhoon. "The Reintegration of the Loyalists and the Disaffected," in Jack Greene, ed. *The American Revolution: Its Character and Limits* (New York: New York University Press, 1987), citing Kettner.

26. *Proceedings of the American International Law Society* (1927), 91.

27. *FRUS* (1873), 1296.

28. *FRUS* (1873), 1301–2. This obligation to protect the sojourner was affirmed in the *Slaughter House Cases*, 83 *U.S.* 36 (1872), which established the precedent that a citizen may properly "demand the care and protection of the Federal government over his life, liberty, and property when on the high seas or within the jurisdiction of a foreign government."

29. John B. Moore, *American Diplomacy: Its Spirit and Achievements* (New York and London: Harpers, 1905), 184, paraphrased.

30. Ibid., 186, paraphrased. See also "Protection to American Citizens," *NYT*, 27 February 1868, 1-5–6; the resolutions and memorials presented to Congress may be found in House and Senate miscellaneous documents for 40.2.

31. "Expatriation and Protection of Naturalized Americans Abroad and in Turkish Dominions," *American Journal of International Law* (January 1908), 2:156–60.

32. Ibid., 1304–5.

33. C. A. Logan, U.S. Legation Guatemala City to Secretary Evarts, 20 August 1879, *FRUS* (1879), 143–45, paraphrased and quoted.

34. The case of Anton Joseph Maassen was illustrative: he had come to Guatemala about 1877, represented himself as a German, mixed with Germans there; he eventually settled near Izabal, where he had occasion to appeal to German authorities for diplomatic intervention to help his children after their mother abandoned the family. Maassen did not like the sort of help he received and declared himself an American, based on a long-ago trip through that country during which he had obtained naturalization papers.

35. Moore, *International Law Digest*, vol. 3, 759.

36. *FRUS* (1873), 1188.

37. Moore, *International Law Digest*, vol. 3, 773–74.

38. *FRUS* (1873), 1276, paraphrased.

39. *Afroyim v. Rusk, Secretary of State*, 387 *U.S.* 253; 1967 *U.S. LEXIS* 2844, 7 and 8/24.

40. Moore, *International Law Digest*, vol. 3, 762.

41. *A Compilation of the Messages and Papers of the Presidents 1789–1907*, James Richardson, ed. (Washington, D.C.: Bureau of National Literature and Art, 1908), vol. 3, 36. President Grant circulated a set of questions about expatriation, protection, and extraterritorial jurisdiction to all executive branch agencies; reproduced in *FRUS* (1873).

42. *FRUS* (1873), 1204.

43. Ibid., 1717.

44. Moore, *International Law Digest*, vol. 3, 765–67.

45. *FRUS* (1873), 1188–89.

46. *FRUS* (1873), 1214, emphasis added.

47. Neuman, *Strangers*, 8, paraphrased.

48. Moore, *International Law Digest*, vol. 2, 232.

49. Lester Langley and Thomas Schoonover, *The Banana Men: American Mercenaries and Entrepreneurs in Central America, 1880–1930* (Lexington: University Press of Kentucky, 1995), 6.

50. Ibid., ch. 1, especially 13–14.

51. Ibid., 28–31.

52. Ibid., 41.

53. *FRUS* (1894), 316–31.

54. *FRUS* (1894), 343; (1906), vol. 2, 870.

55. Clarence Clendenen et al., *Americans in Africa 1865–1900* (Stanford: Stanford University Press, 1966), 18–23, 67; Thomas Noer, *Briton, Boer, and Yankee. The United States and South Africa 1870–1914* (Kent: Kent State University Press, 1978), 4, 7, 75, 81–82.

56. Noer, 12, 18.

57. Arrell Gibson, *Yankees in Paradise: The Pacific Basin Frontier* (Albuquerque: University of New Mexico Press, 1993), 348.

58. Ibid., 349.

59. Curtis Henson, *Commissioners and Commodores: The East India Squadron and American Diplomacy in China* (University: University of Alabama Press, 1982), 13, 181.

60. Edward Graham, *American Ideas of a Special Relationship with China, 1784–1900* (New York: Garland, 1988), 3–5, 7.

61. Graham, 26–27.

62. Te-kong Tong, *United States Diplomacy in China, 1844–60* (Seattle: University of Washington, 1964), 64.

63. Keeton, *The Development of Extraterritoriality*, vol. 1, 49.

64. On the general subject, see Hunt, *The Making of a Special Relationship*.

65. Swisher, *China's Management of the American Barbarians*, 47–51.

66. Graham, *American Ideas of a Special Relationship*, 52–54; Charles C. Stelle, "American Trade in Opium to China, Prior to 1820," *Pacific Historical Review* (December 1940), 9:427.

67. Jacques Downes, "Fair Game: Exploitative Role-Myths and the American Opium Trade," *Pacific Historical Review* (May 1972), 41:141, 146.

68. Graham, *American Ideas of a Special Relationship*, 57–58.

69. Ibid., 13, 15, 21.

70. *Congressional Globe* (1840), 26:172, 275.

71. Factual information here drawn from Ruth Kark, *American Consuls in the Holy Land, 1832–1914* (Detroit: Wayne State University Press, 1994), 68–69, 79.

72. Henson, *Commissioners and Commodores*, 32; U.S. House, "Memorial of R. B. Forbes and Others to the Congress of the U.S.," 26th Cong., 1st sess. (1839), H. Doc. 40; Graham, *American Ideas of a Special Relationship*, 63–64.

73. Wu Meng-hsüeh, *Mei-kuo tsai Hua ling-shih ts'ai-p'an ch'üan pai-nien shih*; Graham, *American Ideas of a Special Relationship*, 26–27; Keeton, *The Development of Extraterritoriality*, vol. 1, 49; John K. Fairbank, "'American China Policy' to 1898: A Misconception," *Pacific Historical Review* (November 1970), 39:409–20.

74. A. Owen Aldridge, *The Dragon and the Eagle: The Presence of China in the American Enlightenment* (Detroit: Wayne State University Press, 1983), 210.

75. Hinckley, *American Consular Jurisdiction*, 27, 30, paraphrased and quoted.

76. U.S. Senate, Kearny to Governor General of Kwangtung and Kwangse, 13 April 1843, 29th Cong., 1st sess., S. Doc. 139, 34.

77. U.S. Senate, "Correspondence of the Late Commissioners to China," 35th Cong., 2d sess.(1858), S. Exec. Doc. 22, 259.

78. Hinckley, *American Consular Jurisdiction*, 81.

79. "Correspondence of the Late Commissioners in China," 737–38.

80. U.S. House, U.S. Minister to State Department, 22 February 1860, H. Doc. 56, 291–93.

81. Opinion of George H. Williams, Department of Justice, "Imprisonment of Convicts of Consular Courts," 14 *Opinions Atty Gen.* 522 (1875). Issued in response to case involving an American convicted at Smyrna for forgery and another at Constantinople, whom consuls want to transfer to the United States.

82. Opinion of W. H. H. Miller, Department of Justice, "Consular Jurisdiction—Service of Sentence," 20 *Opinions Atty Gen.* 391 (1892). Case involved an American sailor (Harkaway) sentenced in Amoy and sent to Shanghai, but consul there released him, fearing lack of jurisdiction.

83. "Letter of the United States Minister at Peking," enc. in George Seward to State Department, 11 July 1864.

84. Ibid., 5–6.

85. U.S. Consul Ningpo (McCartee) to Commissioner of the United States in China (Parker), 19 February 1855.

86. Burlingame to Seward, 1 June 1864, and response, *FRUS* (1864), 376, 392–96; Clarence Osborn, "American Extraterritorial Jurisdiction in China to 1906: A Study of American Policy," Ph.D. dissertation, Stanford University, 1935, 110.

87. Burlingame to Seward, 23 November 1863, 393.

88. Sources of information on Seward include: "Geo. F. Seward Dead, Insurance Head," *NYT*, 29 November 1910, 11:3; Tyler Dennett, *Americans in Eastern Asia* (New York: Barnes and Noble, 1941).

89. "Minister Seward Arraigned. He Is Placed Before the Bar of the House Charged With Contempt—A Scene of Disorder and Excitement," *NYT*, 1 March 1879, 1:2; and "George F. Seward Arraigned," ibid., 2:6.

90. U.S. House,"Investigation of George F. Seward," 45th Cong., 3d sess. (1879), H. Rpt. 134.

91. *NYT*, 28 February 1879, 1-1–2; "The Attack on Minister Seward," *NYT*, 25 January 1879, 1-4; U.S. House,"Letter from the Late Consul-General (John C. Myers) Requesting an Investigation of the Affairs of the Consulate General at Shanghai, China," 45th Cong., 2d sess. (1878), H. Misc. Doc. 10 (1878), 1.

92. "Investigation of George F. Seward," 7–20.

93. Documents pertaining to Bradford's trials on tampering with the mails and on embezzlement are found in the "Investigation of George F. Seward," part 2, pp. 131–250.

94. Minister (Denby) to Secretary (Bayard), 15 December 1887, #527, in Osborn, "American Extraterritorial Jurisdiction," 315.

95. "Extraterritoriality and the United States Court for China" (in Editorial Comment), *American Journal of International Law* (April 1907), 1:469.

96. Seward, "Letter of the United States Minister at Peking." The nature of the surviving records make all case totals approximate. Very few pre-1906 American cases were reported in *North China Herald*, and the analysis here has been drawn from the sometimes confusing and incomplete docket books found in RG 84, NARA.

97. Shanghai Consul to Chefoo Consul, 30 October 1885, 54. Dispatches from U.S. Consuls in Chefoo, China, 1863—1906. NARA, M102.

98. See, for example, the eight or so cases brought by the Chinese Imperial Collector of Customs in 1854 for debt against various companies refusing to pay duties until Taiping rebels in the Shanghai area had been brought under control. These cases were all referred to Commissioner Robert McLane by mutual agreement.

99. In 1862–63, there were 17 cases brought against Chinese, on charges including furious driving, robbery, assault, theft. All were "sent to [the] city," meaning turned over to the Shanghai Municipal Council, and later the Mixed Court. One case against a Chinese brought by one C. Sane ended in 6 days in jail and small fine. In 1864, there were about 152 criminal cases, ten of which involved Chinese plaintiffs and all of these 10 were dismissed or warned.

100. Osborn, "American Extraterritorial Jurisdiction," 187.

101. Consul at Canton to Assistant Secretary of State, 31 May 1900, #7, Reel 14, with enclosed letter from Viceroy Li Hung Chang. Dispatches from U.S. Consuls in Canton, China, 1790—1906. NARA. M101.

102. Opinion of A. H. Garland, Department of Justice, "Jurisdiction of Consular Courts," 18 *Opinions Atty Gen.* (1886). Case involved U.S. consul in Yokohama convicting a German national for aiding and assisting U.S. seaman to escape from custody; Opinion of James Speed, Attorney General's Office, "Jurisdiction of Consular Courts in Japan," 11 *Opinions Atty Gen.* 474 (1866).

103. Hill testimony, "Investigation of George F. Seward," 27 February 1878, vol. 1, 80; misspellings in original.

104. Tong, *United States Diplomacy in China*, 13–16.

105. *Congressional Globe*, 19 April 1848, 648.

106. Osborn, "American Extraterritorial Jurisdiction," 124–25.

107. Analytical point drawn from David Langum, *Law and Community on the Mexican California Frontier: Anglo-American Expatriates and the Clash of Legal Traditions, 1821–1846* (Norman: University of Oklahoma Press, 1987), 270, paraphrased.

108. Eileen P. Scully, "Prostitution as Privilege: The 'American Girl' of Treaty Port Shanghai," *International History Review* (December 1998), 20:855–83.

109. Bredbenner, "Toward Independent Citizenship," 56. Illegitimacy disqualified an American man's child from claiming citizenship if born abroad. *Guyer v. Smith*, 22 *MD* 239 (1864), a standard international rule, in Bredbenner, 44, fn 10.

110. The rule of thumb for consuls was that if a marriage was legal where it occurred, it was legal in the United States; because China permitted polygamy, the United States refused to recognize sexual unions based only on Chinese laws involving Americans. Consular courts were sometimes called upon to police the distinctions here, as in *U.S. v. Burnett*, where the defendant was ultimately acquitted on charges of kidnapping a woman from an inmate from a nearby Buddhist convent. On appeal to the U.S. minister, it was determined that there was insufficient evidence of coercion.

111. There was undoubtedly a double standard, with a greater tolerance for colonial men marrying indigenous women, as suggested in a 1898 spate of letters in the Shanghai *North China Herald* reacting to the marriage in Shansi of a Norwegian missionary from the China Inland Mission to a Chinese male convert. *NCH*, 5 September 1898, 443; 12 September 1898, 494–95.

112. Goodnow to Assistant Secretary (Peirce), 23 June 1904, #589, as to the will of Mary Bennett, being contested by surviving husband.

113. *Charles E. Hill v. Elizabeth Adams Hill* (1882), heard by the U.S. consul and two assessors. After several years of legal separation, Charles sued Elizabeth for a clear declaration of ownership of certain property in French Concession. She did not contest.

114. U.S. Minister (Denby), to Secretary of State (Bayard), 19 October 1888, *FRUS* (1889), 75. For the British comparison, see William Eversley and William Craies, *The Marriage Laws of the British Empire* (Littleton: F. B. Rothman, 1989).

115. Law Reports, *Bridget Williams v. John Williams*, *NCH*, 23 November 1876, 518–19. For Williams's later activities, see: *Rex (Alfred Barnes) v. J. H. Williams*, *NCH*, 24 April 1880, 364; *Rex (Police) v. John Henry Williams*, *NCH*, 5 February 1880, 105.

116. Particularly striking in this regard is the 1886 case of *Jules Bruchard v. Ethel Clinton*, when the U.S. Consul recessed his court to allow the litigants to bring in the dress under dispute for expert examination; when court resumed, there had been an out-of-court settlement favorable to both parties. *NCH*, 20 October 1886. In 1881, Clinton had brought charges against Isaac Duncan for assault. Scully, "Prostitution as Privilege."

117. Scully, "Prostitution as Privilege."

118. *Matheiu (U.S.) v. Mexico*, 4 July 1868, Howard's case and Aubrey's case 1880. Moore, *International Law Digest*, vol. 3.

119. Young to Frelinghuysen, no. 248, 3 September 1883; no. 34, 12 December 1883, cited Osborn, "American Extraterritorial Jurisdiction," 254–56.

120. See, for example, Shanghai Quarterly Reports for 1860 and 1861 for cases involving Peter Cole, an American black who accompanied the Perry mission that opened Japan. For the killing of a black American saloon keeper, Gregory Lemon, by U.S. Marshal James Frame, see Shanghai Consul General (Leonard) to Assistant Secretary of State, 22 June 1892, no. 202; 31 May 1892, no. 198.

121. Randolph Keim, "A Report to the Hon. George S. Boutwell, Secretary of the Treasury, upon the Conditions of the Consular Service of the United States of America" (Washington, D.C.: GPO, 1872), 177. See *U.S. v. Kimball*, "sailor stealing," in Quarterly Reports, Shanghai Consulate, 4 August–31 December 1850. Henceforth, QR, dates.

122. *U.S. v. Bartlett*, found guilty of inducing seamen to desert ships at Shanghai and Woosung, fined $200 or one month, and deportation in either case; he was imprisoned, but escaped. QR, August 1853.

123. George Garbesi, *Consular Authority Over Seamen from the United States Point of View* (The Hague: Martinus Nijhoff, 1968).

124. Briton Busch, *"Whaling Will Never Do for Me": The American Whaleman in the Nineteenth Century* (Lexington: University Press of Kentucky, 1994), 62–64, 85.

125. Everett to Buchanan, 25 January 1847, no. 23.

126. U.S. House, "Ports of China," 32d Cong., 1st sess. (1852), H. Exec. Doc. 80.

127. 36th Cong., 1st sess. (1858), S. Doc. 30, 426–28. See, for example, *U.S. v. Benjamin Sherburn, master et al.*, *NCH*, 11 August 1870, 111.

128. U.S. Senate, "Correspondence of the Late Commissioners . . . ," 536–37.

129. Morse, *International Relations of the Chinese Empire*, 345–46.

130. U.S. Senate, 36th Cong., 1st sess. (1858), S. Exec. Doc. 30.

131. Graham, *American Ideas of a Special Relationship*, 115.

132. U.S. Senate, 49th Cong., 2d sess. (1887), S. Rpt. 1621; Lobingier, *Extraterritorial Cases*, vol. 1, 521–22.

133. U.S. Senate, 55th Cong., 2d sess., (1858/59), S. Exec. Doc. 22.

134. Osborn, "American Extraterritorial Jurisdiction," 46–47.

135. U.S. Senate, 35th Cong., 2d sess. (1958), S. Exec. Doc. 22, 566–68.

136. *FRUS* (1868), vol. 1, 547–57; Seward to Browne, 5 February 1869, no. 17.

137. Moore, *International Law Digest*, vol. 3, 135.

138. Payson Treat, *Diplomatic Relations Between the United States and Japan, 1853–1895* (Stanford: Stanford University Press, 1932), vol. 1, 355.

139. Neuman, "Anomalous Zones."

3. COLONIZING THE COLONIZERS

1. See, for example, Charles Loomis, "Some Americans Abroad," a satirical series that ran in the *Century Magazine*, May to October 1902.

2. Ibid. See also Madame Juliette Adam, "Those American Girls in Europe," *North American Review* (1891), 151:399–407. Reply to Mrs. John Sherwood, "American Girls in Europe," *North American Review* (1890), 150:680–91.

3. Theodore Roosevelt, "What 'Americanism' Means," *The Forum* (1894), 17:196–201.

4. Candice Bredbenner, "Toward Independent Citizenship," 61.

5. Hillevi Toiviainen, *Search for Security: United States Citizens in the Far East, 1890–1906* (Jyvaskyla: University of Jyvaskyla, 1986).

6. Borchard, *Diplomatic Protection of Citizens Abroad*, 432–33.

7. Stephen Skowronek, *Building a New American State: The Expansion of National Administrative Capacities, 1877–1920* (New York: Cambridge University Press, 1982), 4.

8. Ibid., 11.

9. Ibid., 13, paraphrased.

10. Wharton, *A Digest of the International Law of the United States*, 248–49.

11. Ibid.

12. Moore, *Digest of International Law*, vol. 3, 763.

13. Walter LaFeber, "The Constitution and United States Foreign Policy: An Interpretation," in David Thelen, ed., *The Constitution and American Life* (Ithaca: Cornell University Press, 1988), 35–36.

14. The State Department stipulated that the individual must heed Nicaraguan law, show an intent to return eventually to the United States, and demur from taking any oath of allegiance to a foreign government. *FRUS* (1900), vol. 3, 785.

15. "Expatriation and Protection of Naturalized Americans Abroad and in Turkish Dominions," *American Journal of International Law* (January 1908), 2:156–60.

16. Moore, *International Law Digest*, vol. 2, 968–69.

17. "Citizenship of the United States, Expatriation, and Protection Abroad," 59.2 House Document 326 (1906), 211.

18. Ibid., 212; Moore, *International Law Digest*, vol. 3, 777.

19. Moore, *International Law Digest*, 3, 975, 968–69.

20. Ibid., 975, emphasis added.

21. The term "bargaining risks" is from Epstein, *Bargaining with the State*.

22. *Ross v. McIntyre*, 140 *U.S.* 453, 11 *Supreme Court* 897.

23. The "insular cases" embraced nine cases decided by the Supreme Court circa 1901 that collectively reconciled the U.S. Constitution with colonial rule by the United States over territories it acquired through the annexation of Hawaii and the Spanish-American War. Efren R. Ramos, "The Legal Construction of American Colonialism: the Insular cases (1901–1922)," *Revista Juridica Universidad De Puerto Rico* (1996), 65:225–328.

24. *Ross v. U.S.*, 140 *U.S.* 453. Ross first appealed to the 9th Circuit Court in California (the appellate court for extraterritorial American courts) for a writ of habeas corpus, arguing that U.S.–Japanese treaty provisions for criminal trials applied only to crimes against Japanese. This was denied. The case that reached the Supreme Court was an appeal from the adverse decision of the U.S. Circuit Court in the northern district of New York.

25. 88 *U.S.* 162; Rogers Smith, *Civic Ideals*, 166–67.

26. David J. Bederman, "Extraterritorial Domicile and the Constitution," *Virginia Journal of International Law* (Winter 1988), 28:451–94.

27. Ann Stoler, "Making Empire Respectable: The Politics of Race and Sexual Morality in 20th-Century Colonial Cultures," *American Ethnologist* (November 1989), 16:634–60.

28. Philippa Levine, "Rereading the 1890s: Venereal Disease as 'Constitutional Crisis' in Britain and British India," *Journal of Asian Studies* (1986), 45:585–612.

29. "The Foowchow Road Scandal," *NCH* (9 February 1887), 137–38.

30. Mark Peattie, "Japanese Treaty Port Settlements in China, 1895–1937," in Peter Duus et al., *The Japanese Informal Empire in China, 1895–1937* (Princeton: Princeton University Press, 1989), 171.

31. Vassilios Bill Mihalopoulos, "The *Karayuki-san*: Modernisation, Social Administration, and the Making of Overseas Japanese Prostitutes," *Bulletin of Concerned Asian Scholars* (January–March 1993), 25:41–56. Japanese sources reported the numbers in 1896 as follows: Hong Kong, 100; Singapore, 300; Penang, 200; Australia, 200; Tonkin, 80; Saigon, 160; British India, 200; Siam, 40. *Japan Weekly Mail*, 30 May 1896, 609. See the reassurance offered Japanese in "Japanese Reputation Abroad," *Japan Weekly Mail*, 3 October 1891, 54, to the effect that: "Constituted as the world is, the crossing of women of bad character from one country to another, or the wanderings of habitual loafers is unavoidable. Japan is not the only country which has subjects who bring her no credit."

3. COLONIZING THE COLONIZERS

Some Japanese commentators argued that the outward migration of Japanese prostitutes was good for business, and that the women acted as forerunners for Japanese traders.

32. "The Expander's Armor Pierced," *The New Voice* (19 July 1900) :1; "State Regulation of Vice at Manila," *Women's Journal* (September 1900), 1:274.

33. "Murmurs from Mean Streets," *NCH* (9 May 1898), 789.

34. "A Chinese 'English Pale,'" *NYT* (27 March 1892), 17.7.

35. Patrick Brantlinger and Donald Ulin, "Policing Nomads: Discourse and Social Control in Early Victorian England," *Cultural Critique* (Fall 1993), 25:33–63.

36. Peattie, "Japanese Treaty Port Settlements," 184.

37. Ronald Hyam, "Empire and Sexual Opportunity," *The Journal of Imperial and Commonwealth History* (January 1986), 14:68–69; Edward J. Bristow, *Prostitution and Prejudice: The Jewish Fight Against White Slavery, 1870–1939* (New York: Schocken Books, 1983); for parallel developments in South Africa, see Charles van Onselen, *Studies in the Social and Economic History of the Witwatersrand 1886–1914* (New York: Longman, 1982), vol. 1, 103–62.

38. "Chin-chih ching-shih ke hsi-ren chi-kuan an" (Materials on prohibitions regarding Western brothels in the capital), no. 02–26/13(4), Wai-wu-bu Dangan; "Han-jen . . . tsai ching k'ai-shê chi-kuan an" (Materials regarding the opening of a brothel in the capital by a Korean), #02–26/26(9), both circa 1906–7 (*Guang-hsu* 31–32), Archives of the Tsungli Yamen and the Foreign Affairs Bureau, Manuscript Collection, Institute of Modern History, Academia Sinica, Taipei, Taiwan.

39. Mary Fitch et al. to the White House, enclosed in U.S. Shanghai Consul (J. Goodnow) to State Department, 18 January 1900, M-112.

40. Kenton Clymer, *Protestant Missionaries in the Philippines, 1898–1916* (Champaign: University of Illinois Press, 1986), 17; Jerry Israel, *Progressivism and the Open Door: America and China, 1905–1921* (Pittsburgh: University of Pittsburgh Press, 1971).

41. Stoler, "Sexual Affronts. . . ," 550–51.

42. Ronald Robinson, "Imperial Theory and the Question of Imperialism After Empire," in R. F. Holland and G. Rizvi, eds., *Perspectives on Imperialism and Decolonization* (London: Frank Cass, 1984), 44. See also Dean Britten, "British Informal Empire: The Case of China," *Journal of Commonwealth Comparative Politics* (March 1976), 14:64–81.

43. Mary Wright, *The Last Stand of Chinese Conservatism: The T'ung-Chih Restoration, 1862–1874* (Stanford: Stanford University Press, 1957).

44. Michael Hunt, "The Forgotten Occupation: Peking, 1900–1901," *Pacific Historical Review* (November 1979), 48:507–9.

45. Michael Hunt, *Special Relationship*, part 3; Thomas McCormick, *China*

Market: America's Quest for Informal Empire, 1893–1901 (Chicago: Quadrangle Books, 1967); Paul Varg, *The Making of a Myth: The United States and China 1897–1912* (East Lansing: Michigan State University Press, 1968).

46. James Lorence, "Business and Reform: The American Asiatic Association and the Exclusion Laws," *Pacific Historical Review*, (November 1970), 39:421–38; Delber McKee, *Chinese Exclusion versus the Open Door Policy, 1900–1906* (Detroit: Wayne State University Press, 1977); Hunt, *Special Relationship*, chs. 3, 7.

47. Consul General James Rodgers, Shanghai, to Robert Bacon, Assistant Secretary of State, 28 May 1906, no. 163. Dispatches from U. S. Consuls in Shanghai. NARA, M-112.

48. Peter Onuf, "Settlers, Settlements, and New States," in Jack Greene, ed., *The American Revolution: Its Character and Limits* (New York: New York University Press, 1987), 180–81, 184, 194fn41.

49. Rodgers to Robert Bacon, 19 March 1906, no. 131, M-112.

50. Ibid.

51. Rodgers to Bacon, 29 December 1905, no. 85, M-112. See also James Davidson, acting consul general, to Francis Loomis, Assistant Secretary of State, 23 February 1905, no. 646, M-112.

52. Davidson to Loomis, 23 February 1905, no. 646. M-112.

53. For a contemporary discussion of the problem, and a range of examples illustrating it, see Rev. Jacob Speicher, American Baptist Mission, "The Relation of the Missionary to the Magistrates," *The Chinese Recorder* (August 1901): 391–98; Rev. William Ashmore, "Some Bits of Missionary Experience," *The Chinese Recorder* 1899 (February), 1:53–62; (May), 2:209–16; (June), 3:278–87.

54. McWade to Loomis, 13 April 1903, no. 258, Dispatches from U.S. Consuls in Canton, China, 1863–1906. NARA, M-101.

55. See 1892 documents on foreigners smuggling goods in the interior, no. 2248; arms dealing, no. 2282, no. 2284; counterfeiting, no. 3049, no. 3050, *Chung-Mei kuan-hsi shih-liao, Kuang-hsu ch'ao* [Historical Materials in Sino-American Relations, Kuang-hsu reign], vol. 3 (Taipei, Taiwan: Institute of Modern History, Academia Sinica, 1988–89).

56. Israel, *Progressivism and the Open Door*, 58.

57. The 1905 official figure is comprised as follows: 461 male adults, 317 female adults; 107 male children, 106 female children. Population figures vary. A 1902 consular inspection by Minister E. Conger estimates as follows: 50 = Amoy; 300 = Canton; 200 = Chefoo; 60 = Chinkiang; 156 = Fuchau; 1000 = Shanghai; 100 = Tientsin.

58. Rodgers to Loomis, 21 September 1905, no. 48, M-112.

59. J. B. Scott, State Department Solicitor, "Memorandum in Regard to the Jurisdiction of American Consular Officers in China Over Offenses Against Morality and Decency," 26 November 1906.

60. *The United States Passport: Past, Present, Future* (Washington, D.C.: Department of State, 1976), table 220. From 1861 to 1869, about 40,800 passports were issued; during 1869–77, about 30,000.

61. Chefoo Consul (Fowler) to State Department, 12 October 1905, no number, Dispatches from U.S. Consuls in Chefoo, 1863–1906, M-102; *The Shanghai Times*, 29 January 1907.

62. Moore, *International Law Digest*, vol. 3, 1079–80.

63. "Passports," *Opinions of the Attorneys General*, 10, 517.

64. Hunt, *Special Relationship*, 398n71, and chs. 5 and 8 more generally. When those like Reid pointed to wayward Americans in China as the source of difficulties in the bilateral relationship, one motive was likely to diffuse a tendency back home to blame missionaries, as in: "Missionaries in China. Natives Tolerate Their Religion but Resent their Meddling. Few Converts are Sincere," *NYT*, 24 February 1901, 14.1.

65. Goodnow to Loomis, 17 November 1904, no. 619, M-112, forwarding petitions by Americans in China to improve treatment of Chinese entering the United States.

66. Rodgers to Robert Bacon, 10 January 1906. no. 99, M-112; Rodgers to Bacon, 28 May 1906, no. 163, M-112.

67. Rodgers to Bacon, 31 March 1908, no. 154, M-112.

68. Speech by H. B. Morse to the Asian Association, *Journal of the American Association in China*, 2:6.

69. "American Consulate Burned. Fire at Amoy, China. Also Destroyed Most of the Records," *NYT*, 1 November 1904, 9:2.

70. H. H. D. Peirce, *Inspection of U.S. Consulates in the Orient* (Washington, D.C.: GPO, 1906).

71. Kermit Hall "The Civil War Era as a Crucible for Nationalizing the Lower Federal Courts," *Prologue* (Fall 1975), 7:177–86.

72. "Looting" meant passing the estate around to friends and relatives of the consul, until commissions and unauthorized fees had consumed the assets. When A. H. White, consular clerk and Consul General John Goodnow's brother-in-law, died in 1905, for instance, he bequeathed only a debt of $2,695 gold, the amount he had "borrowed" from the estate of Thelma Newton, alias Barbara May Woods, to which he had been appointed executor by Goodnow. Estate of A. H. White, A-223, Shanghai Probate Records, RG 84, Box 20.

73. Estate of Cosette Denvers, A-238, Shanghai Probate Records, RG84, Box 21.

74. Ibid. On Passano, see *Dickinson and Jones v. Bassano* (sic), in the Shanghai U.S. Consular Court, *NCH*, 4 May 1905, *NCH*, 5 May 1905.

75. Estate of Barbara B. Foster, A-230, RG 84, Box 20. See also material on Zella Maynard, alias Martha Zellars, of Kenton, Ohio, who committed suicide on 23 December 1901, leaving an estate valued at approximately 12,305.81 taels.

[James Ragsdale to State, 28 December 1901, no. 80, and Ragsdale to State, 30 January 1902, no. 85, M-114].

76. Emily Moore refused to give Maxine Livingstone an accounting for the finances of a house on Kiangse Road in which they shared an interest and their American lawyers in Shanghai attempted to work out a settlement but failed. Soon thereafter, the two women came to blows on Bubbling Well Road when one struck the other with a riding crop. When each sought to bring charges against the other for assault, U.S. Consul General James Rodgers refused to consider it, for the reasons stated.

77. Davidson to Loomis, 7 February 1905, no. 635, with enclosures.

78. "The Alhambra Case," *NCH*, 6 January 1905, 34–35, containing extracts of consular correspondence on Brown from the previous year.

79. "At the White House," *[Washington] Evening Star*, 5 December 1906, page 7. (NB: *The Washington Star* on weekdays was *The Evening Star* and on Sundays, the *Sunday Star*.)

80. Ibid., and clipping from the *Washington Post*, n.d., in Rodgers to State Department, 6 January 1906, M-112.

81. John Goodnow, former consul general, Shanghai, to Rodgers, 10 January 1906. Enclosure, Rodgers to Robert Bacon, Assistant Secretary of State, 6 January 1906, M-112. The inconsistency between the earlier and later dates is an error in the original documents.

82. W. F. Walker et al. to James Ragsdale, Tientsin, 23 January 1902, Enc. No. 1 in no. 896, Minister E. Conger to John Hay, Secretary of State, 21 January 1902, contained in ibid., no. 36, 214–16. (The discrepancy of dates is in the original.) A few days before, Ragsdale had reported that although Brown had not been long in Tientsin, he had already established a "splendid trade." Ragsdale, Tientsin, to E. H. Conger, U.S. minister, Peking, 21 January 1902, Enc. No. 7 in no. 889. Reproduced in Jules Davids, ed., *American Diplomatic and Public Papers: The United States and China*, series 3, vol. 12, Document 33, pp. 204–5.

83. Conger to Hay, 31 December 1900, no. 491, *FRUS* (1901), 40. See also Hay to Conger, 27 November 1901, no. 417, ibid., 58–59.

84. A handwritten brief memo to Peirce from the assistant solicitor, 9 March 1906, accompanying John Davidson, Shanghai, to State Department, 7 February 1905, no. 635, M-112, Reel 51.

85. "Accuses Consul Goodnow," *NYT*, 29 September 1904, 1:5. For the consular battle against Brown and the Alhambra, see *Municipal Gazette of the Council for the Foreign Settlement of Shanghai* (1908), 237–38, (1909), 113, 175–76, 204, 227. Shanghai Municipal Archives, Shanghai, China.

86. Peirce to William Loeb Jr. (secretary to President Roosevelt), 3 December 1904. Papers of Theodore Roosevelt, Manuscript Collection, Library of Congress, Reel 50. See also Peirce to Loeb, 21 December 1904, ibid., Reel 51.

87. "District Court of the U.S. for China and Korea," U.S. Senate, 59th Cong., 1st sess. (1905), S. Doc. 95; U.S. House, "U.S. District Court for China," 59th Cong., 1st sess. (1906), H. Doc. 4432. The earlier version bill called for a 15-year judge, and applications of the laws of the United States and the District of Columbia. Although the earlier drafts provided that Korea would be included in the Court's jurisdiction, the 1905 Taft-Katsura Agreement, which conceded Japanese preeminence in Korea, appears to explain why the final creation act applied only to China. In 1906, the United States closed its Seoul Legation in acknowledgment of this U.S.–Japanese understanding.

88. U.S. House, "Reorganization of the Consular Service," 59th Cong., 1st sess. (1906), H. Rept. 2281, 14.

89. U.S. Senate, 59th Cong., 2d sess., S. Doc. 359.

90. The Court had original jurisdiction in civil cases involving sums over $500, and in criminal cases where the punishment for the offense could by law exceed $100 fine or 60 days imprisonment, or both. It had supervisory power over the probate of estates by consuls.

91. Richard McCormick, "The Discovery that Business Corrupts Politics: A Reappraisal of the Origins of Progressivism," *American Historical Review* (April 1981), 86:247–74.

92. Bredbenner, "Toward Independent Citizenship,"63–65; U.S. House, "Protection for Citizens of United States Sojourning Abroad," 58th Cong., 2d sess. (1903–1904), H. Rpt. 2531; U.S. House, "Expatriation of American Citizens and Their Protection Abroad," 59th Cong., 2d sess. (1906–1907), H. Rpt. 6431 and S. Rpt. 7299.

93. Borchard, *Diplomatic Protection of Citizens Abroad*, 680, paraphrased.

94. Elihu Root, "The Basis of Protection to Citizens Residing Abroad," *Proceedings of the American Society of International Law* (1910), 18–19.

4. PROGRESSIVISM SHANGHAIED

1. Wilfley to Theodore Roosevelt, 5 September 1907. Numerical Files of the State Department, 1906–10, Microfilm 862, Reel 82, National Archives, Washington, D.C.; hereafter M-862, Reel number; "Wilfley for Chinese Court," *NYT*, 6 July 1906, 6:6.

2. Glenn Anthony May, *Social Engineering in the Philippines: The Aims, Execution and Impact of American Colonial Policy, 1900–1913* (Westport, Conn.: Greenwood Press, 1980).

3. Indicative of the phenomenon, the post of Attorney General vacated by Wilfley in 1906 was filled by Gregorio Araneta, then solicitor general of the Philippines, of a Spanish *mestizo* family, and famed for "the peculiar qualifica-

tion of being able to pick up a volume of United States Supreme Court reports in the course of his argument and translate it freely into Spanish." "Wilfley for Chinese Court," *NYT*, 6 July 1906, 6:6.

4. William Leuchtenburg, "Progressivism and Imperialism: The Progressive Movement and American Foreign Policy, 1898–1916," *The Mississippi Valley Historical Review* (1952), 39:483–504. The term "militant decency" comes from Walter A. McDougall, *Promised Land, Crusader State* (Boston and New York: Houghton Mifflin, 1997), 17.

5. Hunt, *The Making of a Special Relationship*.

6. Israel, *Progressivism and the Open Door*.

7. Lebbeus Wilfley to William H. Taft, 18 June 1907, William Howard Taft Papers, Library of Congress, Manuscript Division, Reel 67.

8. Ibid.

9. Hepner, *Extraterritorial Criminal Jurisdiction*, 18–19.

10. Thomas L. Haskell, "Capitalism and the Origins of the Humanitarian Sensibility," (parts 1 and 2), in Thomas Bender, ed., *The Antislavery Debate; Capitalism and Abolitionism as a Problem in Historical Interpretation* (Berkeley: University of California Press, 1992)

11. *Shanghai Mercury*, 15 February 1907, in M-862, Reel 80.

12. *Journal of the American Association*, M-862, Reel 85.

13. Hinckley, *American Consular Jurisdiction*.

14. John Field, *Toward a Programme of Imperial Life: The British Empire at the Turn of the Century* (Westport, Conn.: Greenwood Press, 1982), 25, 30, 37–82; and Winfried Baumgart, *Imperialism: The Idea and Reality of British and French Colonial Expansionism, 1888–1914* (New York: Oxford University Press, 1982).

15. Westel Willoughby, "Citizenship and Allegiance in Constitutional and International Law," *American Journal of International Law* (July/October 1907), 1:918, 927–28.

16. Consular courts in China had customarily allowed attorneys to practice based upon their affiliation with state or federal higher courts in the United States. Thus, admission before the Supreme Court of any state enabled one to appear before American consuls in the treaty ports, which in turn, according to the principle of "comity," permitted one to appear in other foreign consular and "mixed" (Sino-Western) courts in China.

17. Shanghai Consul (Rodgers) to Secretary (Root) 17 December 1906, M-862, Reel 84.

18. Wilfley to Root, 8 May 1907, Taft Papers, Reel 65.

19. *U.S. v. Biddle*, (1907), *USC-C: ExCases*, vol. 1, 184, reversed on appeal by the 9th Circuit Court in California, which found insufficient evidence of intent to deceive; *Biddle v. U.S.*, 84 C.C.A. (Circuit Court of Appeals) 415, 156 F. 759 (C.C.A. 9, 28 October 1907), (no. 1463). Appellate case files for the USC-C are at

National Archives–Pacific Sierra Region, Leon J. Ryan Federal Archives and Records Center, San Bruno, Calif., Record Group 276 (U.S. Courts of Appeals), retrievable by case number (e.g., *Biddle v. U.S.* (no. 1463). As noted above, the third judge of the USC-C, Charles Lobingier, published the two-volume *United States Court for China: Extraterritorial Cases* (Manila: Bureau of Printing, 1920, 1928), hereafter abbreviated as *USC-C: ExCases*, vol., page).

20. *United States v. Price* (1907), *USC-C: ExCases*, vol. 1, 129, on appeal 156 F. 950, 85 *C.C.A.* 247, 13 *Am. Ann. Cas.* 483. no. 1429, RG 276, NARA (San Bruno).

21. Scully, "Prostitution as Privilege"; *U.S. v. Maxine Livingstone et al.*, *North China Daily News*, 26 January 1907. Wilfley to Taft, 9 May 1907, Taft Papers, Reel 65. Wilfley to Root, 13 June 1907, enc. in Wilfley to Taft, 18 June 1907, Taft Papers, Reel 67.

22. For the theoretical point, see Jack Greene, *Peripheries and Center: Constitutional Development in the Extended Politics of the British Empire and the United States, 1607–1788* (Athens: University of Georgia Press, 1987), xi.

23. Committee to White House, 14 January 1907, M-862, Reel 79.

24. Root to Wilfley, 6 March 1907, M-862, Reel 80. See also *Curtis v. Wilfley*, 9th C.C.A., 165 *Federal Reports* 893, no. 1598 (1908).

25. On the shared quarters of the Consulate and Court, see Rodgers to Secretary of State, 17 December 1906, M-862, Reel 79; and Rodgers to State Department, 3 January 1907, ibid. For appropriations, see miscellaneous correspondence between State Department officials and the Treasury Department Comptroller, ibid. For Washington's early pressure on Wilfley toward gradualism and accommodation, see Edwin Denby to Root, 25 February 1907, M-862, Reel 80; Taft to Wilfley, 8 March 1907, Taft Papers, Reel 490; Wilfley to Taft, 9 May 1907, Taft Papers, Reel 65.

26. State Department Solicitor (Scott) to Assistant Secretary Robert Bacon, 15 February 1907, M-862, Reel 80.

27. Wilfley to Secretary, received 12 February 1907, M-862, Reel 79; Denby to Consular Bureau Chief (Adee); Adee to U.S. Minister (Rockhill), 13 February 1907, and Bacon to Rockhill, 14 February 1907, ibid.

28. Chefoo Consul (Fowler) to Assistant Secretary, 6 March 1907, M-862, Reel 80.

29. *Yao Nee-zee v. Bassett*, NCH, 20 February 1909, 469–71.

30. British officials observed that the consular court's failure to prosecute successfully two free-lance American prostitutes (Trixy Laprieto and Ray Dixon) led to the arrival of "as many as forty old and new 'girls' who would otherwise have feared to come." "American Prostitutes," Confidential/unnumbered, 5 December 1908, Colonial Office-129/349 (CO-129/no.).

31. George Missemer, "Random Reflections . . . ," *China Weekly Review*, 8 February 1936, 333–34, in which this long-time Shanghai resident notes that "local

[British] juries are prone to stretch a point in favor of their fellow countrymen in criminal cases. However, when a Britisher is once sentenced to jail here, he stays put," as seen by the near total absence of appeals to London.

32. "Wilfley's Asininity," *Manila Cablenews*, 6 June 1907; "Americans Object to Judge Wilfley's Methods in China," *New York Daily Tribune*, 9 July 1907, also carried in *The Catholic News*, 13 July 1907.

33. "Charges Against Lebbeus R. Wilfley . . . and Petition For His Removal From Office," 19 November 1907. Addressed to President Roosevelt, from Lorrin Andrews, acting on behalf of "various American citizens residents of Shanghai," reproduced in "Hearings before a Sub-committee of the Committee on the Judiciary of the House of Representatives upon the Articles for the Impeachment of Lebbeus R. Wilfley" (Washington, D.C.: GPO, 1908).

34. Ibid., 101, 105.

35. *Rex. v. O'Shea*, HBM Supreme Court, 13 November 1908, M-862, Reel 84.

36. Hubert O'Brien to Edwin Denby, 20 October 1908, Edwin Denby Papers, Bentley Library, University of Michigan, Ann Arbor.

37. Root to Wilfley, 14 November 1908, M-862, Reel 84.

38. Wilfley to Taft, 21 February 1909, and 19 April 1909, both in Taft Papers, Reel 122. Emphasis in originals.

39. Secretary Root to Consul Denby, 11 December 1908, with enclosures, M-862, Reel 84.

40. "Judge R.H. Thayer Dies of Apoplexy," *NYT*, 13 July 1917.

41. U.S. Attorney General (Bonaparte) to Secretary of State (Root), forwarding telegram from Judge Ira Abbott; Solicitor General (Hoyt) to Assistant Secretary of State (Bacon), 14 November 1908, both M-862, Reel 84. On Thayer's nomination, see William Barnes, Jr., to President Taft, n.d. August 1912, Taft Papers, with enclosed letter from his sister alluding to the circumstances leading to her husband's appointment several years earlier, and inquiring into the possibility of a transfer because of her increasingly poor health.

42. Rufus Thayer to Secretary (Bryan), 15 September 1913, RG 59, 172.2/84; U.S. House, "Charges Against Rufus H. Thayer," 63d Cong., 1st sess. (1913), (Washington, D.C.: GPO, 1913).

43. The ability of treaty port Americans to cause trouble in Washington for the judges sent to the Shanghai Court had, in effect, the same impact upon judges as does the system operative in some areas of the continental United States where judges are elected and depend upon the support of local bar associations. See, for the modern analogue, "Brooklyn Court Experiment Putting Cases on Fast Track," *NYT*, 29 October 1993, 1. According to this report, "New York judges, who are elected and must rely on the recommendations of bar associations, tend to be lax." In such a system, "A judge who is seen as autocratic in case processing knows that translates into the potential for a truncated career."

44. *Cathay Trust Ltd. v. Brooks*, no. 1971, Circuit Court of Appeals, 9th Circuit, 193 F. 973, 5 February 1912, reversing Thayer; *Connell Brothers Co. v. H. Diederich-sen & Co.*, no. 2361, Circuit Court of Appeals, 9th Circuit, 213 F. 737, 18 May 1914, affirming Thayer, both at NARA (San Bruno).

45. An inference drawn from a letter from Rufus Thayer to Third Assistant Secretary of State (Phillips), 19 March 1909, M-862, Reel 84.

46. "American Prostitutes," CO-129/349, PRO.

47. Acting Secretary (Adee) to U.S. Minister (Rockhill), 10 November 1906, Reel 79.

48. Hinckley to State, 24 August 1914, 172.6/135.

49. USC-C to State, 6 February 1914, 172.6/92; Hinckley to State, 24 August 1914, 172.6/135.

50. Gunther, the individual who allegedly slapped a Chinese, was a chronic offender. Arriving in 1898, Gunther became the subject of repeated incidents of physical abuse toward laboring Chinese. In 1923, he reappears in the records as the unemployed defendant charged with assaulting two Chinese newspaper employees at a local post office: *U.S. (Shanghai Municipal Police v. C. Gunther* (1909), assaulting a rickshaw coolie by kicking; several similar complaints had been dismissed; "Fracas in a Post Office," *NCH*, 27 January 1923, 260.

51. Consul General (Denby) to U.S. District Attorney (Bassett), 26 May 1909; Consul General (Wilder) to U.S. District Attorney (Bassett), 8 June 1909. C8-12, vol. 22.

52. *NCH*, 19 October 1904; Consul (Goodnow) to State, with enclosures, 13 January 1904, M-112, Reel 51; *U.S. (SMP) v. Joseph Munz*, *NCH*, 14 August 1909.

53. *U.S. v. B. M. Gery* (*NCH*, 26 April 1913, 289), involved a U.S. sailor who struck a rickshaw coolie, killing him. Carroll P. Lunt (1912) had been in a boat with four Chinese, three of whom were boatmen. Lunt's gun fired, killing one Chinese. The Court agreed with Lunt that it had been an accident, as there had been no trouble leading up to the incident and no apparent motive. *USC-C: ExCases*, vol. 1, 279.

54. *FRUS* (1909), 55.

55. *Rex v. Stephenson*, HMB Supreme Court docket, PRO 656.101.

56. *FRUS* (1909), 55.

57. Borchard, *Diplomatic Protection*, 406; Thomas Bayard, "State Rights and Foreign Relations," *The Forum* 7 (1891), 235–49.

58. Stanley Hornbeck memorandum, 1928, 172/738, NARA.

59. Acting Secretary (Huntington Wilson) to Attorney General, 2 May 1910, RG 59, Box 3056, 172.6. J71/H. The State Department Solicitor's Office supported the petition for pardon.

60. Attorney General Lebbeus Wilfley, Address delivered before YMCA 11 July 1905 (Manila 1905). These remarks applied to Filipino "natives," and represented

Wilfley's general attitude toward Chinese as well, based on an extensive reading of his official and personal correspondence.

61. "American Prostitutes," CO 129/349, PRO.

62. This overview of the Court's early jurisprudence is drawn from contemporary treaty port newspaper clippings, the Court's actual cases, and two very valuable discussions on the subject by individuals directly involved in the Court, namely Crawford M. Bishop, "Jurisdiction of the United States Consular Courts in China (As Affected by the Act of June 30, 1906, and the Decisions of the United States Court for China created thereby)," American Consulate, Chefoo, China. 6 December 1913. RG 59, 172.1/73, Box 3045; and Charles Lobingier, "A Quarter Century of Our Extraterritorial Court," *Georgetown Law Journal* (May 1932), 20:427–56.

63. *U.S. v. Hadley* (gambling, 1910), *USC-C: ExCases*, vol. 1, 207, (threatening to kill, 1910); *U.S. v. Hennage* (gambling, 1910); *U.S. v. Ross* (gambling, 1910); *U.S. v. Kossack* (gambling, 1910), (embezzlement, 1910); *U.S. v. Clark* (gambling, 1910). See also H. Arnold to U.S. Court for China, 17 June 1910, RG 84, vol. 708, 77.

64. See, for example, the case of J. G. B. Hadley, subsequently before the USC-C for on various charges, and ultimately sentenced to one year for fraud.

65. "Arrest of British Subjects by Chinese Police in Peking," (1910) FO371/874, PRO.

66. *NCDN*, 17 April 1911.

67. Hinckley to Secretary, 16 September 1910, 172.6 K84/3; Hinckley to Secretary, 16 July 1910, 172.6 K84. Hinckley to Secretary, 29 June 1912, 172.3/33; H. Arnold to U.S. Consul General, 17 June 1910, RG 84, vol. 708, 8–49, 77l; A. Gilbert, vice consul in charge, to Shanghai consul general, 25 July 1910, 172.6/K84.

68. See, for example, Hinckley to Wilder, 20 March 1911, in re: Shanghai Municipal Council's resolution no. 2095 on tavern license, RG 84, vol. 741, 81; reply, 82.

69. See, for example, Hinckley to W. Roderick Dorsey, vice consul in charge, 28 February 1912, RG 84, vol. 763, 7, requesting that U.S. consular officials in Japan be alerted to the imminent arrival of alleged prostitute Doris Marlow, a.k.a., Marian Maurice, then en route to Nagasaki, and wanted for trial back in Shanghai.

70. *Laura Brown v. S. R. Price*, Civil Action no. 15; *J. H. Brown and L. Brown v. S. R. Price*, no. 30; *Brown v. Sexton*, no. 90, *US-C: ExCases*, vol. 1, 211. Printed copy also found in RG 59, 172.6 B81, Box 3056. In 1907, the Browns sold the Alhambra to Frank Gordon, allegedly an American using nationalities of convenience, and they had registered the mortgage for Mex.$60,000 in the Spanish Consulate at Shanghai. In 1909, when a judgment against Gordon put the Alhambra on the public auction block, manager Robert Sexton had purchased the premises. The

following year, Laura Brown sued Sexton in the U.S. Court to affirm her prior lien on the mortgaged property. Thayer, effectively insuring that the Court would not be used to assert the rights of one bawdy-house owner over another, determined that the matter lay outside of his jurisdiction. As all relevant deeds and documents had been registered under Spanish auspices, it was to those authorities the parties must appeal.

71. *Re application of J. H. Brown for mandamus . . .* , Civil Cause no. 35. In 1912, during its circuit through Tientsin, the Court heard *Louis Duquesne, Agent Mission Catholique du Tchely Sud Est v. J. H. Brown and Fanny Beck,* a civil suit brought against Brown (and his mother-in-law) involving a property transaction. During the course of the trial, Brown asserted that he had already initiated proceedings to repatriate himself to Russia, *USC-C: ExCases,* vol. 1, 280. See also *In re Jurisdiction over Frank Bascom* (1914), vol. 1, 378 on this question of presumptive jurisdiction.

72. *Brown v. Price* (debt/mortgage $12,500); *Brown v. Price* (debt/mortgage $36,197M); *Brown v. Boyd* (mandamus); *Brown v. Sexton* (debt).

73. Hinckley to Secretary, 19 May 1913, 172.6/B812; Huntington Wilson to Hinckley, 19 September 1912, 172.6/36–37; American Legation to Tientsin Consul General, 22 August 1912, referring to Circular 267, 20 July 1912, from State to W. Roderick Dorsey, vice consul general, Shanghai, 172.6/41 and forward.

74. In 1910, Chinese police in Peking had closed and occupied Brown's resort at No. 3 Telegraph Lane. Brown first tried to recoup the loss by having his wife Laura, the title owner, bribe U.S. Deputy Consul General and Land Registrar T. C. White, to re-register the property in his own name, an "indiscretion" for which White was officially reprimanded. Failing that, he managed somehow to get an order in February 1913 from the new Republic of China's Ministry of Foreign Affairs to Peking municipal authorities to return the premises, conditioned upon Brown's promise to foreswear its use for vice. By May 1, No. 3 Telegraph Lane was again open for business, as were Brown's other houses at Nos. 7 and 15.

75. Laura Brown (Chicago) to Clerk of the U.S. Court for China, 11 August 1914, and response 14 September 1914, both enclosed in U.S. Court to Secretary, 15 September 1914, 172.6/136. Hinckley to Secretary, 19 May 1913, 172.6/B812; Hinckley to Wilder, 16 May 1911, C8-14, vol. 30, 89. A final case involving the Browns came up in 1914, in their absence (*Hans & Clara Bahlke v. J. H. Brown* (1914), with plaintiffs seeking an appeal from a consular court decision.

76. "Resident Agents of China Trade Act Companies," Papers of Norwood Allman (American attorney in Shanghai). Hoover Institution on War, Revolution, and Peace, Stanford University, Box 11.

77. *Chui Cheu-tsuan v. Curtis; Tsu Yue-san v. Mooser; Ah Choy v. Woodruff; Ching Chong v. Hallock; Chong Sing v. Connell Bros; Chong Lai-kee v. Zimmerman; Foh Chang (a.k.a. Woo Yung-kwang) v. McMichael; Foh Chang (a.k.a. Woo*

Yung-kwang) v. Fraser and Co.; Ling Yue-dong v. Seitz; Luckan v. Pustau; Shan Fong Bank v. Barlow & Co.; Wong Lu-chong v. Munyon; Y. C. Tong v. Sutterle; Zun Hoong-sun and Jean v. J. S. Dooly and H. J. Black; Zu Yueng-ching v. Zimmerman; MaFel and Co. v. G. Collinwood; Leu Ching-tsau et al. v. Southern Meth Mission et al.; Woo Ah-sung v. Biddle; Woo Ah-sung v. Biddle and Hennage; Sze Hai-ching v. Biddle; Nee Chang Mou v. H. W. Andrews and George; Laou Kai-fook v. Mrs. W. L. Rodgers; Lu Zing-dong v. Danforth; Chen Wong-tai v. A. W. George & Co.; Chu Kun-kee v. A. W. George & Co.; Wong Sun-tien v. John Green; Lao Lai-ting v. Chung Ting-yer and Chas Bennett; Sun Ming Shan (Sun Nan-shang) v. N. A. Viloudak; Yih Yung-an v. Burlington Hotel. Court reports on each can be found in the *North China Herald* (1907–14).

78. See, for example *Lu Zing-dong v. Danforth* (comprador debt 12,719 Tls); *Chen Wong-tai v. A. W. George & Co.* (debt on contract, 12,579 Tls); *Chu Kun-kee v. A. W. George & Co.* (debt on contract, 1601 Tls); *Wong Sun-tien v. John Green* (debt $3055 Mex); *Lao Lai Ting v. Chung Ting Yer and Chas Bennett* (claim for 8999 Tls).

79. *NCH*, 31 October 1908, 281.

80. *NCH*, 24 February 1911, 455–56.

81. *Woo Ah-sung v. Biddle*, judgment for plaintiff, Biddle's comprador, for 6,000 Tls, generating *In re Bankruptcy of Charles Biddle*. This in turn led to *Woo Ah-sung v. Biddle & Hennage*, contesting Biddle's assignment of assets to Hennage to evade USC-C judgments. The Shanghai consular court case, *Sze Hai-ching v. Biddle* (1911), arose when one of Biddle's creditors asked the consul to restrain him from leaving the jurisdiction. Biddle died in Shanghai in 1919, *USC-C: ExCases*, vol. 1, 887. See also *Nee Chang Mou v. H. W. Andrews and George* (1911), an effort to recover a 1903 consular court judgment of 2,300 Tls, *USC-C: ExCases*, vol. 1, 243; *Yih Yung-an v. Burlington Hotel* (1912), debt of $15,036 for goods delivered, defendants fail to appear, *NCH* 4 May 1912. Further, see *U.S. v. Engelbracht* (1909), where the former U.S. consular court marshal was accused of stealing a judgment paid in 1906 for a Chinese plaintiff. Acquitted on the consular level, Engelbracht was brought before the USC-C because: "It was intolerable that such a record should be allowed to stand in an American court of justice and especially in an extraterritorial court in China and in a case in which the plaintiff was a Chinese." *USC-C: ExCases*, vol. 1, 169, 180.

82. American Consulate General Shanghai, Correspondence (1912), C8-15, vol. 22.

83. Fleming and Davies (attorneys) to Clarence Gauss, 4 January 1916, NA, Records of the Shanghai Consulate, RG 84, vol. 1057.

84. *Hildebrandt v. Zimmerman* (1907), *USC-C: ExCases*, vol. 1, 88. Suit to recover money for shortage on a cargo of flour shipped by plaintiff from Shanghai to Vladivostok by defendant's steamship.

85. *In re Stephen Barchet's Estate* (1911), *USC-C: ExCases*, vol. 1, 235–39.

86. *FRUS* (1910), 197–98.

87. *NCH*, 13 December 1907, 654–65. State Department Solicitor (Scott) to Director of the Consular Service (Carr), 19 December 1908, M-862, Reel 84.

88. *Ginsburg and Mess v. S. Zimmerman* (1908), *USC-C: ExCases*, vol. 1, 133.

89. This is more fully covered in Bederman, "Extraterritorial Domicile and the Constitution." In 1907, the Court argued that U.S. nationals who were long-term residents of China, and who had shown no intention of returning to their homes in America, were to be considered "domiciled" in China, and thereby their estates would come under the Court's jurisdiction, rather than that of particular State courts in the United States. The relevant decision was *In re: Young John Allen* (1907), *USC: ExCases*, vol. 1, 92. There were continued clashes between consuls and the USC-C over control of estates. See *In re Hankow Consul General's Report (on estate of James Winn)* (1913), *USC-C: ExCases*, vol. 1, 291.

90. *U.S. v. Jordan* (1912) *USC-C: ExCases*, vol. 1, 259.

5. WILSONIANISM AND AMERICAN IMPERIAL CITIZENSHIP

1. Emily Rosenberg, *Spreading the American Dream: American Economic and Cultural Expansion, 1890–1945* (New York: Hill and Wang, 1982).

2. "The Protection of American Citizens Abroad," *American Law Review* (1916), 50:902.

3. Hunt, *The Making of a Special Relationship*, 217.

4. This formulation of the essential "Wilsonian problem" is borrowed from Gordon Levin, *Woodrow Wilson and World Politics: America's Response to War and Revolution* (New York: Oxford University Press, 1968), 8.

5. Wilson to Lobingier, 30 January 1914, Wilson Papers, series 4, no. 833; Jerry Israel, *Progressivism and the Open Door*, 114–17, on the Wilson administration's standards for filling Far Eastern posts; Li Tien-yi, *Woodrow Wilson's China Policy, 1913–1917* (New York: Twayne, 1952), 16–19; James Reed, *The Missionary Mind and American East Asian Policy, 1911–1915* (Cambridge: Harvard University, Council on East Asian Studies, 1983), 141–42.

Lobingier was born in Lanark, Illinois, 30 April 1866, graduated from the University of Nebraska in 1888, later taking an M.A., L.L.M. and Ph.D. from the university. From 1900 to 1904 he was a member of the Nebraska Supreme Court Commission; in 1904, he was appointed a judge of the Court of First Instance of the Philippines and served until going to Shanghai. During his time in the Philippines, he convened several assemblies for the instruction of native magistrates, prepared a manual for guidance of local justices of the peace, and formulated an act reforming magistrate courts. Sources: "Hon. C. S. Lobingier is Named Judge of U.S. Court for China," unidentified treaty port newspaper clipping, Hornbeck Papers, Hoover Institute, Box 75.

6. Lobingier to Taft, 2 August 1912, referred to in Taft to Lobingier, 17 September 1912, Taft Papers, Reel 514; "Hon. C. S. Lobingier is Named Judge of U.S. Court for China," unidentified treaty port newspaper clipping, Hornbeck Papers, Box 75.

7. Charles S. Lobingier, "America's Torch-bearing in Asia," *Review of Reviews* (December 1914), 50:714.

8. Lobingier, "America's Torch-bearing in Asia," 717.

9. Robert Freeman Smith, *The United States and Revolutionary Nationalism in Mexico, 1916–1932* (Chicago: University of Chicago, 1972).

10. Ibid., 238.

11. Robert J. Kerr, "American Citizens in Foreign Countries," *International Relations of the United States* (July 1914), 54:236–42.

12. Ibid., 238.

13. Rosenberg, *Spreading the American Dream*, 64.

14. Ibid., 64, 72.

15. Ibid., 65.

16. Green H. Hackworth, "Naturalization and Loss of Nationality," *Proceedings of the American Society of International Law*, 19th Annual Meeting (1925), 59–69.

17. U.S. Department of State, *Citizenship, Registration of American Citizens, Issuance of Passports, etc.* (Washington, D.C.: GPO, 1915), 24.

18. *FRUS* (1913), 76–78.

19. "Expatriation of Naturalized Citizens," *FRUS* (1913), 3.

20. Charles Denby, "The Principles and Practice of Extraterritoriality in China," *Peking Leader*, 12 December 1918, in Hornbeck Papers, Box 75; Charles Denby, "Extraterritoriality in China," *American Journal of International Law* (October 1924), 18:667–75.

21. *FRUS* (1919), vol. 1, 674, 680–81.

22. See Rosenberg, *Spreading the American Dream*, on the rise of the "promotional state," and post-World War I transition to a corporatist, cooperative strategy. For the corporatist interpretative framework to developments in this period, see Michael J. Hogan, "Corporatism: A Positive Appraisal," *Diplomatic History* (Fall 1986), 10:363–72.

23. These functions are among the essential elements of Wilsonianism described in Robert Freeman Smith, "American Expansion and World Order," in Thomas G. Paterson, ed., *Major Problems in American Foreign Policy* (Lexington: D.C. Heath, 1984), vol. 2, 121–135.

24. Ibid.

25. Lobingier, "America's Torch-bearing in Asia," 717.

26. Reinsch, "Decennial Anniversary Brochure," 39–40. Reinsch himself was a lawyer, and had a Ph.D. from the University of Wisconsin (1898/89). His doctoral thesis examined "English Common Law in the Early American Colonies."

27. Kathryn Meyer, "Trade and Nationality at Shanghai upon the Outbreak of the First World War, 1914–1915," *The International History Review* (May 1988), 10:246–48; K. Meyer, "Splitting Apart: The Shanghai Treaty Port in Transition, 1914–1921," Ph.D. dissertation, Temple University, 1985, 59–62 (UMI8509357).

28. Marie-Claire Bergére, *The Golden Age of the Chinese Bourgeoisie, 1911–1937*, trans. Janet Lloyd (New York: Cambridge University Press, 1989), 63–83.

29. Mira Wilkins, *The Maturing of Multinational Enterprise: American Business Abroad from 1914 to 1970* (Cambridge: Harvard University Press, 1974), ch. 1. See also Michael Hunt, "Americans in the China Market: Economic Opportunities and Economic Nationalisms, 1890s-1931," *Business History Review* (Autumn 1977), 41:277–307.

30. Bergére, *The Golden Age*, 67.

31. Wilkins, *The Maturing of Multinational Enterprise*, 20–29; Harry N. Scheiber, "World War I as Entrepreneurial Opportunity: Willard Straight and the American International Corporation," *Political Science Quarterly* (September 1969), 84:507–8.

32. *FRUS* (1923), 525–51; *FRUS* (1924), 570–80.

33. See, for example, correspondence relating to protection of Americans from dangers in Yangtze River trade, *FRUS* (1921), 519–34; (1924), 741–51; from general brigandage, *FRUS* (1922), 860–69; and from nontreaty sanctioned internal taxes, *FRUS* (1923), 579–99.

34. Mira Wilkins, *The Maturing of Multinational Enterprise*, 1–108. It took several years to get the China Trade Act (U.S. Statutes at Large, V-44) through Congress, with various drafts as follows: H. Rpt. 5704 (1919), H. Rpt. 7204 (1919), S. Rpt. 4549 (1920), and additional bills drafted by the State Department Solicitor, one by the Chamber of Commerce of the United States, and one by the Treasury Department. The Senate Judiciary Committee seemed to be the primary opponent of the legislation, doubting its constitutionality (Foreign Trade Adviser, "China Companies Act Question," 18 March 1921, attachment, Division of Far Eastern Affairs to Secretary Hughes, 5 April 1921, 893.5034/127). For a full explanation of the regulations and conditions under which American companies could operate in China as of 1919, see Legislative Reference Service, Library of Congress, "Status of American Corporations in China," 11 July 1919, attachment, 893.5034/127. Cf. Legislative Reference Service, "Taxation of Corporations in China," 23 June 1919, ibid.

35. *USC-C: ExCases: U.S. v. Hunter* (1917), vol. 1, 629, in which Hunter was

sentenced to nine months in prison plus payment of court costs for stealing liquor (valued at less than $35 gold) from a local American bar, during which he struck bar personnel; *U.S. v. Nelson* (1918), vol. 1, 786, in which defendant was sentenced to two years for armed robbery; *U.S. v. Leonhardt and Terry* (1918), vol. 1, 790, where defendants (military personnel) received one year and $1,000 fine for stealing seventy-five pairs of shoes from the U.S. Army to sell privately; *U.S. v. Osman* (1916), vol. 1, 540, in which defendant, a native of Guam, was sentenced to pay $100 bond or spend four months in prison for vagrancy; *U.S. v. Hinde*, (1923), vol. 2, 751, where defendant was jailed for a year for embezzling a woman's savings after she entrusted them to him for investment; *U.S. v. Theyken* (1922), vol. 2, 350, where defendant was sentenced to 18 months in prison and fined $1,000 plus costs for embezzling six million cigarettes from his employer, Liggett and Myers Tobacco Co.; *U.S. v. Bowe* (1922), charging the defendant with operating bogus insurance companies, vol. 2, 229. *NCH*, 12 August 1922, 486–87.

36. See also *Hsieh Po-Hsian v. Shippers Commercial Corporation* (1920) *USC-C: ExCases*, vol. 2, 1010; *NCH*, 12 January 1924, 4; *USC-C: ExCases*, vol. 2, 702.

37. Hay, *Albion's Fatal Tree*, 13–14, 22–23; Haskell, "Capitalism and the Origins of the Humanitarian Sensibility," 107–160.

38. For the theoretical point, see David Trubek, "Toward a Social Theory of Law: An Essay on the Study of Law and Development," *The Yale Law Journal* (1972), 82: 1–50. See, for example, *Yu T. Wang v. Sidney Ross* (1921), *USC-C: ExCases*, vol. 2, 96 (wrongful discharge).

39. Haskell, "Capitalism and the Origins of the Humanitarian Sensibility," 107–110.

40. See *USC-C: ExCases: H. D. Rodger v. A. R. Hager* (1915), vol. 1, 444; *Charles Paget v. Canton Christian College, a Corporation,* (1915), vol. 1, 457; *Zee Foh Sung v. Frank Fernandez* (1920), vol. 1, 956.

41. *USC-C: ExCases: Shanghai Tannery Co., Ltd. v. American Trading Co.* (1916), vol. 1, 576; *Steele v. American Trading Co.* (1920), vol. 1,, 964, upheld 9th Circuit Court of Appeals, 274 F. 774, no. 3585 (1921); *S. A. Ransom et al. v. Paul M. Martin* (1920), vol. 2, 31.

42. *USC-C: ExCases: R. W. Steiner v. Frazar and Co.* (1911), vol. 1, 253; *Lung Chu v. Sino-American Trading Corp.* (1920), vol. 1, 1006; *Ransom v. Martin* (1920), vol. 2, 34; *Kitty Ren v. American Drug Co.* (1923), vol. 2, 505.

43. *USC-C: ExCases: Vera Meier and Olga Kaltzoff v. Arkell and Douglas, Inc.* (1919), vol. 1, 904; *In re Assignment of A. S. Fobes* (1920), vol. 1, 950; *Lung Chu v. Sino-American Trading Corp.* (1920), vol. 1, 1006.

44. *USC-C: ExCases: Paget v. Canton College* (1915), vol. 1, 457; *Cecile Raigorodetzkaia v. H. H. Arnold* (1916), vol. 1, 589.

45. *USC-C: ExCases: King Ping Kee v. American Food Manuf Co.*, vol. 1, 735; *John Davis v. Tsu Eu Sung, dba Hoa Sun Iron Works* (1919), vol. 1, 922; *Yu Yar*

Chuan v. Shippers Commercial Corp. (1922), vol. 2, 290; *Chin Hsing Hsun v. Shippers Commercial Corp.* (1922), vol. 2, 307; *George Chiskin v. American Drug Co.* (1922), vol. 2, 343.

46. USC-C: ExCases: *H. Leslie Ford v. Macdonell-Chow Corp.* (1918), vol. 1, 805; *American Trading Co. v. Steele* (1921), vol. 2, 196.

47. USC-C: ExCases: *Star Garage v. H. S. Honigsberg and Co.* (1916), vol. 1, 558.

48. The plaintiff, Frank J. Raven, lost his petition to force the U.S. consular clerk to accept the incorporation papers of a private banking enterprise. Lobingier ruled against him, arguing that the U.S. government specifically prohibited the operation of American banks abroad that did not have home offices subject to inspection and regulation by federal and state authorities. Foreign Trade Adviser, "China Companies Act Question," 18 March 1921, attachment, Division of Far Eastern Affairs to Secretary Hughes, 5 April 1921, NARA, RG 59, 893.5034/127.

49. U.S. House, "Incorporation of Companies to Promote Trade in China," 66th Cong., 3d sess. (1920), H. Rpt. 1312.

50. E. Cunningham to Secretary, 22 December 1919, NA, RG 59, 893.5034/42; Carr to Cunningham, 24 February 1920, ibid. The State Department was concerned about the proliferation of fraudulent companies under the *Raven* precedent, and so instructed Consul General at Large Charles Eberhardt to look into the situation (State Department Instruction, 10 August 1920, 893.5034/83), telling him to investigate the situation, "giv[ing] special attention to the activities of these corporations with a view to discovering whether there is any foundation for the belief that irresponsible persons are taking advantage of the easy methods of incorporation offered to carry on undertakings that might otherwise be illegal or impossible." The results of the investigation are reported in the Eberhardt dispatch cited above (i.e., Eberhardt to State, 14 January 1921, 893.5034/115).

51. M. Perkins, Shanghai, to Eberhardt, 5 January 1921, enclosure 5, 893.5034/115. On the changing Hong Kong Ordinances, see explanation in Foreign Trade Adviser, "China Companies Act Question," 18 March 1921, attachment, Division of Far Eastern Affairs to Secretary Hughes, 5 April 1921, 893.5034/127; cf. Meyer, "Splitting Apart," 180.

52. For the mail fraud case, see *U.S. v. Donohoe* (1914), USC-C: ExCases, vol. 1, 347. Lobingier dismissed the charges on the grounds that it was the Chinese mails Donohoe used, and relevant American laws pertained only to the U.S. postal system.

53. On the company, see: Charles Eberhardt to Secretary, 14 January 1921, 893.5034/115 with enclosures; and Consul, Chungking, to Secretary, 4 December 1919, 893.5034/43; State Department to Cunningham, 10 August 1921, 893.5034/142, approving the consul's refusal to allow the registration; Cunning-

ham to State, 19 August 1921, informing State that the company had now registered under French license; Cunningham to Secretary, 26 May 1921, 873.5034/142,
noting that the Yangtze Transport and Supply Co. was on a list compiled by the
British Consulate of firms owned by Chinese and involved in opium traffic.

54. Cunningham to Secretary, 26 May 1921, 873.5034/142. Other corporations
organized under the auspices of the U.S. Court included: Devin and Co., operated for about three years by an American prostitute fronting for indigenous
opium dealers (Cunningham, Hankow, to Secretary, 2 May 1921, 893.5034/140);
Stewart Crane, Inc., and Reid's, Inc., both bankrupt by 1924, and leaving large
Chinese investors high and dry ("Affairs of Stewart Crane, Inc., bankruptcy,
NCH 31 March 1923; "Affairs of Reid's Ltd. Inc.," *NCH* 22 March 1924, in the latter case one major creditor was Hong Kong merchant C. Lai-hing, who
advanced Tls.100,000); Connolly Land and Oil Company, a concern set up by
the departing clerk of the U.S. Court in 1920 to sell shares in what were actually nonproducing oil lands in the United States (M. Perkins, Shanghai, to Secretary, 28 September 1920, 893.5034/90, enc. "U.S. Court Clerk Leaves for
Home," *The China Press*, 26 September 1920, and enc. Associated Advertising
Clubs to J. B. Powell, 17 November 1920 (reporting on lands listed in Connolly's
prospectus); Eberhardt to Secretary, 25 October 1920, 893.5034/115; George K.
Ward and Co., Inc., an impoverished former consular clerk fronting for Chinese
investors (Eberhardt to State, 14 January 1921, 893.5034/115); the American Sales
Corp., specializing in fraudulently obtaining transit passes (allowing exemp-
tion from certain internal taxes) for Chinese merchants, ibid.; the Chinese-
American Aviation Company, allegedly a front for Sun Yat-sen's clique in South
China used to obtain commercial planes for military use, ibid.; as well as the
Shanghai Motors Corp. and Wilkins Brothers and Co., both widely reputed to
be just more examples of the same combination of Chinese capital and Amer-
ican adventurers.

55. Charles Hughes, Secretary of State, to L. C. Dyer, House of Representatives, 12 April 1921, 893.5034/126, in response to Dyer to Hughes, 9 March 1921.
Dyer had solicited the Secretary's opinion of the draft China Trade bill (H.R.
16043), and Hughes suggested changes that "would allow the Secretary of State
to participate (with the Secretary of Commerce) in the designation of officers
and agents in China, pursuant to the provisions of the Act," and which "would
give the Secretary of State a voice in the regulations to be promulgated for the
purpose of carrying out . . . the Act." See also Dyer to Hughes, 21 April 1921,
893.5034/131, asking for the Secretary's comments on H.R. 4088, the China Trade
Bill.

56. *USC-C: ExCases: Siao King Kee v. Amer Trading Co.* (1920), vol. 1, 940,
where plaintiff was defendant's engineering comprador; and *In re Assignment of
A. S. Fobes* (1920), vol. 1, 950, by the same plaintiff.

57. *Chang Quai Ching et al. v. Dodge and Seymour* (n.d.), *USC-C: ExCases*, vol. 1, 840–42.

58. *NCH*, 25 April 1916; *Ling Ah Choy et al. v. Standard Oil* (1916), *USC-C: ExCases*, vol. 1, 561–73.

59. *NCH*, 2 September 1922, 700; *Hsu Hwa Tang v. Standard Oil* (1922), *USC-C: ExCases*, vol. 2, 245–46.

60. *Sung Kya Yi v. Dodge and Seymour* (1919), *USC-C: ExCases*, vol. 1, 889–90.

61. *Nanyang Bros v. Green Star SS* (1924); *National City Bank of New York v. Harbin Electric Joint-Stock Co., Ltd.* (1928); *Woo King-hsun v. Pemberton and Penn Inc.* (1933); *King Foong Silk Filature v. Globe and Rutgers Fire Insurance* (1924); *Republic of China v. Merchants Fire*; *ROC v. Great American Insurance Co.* (1929). These appealed cases are available at: National Archives, Pacific Sierra Region, Leon J. Ryan Federal Archives and Records Center, San Bruno, Calif., Record Group 276 (U.S. Courts of Appeals).

62. *U.S. v. Homer Darke* (1920), *USC-C: ExCases*, vol. 2, 53.

63. *U.S. v. Welch* (1920), *USC-C: ExCases*, vol. 2, 4.

64. *U.S. v. John Rohrer (alias Thomas Riggs, alias John Cook)*, (1915), *USC-C: ExCases*, vol. 1, 517.

65. *FRUS* (1922), 826. Additional indemnities were authorized for: two Chinese drowned in a collision by the U.S. *Palos* in 1917; $1,500 for sailor Homer Darke's killing of the Chinese cobbler, who had four children; and $2,000 for Private Petticrew's murder of a Chinese wineshop employee.

66. Walter LaFeber, *The American Search for Opportunity, 1865–1913* (Cambridge: Cambridge University Press, 1993).

67. On the subject, see William O. Walker, *Opium and Foreign Policy: The Anglo-American Search for Order in Asia, 1912–1954* (Chapel Hill: University of North Carolina Press, 1991).

68. *Rex v. Lee Ki-lung* (1919), briefed in *USC-C: ExCases*, vol. 1, 349.

69. *USC-C: ExCases*, vol. 1, 520, 520n, and 523n. Americans were prohibited from participating in the opium traffic by virtue of a 17 January 1914 Act of Congress. In transcribing the law from one text to another, a clerk omitted the phrase allowing the judge of the U.S. Court in China to impose *both* a $500 fine and a jail term, leaving the fine as the only legal punishment.

70. For an assessment of foreign involvement in the arms trade during the warlord era, see Anthony Chan, *Arming the Chinese: The Western Armaments Trade in Warlord China, 1920–1928* (Vancouver: University of British Columbia Press, 1982). The quotation in the text is from Chan, 63. For a discussion of the complicated diplomatic maneuvering among the great powers leading up to the Agreement and shaping its enforcement, see Stephen Valone, *A Policy Calculated to Benefit China: The United States and the China Arms Embargo, 1919–1929* (Westport, Conn.: Greenwood Press, 1991).

71. "Shanghai Gun Runners are Given Sentences of Many Years in San Francisco Case Dating From 1924," *China Press*, 20 March 1927, 1. The case involved a former U.S. Customs agent, various Shanghai and San Francisco Chinese, and several other soldiers of fortune. Most of the defendants received the maximum sentence of two years and a $10,000 fine.

72. Chargé d'affaires (Gauss) to State, 7 December 1934, *FRUS* (1935), vol. 4.

73. Ibid.

74. Kearny had incorporated as Kearny, Leicester, and Lee, reputed to be funded by Japanese interests, and later the China Credit and Information Bureau, subsequently renamed Kearny Company. The latter company declared bankruptcy at the time of Kearny's difficulties in the arms sales case. For the arms case, see *U.S. v. Kearny* (1923), *USC-C: ExCases*, vol. 2, 662; "The Arms Case in the U.S. Court," *NCH*, 21 July 1923; "Kearny on Trial in U.S. Court," *NCH*, 29 September 1923. Chan, *Arming the Chinese*, 52–53.

75. Japanese did not do much better in policing arms trafficking, providing only 29 days maximum for arms smugglers.

76. *U.S. v. Slevin* (1923), *USC-C: ExCases*, vol. 2, 460; Ronald Macleay to Foreign Secretary Curzon, FO 371/9197, 20 February 1923, cited in Chan, *Arming the Chinese*, 15n84; *NCH*, 17 February 1923.

77. Chan, 156fn124, 58, 90–92.

78. "American Seizure of Arms," *NCH*, 27 January 1923; "Arms Smuggling in China," *NCH*, 17 May 1924; "Arms Sales in Manila," *NCH*, 21 January 1924; "Arms Seizures in Shanghai,"*NCH*, 16 June 1923; "Smuggled Arms on Str. *Pres. Jefferson*," ibid.; "Smuggled Arms on the *President Wilson*," ibid., 30 June 1923.

79. *U.S. v. Pablo Sonico* (1918), *USC-C: ExCases*, vol. 1, 671–80.

80. Tientsin Consul (Fuller) to State Department, 14 March 1921, nos. 721, 172.1/16; *U.S. v. Furbush* (1921), *USC-C: ExCases*, vol. 2, 81.

81. *U.S. v. Charles Carberry* (1923), *USC-C: ExCases*, vol. 1, 591–95.

82. David Bederman, *Imperialism*, 463. Lobingier affirmed that the Court had jurisdiction in all cases where the defendant was subject to American authority, and in cases brought *in rem*, regardless of the litigants' nationality. *Swayne and Hoyt v. Everett* (1919) established that subject matter jurisdiction did not depend upon the residence of litigants.

83. Allen, an African American ex-sailor, was charged with operating the Oregon Bar without a license. *U.S. v. John T. Allen* (1914), *USC-C: ExCases*, vol. 1, 308, 315. Other information on this individual: John Thomas and Susan were married in 1911; in their divorce case a few years later, she is described as "elderly and infirm," and in a relationship with a man only to get help in opening up a restaurant for "colored" soldiers. She was granted a divorce, neither allowed to remarry, and he had to pay support of US$20 per month, and lawyers fees. He

later unsuccessfully sought to modify the maintenance order, arguing that she has been with other men. Ibid., vol. 1, 621, 495, 533.

84. On the designation of Bilibid, see 30 *Opinions of the Attorneys General* 462 (1915). For illustrative cases, see the following *USC-C: ExCases*: *U.S. v. John T. Allen*, vol. 1, 308, 326 (see note 85); *U.S. v. Crawley*, vol. 2, 654, fined $500 for running gaming tables in Harbin; *U.S. v. Bowe*, vol. 2, 229, sentenced to three years for forging several checks; *U.S. v. Furbush*, vol 2, 74, a ship's engineer given a life sentence for killing a fellow foreigner in Shanghai during a drinking bout; *U.S. v. Osman*, vol. 1, 540), a Guam national sentenced to four months for vagrancy; *U.S. v. Rincon*, vol. 1, 619, a Filipino sentenced to six months and fined $200 for selling forged promissory notes for two diamond rings.

85. "I.W.W. Men on Local Ship," *NCH*, 18 March 1922. A group of seamen from the United States were brought in for refusing to obey orders and slacking on duty during the journey. The U.S. shipping vice consul visited the ship to investigate charges against the first mate, but found them to be "frivolous." The "ringleader" conceded that he was a member of the International Workers of the World (IWW), and was sentenced to 90 days, while the others got 60 days.

86. *U.S. v. Gilbert Reid* (1917), *USC-C: ExCases*, vol. 1, 666; "The Gilbert Reid Case," *Millard's Review*, 16 June 1917, 7; "The Case Against Dr. Reid," *NCH*, 16 June 1917, 631.

87. *NCH*, 29 December 1917, 132–33.

88. *U.S. v. Sin Wan Pao Company* (1920), *USC-C: ExCases*, vol. 1, 983–89. See also ibid., *Banque Belge v. Montgomery Ward and Co.* (1922), vol. 2, 371–87, affirmed on appeal to California. Lobingier applied the common law maxim that "where one of two innocent parties must suffer, he who made possible the loss must bear it," saying that it was "peculiarly applicable in this jurisdiction. . . . where so many of our nationals constantly engage in transactions . . . with those of other nationalities who are unfamiliar with our law."

89. *Jameson v. Jameson*, 176 *F.2d.* 58 (DC Cir 1949), recognition of divorce decree; *Newman v. Basch*, 89 *Misc.* 622, 152 *NYS* 456 (New York City Court, 1915), divorce settlement.

90. "Decennial Anniversary Brochure," 46–47, 52–53; *USC-C: ExCases*, vol. 1, ix–x. The 1922 membership included one woman, Helen McCauley. Branches were in Japan and the Philippines, and the Bar was affiliated with the American Bar Association as of 1915.

91. *Barkley Co. v. William E. Maloney* (1919), *USC-C: ExCases*, vol. 1, 926.

92. Alison Conner, "Soochow Law School and the Shanghai Bar," *Hong Kong Law Journal* (1993), 23:395–411.

93. Robert Bryan Jr., "The Legal Profession," in *American University Men in China* (Shanghai: Comacrib Press, 1936), 84.

94. For tributes to Lobingier, see excerpts in *Twenty Years in the Judiciary* (Shanghai: Far Eastern American Bar Association, 1922), Bulletin 7.

95. Wang Chung-hui to Attorney General Harry Daugherty, 19 December 1921. Justice Department, Numerical Files, no. 215890, Box 3459 (no individual document number). In this same vein, see the letter of support from Wang Chen-t'ing (C. T. Wang) to Harding, 4 October 1923, RG 59, 172.3 Lobingier, Box 3051. C. T. Wang, who attended Lobingier's twenty-year tribute banquet in 1922, moved up in treaty port society through missionary schools and the YMCA. He studied in the United States (University of Michigan, Yale, B.A. 1910), and was granted a law degree from St. John's in Shanghai (1920). He held several key posts in the shifting governments of the post-1911 period, went into the brokerage business in Shanghai, and opened a cotton mill at Woosung around 1920, and was part of the Chinese delegation at the Washington Conference (1921–22). At the time of his letter for Judge Lobingier, he was a chief representative in the Directorate General of Sino-Russian Negotiations. Boorman, vol. 3, 362–64. For biographical information on Wang, see Howard L. Boorman and Richard C. Howard, eds., *Biographical Dictionary of Republican China* (New York: Columbia University Press, 1967–1971), vol. 3, 376–62.

96. Li Yuen [Yuan]-hung to the U.S. President (Calvin Coolidge), 30 September 1923, enclosure; Selden Spencer, U.S. Senate, to Coolidge, 8 November 1923, RG 59, 172.3 (Lobingier), box 3051.

97. Marie-Claire Bergère, "The Consequences of the Post-First World War Depression for the China Treaty Port Economy, 1921–1923," in Ian Brown, ed., *The Economy of Africa and Asia During the Interwar Depression* (London and New York: Routledge, 1989); Jurgen Osterhammel, "Britain and China, 1842–1914," 146–69..

98. Of the 58 China Court companies established under the *Raven* precedent, Fleming was involved in eight, capitalized at a total of $1,850,000; in two of these he served as director or president. As a consequence of his connections, he was a much sought-after attorney, and could claim among his clients leading American China companies, such as Robert Dollar; Connell Brothers; American Trading Co.; American Express; the American Oriental Banking Corp.; Raven Trust; Texas Oil; Fearon, Daniel, and Co.; and Anderson and Meyer. William Fleming to Charles Eberhardt, 25 January 1921, and Eberhardt to State, 14 January 1921, 893.5034/115.

99. William Fleming, "The United States Court for China as an Institution," Stanley Hornbeck Papers, Box 113, "U.S. Court for China."

100. Harding Papers, Reel 194, File 295; Case no. 215890, Boxes 3458–59. RG 60, Straight Numerical Files, Correspondence, NARA.

101. H. Hoover to Attorney General, 18 February 1922, RG 60, 215890–48.

102. L. Dyer to Harding, 19 May 1922, RG 60, no. 215890, Box 3459 (no individual document number).

103. "America Jeopardizes Treaty Rights Because of U.S. Court Deadlock," *Weekly Review of the Far East*, 10 June 1922.

104. David Mulvane to Attorney General, 6 July 1921, RG 60, 215890 (no number); Rush Holland, Report on charges against Lobingier, RG 60, no. 215890-80, Box 3458.

105. Daugherty to Lobingier, 4 April 1922; George B. Christian Jr., secretary to the President, to Attorney General, 5 April 1922, RG 60, no. 215890, Box 3459; Lobingier to Harding, 11 May 1922, 26 June 1922; Harding to Lobingier, 5 September 1922; Lobingier to Harding, January, 1923, Harding Papers.

106. Cunningham to State, 5 September 1922, 30 December 1922, 172.3 Lobingier, Box 3051.

6. INTERWAR DEMISE OF CONSULAR JURISDICTION

1. Charles Bright and Matthew Geyer. "For a Unified History of the World in the Twentieth Century," *Radical History Review* (1987), 39:76–78.

2. Jurgen Osterhammel, "China," in *The Oxford History of the British Empire* (Oxford and New York: Oxford University Press, 1999), vol. 4, 647.

3. Edgar Turlington, "The Settlement of Lausanne," *American Journal of International Law* (October 1924), 18:696–706.

4. "The I.L.O. Meeting and Extraterritoriality," *China Weekly Review*, 29 June 1929, 185.

5. Clifford, *Spoilt Children of Empire*, 6. The May 4th Movement took off in 1919, when the great powers at Versailles gave Japan Germany's possessions in China. The May 25th Incident, leading to a national anti-foreign boycott, occurred in 1925 around violent clashes between Chinese demonstrators and Japanese and (later) British police.

6. ABC-FM to State Department, 18 March 1924, and related documents, *FRUS* (1924), vol. 1, 601–3. See also essays in John Fairbank, ed., *The Missionary Enterprise in China and America* (Cambridge: Harvard University Press, 1974).

7. David Wilson, "Principles and Profits: Standard Oil Responds to Chinese Nationalism, 1925–1927," *Pacific Historical Review* (November 1977), 41:625–47; Osterhammel, "China," 653.

8. Marie-Claire Bergére, *The Golden Age of the Chinese Bourgeoisie, 1911–1937*, trans. Janet Lloyd (New York: Cambridge University Press, 1989), 280–81.

9. "The Shanghai Boom," *Fortune* (January 1935), 2, no. 1:17–18.

10. Lloyd Eastman, *The Abortive Revolution: China Under Nationalist Rule, 1927–1937* (Cambridge: Harvard University Press, 1974); Parks Coble Jr., *The*

Shanghai Capitalists and the Nationalist Government, 1927–1937 (Cambridge: Harvard University Press, 1980).

11. William C. Kirby, "Intercultural Connections and Chinese Development: External and Internal Spheres of Modern China's Foreign Relations," in Frederic Wakeman, Jr. and Wang Xi, eds., *China's Quest for Modernization: A Historical Perspective* (Berkeley: University of California, 1997); Kirby, "The Internationalization of China: Foreign Relations at Home and Abroad in the Republican Era," *The China Quarterly* (June 1997), 150:433–58; John Fitzgerald, "The Misconceived Revolution: State and Society in China's Nationalist Revolution, 1923–26," *Journal of Asian Studies* (May 1990), 49, no. 2:323–43.

12. On British Far Eastern policy in this period, see Peter Lowe, *Great Britain and Japan, 1911–1915* (New York: St. Martin's Press, 1969) and Ian Nish, *Alliance in Decline: A Study of Anglo-Japanese Relations* (London: Athlone Press, 1972).

13. Russell D. Buhite, "The Open Door in Perspective: Stanley K. Hornbeck and American Far Eastern Policy," in Frank Merli and Theodore Wilson, eds., *Makers of American Diplomacy: From Theodore Roosevelt to Henry Kissinger* (New York: Scribners, 1974).

14. For the international context of the Shanghai crisis of 1932, see Christopher Thorne, "The Shanghai Crisis of 1932: The Basis of British Policy," *American Historical Review* (October 1970):1616–39. For a typical illustration of Shanghai Americans' view, see "Protection of American Life and Property in China: Important Deliverance by Mr. George Bronson Rea Before the National Foreign Trade Council of America," *NCH*, 13 August 1927, 305.

15. Undoubtedly, the most succinct and authoritative summary of these concessions remains John Carter Vincent, *The Extraterritorial System in China: Final Phase* (Cambridge: Harvard University Press, 1973).

16. Thomas McCormick, *America's Half Century: United States Foreign Policy in the Cold War* (Baltimore: Johns Hopkins University Press, 1989), 24–25; Thomas Ferguson, "From Normalcy to New Deal: Industrial Structure, Party Competition, and American Public Policy in the Great Depression," *International Organization* (Winter 1984), 38:41–94.

17. Nym Wales, "Analyzing the 'Shanghai Mind,' " *CWR* 9 September 1933, 57–58.

18. "Coolidge Defines Our World Policies," *NYT*, 26 April 1927, 1, 10.

19. "American Firms Registered with American Consulate General," Records of Attorney Generals and Marshals, RG 118, Box 1.

20. "The Americans, Japanese and Chinese at Shanghai," *CWR*, 1 May 1937, 317–19.

21. Population figures for treaty port Americans are inexact at best and diverge significantly across sources. Feuerwerker, relying on records of the Inspectorate General of Customs, indicates a total of 5,580 American residents in

China, and 8,230 in 1921. Feuerwerker, *The Foreign Establishment in China*...., 17; and explanatory text, 16–18. A War Department document (no. 2055–436), 9 April 1921) roughly estimates a total of 6,389 Americans residing in China, about 2,630 of them in Shanghai. The Shanghai Consulate General estimated 2,999 Americans in Shanghai in 1921, with the caveat that those figures were 10 to 15 percent lower than the actual totals. James L. Huskey, "Americans in Shanghai: Community Formation and Response to Revolution, 1919–1928," Ph.D. dissertation, University of North Carolina, Chapel Hill, 1985, 189n5. On the CPI, see: Hans Schmidt, "Democracy for China: American Propaganda and the May Fourth Movement," *Diplomatic History* 22.1 (Winter 1998), 1–28.

22. A process well covered in Huskey, "Americans in Shanghai.."

23. U.S. House, "Incorporation of Companies to Promote Trade in China," 66th Cong., 3d sess. (1921), H. Rpt. 1312, 6.

24. "Shanghai Americans Turn on Periodical," *NYT*, 27 April 1927, 5; James Huskey, "The Cosmopolitan Connection," *Diplomatic History* (Summer 1987), 11:227–42; "The American Minister's Visit to Shanghai," *NCH*, 15 September 1925, 555: "The 'Omnia-Juncta-in-Uno' and the Rest of Us," *CWR*, 29 April 1933, 1.

25. "Some Significant Elements in the Municipal Election," *CWR*, 7 April 1934, 199–200. William Fleming, Raven's attorney, and Lobingier's nemesis, had died in 1932: "Mr. W. S. Fleming [obituary]," *NCH*, 7 September 1932, 379. Cornell Franklin and Norwood Allman had been Fleming's law partners; "Interlocking Directorate of S.M.C. and Transit Interests," *CWR*, 19 May 1934, 441–42.

26. "American Chamber of Commerce Holds Its Annual Meeting and Elects Directorate for Year," *China Press*, 27 April 1927.

27. "Struggle for Jurisdiction Over 'Extra-Settlement' Roads," *CWR*, 10 February 1934, 399; "Joint Administration of Extra-Settlement Area is Practically Arranged," 7 July 1934, 234–35.

28. Nicholas Clifford, "A Revolution Is Not a Tea Party: The 'Shanghai Mind(s)' Reconsidered," *Pacific Historical Review* (November 1990), 59:501–26; Edgar Snow, "The Americans in Shanghai," *The American Mercury* (August 1932), 20:437–45; Arthur Ransome, "The Shanghai Mind," reprinted *CWR*, 28 May 1927, 339–41; *Shang-hai kung-kung tsu-chieh shih-kao* (A Historical Sketch of the Shanghai International Settlement) (Shanghai: Jen min ch'u pan she, Hsin hua shu tien Shang-hai fa hsing so fa hsing, 1980), 532–37. For the defense of the "Shanghai mind," see "What the Treaties did for China," *NCH*, 28 September 1929, 508.

29. "The 'Independent-Free-City State' Scheme for Shanghai," *CWR*, 23 April 1932, 240–42; "Shanghai's Spokesman and the Diehards," 9 July 1932, *CWR*, 194–95; "The Free-City and Demilitarized Zone Ideas are Bound to Fail," *CWR*, 25 June 1932, 113–14; "The 'Independent-Free-City State' Scheme for Shanghai," 23 April 1932, *CWR*, 240–42; "Free City," *CWR*, 28 May 1932, 429–30.

30. Those who rose to defend Husar and supply him with an alibi later proved to be patently false, were the very same individuals responsible for driving Judge Lobingier out three years previously. Husar was given two years in jail and a $3,000 fine, a verdict upheld on appeal to the 9th Circuit Court in San Francisco. RG 59, 172.3/Husar, Box 3050; *NCH* 16 April 1927, 127–28; 23 April 1927, 175–76; 30 April 1927, 214–16; 7 May 1927, 257–59; *Husar v. U.S.* no. 5297. 11 June 1928, 26 *F.2d* 847.

31. Around this same time, Court Clerk William Chapman was found to have embezzled tens of thousands of dollars in court fees, and Henry Krenz, disbursing officer at the U.S. Legation in Peking, allegedly fled China with $30,000 of U.S. government funds. On Chapman, see RG 59, 172.3 Chapman. For Krenz, see 172.8/99, and "Serious Charge Against U.S. Official Henry Krenz," *NCH*, 19 November 1927, 322.

32 *"Chung wai lü-shih ke shih cheng lun hu hsieh"* ([Right of] Foreign Lawyers in China to Argue All Types of Cases in the Shanghai Court), *Shih-pao*, 13 July 1926; *"Wai-chi lü-shih tai-piao ch'u ching"* (Foreign Lawyers Send a Representative to Peking), *Shih-pao*, 30 July 1926; "Chinese Lawyers and the Rendition of the Mixed Court," *NCH*, 24 July 1926, 158.

33. His decision may have been affected by the sudden death of his wife in 1932. "Mrs. Milton Purdy [obituary]," *NCH*, 27 July 1932, 137.

34. See, for example: *Li and Li v. Andersen Meyer and Co.* (1925), *NCH*, 21 February 1925, 318; *Ah Hong v. Nanking Univ* (1925), where the plaintiff successfully sought $9,100 for work done and material supplied on Ginling College in Nanking; or *Wong Paoding v. Anderson* (1929), where the plaintiff collected $1,271 for an overdue promissory note for $1271 (*NCH*, 19 October 1929, 103); *Yu Shing and Partners v. Rudolph Mayer*, a claim for $6,000 brought by group of compradors (*NCH*, 23 December 1936, 506); *Hwa Tung Elec and Gen Eng v. Home Insurance Co.*, an insurance claim for $27,171 (*NCH*, 27 March 1940, 503).

35. Primary source material for cases from 1924 to 1929 (with some information on later cases as well) can be found in NARA, RG 59, State Department Central Files, Decimal Files 172.XXX. Material for 1929–1934 material is lacking; thus, cases have been reconstructed from the *NCH* and other relevant indirect sources. Material for the 1935–1941 period can be found in NARA, RG 118, Records of Attorney Generals and Marshals, District of China. As noted earlier, there is no relevant material on the USC-C to be found at the Shanghai Municipal Archives, or the Tsungli-Yamen archives at the Academia Sinica in Taiwan.

36. See the symposium "Coping with Shanghai: Means to Survival and Success in the Early Twentieth Century," *The Journal of Asian Studies* (February 1995), 54:3–123.

37. *NCH*, 15 May 1926, 314.

38. "The Foreign Women in the Orient," *Millard's Review*, 10 November 1917, 303–5.

39. Though in practice, married women had contracted, the USC-C gave the custom legal standing in 1923, applying a 1901 U.S. law. *U.S. (SMP) v. Elmonts* (1923), to recover costs for her hospitalization in a municipal nursing home.

40. Customers: *Black and Co. v. Mary Williamson* (1927), for hospital bills; *Anna Istomine v. Ford Hire* (1929), for contract; *John Wanamaker N.Y. v. Mrs. R. N. Williams* (1926), for bills; *Mrs. J. C. West v. China Finance Corp.* (1935), for fraud; *Mrs. E. Mariepolsky v. Shanghai Telegraph Co.* (1937); *Vera Meier and Olga Kaltzoff v. Arkell and Douglas* (1919). Creditors: *Katherine Massey v. Robert Rene Fernbach* (1923), where the plaintiff returned to the USC-C to recover interest on an earlier judgment of $18,000 (Mex), II *ExCases* 639–41 (1923). Victims: *Cecila Raigorddetzkaia v. H. Arnold* (1916), *USC-C: ExCases*, vol. 1, 589, appeal from consular court. Employees: *Roy Allman v. Miss Ann Summers* (1937); *Mrs. Betty Spunt v. Julius Rosenfeld* (1936); *Mrs. Nellie Richie v. Montgomery Ward and Co.* (1922), *NCH*, 21 January 1922, 192–93. Employers: *Kitty Ren v. American Drug Co.* (1922), where the plaintiff was granted 20,000 Tls. *NCH*, 23 December 1922, 823; 24 March 1923, 833.

41. *Henrietta Weil v. J. Thomas Wright* (1921), *USC-C: ExCases*, vol. 2, 395–402. For a similar case in the British court, see *Mrs. Sarah E. Senna v. V. Britto*, HMS, 15 April 1923, 126, for breach of promise. The 56-year-old Senna lent Britto money on his implicit promise of future marriage. She got only $115 in damages, *NCH*, 21 April 1923, 193.

42. "British Women Remain British after Marrying Americans," *CWR*, 24 February 1934, 465.

43. Bredbenner, *A Citizenship of Her Own*, iii–iv.

44. *NCH*, 9 December 1922, 693.

45. *U.S. v. Elrod*, NCH, 11 August 1928, 246–47. Clifford Elrod was charged with assault with intent to kill his wife Mrs. Eulalie Elrod; he got the Court's mercy when doctors testified on his behalf that a blow on the head during the mob riots of the May 30th Incident had left him violent and mentally unstable. The two were married in 1917 in Tientsin and came to Shanghai in 1920.

46. The USC-C used the divorce laws in effect for the District of Columbia. In the 1930s, this brought changes to the effect that a decree could be handed down immediately, although it would not become effective until after six months. Further, where before all petitioners were subject to a one-year residency requirement, this was increased to two years in cases where the grounds for divorce arose outside of the jurisdiction. Absolute divorce was granted for adultery, desertion for two years, voluntary separation for five years, conviction on a felony resulting on nonsuspended sentences over two years. "US Court Divorce Law is Changed," *CWR*, 20 September 1935, 1.

47. *Lily Thomas v. James Ching, NCH*, 14 November 1925, 306.

48. Earlier such cases, few though they were, had been criminally prosecuted. See, for example, *U.S. v. Ollerdessen* (1909), where the defendant, son of a prominent treaty port American family, who killed a Chinese telephone company worker when he, Ollerdessen, was momentarily distracted while driving down a main street in Shanghai. The victim's wife was permitted to come in and testify as to what would be equitable, and in the end agreed—what choice did she have?—to an arrangement whereby Ollerdessen would not go to jail, but rather would pay her (and her five children) $20 per month for 19 years, a figure derived from calculating the deceased's income ($19 p/m) and anticipated mortality.

49. *Han Pai-chi v. F.R. Welch, NCH*, 3 April 1935, 34, claim for US$5,000 for damages and medical bills.

50. *NCH*, 14 September 1929, 417.

51. *NCH*, 25 January 1933, 143.

52. *NCH*, 8 May 1940, 225.

53. *NCH*, 12 August 1936, 287; *NCH*, 26 July 1936, 198–99. Non-Chinese female plaintiffs fared no better, as in: *Nadeja S. Maximenko v. Shanghai Power Co., NCH*, 12 August 1936, 286. This was a claim for $10,000 for the death of plaintiff's husband, electrocuted while in company employ. The USC-C urged the defendant company to raise its offer of compensation, but determined that the deceased had taken upon himself to do something dangerous and uncalled for.

54. *NCH*, 10 March 1923, 655.

55. *U.S. v. Enders, NCH*, 19 January 1938, 103; "Americans who are involved in the Dope Traffic," *CWR*, 24 July 1937, 263–65.

56. "Social Disease, Prostitution Have Been Investigated Many Times in City, Official Says," *China Press*, 16 July 1935, 9; "Commercialized Vice in Shanghai: An International Problem in an International Settlement," Shanghai Municipal Archives, W1-0-575.

57. Percy Finch, *Shanghai and Beyond* (New York: Scribners, 1953), 37; Henry Champly, *The Road to Shanghai* (London: John Long, 1934).

58. Hankow Consul General (Cunningham) to State Department, 21 January 1919, and 9 March 1921, 893.5034/120–21. See also *U.S. v. Katherine de Salas*, involving "larceny by trick." Records of U.S. Attorney, China, RG 118, Box 7.

59. See *L. E. Hudec v. Grant Mark, NCH*, 21 June 1935, 9, for discussion of Mark's mother's activities.

60. *NCH*, 19 June 26, 552.

61. "Maria Wendt Guilty in Heroin Case," *CWR*, 16 December 1936, 448; "2 Suicides, 1 Jailed in Latest Shanghai-U.S. Dope Deal," *CWR*, 26 September 1936, 1.

62. *NCH*, 19 September 1934, 436–37.

63. *Shanghai Times*, 6 February 1929, 2; *NCH*, 20 July 1929, 94; 14 August 1940, 258; 28 September 1929, 444. See also *Yu Chang-mei v. Henry Bagman.* Bagman

was an American-born Chinese, ordered to pay $2,000 and costs to Yu over a disputed purchase. "Dual nationals US-China," RG 59, 893.012/43, 9 October 1929.

64. *In re Robert E. Lee's Estate* (1918), *USC-C: ExCases*, vol. 1.

65. *In re Adoption of Pearl Covert Wu, minor* (1918), where Charles and Jane Bromley adopted a 6-year-old in their custody after both Chinese parents had died, leaving a document approving the arrangement. See also *In re adoption of Alice Alford* (1915), *USC-C: ExCases*, vol. 1, 441. "Chinese Acquisition of American Nationality," *CWR*, 28 June 1924, 115. The District Court of Washington, North Dakota, ruled in 1927 that the daughter of an American man in China and his Chinese concubine was not entitled to citizenship. *Ex parte Ng Suey Hi*, no. 11520, District Court, W. D. Washington, ND, 20 *F.2d* 266 (1927).

66. In 1932, there were approximately 3,614 Americans in Shanghai; 1,608 of whom were in the International Settlement; 1,541 in the French Concession; and 465 in the Chinese district. There were 387 Filipinos among the total. "Civilian Foreigners in Shanghai," 3 February 1932, Stanley Hornbeck Papers, Hoover Institution, Box 8.

67. "Introduction," in Frederic Wakeman Jr. et al., eds., *Shanghai Sojourners* (Berkeley: University of California Press, 1992), 9; Wakeman, "Policing Modern Shanghai," *China Quarterly* (September 1988), 115:412. For a contemporary view, see M. K. Han, "French Colonial Policy in China as Reflected in the Shanghai French Concession," *CWR*, 23 January 1932, 239–40.

68. Gail Hershatter, "Regulating Sex in Shanghai: The Reform of Prostitution in 1920 and 1951," in Wakeman, *Shanghai Sojourners*, 145–85.

69. Nien Ch'eng (pseud.), ed., *Nan-wang te sui-yueh* (Unforgettable Times) (Hong Kong: Chih cheng ch'u pan she, 1972), 80–89; Lin Chih-san, "Hai jen bu ch'ien te hui-li ch'iu-ch'ang" (The Damage Done Is Not Just on the Jai-lai Field), in *Shang-hai te ku-shih*, (Shanghai Stories) vol. 3 (Shanghai: Jen-min ch'u pan, 1963); "Will Shanghai Remain 'Safe' for Dog-Race-Gambling," *CWR* 15 November 1930, 382–83; "Dog-Race-Gambling and the Question of Extraterritoriality and the Status of the Foreign Settlement," *CWR*, 15 November 1930, 384–85; Rose Leibrand, "How Foreign Shanghai Plays," *CWR*, 26 July 1930, 293–94; Lowe Chuan-hua, "So This Is Shanghai?" *CWR* 14 December 1919, 60; "Still Dilly-Dallying with Dog-Race-Gamblers," *CWR*, 29 November 1930, 459;"The Council Under Fire," *China Critic*, reproduced in *CWR*, 20 November 1930, 459–60; "The Matter of Closing the Dog-Race-Gambling Joints," *CWR*, 22 November 1930, 424–25.

70. Brian Martin, " 'The Pact with the Devil' ": The Relationship Between the Green Gang and the French Concession Authorities, 1925–1935," in Wakeman, *Shanghai Sojourners*, 266–304.

71. Wakeman, "Policing Modern Shanghai." On French China policy more generally, see John F. Laffey, "Lyonnais Imperialism in the Far East, 1900–1932," *Modern Asian Studies* (April 1976), 10:225–48.

72. Jonathan Marshall, "Opium and the Politics of Gangsterism in Nationalist China, 1927–1945," *Bulletin of Concerned Asian Scholars* (July–September
1976), 8:41–42.

73. Marshall, ibid., 19.

74. Walker, *Opium and Foreign Policy*, 48–58, 80; Marshall, "Opium and the
Politics of Gangsterism," 19, 25–27; O. Edmund Clubb, "The Opium Traffic in
China," 24 April 1934, no. 893.114 Narcotics/738, RG 59; "Opium in Shanghai,"
enclosure in Edwin Cunningham to State, 3 March 1930, 893.114 Narcotics/105.
See also "The Local Opium Scandal," *NCH*, 8 December 1928, 396–97, discusses
a Chinese police opium seizure which seemed to most to involve the competitive use of state power among highly placed opium dealers.

75. *NCH*, 15 May 1934, 253.

76. *U.S. v. Maloney and Barrett, NCH*, 26 January 1926, 600; *U.S. v. J. W. Maloney, NCH*, 28 February 1926, 360; 21 March 1925, 494.

77. *FRUS* (1933), vol. 2; *NCH*, 13 November 33, 271; *Bert Hall v. Douglas Aircraft Co., 23 Cal. App. 2d* 498.

78. For illustrative insanity cases, see Mary Margaret Matlack, committed to
an asylum in California in 1936, for "paranoid" claims that the British and Chinese were conspiring to kill her; Amado Lagua Roque, 1935, for general distur-
bances; Edward May Bostick, 1936, a missionary appointed by the Foreign Mission Board of the Southern Baptist Convention who "went nuts," from over-
work. RG 118, Records of U.S. Attorneys and Marshals, China.

79. Consul General Edwin Cunningham to State Department, 25 October
1934, 893.5017/12, enc "Report on Employment and Living Conditions in Shanghai"; annual update, Cunningham to State, 1 October 1935, 893.5017/14.

80. *NCH*, 19 January 1932, 97.

81. *NCH*, 5 September 1925, 316; 10 April 1926, 76; 17 April 1926, 126.

82. "The Shanghai Boom," *Fortune* (January 1935), 2, no. 1:30–40, 99–120.

83. For the information from which this inference is drawn, see "Reports of
American Citizens Residing in Outposts," Record Group 118, Box 5, showing
nationality and occupations of those registered U.S. nationals, with an indica-
tion of which were Filipino. The impact of this labor market on Russian emigres
in Shanghai is noted in Victor Petrov, "Russian Shanghai," *Far Eastern Affairs*
(1992), 2:140–56, 3:131–41.

84. On Sully, *NCH*, 3 May 1932, 183.

85. Case is in Record Group 118, Box 1, no. 3.

86. "Resident Agents of China Trade Act Companies," no date, Norwood F.
Allman Papers, Hoover Institution, Box 11, China Trade Act Companies.

87. Miss Edith Wolfe was convicted in the American Consular Court for
"furiously and recklessly driving a gig" (owned by J. H. "Tientsin" Brown), when
she ran over a Chinese amah carrying a child. She was among those bawdy

house inmates brought in on charges before Judge Wilfley, but at that time claimed German citizenship, giving her birth name as Dorothy Elizabeth Hawage. (Consular Court Case No. 35, 16 January 1906, noted Shanghai Consulate, Correspondence, Record Group 84, C8-10, vol.14; USC-C, District Attorney's files, 1907). Wolfe's later success, under American registry, is indicated by a brief mention of her eminent brothel in Edgar Snow's scathing critique of the Shanghai American community: Snow, "The Americans in Shanghai." Dorothy Grant is described in Shanghai Municipal Police Report 6459 (5 November 1935), Records of the Shanghai Municipal Police, 1894–1949, RG 263.

88. 172/738 (1928), RG 59, Box 3040.

89. Legation to State Department, 23 July 1924, no. 2411, RG 59, 172.1/57.

90. The bill was HR 9292, and did not pass, largely due to State Department objections. See RG 59, 172/739.

91. "The Sheinbein Ruling," *The Jerusalem Post*, 26 February 1999, 8.

92. *NCH*, 12 February 1936, 281.

93. *Dorr and O'Brien v. U.S.*, 24 S. Ct. 808 (1904). O'Brien later went on to Shanghai to become one of the most vicious press critics of Lebbeus Wilfley, discussed in the congressional impeachment documents cited in chapter 4.

94. Vincent, *The Extraterritorial System in China*, 70.

95 Ibid., 78.

96. Ibid., 76.

97 "An Appeal to Shanghai Americans," 23 June 1927; Consul General Cunningham to American Consulate General Staff, 29 June 1927, 1927/843/137; *CWR*, 10 January 1925.

98. "The Shanghai Boom," 120.

99. *NCH*, 24 April 1926, 169.

100. The records of the case can be found in Oriental Banking Corporation, RG 59, 172.6, Box 3056; and RG 118, #26, Oriental Banking Corporation, Investigation.

101. "Lone American on New Council in International Settlement," *NYT*, 24 March 1932, 4:3; "American Bankers [Raven and his associate Warner Brown] Convicted in China," *NYT*, 1 February 1936, 7:5; "Convicted Banker was Myth in China," *NYT*, 2 February 1936, 86; "Banker Sets a New Low for American 'Face' in Shanghai," *Newsweek*, 8 February 1936. Raven began as a partner in the British-run China Realty Company, but assumed control of that firm in 1917, registering it locally under the auspices of the U.S. Court (i.e., using the provision for local incorporation offered by *Raven v. McRae*).

102. This argument was also made by contemporaries: "Shanghai Landlords at Bay," *CWR*, 31 August 1935, 459–60.

103. "Element of American 'Prestige' in Raven Liquidation," *CWR*, 27 July 1935, 279–80, characterized Raven as staunch defender of treaty port privilege.

104. "Rev. Boynton's Circular—Missionary Interest in Collapse of Raven Enterprises," *CWR*, 15 June 1935, 76; "Creditors of Raven Group Given Advice. Long Statement Tells Missionaries What to Do . . . ," *CWR*, 9 June 1935, 1. J. Warner Brown's background is given in "A.O.F.C. Used Bucket-Shop Methods, J. W. Brown Admits, in Cross-Examination; Then Denies," *CWR*, 1 February 1936, 303–4. See also "Financial Troubles of [the Shanghai] American School from Raven Collapse," *CWR*, 11 April 1936, 182–83.

105. See the discussion of Raven's portfolio in "A.-O. Liquidator Has Only Collected $355,655 Out of Nominal Eleven Million of Assets," *CWR*, 27 June 1935, 293.

106. "Collapse of Raven Interests—Cause, Probable Effect, and Possibility of Recovery," *CWR*, 1 June 1935, 4–7.

107. Judge Purdy's situation is noted in "Frank J. Raven Sentenced to Five Years, J. W. Brown to Two Years, for Embezzlement," *CWR*, 8 February 1936, 352–53.

108. The Executive Order transferring the Court put the Judge and clerk of the court and their staffs under the Administrative Office of the United States Courts, and the district attorney and marshal and their staffs directly under the Department of Justice. "Proposed Provisions Pertaining to Appropriations for the Judicial Establishment, 1942," 77th Cong., 1st sess. (1941), House Document 124.

109. Hsieh Chu-ts'eng, "Lei-wen he hua-t'ou yin-hang–mei-feng yin-hang," (Raven and his slippery bank–the American Oriental Bank), in *Shang-hai te ku-shih* (Shanghai Stories) (Shanghai, 1982), 290–99.

110. "Convicted Banker was Myth in China," *NYT*, 2 February 1936, 86; "Rough on Raven," *Time*, 10 February 1936; "Lone American on New Council in International Settlement," *NYT*, 24 March 1932, 4:3.

111. "Chinese Interests in A.-O. Bank," *China Press*, 25 September 1935, 512.

112. "A.-O.B.C. to Pay 7′ P.C. to Creditors," *NCH*, 13 November 1935, 277; "American Oriental Banking Corporation and Allied Financial Institutions Close Doors," *CWR*, 1 June 1935, 8–9; "A.-O. Bank Chinese Creditors Represented," *China Press*, 17 September 1935, 1; "Conference on Finances held by Dr. Kung, *China Press*, 28 May 1935, 12; Andrea Lee McElderry, *Shanghai Old-Style Banks (Ch'ien-Chuang), 1800–1935: A Traditional Institution in a Changing Society* (Ann Arbor: University of Michigan, 1976), 170–80; Cheng I-fang, *Shang-hai ch'ien-chuang, 1843–1937* (Shanghai's Native Banks, 1843–1937) (Taipei: Taipei Academia Sinica, 1981), chs. 3–5.

113. "American Bankers Convicted in China," *NYT*, 1 February 1936, 7:5.

114. Kirby, "Intercultural Connections and Chinese Development," 225.

115. Kirby, "Intercultural Connections," 222; Tahirih V. Lee, "Coping with Shanghai," 11; Rudolf G. Wanger, "The Role of the Foreign Community in the Chinese Public Sphere," *China Quarterly* (June 1995), 142:441; Christian Henriot, *Shanghai, 1927–1937: Municipal Power, Locality, and Modernization*

(Berkeley: University of California Press, 1993), translated by Noel Castelino, 1, 235.

116. Parks M. Coble Jr., *The Shanghai Capitalists and the Nationalist Government, 1927–1937* (Cambridge: Harvard University Press, Council on East Asian Studies, 1980).

117. Ibid., 188, and ch. 7 more generally. See also Bergére, *The Golden Age*, 281–84.

118. In *Blackmer v. U.S.*, 284 *U.S.* 421; 52 *S.Ct.* 252 (1932), the Supreme Court upheld a $30,000 judgment against an American residing in Paris, found guilty of contemptuous disobedience of two subpoenas to testify as a witness in a criminal case back home. To the defense's claim that allegiance has territorial limits, and consuls cannot 'round up' citizens abroad, the Justices proclaimed that a sojourning national "continues to owe allegiance to the United States and is bound by its laws made applicable to his situation." In short, inherent in sovereignty is "the power to require the return of absent citizens in the public interest."

119. This critical distinction is drawn in William Lockwood Jr., "The International Settlement at Shanghai, 1924–34," *American Political Science Review* (December 1934), 28:1030–46.

120. "Element of American 'Prestige,'" *CWR*.

121. Ibid., and "Problem of Improving Prestige of American Business," *CWR*, 2 November 1935, 287–88.

122. "U.S. Comment on China Vitally Concerns Local Americans," *CWR*, 13 November 1935, 235–36.

123. Frederic Wakeman, Jr., *The Shanghai Badlands. Wartime Terrorism and Urban Crime, 1937–1941* (Cambridge and New York: Cambridge University Press, 1996)

124. Helmick reported about 70 cases still pending. He later served as Judge of the Consular Court at Casablanca, and was subsequently transferred to the analogous court in Tangier. See Edwin Smith, "The End of the Consular Courts." The 1942 case involved Boatner R. Carney, an American aviation instructor with the Chinese Air Force, who killed Sgt. W. R. Reichmann. The U.S. Army declined jurisdiction, committing Carney to the USC-C. "Memorandum of Conversation," 30 September 1942, Hornbeck Papers, Box 113.

EPILOGUE

1. Edward Littleton, 1689, "The Groans of the Plantations." Quoted in Jack Greene, *Peripheries and Center: Constitutional Development in the Extended Politics of the British Empire and the United States, 1607–1788* (Athens: University of Georgia Press, 1987), 19–20.

2. This section on post-World War II Americans in China relies wholly on the work of Mark Wilkinson of the Virginia Military Institute: Wilkinson, "The Shanghai American Community, 1937–1949," 1997 draft in my possession, cited with permission; Wilkinson, "At the Crossroads: Shanghai in Sino-American Relations, 1945–1950," Ph.D. dissertation, University of Michigan, 1982 (University Microfilms, Inc., UM 8215105).

3. Warren Tozer, "Last Bridge to China: The Shanghai Power Company, the Truman Administration, and the Chinese Communists," *Diplomatic History* (Winter 1977), 1:66.

4. "Claims of Nationals of the United States Against the Chinese Communist Regime," 89th Cong., 2d sess. (Washington, D.C.: GPO, 1966).

5. "High Court Rules U.S. Can Release Girard to Japan," *NYT*, 12 July 1957, 1, 7; "Girard's Home Town Sends a Petition to White House," *NYT*, 11 June 1957, 1, 15

6. National Security Council Progress Report, 3 July 1957, on U.S. Policy Toward Taiwan and the Government of the Republic of China, NSC 5503 by Operations Coordinating Board, Top Secret, 24 May 1957; Frank C. Nash, Report to the President on U.S. Overseas Military Bases," December 1957, Secret, Dwight D. Eisenhower Papers, Administrative Series. All from Declassified Documents.

7. National Foreign Assessment Center, III CI-10, 398 11/29; Iranian Socioeconomic Interest Groups: An Intelligence Assessment. ER 79–10620 11/79. All from Declassified Documents.

8. Louis Henkin, *Foreign Affairs and the United States Constitution* (Oxford: Clarendon Press, 1996), 284–85.

9. U.S. Senate, Committee on Foreign Relations, "Department of State Passport Policies," 85th Cong., 1st sess. (1957).

10. *Kent v. Dulles*, 357 *U.S.* 116 (1958); *Aptheker v. Secretary of State*, 378 *U.S.* 500 (1964); *Zemel v. Rusk*, 381 *U.S.* 1, 382 *U.S.* 873 (1965).

11. *Reid v. Covert*, 351 *U.S.* 487 (1956) and *Kinsella v. Krueger*, 351 *U.S.* 470 (1956) were consolidated for reconsideration (and reversal) under *Reid v. Covert*, 354 *U.S.* 1 (1957). "The Law," *Time*, 4 December 1955, 30–31.

12. *Toth v. Quarles*, 350 *U.S.* 11 (1955), overturned court-martial sentence over ex-serviceman for murder committed in Korea while on active duty.

13. *Kinsella v. U.S. ex. rel. Singleton* (1960), 361 *U.S.* 234; 80 *Sup. Ct.* 297. Mrs. Joanna Dial and her serviceman husband were arrested in Baumholder, Germany, and tried by court martial for the unpremeditated murder of their child. The Supreme Court decision led to her release from the Federal Reformatory for Women in Alderson, West Virginia. Kinsella was the warden of the prison. *Grisham v. Hagan*, 361 *U.S.* 278 (1960) and *McElroy v. Guagliardo*, 361 *U.S.* 281 (1960).

14. By and large, most arrests have been for drug possession and trafficking; figures typically run in the low thousands, and most occur in Canada, Germany,

Jamaica, and Mexico. Karen Fawcett, "Drug Offenses Lead List of Charges Against U.S. Citizens Abroad," *USA Today*, 18 May 1994, A2.

15. American Law Institute, *Restatement of the Law Third: The Foreign Relations Law of the United States* (St. Paul: American Law Institute Publishers, 1986), vol. 1, 237.

16. Christopher L. Blakesley, "Criminal Law: United States Jurisdiction Over Extraterritorial Crime," *Journal of Criminal Law and Criminology* (Fall 1982), 73:1109–63; Lea Brilmayer and Charles Norchi, "Federal Extraterritoriality and Fifth Amendment Due Process," *Harvard Law Review* (April 1992), 105:1217–63; A. Mark Weisburd, "Due Process Limits on Federal Extraterritorial Legislation?" *Columbia Journal of Transnational Law* (1997), 35:379–428.

17. Epstein, *Bargaining with the State*.

18. Malley, "Constructing the State Extra-territorially."

19. *U.S. v. Verdugo-Urquidez*, 856 F.2d 1214 (9th Cir. 1988), reversed 494 *U.S.* 259 (1990); Jennifer J. Dacey, "U.S. Citizens' Fourth Amendment Rights: Do They Extend Only to the Waters' Edge? *United States v. Barona*," *George Mason Law Review* (Summer 1997), 5:761–97.

20. Andreas F. Lowenfeld, "U.S. Law Enforcement Abroad: The Constitution and International Law," *The American Journal of International Law* (April 1990), 84:444–493.

21. Patrick Quilligan, "International Community Acts to Combat Child Sex Exploitation," *Irish Times*, 1 June 1995, 10; "Paedophile Tourists Face Crackdown," *The Independent*, 2 July 1995, 5; David Wallen, "Britain Joins the Move Against Child Sex Tours," *South China Morning Post*, 15 July 19995, 18. All items cited here accessed through Lexis-Nexis.

22. *Perez v. Brownell* (1958), overturned in *Afroyim v. Rusk* (1967) and *Vance v. Terrazas* (1980), wherein the Supreme Court held that Congress cannot revoke a person's U.S. citizenship without evidence of his or her explicit intent to give up that citizenship.

23. "One Citizen, Two Passports," *Denver Rocky Mountain News*, 14 June 1998, B-2; Linda Chavez, "Dual Citizenship Claim by Mexico Natives Raises Questions about Loyalty to America," *Baltimore Sun*, 8 April 1998, A-19. All accessed through Lexis-Nexis.

24. Patrick McDonnell, "Mexico Delays Dual-Nationality Plan 1 Year," *Los Angeles Times*, 6 March 1997, A-3; John Miller, "Loyalty Duel," *National Review*, 18 May 1998, paraphrased; "Dual Citizenship a Dubious Deal," *The Tampa Tribune*, 2 January 1997, 9. All accessed through Lexis-Nexis.

25. Samuel Sheinbein, a Maryland teenager wanted for murder, claimed Israeli citizenship through his father, who was born in the British-controlled portion of Palestine that later became Israel. The Supreme Court of Israel determined that a 1978 law prohibiting extradition of citizens trumped treaty agreements between

the United States and Israel. "The Sheinbein Ruling," *The Jerusalem Post*, 26 February 1999, 8. Chaim Berger is a 73-year-old Hasidic man wanted on charges of embezzlement, fraud, and other charges. "American Fights U.S. Extradition," *Pittsburgh Post-Gazette*, 8 March 1999, A4. Goldberg, 20, was indicted in Texas in the stabbing death of a store clerk. "Suspect Could be Beyond Reach," *Houston Chronicle*, 20 February 1999, A-1. All accessed through Lexis-Nexis.

26. John J. Miller, "Loyalty Duel," *National Review*, 18 May 1998. "U.S.-Africa Talks Boost Dual Citizenship," *The Herald* (Glasgow), 6 May 1995, 8-A, reported that a seminar in Dakar "ended today with a call for black Americans to take a stake in their ancestral home by applying for dual citizenship in an African country." Accessed through Lexis-Nexis.

27. "Vietnamese Expats get Deal from Hanoi," *Bangkok Post*, 7 January 1999. The Korean Justice Ministry recently considered a plan opposed by the Ministry of Foreign Affairs and Trade to issue certificate of residence registration to overseas Koreans, allowing them full equality with resident citizens, except suffrage and public office. "Planned Legislation for Overseas Koreans to be Revised," *Korea Herald*, 9 September 1998. Accessed through Lexis-Nexis.

28. Reported in "U.S.-Africa Talks Boost Dual Citizenship."

29. Ireland passed a law in 1956 allowing grandchildren of people born there to obtain dual citizenship; Canada passed similar legislation in the 1970s. Currently about 50 countries—including the United Kingdom, Poland, France, Ecuador, Colombia, the Dominican Republic and Brazil—do not take naturalization elsewhere as expatriation back home. Lilia Velasquez, "Mexican Dual Nationality," *San Diego Union-Tribune*, 20 March 1998, B-7; James Edwards, "Dual Citizenship is Dangerous," *Christian Science Monitor*, 29 April 1998, 20.

30. Philip Sherwell, "Foreign Crisis Refugee Explosion: Europe Besieged," *Sunday Telegraph*, 6 June 1993, 24; Michael Binyon, " 'Blood Right' basis of German Citizenship Laws Under Attack," *The Times*, 15 February 1993. Accessed through Lexis-Nexis.

31. "Tourist hoping Holiday Won't include Army Duty," *Toronto Star*, 22 August 1998, L15. See also Stephen Farrell et al., "French Relent Over Briton Seized for National Service," *The Times*, 12 June 1997. See also an advisory that U.S. citizens born in Cambodia and their offspring could be subject to obligations should they go back. "Dual Citizenship Raises Questions," *San Diego Union-Tribune*, 19 January 1992, Ed. 1, 2; G-5. All accessed through Lexis-Nexis.

32. T. Alexander Aleinifoff, "A Multicultural Nationalism?" *The American Prospect* (January–February 1998), 80–86.

33. Jean-Marie Guehenno, *The End of the Nation State* (1995), 19, quoted in: Alfred Aman, "The Globalizing State: A Future-Oriented Perspective on the Public/Private Distinction, Federalism, and Democracy," *Vanderbilt Journal of Transnational Law* (October 1998), 31:769–870.

34. For example, in New York City, seven of the 10 largest immigrant groups now have the right to be dual nationals. Georgie Anne Geyer, "Dual Nationality, Divided Loyalty," *The Times-Picayune*, 15 January 1997, B7. "According to one estimate, about half a million children are born in the United States each year with automatic dual citizenship." John J. Miller, "Loyalty Duel," *National Review*, 18 May 1998. Since 1995, 1.2 million immigrated to US, about 1/4th illegally. One of every ten people in the U.S. was born elsewhere; almost half, in one of seven developing countries (Mexico, Philippines, India, Vietnam, China, Dominican Republic, Cuba). The vast majority are unskilled and require major public support. Ronald Steel, "Who is Us," *The New Republic*, 14 and 21 September 1998, 13–14. All accessed through Lexis-Nexis.

35. Geyer's other metaphor is worth noting: the rhetoric about dual-nationality "equates the United States with a carcass to feed off until you can have some of your Motherland's good home cooking again. . . ." Georgie Anne Geyer, "Dual Nationality, Divided Loyalty," *The Times-Picayune*, 15 January 1997, B7. See also, Pat Truly, "Dual Citizenship; Dueling Loyalties?," *Houston Chronicle*, 29 December 1996, 1. Lexis-Nexis.

36. James Fallows review of Georgie Anne Geyer's *Americans no More: The Death of Citizenship*, in *The Washington Monthly* (October 1996).

37. Somini Sengupta, "Immigrants in New York Pressing Drive for Dual Nationality," *NYT*, 30 December 1996, B1. Quoting Dan Stein, executive director of Federal for American Immigration Reform.

38. Quoted in Aleinifoff, "A Multicultural Nationalism?"

39. Quoted in Spiro, "The Citizenship Dilemma," 624.

40. Mark Fritz, "Dual Citizenships Create Dueling Family Allegiances," *Los Angeles Times*, 6 April 1998, A15. Lexis-Nexis.

41. Alejandro Portes, "Global Villagers: the Rise of Transnational Communities," *The American Prospect* (March-April 1996), 74.

42. Steel, "Who Is Us," 14.

43. Aman, "The Globalizing State," 28, quoting Saskia Sassen, *Losing Control* (1996).

44. Evelyn Tan Powers, "Cyberworld Grows for U.S. Expats," *USA Today* (14 June 1995), 2A, Lexis-Nexis.

45. David Martin, "The Civic Republican Ideal for Citizenship, and for Our Common Life," *Virginia Journal of International Law* (Fall 1994), 35:237–278.

46. *Edmund S. Muskie, Secretary of State, Petitioner v. Philip Agee*, nos. 80–83 (1981); *Haig v. Philip Agee*, 453 *U.S.* 280 (1981).

47. The attorney did not, however, know the identity of the unnamed "notorious" gambling casino operator of coastal China circa 1906 described in the precedents for passport revocation.

BIBLIOGRAPHY

A. Documentary and Archival Sources
B. Newspapers and Serials
C. Books, Articles, and Government Publications

A. DOCUMENTARY AND ARCHIVAL SOURCES

Ch'ing-tai wai-ch'ao shih-liao, Tao-kuang chao (Historical Materials on Ch'ing Dynasty Foreign Relations, Tao-kuang reign) nos. 7–9.

Denby, Edwin. Papers. Bentley Library, University of Michigan, Ann Arbor.

Harding, Warren G. Papers. Manuscript Division, Library of Congress, Washington, D.C.

Hornbeck, Stanley K. Papers. Hoover Institution, Stanford University, Stanford, Calif.

Roosevelt, Theodore. Papers. Manuscript Division, Library of Congress, Washington, D.C.

Root, Elihu. Papers. Manuscript Division, Library of Congress. Washington, D.C.

Shanghai Municipal Police. Shanghai Municipal Police Files, 1894–1947 (formerly Security Classified Investigation Files, 1916–1947). U.S. National Archives, College Park, Md., Record Group 263 (Central Intelligence Agency).

Taft, William H. Papers. Manuscript Division, Library of Congress, Washington, D.C..

Tsung-li ko-kuo shih-wu ya-men ch'ing-tang, Ch'ing-chi-pu, Mei-kuo-men (Clean files of the Tsungli-yamen, late Ch'ing section, United States files, various categories), manuscript archive housed at Institute of Modern History, Academia Sinica, Taipei, Taiwan.

U.S. Court of Appeals, Ninth Circuit, California. Records. National Archives: Pacific Sierra Region, Leo J. Ryan Federal Archives and Record Center, San Bruno, Calif., Record Group 276.

U.S. Department of Justice. Records of the U.S. Attorneys and Marshals: U.S. District Court of China, 1935–41. National Archives, Record Group 118.

U.S. Department of State. Central Records of the Department of State, 1910–1943. National Archives, Record Group 59.

——. Despatches from U.S. Consuls in Canton, China, 1790–1906. National Archives, Microfilm-101.

——. Despatches from U.S. Consuls in Chefoo, China, 1863–1906. National Archives, Microfilm-102.

——. Despatches from U.S. Consuls in Hong Kong, 1844–1906. National Archives, Microfilm-108.

——. Despatches from U.S. Consuls in Shanghai, China, 1847–1906. National Archives, Microfilm-112.

——. Records of the Foreign Service Posts. National Archives, Record Group 84.

U.S. Military Intelligence Division Files: China, National Archives, Record Group 165, Microfilm 649, 1930–49.

Wilson, Huntington. Papers, Ursinus College, Collegeville, Pa.

Wilson, Woodrow. Papers. Manuscript Division, Library of Congress, Washington, D.C.

B. NEWSPAPERS AND SERIALS

China Weekly Review (Shanghai), selected years.

China Press (Shanghai), selected years, 1920–1943.

Fortune, selected years, 1930s.

Japan Weekly Review (Yokohama), selected years.

Japan Weekly Mail (Yokohama), 1890s.

Journal of the American Association in China

Newsweek, selected years.

North American Review, selected years, 1830–1900.

North China Daily News, selected years.

North China Herald, Supreme Court and Consular Gazette (Shanghai), selected years, 1900–1944.

Proceedings of the American International Law Society, various years.

Shen Pao (Shanghai), selected years, 1906–1943.

Shih Pao (Shanghai), selected years, 1906–1943.

The Chinese Recorder, various years, 1890–1901

The Forum, selected years, 1890–1910.

The New Voice, 1900.

The New York Times, selected years, 1900–1944.

The Shanghai Times, 1907.

The [Washington] Evening Star, selected years.

Time, selected years, 1930–1960.

Women's Journal, 1900.

C. BOOKS, ARTICLES, AND GOVERNMENT PUBLICATIONS

Adams, John, ed. *Works of John Adams*. 10 vols. Boston: Little, Brown, 1854.

Aldridge, A. Owen. *The Dragon and the Eagle: The Presence of China in the American Enlightenment*. Detroit: Wayne State University Press, 1983.

Allman, Norwood. *Shanghai Lawyer*. New York: McGraw-Hill, 1943.

Aman, Alfred. "The Globalizing State: A Future-Oriented Perspective on the Public/Private Distinction, Federalism, and Democracy." *Vanderbilt Journal of Transnational Law* (October 1998), 31:769–870.

American Law Institute. *Restatement of the Law Third: The Foreign Relations Law of the United States*. 2 vols. St. Paul: American Law Institute, 1986.

American University Men in China. Shanghai: Comacrib Press, 1936.

Anderson, David L. *Imperialism and Idealism: American Diplomats in China, 1861–1898*. Bloomington: Indiana University Press, 1985.

Angell, James B. "The Turkish Capitulations." *American Historical Review* (January 1901), 6:254–59.

Anghie, Antony. "Finding the Peripheries: Sovereignty and Colonialism in Nineteenth-Century International Law." *Harvard International Law Journal* (Winter 1999), 40:1–80.

Arnold, David. "European Orphans and Vagrants in India in the Nineteenth Century," *The Journal of Imperial and Commonwealth History* (January 1979), 7:104–27.

Balsdon, John P. V. D. *Romans and Aliens*. Chapel Hill: University of North Carolina Press, 1979.

Barnes, William and John Heath Morgan. *The Foreign Service of the United States*. Westport, Conn.: Greenwood Press, 1981.

Baumgart, Winfried. *Imperialism: The Idea and Reality of British and French Colonial Expansionism, 1888–1914*. New York: Oxford University Press, 1982.

Bederman, David J. "Extraterritorial Domicile and the Constitution." *Virginia Journal of International Law* (Winter 1988), 28:451–94.

Bergére, Marie-Claire. "The Consequences of the Post-First World War Depression for the China Treaty Port Economy, 1921–1923." In Ian

Brown, ed., *The Economy of Africa and Asia During the Interwar Depression*. London and New York: Routledge, 1989.

——. *The Golden Age of the Chinese Bourgeoisie, 1911–1937*. Translated by Janet Lloyd. New York: Cambridge University Press, 1989.

——. "The Other China, Shanghai 1911–1919." In Christopher Howe, ed., *Shanghai: Revolution and Development in an Asian Metropolis*. Cambridge: Cambridge University Press, 1981.

Bickers, Robert A. and Jeffrey N. Wasserstrom. "Shanghai's 'Dogs and Chinese Not Admitted' Sign: Legend, History and Contemporary Symbol." *China Quarterly* (June 1995), 142:444–466.

Biggerstaff, Knight. "The Secret Correspondence of 1867–1868: Views of Leading Chinese Statesmen Regarding the Further Opening of China to Western Influence." *Journal of Modern History* (June 1950), 22:122–36.

Bishop, Crawford M. "American Extraterritorial Jurisdiction in China." *American Journal of International Law* (April 1926), 20:281–99.

Blakesley, Christopher L. "Criminal Law: United States Jurisdiction Over Extraterritorial Crime." *Journal of Criminal Law and Criminology* (Fall 1982), 73:1109–63

Boorman, Howard L. and Richard C. Howard, eds. *Biographical Dictionary of Republican China*. New York: Columbia University Press, 1967–1971.

Borchard, Edwin. "Basic Elements of Diplomatic Protection of Citizens Abroad." *American Journal of International Law* (July 1913), 7:497–520.

——. *The Diplomatic Protection of Citizens Abroad*. New York: Banks Law Publishing, 1916.

Boudin, Leonard B. "The Right to Travel." In Norman Dorsen, ed., *The Rights of Americans: What They Are—What They Should Be*. New York: Pantheon Books, 1971.

Bozeman, Adda B. *Politics and Culture in International History*. New Brunswick: Transaction Publishers, 1994 [1960].

Braeman, John. "Power and Diplomacy: The 1920s Reappraised." *The Review of Politics* (July 1982), 44:342–69.

Braddick, Michael J. "The English Government, War, Trade, and Settlement,

1625–1688." In *Oxford History of the British Empire*. Vol. 1. Oxford and New York: Oxford University Press, 1998.

Brands, H. W. "The Idea of the National Interests." *Diplomatic History* (Spring 1999), 23:239–261.

Brantlinger, Patrick and Donald Ulin. "Policing Nomads: Discourse and Social Control in Early Victorian England." *Cultural Critique* (Fall 1993), 25:33–63.

Bredbenner, Candice. *A Nationality of Her Own: Women, Marriage, and the Law of Citizenship*. Berkeley: University of California Press, 1998.

——. "Toward Independent Citizenship: Married Women's Nationality Rights in the United States: 1855–1937." Ph.D. dissertation, University of Virginia, 1990. Ann Arbor: University Microfilms, 1997.

Brewer John and John Styles, eds. *An Ungovernable People: The English and Their Law in the Seventeenth and Eighteenth Centuries*. New Brunswick: Rutgers University Press, 1980.

Bright, Charles and Matthew Geyer. "For a Unified History of the World in the Twentieth Century." *Radical History Review* (1987), 39:69–91.

Brilmayer, Lea and Charles Norchi. "Federal Extraterritoriality and Fifth Amendment Due Process." *Harvard Law Review* (April 1992), 105:1217–63.

Bristow, Edward J. *Prostitution and Prejudice: The Jewish Fight against White Slavery 1870–1939*. New York: Schocken Books, 1983.

"British Colonial Societies." A Symposium, *The International History Review* (February 1990).

Bryan, Robert, Jr. "The Legal Profession." In *American University Men in China*. Shanghai: Comacrib Press, 1936.

Buhite, Russell D. "The Open Door in Perspective: Stanley K. Hornbeck and American Far Eastern Policy." In Frank Merli and Theodore Wilson, eds., *Makers of American Diplomacy: From Theodore Roosevelt to Henry Kissinger*. New York: Scribners, 1974.

Bull, Hedley, ed. *The Expansion of International Society*. Oxford: Clarendon Press, 1984.

Burgess, John William. "How May the United States Govern Its Extra-Continental Territory." *Political Science Quarterly* (1899), 14:1–18.

Burroughs, Peter. "The Law, the Citizen, and the State in Nineteenth-Century Australia." *Journal of Imperial and Commonwealth History* (September 1994), 22:542–54.

——. "Imperial Institutions and the Government of Empire." In *Oxford History of the British Empire*. Vol. 3. Oxford and New York: Oxford University Press, 1999.

Busch, Briton Cooper. *"Whaling Will Never Do for Me": The American Whaleman in the Nineteenth Century*. Lexington: University Press of Kentucky, 1994.

Calhoon, Robert. "The Reintegration of the Loyalists and the Disaffected." In Jack Greene, ed., *The American Revolution: Its Character and Limits*. New York: New York University Press, 1987.

Canny, Nicholas. "The Permissive Frontier: The Problem of Social Control in English Settlements in Ireland and Virginia, 1550–1650." In K. R. Andrews et al., eds., *The Westward Enterprise: English Activities in Ireland, the Atlantic, and America, 1480–1650*. Detroit: Wayne State University Press, 1979.

Ch'en Kuo-huang. *Ling-shih ts'ai-p'an ch'üan tsai Chung-kuo chih hsing-ch'eng yü fei-ch'u* (The Formation and Abrogation of Consular Jurisdiction in China). Taipei: Chia hsin shui ni kung ssu wen hua chi chin hui, 1971.

Chamberlain, Heath B. "On the Search for Civil Society in China." *Modern China* (April 1993), 19:199–215.

Champly, Henry. *The Road to Shanghai*. London: John Long, 1934.

Chan, Anthony. *Arming the Chinese: The Western Armaments Trade in Warlord China, 1920–1928*. Vancouver: University of British Columbia Press, 1982.

Chan, F. Gilbert and Thomas H. Etzold, eds. *China in the 1920's: Nationalism and Revolution*. New York: New Viewpoints, 1976.

Chang, Richard. *The Justice of the Western Consular Courts in Nineteenth-Century Japan*. Westport, Conn.: Greenwood Press, 1984.

Cheng Tsuan. "Shang-hai tsu-chieh hsing wang lun" (A Discussion of the Rise and Fall of the Concessions in Shanghai), *Shang-hai she-hui k'e-hsüeh yuan-hsüeh shu chi-k'an* (Quarterly Journal of the Shanghai Academy of Social Sciences) (1988), 4:66–76.

Chung, Tan. "The Unequal Treaty System: Infrastructure of Irresponsible Imperialism." *China Report* (September–October 1981), 17:3–34.

Chung Mei Kuan-hsi Shih-liao, *Kuang-hsu chau* (Historical Material on Sino-American Relations, Guang-hsu Period). Taipei: Institute of Modern History, Academia Sinica, 1988–89.

Clendenen, Clarence et al. *Americans in Africa 1865–1900*. Stanford: Stanford University Press, 1966.

Clifford, Nicholas R. "A Revolution Is Not a Tea Party: The 'Shanghai Mind(s)' Reconsidered." *Pacific Historical Review* (November 1990), 59:501–26.

——. *Spoilt Children of Empire: Westerners in Shanghai and the Chinese Revolution of the 1920s*. Hanover: University Press of New England, 1991.

Clymer, Kenton. *Protestant Missionaries in the Philippines, 1898–1916*. Champaign: University of Illinois Press, 1986.

Coates, P. D. *The China Consuls: British Consular Officers, 1843–1943*. Hong Kong: Oxford University Press, 1988.

Coble, Parks M., Jr. *The Shanghai Capitalist and the Nationalist Government, 1927–1937*. Cambridge: Harvard University Press, 1989.

Cohen, Jerome and Hungdah Chiu, eds. *People's China and International Law: A Documentary Study*. Princeton: Princeton University Press, 1974.

Conner, Alison. "Soochow Law School and the Shanghai Bar." *Hong Kong Law Journal* (1993), 23:395–411.

Cooper, Frederic and Ann L. Stoler, eds. "Tensions of Empire." *American Ethnologist* (November 1989), 16:609–765.

"Coping with Shanghai: Means to Survival and Success in the Early Twentieth Century." *The Journal of Asian Studies* (February 1995), 54:3–123.

"Correspondence, Ordinances, Orders in Council . . . Respecting Consular Establishments in China, 1833–81." In *British Parliamentary Papers*, China-26. Shannon: Irish University Press, 1974.

Crane, Daniel M. and Thomas A. Breslin. *An Ordinary Relationship: American Opposition to Republican Revolution in China*. Gainesville: Florida International University Press, 1986.

Crapol, Edward. "Coming to Terms with Empire: The Historiography of Late-Nineteenth-Century American Foreign Relations." *Diplomatic History* (Fall 1992), 16:573–97.

Dacey, Jennifer J. "U.S. Citizens' Fourth Amendment Rights: Do They Extend Only to the Waters' Edge? *United States v. Barona*." *George Mason Law Review* (Summer 1997), 5:761–97.

Davids, Jules, ed. *American Diplomatic and Public Papers: The United States and China*. Wilmington: Scholarly Resources, 1979.

Dean, Britten. "British Informal Empire: The Case of China." *Journal of Commonwealth and Comparative Politics* (March 1976), 14:64–81.

Denby, Charles, Jr. "Extraterritoriality in China." *American Journal of International Law* (October 1924), 18:667–75.

Dennett, Tyler. *Americans in Eastern Asia*. New York: Barnes and Noble, 1941.

Downs, Jacques M. "Fair Game: Exploitative Role-Myths and the American Opium Trade." *Pacific Historical Review* (May 1972), 41:133–49.

Duara, Prasenjit. "Transnationalism and the Predicament of Sovereignty: China, 1900–1945." *American Historical Review* (October 1997), 102:1030–1051.

Dunn, Frederick. *The Protection of Nationals*. Baltimore: Johns Hopkins University Press, 1932.

Edwards, R. Randle. "Ch'ing Legal Jurisdiction Over Foreigners." In Jerome Cohen et al., eds. *Essays on China's Legal Tradition*. Princeton: Princeton University Press, 1980.

Elvin, Mark. "The Administration of Shanghai, 1905–1914." In William Skinner and Mark Elvin, eds., *The Chinese City Between Two Worlds*. Stanford: Stanford University Press, 1974.

——. "The Gentry Democracy in Chinese Shanghai, 1905, 1914." In Jack Grey, ed., *Modern China's Search for a Political Form*. London: Oxford University Press, 1969.

Epstein, Richard. *Bargaining with the State*. Princeton: Princeton University Press, 1993.

Etzold, Thomas H., ed. *Aspects of Sino-American Relations Since 1784*. New York: New Viewpoints Press, 1978.

Everett, Edward. "The Execution of an Italian at Canton." *North American Review* (1835), 40:58–68.

"Expatriation and Protection of Naturalized Americans Abroad and in Turkish Dominions." *American Journal of International Law* (January 1908), 2:156–60.

"Extraterritoriality and the United States Court for China" (in Editorial Comment). *American Journal of International Law* (April 1907), 1:469–80.

Fairbank, John K. " 'American China Policy' to 1898: A Misconception." *Pacific Historical Review* (November 1970), 39:409–20.

——. *Trade and Diplomacy on the China Coast: The Opening of the Treaty Ports, 1842–1854*. Cambridge: Harvard University Press, 1953.

Feetham, Richard. *Report of the Hon. Justice Feetham to the Shanghai Municipal Council*. Shanghai: North China Daily News and Herald, 1931–32.

Ferguson, Thomas. "From Normalcy to New Deal: Industrial Structure, Party Competition, and American Public Policy in the Great Depression." *International Organization* (Winter 1984), 38:41–94.

Feuerwerker, Albert. *The Foreign Establishment in China in the Early Twentieth Century*. Ann Arbor: University of Michigan Press, 1976.

——. "The Foreign Presence in China." In J. K. Fairbank, ed., *The Cambridge History of China*, vol. 12, part 1. Cambridge: Cambridge University Press, 1983.

Fewsmith, Joseph. *Party, State, and Local Elites in Republican China: Merchant Organizations and Politics in Shanghai, 1890–1930*. Honolulu: University of Hawaii Press, 1985.

Field, John H. *Toward a Programme of Imperial Life: The British Empire at the Turn of the Century*. Westport, Conn.: Greenwood Press, 1982.

Finch, Percy. *Shanghai and Beyond*. New York: Scribners, 1953.

Flournoy, Richard W. "International Problems in Respect to Nationality by Birth." *American Society of International Law Proceedings* (1926).

Franck, Thomas. "Legitimacy in the International System." *American Journal of International Law* (October 1988), 82:705–59.

Frey, Linda S. and Marsha L. Frey. *The History of Diplomatic Immunity*. Columbus: Ohio State University Press, 1999.

Frieden, Jeffry A. "The Economics of Intervention: American Overseas Investments and Relations with Underdeveloped Areas, 1890–1950." *Comparative Studies in Society and History* (January 1989), 21:55–80.

"The Functionality of Citizenship." *Harvard Law Review* (June 1997),

110:1814–1831.

Gallagher, John and Ronald Robinson. "The Imperialism of Free Trade." *Economic History Review*, 2d series (August 1953), 6:1–15.

Galsterer, H. "The Administration of Justice." *Cambridge Ancient History*, vol. 10. New York: Macmillan, 1996.

Galtung, Johan. "A Structural Theory of Imperialism." *Journal of Peace Research* (1971), 8:81–117.

Garbesi, George C. *Consular Authority Over Seamen from the United States Point of View*. The Hague: Martinus Nijhoff, 1968.

"General Correspondence; and Papers Relating to Naturalization and Expatriation." In *Foreign Relations of the United States* (FRUS). Washington, D.C.: GPO, 1873.

Gibson, Arrell. *Yankees in Paradise: The Pacific Basin Frontier*. Albuquerque: University of New Mexico Press, 1993.

Gilissen, John, ed. *L'Etranger*. Brussels: Librairie Encyclopèdique, 1958.

Gong, Gerrit W. *The Standard of "Civilization" in International Society*. Oxford: Clarendon Press, 1984.

Graham, Edward. *American Ideas of a Special Relationship with China, 1784–1900*. New York: Garland, 1988.

Greenberg, Douglas. "Crime, Law Enforcement, and Social Control in Colonial America." *American Journal of Legal History* (1982), 26:293–325.

Greenberg, Michael. *British Trade and the Opening of China, 1800–1842*. Cambridge: Cambridge University Press, 1951.

Greene, Jack. "Competing Authorities: The Debate Over Parliamentary Imperial Jurisdiction, 1763–1776." In Philip Lawson, ed., *Parliament and the Atlantic Empire*. Edinburgh: Edinburgh University Press, 1995.

Greene, Jack, ed. *Negotiated Authorities: Essays in Colonial Political and Constitutional History*. Charlottesville: University of Virginia, 1994.

———. *Peripheries and Center: Constitutional Development in the Extended Politics of the British Empire and the United States, 1607–1788*. Athens: University of Georgia Press, 1987.

Hall, John A. and G. John Ikenberry. *The State*. Minneapolis: University of Minnesota Press, 1989.

Hall, Kermit. "The Civil War Era as a Crucible for Nationalizing the Lower Federal Courts." *Prologue* (Fall 1975), 7:177–86.

Hammar, Tomas. "State, Nation, and Dual Citizenship." In William R. Brubaker, ed., *Immigration and the Politics of Citizenship in Europe and North America*. Lanham, Md.: University Press of America, 1989.

"The Hansa." *Cambridge Medieval History*, vol. 7. New York: Macmillan, 1932

Hao Li-yu. *Ling-shih ts'ai-p'an ch'üan wen-t'i* (The Problem of Consular Jurisdiction). Shanghai: Shang wu yin shu kuan, 1930.

Haskell, Thomas L. "Capitalism and the Origins of the Humanitarian Sensibility (Parts I, II)." In Thomas Bender, ed. *The Antislavery Debate: Capitalism and Abolitionism as a Problem in Historical Interpretation.* Berkeley: University of California Press, 1993.

Hay, Douglas et al., eds. *Albion's Fatal Tree: Crime and Society in Eighteenth-Century England.* London: Pantheon Books, 1975.

Helmick, Milton. "The United States Court for China." *American Bar Association Journal* (September 1941), 27:544–46.

Henkin, Louis. *Foreign Affairs and the United States Constitution.* Oxford: Clarendon Press, 1996.

Henriot, Christian. *Shanghai, 1927–1937: Municipal Power, Locality, and Modernization.* Translated by Noel Castelino. Berkeley: University of California Press, 1993.

Henson, Curtis T., Jr. *Commissioners and Commodores: The East India Squadron and American Diplomacy in China.* University: University of Alabama Press, 1982.

Hepner, Adolph. *Extraterritorial Criminal Jurisdiction and Its Effects on American Citizens.* Washington, D.C.: GPO, 1890.

Hershatter, Gail. *Dangerous Pleasures: Prostitution and Modernity in Twentieth-Century Shanghai.* Berkeley: University of California Press, 1997.

Hinckley, Frank E. *American Consular Jurisdiction in the Orient.* Washington, D.C.: W. H. Lowdermilk, 1906.

Hobsbawm, Eric J. *Nations and Nationalism Since 1780: Programme, Myth, Reality.* Cambridge: Cambridge University Press, 1990.

Hogan, Michael J. "Corporatism: A Positive Appraisal." *Diplomatic History* (Fall 1986), 10:363–72.

Holt, Wythe, ed. *Essays in Nineteenth-Century American Legal History.* Westport, Conn.: Greenwood Press, 1976.

Hoyt, Frederick B. "The Open Door Leads to Reluctant Intervention: The Case of the Yangtze Rapid Steamship Company." *Diplomatic History* (Spring 1977), 1:155–69.

——. "The Summer of '30: American Policy and Chinese Communism." *Pacific Historical Review* (May 1977), 46:229–49.

Hunt, Michael. "The American Remission of the Boxer Indemnity: A Reappraisal." *Journal of Asian Studies* (May 1972), 31:539–59.

——. "Americans in the China Market: Economic Opportunities and Economic Nationalism, 1890's–1931." *Business History Review* (Autumn 1977), 41:277–307.

——. "The Forgotten Occupation: Peking, 1900–1901." *Pacific Historical Review* (November 1979), 48:501–29.

——. *The Making of a Special Relationship: The United States and China to 1914.* New York: Columbia University Press, 1983.

Hunt, Michael and Steven Levine. "The Revolutionary Challenge to Early U.S. Cold War Policy in Asia." In Warren I. Cohen and Akira Iriye, eds., *The Great Powers in East Asia, 1953–1960*. New York: Columbia University Press, 1990.

Huskey, James L. "Americans in Shanghai: Community Formation and Response to Revolution, 1919–1928." Ph.D. dissertation, University of North Carolina at Chapel Hill, 1985. Ann Arbor: University Microfilms (86–05606).

——. "The Cosmopolitan Connection." *Diplomatic History* (Summer 1987), 11:227–42.

Hyam, Ronald. "Empire and Sexual Opportunity." *The Journal of Imperial and Commonwealth History* (January 1986), 14:34–90.

Ichioka, Yuji. "Ameyuki-san: Japanese Prostitutes in Nineteenth-Century America." *AmerAsia* (1977), 4:1–21.

Israel, Jerry. *Progressivism and the Open Door: America and China, 1905–1921*. Pittsburgh: University of Pittsburgh Press, 1971.

Johnstone, W. C. "The Feetham Report: A New Plan for Shanghai." *American Political Science Review* (November 1931), 25:1044–50.

——. "Status of Foreign Concessions and Settlements in the Treaty Ports of China." *American Political Science Review* (October 1937), 31:942–48.

"Judge Feetham Surveys Shanghai: A Digest." *Pacific Affairs* (July/September 1931), 4:586–614.

Kark, Ruth. *American Consuls in the Holy Land, 1832–1914*. Detroit: Wayne State University Press, 1994.

Kasaba, Resat. "Treaties and Friendships: British Imperialism, the Ottoman Empire, and China in the Nineteenth Century." *Journal of World History* (Fall 1993), 4:215–42.

Kassan, Shalom. "Extraterritorial Jurisdiction in the Ancient World." *American Journal of International Law* (April 1935), 29:237–47.

Kearney, Kevin M. "Private Citizens in Foreign Affairs: A Constitutional Analysis." *Emory Law Journal* (Winter 1987), 36:285–355.

Kearny, Thomas. "Tsiang Documents: Elipoo, Ke-ying, Pottinger, and Kearny and the Most Favored Nation and Open Door Policy in China in 1842–44." *Chinese Social and Political Science Review* (1932), 16:73–104.

Keeton, George W. *The Development of Extraterritoriality in China*. London: Longmans, Green, 1928, vols. 1 and 2.

——. "The International Status of Macao Before 1887." *Chinese Social and Political Science Review* (1927), 11:404–13.

Kennedy, David. "International Law and the Nineteenth Century: History of an Illusion." *Quinnipiac Law Review* (Spring 1997), 17:99–138.

Kens, Paul. "The Source of a Myth: Police Powers of the States and Laissez Faire Constitutionalism, 1900–1937." *The American Journal of Legal History* (1991), 35:70–98.

Kerber, Linda K. "The Meanings of Citizenship." *Journal of American History* (December 1997), 84:836–37.

Kerr, Robert J. "American Citizens in Foreign Countries." *International Relations of the United States* (July 1914), 54:236–42.

Kettner, James H. *The Development of American Citizenship, 1608–1870.* Chapel Hill: University of North Carolina Press, 1978.

Khadduri, Majid and Herbert J. Liebesny. "The Development of Western Judicial Privileges." *Law and the Middle East.* Washington, D.C.: Middle East Institute, 1955.

Kirby, William C. "Intercultural Connections and Chinese Development: External and Internal Spheres of Modern China's Foreign Relations." In Frederic Wakeman, Jr. and Wang Xi, eds. *China's Quest for Modernization: A Historical Perspective.* Berkeley: Institute of East Asian Studies, University of California, 1997.

——. "The Internationalization of China: Foreign Relations at Home and Abroad in the Republican Era." *The China Quarterly* (June 1997), 150:433–58.

Koo, Wellington. *Status of Aliens in China.* New York: Columbia University Press, 1912.

Kotonev, Anatol. *Shanghai: Its Court and Council.* Shanghai: North China Daily News and Herald, 1927.

LaFeber, Walter. *The American Search for Opportunity, 1865–1913.* Cambridge: Cambridge University Press, 1993.

——. "The Constitution and United States Foreign Policy: An Interpretation." In David Thelen, ed., *The Constitution and American Life.* Ithaca: Cornell University Press, 1988.

Lamson, H. D. "Sino-American Miscegenation in Shanghai." *Social Forces* (May 1936), 14:573–81.

——. "Sociological Study of the American Community in Shanghai." *Sociological and Social Research* (March 1932), 16:395–96.

Langley, Lester and Thomas Schoonover. *The Banana Men: American Mercenaries and Entrepreneurs in Central America, 1880–1930.* Lexington: University Press of Kentucky, 1995.

Langum, David J. *Law and Community on the Mexican California Frontier: Anglo-American Expatriates and the Clash of Legal Traditions, 1821–1846.* Norman: University of Oklahoma Press, 1987.

Latourette, Kenneth Scott. "Chinese Historical Studies During the Past Nine Years." *American Historical Review* (July 1930), 35:778–97.

"Law in the West." *Journal of the West* (January 1985), 24:3–94.

Law Officers' Opinions to the Foreign Office, 1793–1860. Westmead: Gregg International, 1970–73.

Lee, Tahirih V. "Coping with Shanghai: Means to Survival and Success in the

Early Twentieth Century–[Introduction to] A Symposium." *Journal of Asian Studies* (February 1995), 54:3–18.

Legomsky, Stephen H. "Why Citizenship?" *Virginia Journal of International Law* (Fall 1994), 35:279–300.

Leuchtenburg, William E. "Progressivism and Imperialism: The Progressive Movement and American Foreign Policy, 1898–1916." *The Mississippi Valley Historical Review* (1952), 39:483–504.

Levenson, Joseph. "Western Powers and Chinese Revolutions: The Pattern of Intervention." *Pacific Affairs* (September 1953), 26:230–35.

Levin, N. Gordon. *Woodrow Wilson and World Politics: America's Response to War and Revolution*. New York: Oxford University Press, 1968.

Levine, Philippa. "Rereading the 1890s: Venereal Disease as 'Constitutional Crisis' in Britain and British India." *Journal of Asian Studies* (1986), 45:585–612.

Lewis, George. *On Foreign Jurisdiction and the Extradition of Criminals*. New York: Parker, 1859.

Li Tien-yi. *Woodrow Wilson's China Policy, 1913–1917*. New York: Twayne, 1952.

Lilley, Charles and Michael Hunt. "On Social History, the State, and Foreign Relations: Commentary on [James Huskey's] 'The Cosmopolitan Connection.'" *Diplomatic History* (Summer 1987), 11:–

Lobingier, Charles Sumner. "America's Torch-bearing in Asia." *Review of Reviews* (December 1914), 50:714–16.

——. "A Quarter Century of Our Extra-Territorial Court." *Georgetown Law Journal* (May 1932), 20:427–56.

Lobingier, Charles Sumner, comp. and ed. *United States Court for China: Extraterritorial Cases*. 2 vols. Manila: Bureau of Printing, 1920, 1928.

Lockwood, W. W., Jr. "The International Settlement at Shanghai, 1924–34." *American Political Science Review* (December 1934), 28:1030–46.

Lorence, James. "Business and Reform: The American Asiatic Association and the Exclusion Laws." *Pacific Historical Review* (November 1970), 39:421–38.

Loring, Charles. "American Extraterritoriality in China." *Minnesota Law Review* (1926), 10:407–416.

Lo-shu Fu, ed. *A Documentary Chronicle of Sino-Western Relations (1644–1820)*. Tucson: University of Arizona Press, 1966.

Lowenfeld, Andreas F. "U.S. Law Enforcement Abroad: The Constitution and International Law." *The American Journal of International Law* (April 1990), 84:444–493.

Lutz, Jessie. "Chinese Nationalism and the Anti-Christian Campaigns of the 1920's." *Modern Asian Studies* (July 1976), 10:395–416.

Mah, N. Wing. "Foreign Jurisdiction in China." *American Journal of International Law* (October 1924), 18:676–95.

Malley, R. et al. "Constructing the State Extraterritorially." *Harvard Law Review* (1990), 103:1273–1305.

Marshall, P. J. "The Whites of British India, 1780–1830: A Failed Colonial Society?" *International History Review* (February 1990), 12:26–44.

——. "Introduction." *Oxford History of the British Empire*, vol. 2. Oxford and New York: Oxford University Press, 1998.

——. "The British in Asia: Trade to Domination, 1700–-1765." *Oxford History of the British Empire*, vol. 2. Oxford and New York: Oxford University Press, 1998.

May, Glenn A. *Social Engineering in the Philippines: The Aims, Execution, and Impact of American Colonial Policy, 1900–1913*. Westport, Conn.: Greenwood Press, 1980.

McCormick, Richard L. "The Discovery that Business Corrupts Politics: A Reappraisal of the Origins of Progressivism." *American Historical Review* (April 1981), 86:247–74.

McCormick, Thomas. *America's Half Century: United States Foreign Policy in the Cold War*. Baltimore: Johns Hopkins University Press, 1989.

——. *China Market: America's Quest for Informal Empire, 1893–1901*. Chicago: Quadrangle Books, 1967.

McDougall, Walter A. *Promised Land, Crusader State*. Boston and New York: Houghton Mifflin Company, 1997.

McElderry, Andrea Lee. *Shanghai Old-Style Banks (Ch'ien-Chuang), 1800–1935: A Traditional Institution in a Changing Society*. Ann Arbor: University of Michigan Press, 1976.

McKee, Delber L. *Chinese Exclusion versus the Open Door Policy, 1900–1906*. Detroit: Wayne State University Press, 1977.

Merry, Sally Engle. "Law and Colonialism. A Review Essay." *Law and Society Review* (Winter 1991), 25:889–922.

Meyer, Kathryn. "Splitting Apart: The Shanghai Treaty Port in Transition, 1914–1921." Philadelphia: Temple University Press, 1985. Ann Arbor: University Microfilms, 85–09357.

——. "Trade and Nationality at Shanghai upon the Outbreak of the First World War, 1914–1915." *International History Review* (May 1988), 10:238–60.

Mihalopoulos, Vassilios Bill. "The *Karayuki-san*: Modernisation, Social Administration, and the Making of Overseas Japanese Prostitutes." *Bulletin of Concerned Asian Scholars* (January–March 1993), 25:41–56.

Miller, Stuart C. *"Benevolent Assimilation": The American Conquest of the Philippines, 1899–1903*. New Haven: Yale University Press, 1982.

Mitchell, Timothy. "The Limits of the State: Beyond Statist Approaches and their Critics." *American Political Science Review* (March 1991), 85:77–96

Mommsen, Wolfgang and J. A. De Moor, eds. *European Expansion and Law: The*

Encounter of European and Indigenous Law in 19th- and 20th-Century Africa and Asia. New York: Berg, 1992.

Mommsen, Wolfgang and Jürgen Osterhammel, eds. *Imperialism and After: Continuities and Discontinuities.* London: Allen and Unwin, 1986.

Moore, John Bassett. *American Diplomacy: Its Spirit and Achievements.* New York and London: Harpers, 1905.

——. *A Digest of International Law.* 3 vols. Washington, D.C.: GPO, 1906.

——. *Report on Extraterritorial Crime and the Cutting Case.* Washington, D.C.: GPO, 1887.

Morse, Hosea. *The International Relations of the Chinese Empire.* London: Longmans, Green, 1918, 3 vols.

——. *The Trade and Administration of the Chinese Empire.* London: Longmans, Green,, 1908.

Municipal Gazette of the Council for the Foreign Settlement of Shanghai, 1908–1943. Shanghai Municipal Archives, U1-1-973-1008.

Nadelmann, Ethan A. "The Role of the United States in the International Enforcement of Criminal Law." *Harvard International Law Journal* (1990), 31:37.

Naff, Thomas. "The Ottoman Empire and the European States System." In Hedley Bull, ed., *The Expansion of International Society.* Oxford: Clarendon Press, 1984.

Nagle, D. Brendan. *The Ancient World: A Social and Cultural History.* Englewood Cliffs, N.J.: Prentice Hall, 1989 [1979].

Neuman, Gerald L. "Surveying Law and Borders: Anomalous Zones." *Stanford Law Review* (1998), 48:1197.

——. *Strangers to the Constitution: Immigrants, Borders, and Fundamental Law.* Princeton: Princeton University Press, 1996.

Nien Ch'eng (pseud.), ed. *Nan Wang te sui-yueh* [Unforgettable Times]. Hong Kong: Chih cheng ch'u pan she, 1972.

Noer, Thomas. *Briton, Boer, and Yankee: The United States and South Africa 1870–1914.* Kent, Ohio: Kent State University Press, 1978.

Onselen, Charles van. *Studies in the Social and Economic History of the Witwatersrand 1886–1914,* 2 vol. New York: Longman, 1982.

Onuf, Peter. "Settlers, Settlements, and New States." In Jack Greene, ed., *The American Revolution: Its Character and Limits.* New York: New York University Press, 1987.

Osborn, Clarence G. "American Extraterritorial Jurisdiction in China to 1906; A Study of American Policy." Ph.D. dissertation, Stanford University, 1935.

Osterhammel, Jürgen. *Colonialism.* Princeton: Markus Wiener, 1997.

——. "China." *Oxford History of the British Empire,* vol. 4. Oxford and New York: Oxford University Press, 1999.

——. "Britain and China, 1842–1914." *Oxford History of the British Empire*, vol. 3. Oxford and New York: Oxford University Press, 1999.

Packer, Herbert L. "Two Models of the Criminal Process." *University of Pennsylvania Law Review* (1964), 113:1–68.

"Passport." In *Encyclopedia of the Social Sciences*, vol. 12. New York: Macmillan, 1936.

Peattie, Mark. "Japanese Treaty Port Settlements in China, 1895–1937." In Peter Duus et al., *The Japanese Informal Empire in China, 1895–1937*. Princeton: Princeton University Press, 1989.

Peirce, H. H. D. *Inspection of U.S. Consulates in the Orient*. Washington, D.C.: GPO, 1906.

Pelcovits, Nathan. *Old China Hands and the Foreign Office*. New York: Kings Crown Press, 1948.

Petrov, Victor. "Russian Shanghai." *Far Eastern Affairs* [Russia] (1992), 2:140–56 and 3:131–41.

Perritt, Henry H. "Jurisdiction in Cyberspace." *Villanova Law Review* (1996), 41:64–128.

Pfeffer, Richard M. "Crime and Punishment: China and the United States." In Jerome Cohen, ed., *Contemporary Chinese Law: Research Problems and Perspectives*. Cambridge: Harvard University Press, 1970.

Phillipson, Coleman. *The International Law and Custom of Ancient Greece and Rome*, 2 vols. London: Macmillan, 1911.

Ramos, Efren R. "The Legal Construction of American Colonialism: The Insular Cases (1901–1922)." *Revista Juridica Universidad de Puerto Rico* (1996), 65:225–328.

Ratner, Joseph, ed. *Intelligence in the Modern World: John Dewey's Philosophy*. New York: Modern Library, 1939.

Reed, James. *The Missionary Mind and American East Asian Policy, 1911–1915*. Cambridge: Harvard University, Council on East Asian Studies, 1983.

Report of the Commission on Extra-territoriality in China. London: H.M.S.O., 1926; reprint, San Francisco: Chinese Materials Center, 1975.

Richardson, James, comp. *A Compilation of the Messages and Papers of the Presidents, 1789–1907*. Washington, D.C.: Bureau of National Literature and Art, 1908.

Robinson, Ronald. "Imperial Theory and the Question of Imperialism After Empire." In R. F. Holland and G. Rizvi, eds., *Perspectives on Imperialism and Decolonization*. London: Frank Cass, 1984.

——. "Non-European Foundations of European Imperialism: Sketch for a Theory of Collaboration." In Roger Owen and Bob Sutcliffe, eds., *Studies in the Theory of Imperialism*. London: Longman Group, 1972.

——. "The Eccentric Idea of Imperialism, with or without Empire." In Wolfgang

Mommsen and Jürgen Osterhammel, eds. *Imperialism and After: Continuities and Discontinuities*. London: Allen & Unwin, 1986.

Roosevelt, Theodore. "What 'Americanism' Means." *The Forum* (1894), 17:196–206.

Russell-Wood, A. J. R. "Seamen Ashore and Afloat: The Social Environment of the *Carreira da India*, 1550–1750." In Ursula Lamb, ed., *The Globe Encircled and the World Revealed*. Brookfield: Variorum, 1995.

Sayre, Francis Bowes. "The Passing of Extraterritoriality in Siam." *American Journal of International Law* (January 1928), 22:7–88.

Scheiber, Harry N. "World War I as Entrepreneurial Opportunity: Willard Straight and the American International Corporation." *Political Science Quarterly* (September 1969), 84:484–511.

Schmidt, Hans. "Democracy for China: American Propaganda and the May Fourth Movement." *Diplomatic History* (Winter 1998), 22:1–28.

Scott, James C. *Comparative Political Corruption*. Englewood Cliffs, N.J.: Prentice-Hall, 1972.

Scully, Eileen P. "Crime, Punishment, and Empire: The U.S. Court for China, 1906–42." Ph.D. dissertation, Georgetown University, 1994.

——. "Prostitution as Privilege: The 'American Girl' of Treaty Port Shanghai." *International History Review* (December 1998), 20:855–83.

——. "Taking the Low Road to Sino-American Relations: 'Open Door Expansionists' and the Two China Markets." *Journal of American History* (June 1995), 82:62–83.

Shang-hai ti ku-shih (Tales of Shanghai). 3 vols. Shanghai: Jen min ch'u pan she, 1965.

Skowronek, Stephen. *Building a New American State: The Expansion of National Administrative Capacities, 1877–1920*. New York: Cambridge University Press, 1982.

Smith, Edwin L. "The End of the Consular Courts." *Foreign Service Journal* (January 1960), 37:44–49.

Smith, Robert Freeman. *The United States and Revolutionary Nationalism in Mexico, 1916–1932*. Chicago: University of Chicago Press, 1972.

Smith, Rogers. *Civic Ideals: Conflicting Visions of Citizenship in U.S. History*. New Haven: Yale University Press, 1997.

Snow, Edgar. "The Americans in Shanghai." *The American Mercury* (August 1932), 20:437–45.

Sofka, James R. "The Jeffersonian Idea of National Security: Commerce, the Atlantic Balance of Power, and the Barbary War, 1786–1805." *Diplomatic History* (Fall 1997), 21:519–44.

Sohn, Louis. "The New International Law: Protection of the Rights of Individuals Rather than States." *American University Law Review* (Fall 1982), 32:1–64.

Spiro, Peter. "Dual Nationality and the Meaning of Citizenship." *Emory Law Journal* (Fall 1997), 46:1411–85.

Steensgaard, N. "Consuls and Nations in the Levant from 1570 to 1650." *The Scandinavian Economic History Review* (1967), 15:13–55.

Stelle, Charles C. "American Trade in Opium to China, Prior to 1820." *Pacific Historical Review* (December 1940), 9:425–444

Stephens, Thomas. *Order and Discipline in China: The Shanghai Mixed Court, 1911–27.* Seattle and London: University of Washington Press, 1992.

Stevenson, G. H. "The Provinces and Their Government." *Cambridge Ancient History,* vol. 9. London: Cambridge University Press, 1932.

Stoecker, Helmuth. "Germany and China, 1861–94." In John A. Moses and Paul M. Kennedy, eds. *Germany in the Pacific and Far East, 1870–1914.* St. Lucia: University of Queensland Press, 1977.

Stoler, Ann L. "Making Empire Respectable: The Politics of Race and Sexual Morality in 20th-Century Colonial Cultures." *American Ethnologist* (November 1989), 16:634–60.

——. "Rethinking Colonial Categories: European Communities and the Boundaries of Rule." *Comparative Studies in Society and History* (January 1989), 13:134–61.

——. "Sexual Affronts and Racial Frontiers: European Identities and the Cultural Politics of Exclusion in Colonial Southeast Asia." *Comparative Studies in Society and History* (July 1992), 34:514–551.

Swisher, Earl, ed. and trans. *China's Management of the American Barbarians: A Study of Sino-American Relations, 1841–1861, with Documents.* New Haven: Yale University Press, 1972.

Thelen, David. "The Nation and Beyond: Transnational Perspectives on United States History." *Journal of American History* (December 1999), 86:965–75.

Thieme, Hans. "Die Rechtsstellung der Fremden in Deutschland Bis zum 18: Jahrhundert." In John Gilissen, ed., *L'Etranger.* Brussels: Librairie Encyclopèdique, 1958.

Thomson, James C., Jr. *While China Faced West: American Reformers in Nationalist China, 1928–1937.* Cambridge: Harvard University Press, 1969.

Thomson, Janice E. *Mercenaries, Pirates, and Sovereigns: State-Building and Extraterritorial Violence in Early Modern Europe.* Princeton: Princeton University Press, 1994.

Tilly, Charles. "Citizenship, Identity, and Social History." In Charles Tilly, ed., *Citizenship, Identity, and Social History.* Cambridge: Cambridge University Press, *International Review of Social History Supplement 3,* 1996.

Tong, Te-kong. *United States Diplomacy in China, 1844–60.* Seattle: University of Washington Press, 1964.

Torpey, John. *The Invention of the Passport. Surveillance, Citizenship and the State*. Cambridge: Cambridge University Press, 2000.

Tozer, Warren. "Last Bridge to China: The Shanghai Power Company, the Truman Administration, and the Chinese Communists." *Diplomatic History* (Winter 1977), 1:64–78.

Treat, Payson. *Diplomatic Relations Between the United States and Japan, 1853–1895*. Stanford: Stanford University Press, 1932.

Treggiari, Susan. "Social Status and Social Legislation." *Cambridge Ancient History*, vol. 10. New York: Macmillan, 1996.

Trubek, David. "Toward a Social Theory of Law: An Essay on the Study of Law and Development." *The Yale Law Journal* (1972), 82:1–50.

Tsiang, T. F. "The Extension of Equal Commercial Privileges to Other Nations than the British After the Treaty of Nanking." *Chinese Social and Political Science Review* (1931), 15:422–44.

——. "Difficulties of Reconstruction After the Treaty of Nanking." *Chinese Social and Political Science Review* (1932), 16:319–27.

Turlington, Edgar. "The Settlement of Lausanne." *American Journal of International Law* (October 1924), 18:696–706.

"The United States Court for China." *Harvard Law Review* (1936) 49:793.

Turnbull, C. M. "Formal and Informal Empire in East Asia." *Oxford History of the British Empire*, vol. 5. Oxford and New York: Oxford University Press, 1999.

Tyrrell, Ian. "Making Nations/Making States: American Historians in the Context of Empire." *Journal of American History* (December 1999), 96:1015–44.

U.S. Congress: House of Representatives

——. *Charges Against Rufus H. Thayer*. Washington, D.C.: GPO, 1913.

——. "Chinese Court Bill: Jurisdiction Extension." 60th Cong., 1st sess., 1908, Committee on Foreign Affairs, on House Report 17142.

——. "Commission to Inquire into Citizenship of U.S. Expatriation and Protection Abroad." 59th Cong., 1st sess., 1905/6, House Report 4784.

——. "Correspondence of the Late Commissioners in China." 35th Cong., 2d sess., 1858, Executive Document 22.

——. Hearings Before a Subcommittee of the Committee on the Judiciary of the House of Representatives upon the Articles for the Impeachment of Lebbeus R. Wilfley. Washington, D.C.: GPO, 1908.

——. "Incorporation of Companies to Promote Trade in China." 66th Cong., 3d sess., 1921, House Report 1312.

——. "Investigation of George F. Seward." 45th Cong., 3d sess., 1879, House Report 134.

——. "Letter from the Late Consul-General (John C. Myers) Requesting an

Investigation of the Affairs of the Consulate General at Shanghai, China." 45th Cong., 2d sess., 1879. House Miscellaneous Document 10.

———. "Political Relations Between the United States and China." 26th Cong., 2d sess., 1840, Executive Document 71.

———. "Proposed Provisions Pertaining to Appropriations for the Judicial Establishment, 1942." 77th Cong., 1st sess., 1941, House Document 124.

———. "Reorganization of the Consular Service." 59th Cong., 1st sess., 1906, House Report 2281.

———. "To Amend the China Trade Act of 1922 and the Revenue Act of 1921." 68th Cong., 1st sess., 1924, House Report 354–58, on H.R. 16043, H.R. 4810.

———. "Trade with China." 26th Cong., 1st sess., 1840, House Document 119.

———. "U.S. Court for China: Reorganization and Jurisdiction Clarification." 65th Cong., 1st sess., 1917, House Committee on Foreign Affairs 65-H, on H.R. 4281.

U.S. Congress: Senate

———. "American Nationals, Troops, and Capital in China." 75th Cong., 3d sess., 1938, Senate Document 131.

———. "Extend the Jurisdiction of the United States Court for China." 74th Cong., 2d sess., 1936, Senate Report 2424.

———. "For the Relief of American Employees of the Former Shanghai Municipal Council." 83d Cong. 2d sess., 1954, Senate Judiciary Committee 175 on S. 2429.

———. "Promotion of Trade in China." 67th Cong., 1st sess., 1921, Senate 180–82 on H.R. 16043, H.R. 4810

U.S. Court for China. *Decennial Anniversary Brochure.* Shanghai: Far Eastern American Bar Association, 1916.

U. S. Department of State. *Citizenship, Registration of American Citizens, Issuance of Passports, Etc.* Washington, D.C.: GPO, 1915.

———. Records of the Foreign Service Posts. National Archives, Record Group 84.

———. *The United States Passport: Past, Present, Future.* Washington, D.C.: GPO, 1976.

Valone, Stephen J. *A Policy Calculated to Benefit China: The United States and the China Arms Embargo, 1919–1929.* Westport, Conn.: Greenwood Press, 1991.

Varg, Paul. *The Making of a Myth: The United States and China 1897–1912.* East Lansing: Michigan State University Press, 1968.

Vattel, Emmeric de. *The Law of Nations,* Joseph Chitty, ed. London: T. and J. W. Johnson, 1861.

Vincent, John Carter. *The Extraterritorial System in China: Final Phase.* Cambridge: Harvard University Press, 1970.

Wagner, Rudolf G. 'The Role of the Foreign Community in the Chinese Public Sphere." *China Quarterly* (June 1995), 142:422–43.

Wakeman, Frederic, Jr. "Policing Modern Shanghai." *China Quarterly* (September 1988), 115:408–40.

——. *The Shanghai Badlands. Wartime Terrorism and Urban Crime, 1937–1941.* Cambridge and New York: Cambridge University Press, 1996.

Wakeman, Frederic, Jr. and Wen-hsin Yeh, eds. *Shanghai Sojourners.* Berkeley: University of California Press, 1992.

Walker, William O. *Opium and Foreign Policy: The Anglo-American Search for Order in Asia, 1912–1954.* Chapel Hill: University of North Carolina Press, 1991.

Wansbrough, J. and Inalcik Halil, "Imtiyazat." *Encyclopaedia of Islam*, vol. 3. Leiden: E. J. Brill, 1971.

Watson, Geoffrey R. "Offenders Abroad: The Case for Nationality-Based Criminal Jurisdiction." *Yale Journal of International Law* (Winter 1992), 17:41–84.

Weisburd, A. Mark. "Due Process Limits on Federal Extraterritorial Legislation?" *Columbia Journal of Transnational Law* (1997), 35:379–428.

Wharton, Francis. *A Digest of the International Law of the United States.* Washington, D.C.: GPO, 1887.

Wheeler, Everett P. "The Relation of the Citizen Domiciled in a Foreign Country to His Home Government." *American Journal of International Law* (October 1909), 3:869–84.

Who's Who in China. Shanghai: China Weekly Review, 1931.

Wilkie, Mary E. "Colonials, Marginals, and Immigrants: Contributions to a Theory of Ethnic Stratification." *Comparative Studies in Society and History* (January 1977), 19:67–95.

Wilkins, Mira. *The Maturing of Multinational Enterprise: American Business Abroad from 1914 to 1970.* Cambridge: Harvard University Press, 1974.

Wilkinson, Mark. "At the Crossroads: Shanghai in Sino-American Relations, 1945–1950." Ph.D. dissertation, University of Michigan, 1982. Ann Arbor: University Microfilms, UM 8215105.

——. "The Shanghai American Community, 1937–1949." (unpublished, 1997) cited with permission.

Willoughby, Westel W. "Citizenship and Allegiance in Constitutional and International Law." *American Journal of International Law* (October 1907), 1:914–29.

——. *Foreign Rights and Interests in China.* 2 vols. Baltimore: Johns Hopkins University Press, 1927 [1920].

Wilson, David. "Principles and Profits: Standard Oil Responds to Chinese Nationalism, 1925–1927." *Pacific Historical Review* (November 1977), 46:625–47.

Wolfe, Patrick. "Review Essay. History and Imperialism: A Century of Theory, from Marx to Postcolonialism." *American Historical Review* (April 19976), 102:388–420.

Wright, Mary. *The Last Stand of Chinese Conservatism: The T'ung-Chih Restoration, 1862–1874*. Stanford: Stanford University Press, 1957.

Wu Chün-yi, ed. *Shang-hai tsu-chieh wen-t'i* (The Problem of the Shanghai International Settlement). Taipei: Cheng Chung shu ch'u, 1981.

Wu Meng-hsüeh. *Mei-kuo tsai Hua ling-shih ts'ai-p'an ch'üan pai-nien shih* (One Hundred Years of American Consular Jurisdiction in China). Beijing: She-hui ko-hsüeh wen hsien chu-p'an she, 1992.

Wunder, John. "The Chinese and the Courts in the Pacific Northwest: Justice Denied?" *Pacific Historical Review* (May 1983), 3:191–211.

Yen-p'ing Hao and Erh-min Wang. "Chinese Views of Western Relations, 1840–95." In John K. Fairbank and Kwang-ching Liu, eds., *Cambridge History of China*, vol. 11, part 2. Cambridge: Cambridge University Press, 1980.

Young, Marilyn B. *The Rhetoric of Empire: American China Policy, 1895–1901*. Cambridge: Harvard University Press, 1968.

INDEX

for China case against, 237*n*70,
238*nn*71&74
Brown, Laura, 135, 237*n*70,
238*nn*70&74
Brown v. Sexton, 237*n*70, 238*n*70
Bruchard, Jules, 225*n*116
Bryan, William Jennings, 135, 140
Buchanan, James, 67
Buckley, John, 68, 69, 70
Burlingame, Anson, 68, 69
Busch, Briton, 77

Cable Act (1922), 75, 174
Cambodia, 263*n*31
Canada, 142, 199
Canton, 31, 32, 36–38, 42
"Canton System," 32–33
capitalism, extrality as vehicle for,
12–13, 112–13
capital punishment: of Chinese in
opium trade, 41; under Ch'ing
dynasty, 33, 34–36; in consular
courts, 68–69; in homicides, 37–38,
214*n*65 (*see also* sacrificial lamb
syndrome); in rape cases, 216*n*102
capitulations: abrogation of, 48; con-
cept entrenched in Western world,
25, 196; definition of, 24
Caribbean, 60, 61, 142
Carlowitz and Co., 154
Carter, James, 152
CCP. *See* Chinese Communist Party
Cecilia Raigorddetzkaia v. H. Arnold,
254*n*40
censorship, 186
Central America, 60–61, 142
Chaio Van Sing v. Mason, 74
Chang, Daisy, 178
Chang, Richard, 15
*Chang Quai Ching et al. v. Dodge and
Seymour*, 150

Chapman, William, 253*n*31
Char, Nick Wai-yuen, 177–78
*Charles E. Hill v. Elizabeth Adams
Hill*, 224*n*113
charter companies, 22, 31–32, 39–40
Chase National bank, 196
Chiang Kai-shek, 179
children, 178, 256*n*65
China Credit and Information
Bureau, 247*n*74
China Forum, 185
China Investment Corporation, 137
China Merchants Steam Navigation
Company, 150
China Pipe and Tile Company, 101
China Squadron, 63
China Trade Act (1922/1925), 146, 150,
242*n*34, 245*n*55
"China Trade Act Services," 183
Chinese-American Aviation Com-
pany, 245*n*54
Chinese Americans, cases involving,
177–78
Chinese Communist Party (CCP),
196
Chinese Imperial Collector of Cus-
toms, 223*n*98
Chinese Officer v. Eaton and Gilfillin,
76–77
Ch'ing dynasty, 5; Boxer rebellion
and, 92; extrality and, 42; foreigner disputes and, 31; on foreigners' characteristics, 63; homicides
and, 33, 34–36; immigration treaty
revocation by, 93; objections to
rulings of U.S. Court for China,
130–31; opening of China and, 30;
Opium War and, 5, 30, 41, 65; out-
castes and, 215*n*75; overthrow of,
140; on *U.S. v. Demenil*, 130; on
Western vice, 90

citizenship: versus allegiance, 53; beginning of modern state and, 22–23, 27; of children, 178, 256*n*65; during Civil War and after, 54–56; commercial interests and, 85–86; Enlightenment view of, 27–28; expatriation and, 57–58, 84–85; extrality and, 17, 18–19; "federal," 87–88; federal U.S. policy and extraterritorial, 54; identity and, 2, 27; illegitimacy and, 224*n*109; military service and, 55, 59–60, 142; naturalization and, 85, 200; post-World War II and overseas, 196–98; revocation of, 262*n*22; Roman *civitas* legacy and, 22, 23–24; *Ross v. United States* and, 87–88, 113; State Department regime for, 58–59, 85; U.S. constitution and, 51, 113
Civic Ideals (Smith), 1
civil cases: Americans in, 219*n*11; assessor system in, 66, 120; equity in, 74; Lobingier and, 147–50, 156, 244*n*52; Purdy and, 175; in U.S. Court for China, 115, 136–38, 147–50, 156, 232*n*87; women in, 175
Civil War, U.S., 54–56
class: charter companies and, 32; of Japanese in treaty ports, 217*n*113; justice and extrality, 43–45; merchant houses and, 30–31; seamen pressure groups and, 39; white-collar, 182; white overseas communities and, 11–12, 89; Wilfey use of second-class federal citizenship category, 113–16
Clinton, Ethel, 225*n*116
Cloud, Frederick, 137
co-hong system, 37, 39–40
Cole, Peter, 225*n*120

Colombia, 200–201, 263*n*29
comity, principle of, 233*n*16
Commercial Bank of China, 191
Commissioner's Court, 157
Committee on Public Information, 170
companies: abuse of *Raven* ruling, 149–50, 244–45*nn*50&53; charter, 22, 31–32, 39–40; China court, 148–49, 190, 245*n*54, 249*n*89; Chinese government and agreements on taxes and jurisdiction, 165; consular courts and, 73–74; definition of "American," 137; domestic laws and foreign-based, 198–99; extrality and, 72–73, 112–13, 137; federal assistance to American, 145–46; as "good citizens," 156–57; indigenous collaborators and, 166; insurance, 175; local Chinese conditions and investors, 145; Progressives on legitimate versus shady, 137, 141; State Department on American, 137, 149, 244–45*n*53; State Department on fraudulent American, 244*n*50; use of extrality by, 72–73, 112–13. *See also specific companies*
Conger, Edwin, 103, 229*n*57, 231*n*82
Congress: Acts of (*see specific Acts*); anti-imperialism of, 71–72; labor versus management legislation of, 77; Wilfey impeachment hearings, 122
Connell Brothers, 249*n*98
Connolly Land and Oil Company, 245*n*54
constitution, U.S.: citizenship and, 51, 113; diplomatic protection and, 56–59, 84, 87–88, 113; State Department on constitutionality of rights and, 199
consular courts: arbitration in, 72;

Shanghai Missionary Association,
90–91
Shanghai Motors Corp., 245n54
Shanghai Municipal Council (SMC),
166, 171, 178–79
Shanghai Power, 196
Shanghai Telephone, 196
Sheinbein, Samuel, 262–63n25
Shing Ho v. Wetmore, 73
Siam (Thailand), 65, 83
Silver Purchase Act (1934), 192
Sino-American Cooperation Organi-
zation (SACO), 179
Sino-American treaties, 207n16
Sino-Belge Tientsin Carpet Factory,
176
Sino-Russian Treaty (1689), 33
Slaughter House Cases, 56, 220n28
SMC. *See* Shanghai Municipal Coun-
cil
Smith, Rogers, 1
Soochow School of Comparative Law,
158
Soong, T. V., 192
South African Republic, 62
Southern Methodist Mission Board,
158
sovereignty: China and loss of, 30;
concept(s) of, 27, 202; on high
seas, 29, 51, 54
Soysal, Yasmin, 202
Spain, 42
Springer, William, 69
Squires, R. W., 175
Standard Oil, 150, 165
Standard Vacuum Oil, 196
state: allegiance to (*see* allegiance: to
nation-state); beginning of mod-
ern, 22, 27; citizenship and begin-
ning of modern, 22–23, 27; concepts of sovereignty and, 27; elites

and (*see* elites); extension of sov-
ereign justice and, 29; extrality
and, 2–3; extra-territorial policing
and, 28–30; long-term survival of,
201–202
State Department, U.S. *See* U.S.
Department of State
status-of-forces agreements, versus
extrality, 195, 196
statutes of limitations, 67
Steel, Ronald, 202
Stephens, Thomas B, 14–15, 209n37
Stimson, Henry, 168
Stoler, Ann, 88, 91
Strangers to the Constitution (Neu-
man), 1
Styles, John, 39
Sublime Porte treaty, 64–65
Sullivan, Ruth, 173–74
Sully, C. S., 183
Sun Kau-sz, 129
Sun Yat-sen, 140, 154, 245n54
supercargoes, 33
Supreme Court and Consular Gazette,
209n40
Swayne and Hoyt v. Everett, 247n82
Sweden-Norway, 42, 199
Sze Hai-ching v. Biddle, 239n81

Taft, William Howard: creation of
U.S. Court for China and, 7, 110;
on expatriates, 141; Philippines
and, 94; on prostitution in treaty
ports, 96; service on Supreme
Court, 161; Wilfey and, 111, 121, 124,
140
Taft-Katsura Agreement (1905),
232n87
taipans, 32–33
Talbot v. Janson, 53
Tangier, 5

tax policies, 50, 146, 165
"Teapot Dome" affair, 162
Terranova, Franceso "Frank," 36–38, 131
Terranova solution, 36–38, 98
terrorism, 199
Texas Company, 165
Texas Oil, 249*n*98
Thailand (Siam), 65, 83
Thayer, Rufus: appellate court use under, 125; appointment of, 235*n*41; background of, 124–25; Brown case ruling, 135; corruption charges against, 125, 126; on land titles, 137; *U.S. v. Jones* and, 16
Torres, Victorino, 129
Toth v. Quarles, 197–98, 261*n*12
trade stoppages, 33–34, 39–40
treaties: extradition, 30, 66, 262–63*n*25; immigration, 93; legal impact of, 16; most-favored nation clauses and, 42, 65, 142–43; opening of China and, 30, 42; post-Tientsin era, 48; signed by U.S., 4–5, 51, 53, 59, 64–65, 79; U.S. national interest and, 67. *See also specific treaties and agreements*
Treaties of Tientsin (1858), 47, 48, 78
Treaty of Nanking (1842), 5, 30
Treaty of Paris (1856), 48
Treaty of Wanghia (1844), 6, 30, 50
treaty ports: class of Japanese in, 217*n*113; consular courts in (*see* consular courts); dual nationals in, 94; expatriate population in, 251–52*n*21; justice in, 235*n*31; labor market structure in, 182, 257*n*83; opening of, 42–43; prostitution influx into China, 90, 234*n*30; as U.S. bargaining chips with China, 168–71; Western scholarship on, 14–15

Tripoli, 5, 51, 62, 83
Tsungli Yamen, 47
Tunis, 5, 51, 62, 83
Turkey: criminal cases and, 65; on end of extrality, 164; extrality and, 83; missionaries in, 142; naturalized U.S. citizens in, 85–86; Sublime Porte Treaty and, 64–65; treaties with U.S., 5; Treaty of Paris and, 48
Tu Yue-sheng, 179

Underwood, Dorothy, 177
Underwood, James, 177
United States: anti-imperialist imperialism, 71–72, 82, 93; Ch'ing characterization of, 63; citizenship and, 51, 54, 113, 174–75 (*see also* naturalized citizens); concessions to Kuomintang, 168; consular service (*see* consular service); dual nationals in early, 52; expatriation views of, 52–54, 56; extrality and (*see* extrality); extrality for naturalized citizens of, 207*n*17; foreign policy and Progressives, 83; interwar policy toward Asia, 169; Japan and, 5, 83; Korea and, 232*n*87; local authority and, 61, 63, 208*n*33; local conditions and policy of, 144–45; modernization of China and, 48; nationality and issues of prostitution, 100–101; non-consular courts of, 207*n*16; passports and, 51, 96–97, 197; policy in underdeveloped areas, 61; privateers of, 52–53; Progressives in (*see* Progressives); public opinion of expatriates, 81, 205–206*n*3, 230*n*64; as replacement for British in East Asia, 167–72; role in Boxer rebellion, 92–93; sexual offenses and,

99–100; local businessmen and
foreign, 44–45; as "Other," 89–91,
93–96; U.S. Court for China and,
115, 155, 180–83
Vance v. Terrazas, 262*n*22
Vanderlip, Frank, 145
Vattel, Emmeric de, 26, 29, 51, 66
*Vera Meir and Olga Kaltzoff v. Arkell
and Douglas*, 254*n*40
vice cases: in U.S. Court for China,
115–16, 132–36
violence: antiforeign, 89; against Chinese by foreigners, 236*nn*50&53;
Chinese gangs and, 179; indigenous elites and, 9–10; U.S. Court
for China and, 128–29

"wage bargain," 148
Wakeman, Frederic, 14
Walker, William, 60, 61
Wallace, Emma, 174
Walsh, Harry, 181
Walzer, Michael, 202
Wang, C. T., 249*n*95
Wang Chung-hui, 158–59
Wang King Kee v. Bull & Company, 74
War Department, 207*n*16
Warner, Murray, 97
War of 1812, 53–54, 63
Washington, George, 62, 219*n*16
Webb-Pomerene Act (1918), 145–46
Wells, G. Wiley, 70
Wen(dt), Maria, 177
West China Navigation Company, 149
Wheaton, Henry, 54
Wheeler, Belle, 100
White, A. H., 230*n*72
White, James, 68
White, T. C., 238*n*74
Wiebe, Robert, 83
Wilcox, B. C., 36–37

Wilder, Amos, 133, 134
Wilfey, Lebbeus Redman: on American companies in questionable
cases, 137; anti-Catholic charges
against, 121; attitude toward
natives, 236–37*n*60; background
of, 110–12; British support of,
122–23; criminal charges against,
121–22; critics of, 116–17, 258*n*93;
definition of "crime," 180; demise
of, 123–24; on "good" Chinese, 132;
impeachment hearings on, 122;
issues between U.S. Department
of State and, 119–20; lawyers and,
114–15, 120, 121; mission of, 7, 141;
resignation of, 124; 9th Circuit
Court and, 117; *U.S. v. Demenil*
ruling, 129–30; use of second-class
federal citizenship category, 113–16
Wilkie, Mary, 11–12
Wilkins Brothers and Co., 245*n*54
Williams, Bridget, 75
Williams, David, 68
Williams, Hilton A., 152
Williams, John, 75
Wilson, Woodrow, 140, 142
Wolfe, Edith, 183, 257–58*n*87
women, respectable white, 90–91. *See
also* prostitution
Wong Kim Ark case, 178
Wong Paoding v. Anderson, 253*n*34
Woo Ah-sing v. Biddle, 115, 239*n*81
Woo Ah-sing v. Biddle & Hennage,
239*n*81
Woods, Barbara May, 230*n*72
*Woo Lan-ying Estate v. Drs. Mourer &
Dale*, 175–76
World War I, U.S. Court for China
after, 164–67
Wright, Mary, 48
Wu, John C. H., 158